Solomon,

Falcon of Sheba

Cover image: The solid gold death-mask of King Solomon.

Solomon,

Falcon of Sheba

The tombs of King David, King Solomon and the Queen of Sheba discovered.

by
Ralph Ellis

Edfu Books

Adventures Unlimited

Solomon, *Falcon of Sheba*
First published in 2002 by Edfu Books

Published in the U.K. by:
Edfu Books
PO Box 165
Cheshire
CW8 4WF
info@edfu-books.com
U.K.

Published in the U.S.A. by:
Adventures Unlimited
PO Box 74
Kempton, Illinois
60946
auphq@frontier.net
U.S.A.

Prototype edition Nov 2002
First Edition Dec 2002

U.K. paperback edition
ISBN 0-9531913-4-6

U.S.A. paperback edition
ISBN 1-931882-12-6

Printed in the United Kingdom by T.J. International, Padstow.

Her I loved and sought out from my youth,
And I sought to take her for my bride,
And I became enamoured by her beauty,
She glorifies her noble birth in that it is given her to live with god,
And the sovereign Lord of all loved her,
For she is initiated into the knowledge of god,
But if riches are a desired possession in life,
What is richer than wisdom?

A tribute to the wisdom of the Queen of
Sheba in her role as the goddess Ma'at.
Wisdom of Solomon 8:2.

To Yosser. A friend in need is a friend indeed.

Acknowledgements

My thanks have to go to a trashy T.V. programme that purported to show the origins of the legendary Queen of Sheba. I couldn't bear to watch more than 20 minutes of its diatribe, but it did set me thinking that 'there has to be a better explanation than this!'

Thanks are due to the following: Jane Tatam, who has to interest the media and sort out the UK distribution. David Hatcher Childress at Adventures Unlimited, who has done some sterling work in controlling the USA distribution. Eric Aubourg of Utrecht University, Nederlands, who supplied the Hieroglyphic Text Processing programme. This simple-to-use hieroglyphic font set not only looks more professional than my previous fonts, it also freed up a great deal of time for other research. The e-mail address for this software is: ccer@ccer.nl

I would also like to thank the curators of the Cairo Museum, who went to great trouble to provide extra lighting in order that I could take some photographs of their exhibits. Their time and efforts were greatly appreciated.

Finally, I should not forget to thank Random House, the international consortium of publishers who plagiarised my book *Thoth*, and whose belated out-of-court settlement for damages paid for the publication of this book. Plagiarism is, of course, the sincerest form of flattery, and if Random House would like to endorse our products again we would be happy to oblige in like fashion.

Ralph Ellis
November 2002
Cheshire.

www.edfu-books.com

Contents

Deception

The literary trail that had led me to the site of the tombs of King David and King Solomon had been long and complex, involving every last nook and cranny of the Biblical and historical archives. But here, at last, I was striding across the desert sands in one small corner of the Arabian Desert in search of those very same tombs.

Suddenly, there they were; a small heap of roughly hewn stones that had obviously been borrowed from previous constructions. The tombs had already been discovered and opened some years previously and, upon looking through these entrance holes, the vague outlines of granite sarcophagi could be seen. Torch in hand, I crawled into the tomb complex through the short and narrow passageway and found myself in a small vestibule that was covered in inscriptions. Picking these characters out one by one with my torch, I finally found what I was looking for – *Duad* דוד, the Hebrew pronunciation for King David.

While this discovery was dramatic and unprecedented, it was perhaps a little disappointing to know that all of these granite sarcophagi were empty. However, having fully researched this era and area, this was not a great surprise to me. The text books that detail this region indicated that these very tombs had been excavated in the 1930s and that the intact sarcophagi of these monarchs had been transferred to a local museum. Unfortunately, these sarcophagi had been mis-identified, which is why very little was made of their discovery and why these priceless artifacts had managed to lie in complete obscurity for more than sixty years.

Having arranged a visit to this same museum, I then discovered another reason for these sarcophagi being so obscure. I had finally traced their catalogue numbers to a small side-room in the museum. Upon entering the room, however, I was stunned to see that these beautiful solid silver sarcophagi resided in complete darkness. I sat and watched as the one or two visitors who did enter this small annex just walked past, completely unaware that these coffins were even there!

Never mind the proposed historical associations that are about to be made for these artifacts, they are magnificent pieces of craftsmanship in their own right. Both of these sarcophagi were hand-crafted in solid silver, and each bears a haunting image of the long-deceased king. In fact, the coffin of King Solomon is crafted into the image of a falcon, and is absolutely unique in the ancient world.

So why are these magnificent treasures, which date from the tenth century BC, left in darkness and obscurity? Is there something that the authorities wish to hide? Does someone know of their true identity and has done everything within their power to keep them out of the public eye?

History

Having already written so much about the early generations of the Biblical family, I was relatively certain that there was little more of interest to be found in these ancient Biblical texts. But there was always the troubling reality that both King David and King Solomon, the most celebrated kings of Judaic history, could not be found in the historical record. So how could this be so? How could a wealthy and influential empire suddenly disappear from the archaeological record? The physical evidence, or rather the lack of it, was deeply troubling.

This particular investigation began with a quick look at the life of the Queen of Sheba, but it rapidly diverged into a major research project looking at the complete history of the United Monarchy, as I could not believe what these texts actually said. In short, it quickly became evident that every page in the Bible that was turned could be read on two completely different levels: there was the conventional history and the coded, alternative history.

In the introduction for the book *Jesus, Last of the Pharaohs*, I wondered why historians and theologians alike had not commented upon the obvious similarities between the Hyksos pharaohs of Egypt and the Biblical patriarchs. I finally concluded that this omission must have been a simple oversight due to the unexpected nature of this textual synchrony. While that may have been a reasonable assumption for the less reliable history of the Biblical exodus era, I do not believe that the same is possible for the relatively well-documented reigns of King David and King Solomon. That theologians have not been able to deduce in six centuries what I have been able to glean in six short months, is a staggering indictment of their narrow-minded research techniques; and it also infers that Biblical scholars must have deliberately turned a collective blind eye to the facts. In reality, the Biblical books of Kings and Chronicles give us the true identities of these two famous Judaic kings, and they also spell out the true identity of the Queen of Sheba – but not quite in the way that the reader might have been expecting.

The true history of these famous 'Judaic' kings and this legendary 'Ethiopian' queen is stunningly controversial; and this great revolution in history and theology will clearly demonstrate that the origins, history, and the convoluted family relationships of the United Monarchy were diametrically opposed to the standard interpretation of Judaic history. Make no mistake, the evidence that will shortly be presented all points in one clear and unmistakable direction – the educational deficiencies that can be observed all around us must represent a global cover-up of gargantuan proportions.

The events that occurred during the Egyptian twenty-first and twenty-second dynasties, and their relationships with the neighbouring Judaic United Monarchy, have always been shrouded in mystery, but they will shortly be exposed in all their bloody and conspiratorial glory. Prepare for a new window on history that provides not only a crystal-clear view of Biblical history, but also provides a dramatic new perspective on the secular history of Egypt and the Near East.

Notes to the reader

a.   This book represents the sequel to the titles *Jesus, Last of the Pharaohs* and *Tempest & Exodus*. While it can be read as a stand-alone title without reference to the previous works, there will inevitably be occasions when it is assumed that the reader has already read, digested and understood certain concepts – primarily that there are innumerable pieces of evidence that point towards an Egyptian heritage for the Israelites, and that their leaders were actually the Hyksos pharaohs of Egypt.

      To have read the other two titles in advance will prepare the reader for some of the more difficult sections that lie ahead. This is not a hard sell, just a well-intended warning that the history of the United Monarchy becomes rather convoluted at times, and readers need to arm themselves with as much information as possible to understand the full implications of this research.

b.   Because of the radical nature of this book, it has been necessary to highlight the difference between standard orthodox assumptions and those generated by my lateral view of theology. Throughout this book, therefore, I have used curved brackets ( ) to denote orthodox assumptions and square brackets [ ] to denote my radical new assumptions. I hope that this serves to clarify the text.

c.   As readers of the book *Jesus, Last of the Pharaohs* will have noticed, the history of the Biblical exodus is not quite as it seems. Not only were the circumstances and nations involved not quite as advertised in the Bible, but, in fact, there were two exoduses from Egypt. Because there is no longer one definitive Exodus to refer to, the term 'exodus' has been left in lower case.

d.   The references in the text are numerous. To ease the problem of continuously referring to the reference section at the back of the book, some references have been prefixed. Prefixes are as follows:

    B = Bible, K = Koran, J = Josephus, T = Talmud, S = Strabo

    M = Manetho, N = Nag Hammadi, KN = Kebra Nagast.

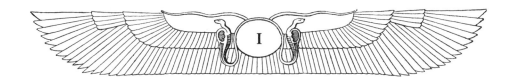

United Monarchy

Most people in the Judaeo-Christian world have probably heard of the Queen of Sheba at some point in their lives, but I suspect that few of us can place her with any confidence within the greater scheme of Near Eastern history. Some may recall a hazy memory of a children's story about an exotic eastern queen, of camels laden with gold and spices, and a titillating subplot about this queen's illicit tryst with King Solomon of Israel. But even this brief summary of the story begs an important question: King Solomon was not terribly important in the greater scheme of Near Eastern politics, so why was this wealthy foreign monarch paying respects and tribute to a king of Israel? King Solomon may have been a key figure in Judaic history, but in the wider context of Near and Middle Eastern power-brokering, in this era, he was not much more than a minnow; a pawn sandwiched between the wider conflicts of Sumer, Assyria and Egypt.

To understand the events of the tenth century BC, which culminated in the Queen of Sheba's caravan winding its way slowly northwards towards Jerusalem, we need to know how the Biblical story arrived at the reign of King Solomon. The books *Jesus, Last of the Pharaohs* and *Tempest & Exodus*, as advertised in the forepages, have revised and amended the early chapters of the Bible to dramatically show the Egyptian heritage of the Israelite people. Having conclusively demonstrated the Israelite's Egyptian ancestry in these two books, the story I have been telling now skips some four hundred years of history, from the reign of the pharaoh Akhenaton, to arrive at the court of Solomon; but what happened in between? Perhaps it is worth having a very quick look at the history of Israel and explaining a few of the basic assumptions that will underpin the staggering revelations and the dramatic new story that will shortly unfold.

1

The basic thrust of the two books, *Jesus* and *Tempest*, is that the Israelite people were not simple slaves in Egypt; they were instead the Hyksos nation. The Hyksos people were a fully integrated part of the population of Egypt, who inhabited the Delta area of Lower Egypt and established major cities at Avaris and Memphis. These people were not only influential and powerful, having a substantial army, they also ran a parallel kingship to that of Thebes in Upper Egypt. These Hyksos leaders were nothing less than pharaohs of Egypt, who were powerful enough to challenge the rule of the Theban monarchs.

Despite their power, however, the Hyksos were eventually pushed out of Egypt by the Theban pharaoh Ahmose I and, according to the third century BC historian Manetho, they then made their way in a great exodus to Jerusalem. Since Manetho's history, which was written some 2,300 years ago, appears to be so similar to the account of a Biblical exodus, I have quite reasonably assumed that they were, in fact, one and the same story. While many historians and theologians see this assertion as being absurd and unsubstantiated, it actually answers many of the problems that the classical explanations for the history of this era simply fail to address.

The problem that classical writers have with the Biblical accounts is that these ancient texts purport to give the history of a tribe of shepherds and their flocks of half-starved sheep. The Egyptologist, Donald Redford, notes these contextual absurdities in the Bible but, instead of seeing them as being signs of our chronological misunderstandings and of deliberate Biblical obfuscation, he merely champions them as evidence of Biblical ignorance:

> But even a cursory reading of this account (in the Bible) is bound to excite suspicion. Cities with massive fortifications fall easily to rustic nomads ... a feat pharaoh's armies had great difficulty in accomplishing ... A detailed comparison of (the Biblical) version ... with extra-Biblical evidence totally discredits the former. [1]

In other words, if the text disagrees with the archaeology, then the text must be wrong. Sometimes this line of reasoning may well be a truism, but on other occasions it may be a sign of our own ignorance. Rather than these Biblical accounts being in error, they are easily explainable if the Biblical exodus was the Hyksos exodus. Of course, 'cities with massive fortifications' fell easily to 'rustic nomads' because these rustic Biblical 'shepherds' were actually the Hyksos Shepherd Pharaohs of Lower Egypt, and they commanded one of the most formidable fighting forces in the region. Although this simple grain of lateral thinking has greatly altered the import of the Bible's message, it has left the basic information that this book presents completely intact; indeed, if this technique is continued throughout the Bible then its stories make a great deal more sense than they ever did before.

If the Israelites were the Hyksos, as seems likely, then it is axiomatic that some of the rites, rituals and beliefs of the priesthood in Jerusalem would have been firmly based upon Egyptian principles. In addition, this same assumption would mean that the Israelite people would have had strong cultural links with Lower Egypt. They would certainly have had much in common with those few Hyksos people who decided to remain in the Delta region during the exodus era, and they may have even had associations with the ruling elite in Thebes. Despite the antipathy and skirmishes between the armed forces of Lower and Upper Egypt during the fifteenth to seventeenth dynasties, it is highly probable that there were strategic marriage alliances between these two separate nations; in which case, the defeated Hyksos leaders may well have had strong family ties with the victorious Theban pharaohs.

While this whole concept of Egypto-Israelites is heretical to both the historical and the theological fraternities, and is commonly dismissed out of hand as being nonsense, this was not always the case. Manetho, as I have already said, stated that the Israelites were the Hyksos people, and the first century AD historian, Josephus, readily agreed with him. Strabo, another historian of the ancient world, had a similar tale to tell. Strabo's travels of the world spanned the first century BC, and he wrote a detailed account of these travels in his book *Geography*. The accounts he gave were largely first hand and for the most part they are thought to be reliable, but of Jerusalem and the province of Galilee he says:

> This region lies towards the north; and it is inhabited ... by mixed stocks of people from Egyptian and Arabian and Phoenician tribes ... But though the inhabitants are mixed up thus, the most prevalent of the accredited reports in regard to the Temple at Jerusalem, represents the ancestors of the present Judaeans as Egyptians. [52]

Thus, there was a consistent and unmistakable opinion abroad, in the centuries before the Christian era, that the Israelites were not simply emigrants who had escaped Egypt, but that they were actually of Egyptian stock themselves. While seemingly radical, this actually makes rather more sense than the Biblical story-line. The Bible wants us to believe that the Biblical patriarch, Abraham, came from Ur in Sumer and eventually settled in Shechem in Canaan, which is effectively the land that lies between

Jerusalem and Galilee. Apparently, these early Israelites were eventually driven out of this land by several famines and this fledgling nation went down into Lower Egypt to find a better life.

After a few centuries of life in Egypt and the supposed 'oppression' of their people by the native Egyptians, the Israelites then fled *back* to Canaan. This land is then described to us as being the new 'promised land' that is supposed to be 'flowing with milk and honey', but the scribes have conveniently forgotten that the Israelites used to live in this country previously, and only left because of repeated famines. The Biblical arguments do not make sense, whereas the alternative explanation in the book *Tempest* – that Abraham came from Ur on the Nile, the Babylon of Egypt – is much more credible. If the Israelites were actually native Egyptians from the Egyptian Ur, then the land of Canaan would indeed have been a new 'promised land' for these people, and they may well have expected the land to be more fruitful than it actually was.

Open mind

This radical new Egyptian slant to the early history of the Israelites is not absolutely necessary in order to follow the arguments in this book, but the evidence that will shortly be presented will be shown to agree with and fully support this concept. These two separate strands of the same story – originating as they do from radically different eras in Israelite history – coming together and dovetailing so nicely, will soon provide an irrefutable argument in favour of the Egyptian ancestry theory.

What may be required by the reader in this investigation, above all else, is an open mind to new ideas and arguments. Unfortunately, my previous two books, which revise the chronology and nationality of the Israelites, have been largely brushed aside by classical historians. Their comments have varied from "the chronology is wrong, therefore his thesis is worthless", to "his contempt for Christianity and its beginnings was obvious". But with all due respect to the reviewers of these books, they missed the whole point about an open-minded revision of history. The first reviewer simply refused to entertain an argument that undermined the classical chronology of Judaea, while the second assumed that any challenge to the orthodox interpretation of the New Testament represented 'contempt'. Significantly, this same reviewer was quite approving of my revisions to the Old Testament; but there again, that is only the 'Jewish' bit of the Bible, so perhaps that does not matter.

The entire empires of the historical and theological fraternity seem to be jammed into an intellectual tunnel, where the only source of light appears to be dead ahead. One might expect this attitude from the theological cabal as they only have one fixed doctrine to peddle, and any deviation from it would undermine their whole facade. But for the historical fraternity to be following in their footsteps, with the same rigid structures, is rather disappointing. Donald Redford shows how this process begins in his dissertation, which discussed the external influences upon early Israel. As a student, he apparently declared his intention to investigate this subject to his tutor and the reply from the learned sage was:

> ... the old man muttered: "Very well, you may do it. But I'll not have you concluding it all came from Egypt!" [3]

Since the 'old man' would have been marking the young Redford's dissertation, and since the 'old man' could have greatly influenced his final exam grades, the result of this warning represents a complete abandonment of free thought. Assuming an answer before the investigation has begun is an all-too-common human failing; we like to reinforce our present belief systems rather than continually challenging them: familiarity is comforting, whereas discord is distressing. But that same comforting sensation also represents an abandonment of the intellectual process; we stop thinking for ourselves.

Like science, history cannot afford to be a closed shop. Whilst the basic tenets and structure of the historical framework may appear secure, they need testing every now and then, to see if they stand up to independent scrutiny. Rather than threatening the entire historical edifice, such challenges should be viewed as strengthening the foundations of our historical structures – as long as it can weather these storms, the framework of history should emerge invigorated and vibrant.

In the case above, the 'old man' should have let the young buck have free reign to devise his own strategy. The student, having fatally committed himself on paper, would then have to justify his conclusions to the critical glare of the 'old man's' marking, and argue his points to the best of his ability. As in science, the grade of a historical qualification should not simply be decided on the ability to copy work from established reference books, but also the ability to make revisions and suggestions that aid our understanding. The astronomer, Galileo, summed up this process rather succinctly when he wrote:

> I believe that good philosophers fly alone, like eagles, and not in flocks like starlings. It is true that because eagles are rare birds they are little seen and

less heard, while birds that fly like starlings fill the sky with shrieks and cries, and wherever they settle they foul the earth beneath them.[4]

Beware the approaching flock of academics!

Judges

The historical revisions that I made in the book *Jesus* effectively left us at the time of Moses, when the Israelite people had left Egypt and settled in Jerusalem. This book then jumped on to the first century BC and the era of Herod the Great, effectively leaving out a massive twelve or fifteen centuries of Israelite history. So what happened during that vast expanse of time, and exactly when did the Queen of Sheba make her historic visit to King Solomon?

The first line of research into this era may seem to be the great authoritative tomes of the Jewish historians. This, after all, is not the hazy historical apparition that is the Biblical book of Genesis, where every tale appears to be more myth than fact; these are instead the relatively recent accounts of Kings and Chronicles, which abound with drama and fine detail. While these events may have occurred some nine hundred years before the Christian era, this is still recent history in terms of the Egyptian, Hittite and Sumerian cultures that sandwiched the fledgling Israelite state. Being immersed in the middle of such well-documented civilisations, surely the Biblical events of Israel in this era must abound with verifiable historical detail.

Unfortunately, this line of reasoning is as far from the reality of the situation as one could possibly travel. The real mystery abut this era of Biblical investigation is that there is no mention or evidence *whatsoever* of these famous Israelite kings. There is not one inscription, seal, image or burial artifact that mentions the kings of the United Monarchy. Despite the apparent wealth and international influence of these famous monarchs, as far as the historical record is concerned, King David and King Solomon simply did not exist:

> Curiously, no reference to (Solomon) or his father David, or their empire in a non-Israelite source is known, although, inscriptions from this period being scarce, this need not be significant.[5]

Isserlin's confidence that this lack of historical evidence 'need not be significant' is not necessarily shared by other Israelite historians. The

I   *United Monarchy*

Dictionary of the Near East does not even have entries for King David or King Solomon; while Michael Massing, an American religious author, ran an article in the New York Times on 9th March 2002 – under the title 'Rabbis Face Facts, Bible Tales Are Wilting' – which argued that the entire Old Testament has no historical value whatsoever, and that it was nothing more than an elaborate myth.

Jewish theologians would reject this notion out of hand, but they are then faced with a difficult task: how does one write a history of the United Monarchy when there is no historical data whatsoever to draw upon for evidence? The answer is that the thick volumes produced by the likes of Louis Finkelstein and Yehezkel Kaufmann are no more than Bible commentaries. The material in the Torah and Talmud is scrutinised, analysed, translated, twisted and turned, and finally a thesis is developed that most of these historians seem to agree upon. However, it is all conjecture based upon one single, contentious source of data – the Bible. The fact that this Biblical evidence is not backed up by the archaeological record is glossed over, presumably because it is assumed that the Bible cannot be wrong.

So, in what way, if any, can this impasse be overcome? How can this era be investigated if there is nothing to investigate? The answer, as with all my previous works, is to take the lateral viewpoint. Although historians would abhor the following opinion, I have nevertheless come to trust the Bible as a reliable, if distorted, historical text. Like the brief history of Manetho, the Bible also seems to be unreliable on the surface, but when read at a deeper level it nevertheless comes up with verifiable events and details time and time again. Turning Biblical rustic shepherds into historical, royal Hyksos Shepherd Kings of Lower Egypt is a minor linguistic twist, but one that clarifies great swathes of Biblical material.

Taking this viewpoint into account, my initial assessment of the problem was that the accounts of Chronicles and Kings are far too detailed and far too embarrassing to be the great fictional accounts that the Biblical detractors so loudly claim. If a scribe was inventing a new utopian history, to provide a fictional backdrop to a new religion, would he want to say that the most famous royal ancestor of the Israelites came to the throne in a bloody military coup? That this king's son killed his own brother? That this same king then killed his wayward son in order to marry his son's wife? That this same wife also happened to be this king's own daughter?

The problem with the common 'Bible is myth' assertion, is that the facts don't add up. Nobody would invent something as embarrassing and as contradictory as the Biblical Old Testament as the basis upon which to build a new religion. The leaders of the Catholic Church recognised this problem a long time ago, and it was for this reason that they so strongly resisted the publication of the Bible in the languages of the common people. As long as the clergy were the only people capable of reading and distilling these texts, the secrets of their confusing and humiliating content were secure. The last thing that the Catholic leadership wanted was for the common people to read these embarrassing passages and start asking difficult questions. This is made perfectly clear in the 1633 Vatican transcripts from the trial of the Florentine astronomer Galileo, where the astronomer was criticised for writing in the vulgar tongue:

> ... and he writes in Italian, certainly not to extend the hand to foreigners or other learned men, but rather to entice to that view common people in whom errors very easily take root. [6]

The clergy were alarmed that, by Galileo writing his book in Italian, the common people would be able to read profound and arcane secrets such as the motions of the planets. Perhaps more importantly, these same plebeians might then also be able to note Galileo's veiled assertions that the position and pronouncements of the Catholic Church on this topic were totally wrong.

If some of the general edicts of the Church being in error was viewed as a grave embarrassment to the clergy, then the possibility of the common people finding fault with the Bible itself must have fomented paranoia at the heart of the Vatican. It was for this reason that William Tyndale, the author of the first printed Bibles in the vulgar tongue of English, was burned at the stake in Vilvorde, Belgium, in 1535. Although at that time the nightmare prospects of *1984* and the rule of Big Brother lay a long way in the future, in many respects this scenario could have been applied directly to the Catholic Church and its Inquisition. The only beliefs allowable in the sixteenth and seventeenth centuries were those that were disseminated by the Thought Police of the Catholic Church, and so Galileo was forced to recant his heresy daily with the words:

> I, Galileo ... kneeling before You – Most Eminent and Reverend Lord Cardinals, Inquisitors-General against heretical depravity throughout the Christian Commonwealth ... swear that I have always believed, I believe now, and with god's help I will in the future believe in all that is held, preached, and taught by the Holy Catholic and Apostolic Church. [7]

However, the clergy need not have been so alarmed about the Bible being translated into the vulgar languages of Europe, and it was the Biblical texts themselves that eventually came to the Church's rescue. What the Vatican had not taken into account was the confusing and impenetrable nature of the Biblical stories. When distilled and purified by the clergy, many of these Bible stories may seem interesting and thought-provoking; but when read in the original script they are turgid, boring and largely incomprehensible. The upshot of this was that the only people prepared to penetrate these texts were the clergy and other committed theosophists; whereas individuals with more open and critical minds simply treated these same texts with disdain or indifference. It was for this reason, perhaps aided and abetted by the laws of blasphemy, that true critical analysis of the Biblical texts has only arisen in the last fifty years or so.

The whole point that is being made here is that the Biblical texts do not appear to represent a fictional account; the many lurid details and the embarrassing foibles of the Israelite royal dynasty point instead towards this being a documentary drawn from the daily life of a real royal court. But if this court was a historical reality, and if it was supposed to be so influential in the politics of the Near East, then why cannot this influential dynasty of kings be found in the historical record? The lateral answer to this conundrum is not that the Bible is fictional, nor that the archaeology is inadequate; the true answer to all of this is that there has been another cover-up.

Whenever the Bible gets into difficult waters it has the habit of changing the odd name or location, and suddenly a new and acceptable story evolves. Mam-Aybre was a Hyksos Shepherd King of Lower Egypt, but the Israelites later despised the Egyptians and so Mam-Aybre's pedigree was a bit of an embarrassment. But what should be done about this situation? The simple answer was to change the name Mam-Aybre to Abra-Ham and make him a pastoral 'shepherd' instead of a Shepherd King. (See the book *Jesus* for details.) Another perceived problem was that the sacred monument of the Israelites was the Great Pyramid at Giza. But the Israelite disdain for all things Egyptian made this association unacceptable once more, and so the simple answer was a quick textual alteration to make the pyramid a 'mountain' and to locate this 'mountain' well away from Egypt. In reality, Mt Sinai was the Great Pyramid at Giza. (See the book *Tempest* for details.)

My previous experience of uncovering so many of these textual amendments suggests that this new Biblical cover-up, in the later books of Chronicles and Kings, has to involve yet more Egyptian content in this story. The obvious supposition would be that the Queen of Sheba was Egyptian, and perhaps that King David and King Solomon were also related in some manner to the royal dynasties of Egypt. The reason for the missing archaeology would then be that historians are looking for the wrong names in the wrong locations.

Under this new scenario, the Queen of Sheba would not have been from Arabia or Ethiopia; evidence for her reign will instead be found somewhere in the great expanse of Egyptian history. Likewise, the names given for King David and King Solomon may well have been Hebrew renditions of equivalent Egyptian names. The Egyptian name of the patriarch Joseph was said to have been 'Sothom Phanech', and if one wanted to find this character in the historical record – much of the surviving details of which reside in Egypt – there would be no point looking for the name Joseph inscribed upon the walls of Karnak. There is a distinct possibility, the reasons for which will be given shortly, that the Kings of Israel were originally known by Egyptian names and it is for this reason that archaeologists have failed to find any details of this famous royal dynasty.

Pentateuch

In order to discover the true identities of these Israelite kings, we need to have a good understanding of the underlying history of this region, and for that we have to go back to the primary record that details their lives – the Bible. The summary that follows is a brief résumé of the three or four centuries that lie between the Amarna period, which has been associated with the second exodus from Egypt, and the era of the United Monarchy of Israel. While this material may be essential to set the scene for the coming revelations, it is, by necessity, fairly boring. If this era is well understood, then it may be worth speed-reading until chapter two is reached.

The United Monarchy of Judaea and Israel comprises the reigns of just three monarchs, King Saul, King David and King Solomon, who also happen to be the three most famous kings in Judaic history. These three kings were supposed to have ruled the two lands of Judaea and Israel during the tenth century BC. There are two independent records of the United Monarchy and these are contained in the Biblical books of Kings and Chronicles. The era just prior to the United Monarchy is not so well documented, but the Biblical books of Judges and Samuel attempt to fill the gap. The general thrust of the narrative in these two books is as follows.

After Moses had been laid to rest and the Israelites had settled in the lands of Jerusalem and Galilee, the concept of an Israelite kingship was abandoned for a while. Instead, the people were ruled by the Judges, a series of leaders who were appointed by god and who were probably not linked to each other by a bloodline: the Judges were *not* supposed to have been a royal dynasty.* If Moses is to be associated with the exodus of the Amarna dynasty from Egypt, then the period of the Judges must have lasted some 350 years; but if Moses were to be placed back into the era of the Hyksos exodus from Egypt, then this same period could represent up to 600 years of Biblical history.

There were apparently twelve Judges during this period, but this is likely to have been a symbolic number based upon the all-important twelve tribes of Israel, a figure which was in turn originally based upon the twelve signs of the Zodiac. The twelve Judges that are recorded in the Bible are hardly enough to cover the three to four hundred years of standard Biblical history, let alone span the six hundred odd years of the fully revised chronology. In fact, the length of each Judge's rule is often given as being 40 years, which is another common symbolic number within the Bible, and it will be shown later that Moses, King Saul, King David and King Solomon all had reign lengths of exactly 40 (or 80) years.

The reason for this forty-year reign length was, I believe, not simply that it was symbolic of a long reign; it is likely that it was also symbolic of an initiation into the finer workings of the early Israelite religion. This theory started to evolve in the book *Thoth*, where I showed beyond all reasonable doubt that the external dimensions of the Great Pyramid of Giza were, in fact, designed around the principle of a forty-times multiple of the fractional approximation of Pi. The Pi ratio that is used when calculating the perimeter length of a circle is 44:7, while the actual measurements used in the external dimensions of the Great Pyramid are 1760:280 (cubits). The pyramid ratio of 1780:280 is, of course, an exact forty-times multiple of the Pi ratio of 44:7.

This observation strongly links the design of the Great Pyramid with the multiple of 40, but then a further observation also linked this same pyramid with the Israelite nation. In the subsequent book, *Tempest*, I went on to demonstrate that the Biblical Mt Sinai, the sacred mountain of the Israelites, was actually a pseudonym for the Great Pyramid of Giza. It would appear that the Great Pyramid itself may have played a central role in some of the early Hyksos-Israelite rituals. This pyramid not only determined the seasons through astronomical observations, and thereby 'regulated' the flooding of the Nile,□ it also contained the god of the Israelites.

If the number forty was important in pyramid metrology, and if, in

---

* Classical theology does not allow for Israelite kings prior to Moses, but the whole thrust of my previous works is that Abraham, Isaac and Jacob were all Hyksos kings of Lower Egypt.

turn, the Great Pyramid was central to Israelite mythology, then surely the number 40 should appear as a regular feature in the Biblical texts. This is exactly what we find; the number 40 was clearly central to early Israelite mythology and it has been used throughout the Old Testament.

John Crowe has made a statistical analysis of the numerology that is contained in the Old Testament. [8] The result of this analysis was that, when looking at time periods, the number 40 was used far more frequently than any other number. It is apparent from the statistics that Crowe produced, that periods of time were often rounded to the nearest ten years, and so intermediate time-spans hardly feature at all in his table. Of the remaining entries in the table, the time-span of 50 years had ten references, the time-span of 30 years had eighteen mentions, while the period of 40 years was used on no less than sixty three occasions. This observation, that the number 40 was in some way special to the Biblical authors, not only supports my earlier assertion of there being links between Israelite theology and the Great Pyramid, it also gives a logical reason for this peculiar obsession with the number 40.

Simply put, I believe that the mention of a reign length or life-span of forty years inferred – to 'those who had ears to hear', as Jesus used to say – that this individual had been instructed in the mathematical design and symbolism of the Great Pyramid. This is similar to a modern Mason saying that 'he is 33 years old', or that 'he was born on October 13th': it is simply a coded declaration of initiation. It is of no coincidence that the Magen David מָגֵן דָּוִד – which is more popularly known as the Star of David, the most potent symbol of modern Judaism – is formed from two interlocking pyramids (one being inverted). It is also no coincidence that the pyramid multiple of forty was primarily used in conjunction with the Israelite royalty and high priesthood, the very people who would have been initiated into these arcane myths and rites. The one example of Israelite pyramid symbology is intimately related to the other, and this is a topic that will be discussed in more detail later.

Judges

It is apparent from the text of Judges that the history of Israel was not maintained with any great enthusiasm during this era, a fact that probably betrays the Israelites' relative economic poverty and lack of political influence in this era. The story of Judges revolves around a standard layout of oppression by enemies (normally the Philistines), the appointing of a new judge who vanquishes the enemy, and then a period of stability under his or her rule. Many of these judges are phantom individuals who are reserved no more than a few lines of text within the Bible; these include Othniel, Ehud, Tola, Jair, Ibzan, Elon, and Abdon. There is no way, from the information given in the Bible, that these characters can be placed within the historical record and no evidence of their lives has been found.

Other judges, like Gideon, Abimalech and Jephthah have more detailed lives but, not surprisingly, they are again absent from the historical record. The three remaining judges are perhaps slightly more famous. Deborah, the only female judge, was famed for the 'Song of Deborah', which celebrated the Israelite victory in the battle of Jezreel against the Canaanites. Samson was perhaps the most famous judge, who was renowned for being duped by Delilah into revealing that the secret of his strength lay in his long hair, and his subsequent capture by the Philistines. But Samson's hair regrew, and he was able to pull down the temple of Dagon by pushing against its pillars. However, in the book *Tempest*, I was able to show that the story of Samson was based upon the Egyptian myth of the fifth pillar *Heh* ⌀ , the pillars of which resided in the 'hair of Horus'. If this were so, it suggests that the story of Samson was based upon a myth and so he may not have been a historical character at all.

The last in the line was another of the more famous judges, Samuel. The account of Samuel's life is again fragmentary and contradictory, but his primary fame lay in his decision to anoint the 'first' king of Israel, Saul. While the Bible indicates that King Saul was supposed to have been the first ever king of Israel, many theologians and historians have pointed out that the texts actually seem to infer that kingship had enjoyed a long heritage in Israelite society. Historians are at a loss to explain this apparent dichotomy, but the Egyptian heritage of the Israelites, as detailed in the book *Jesus*, gives us all the answers that we need. The Israelites had indeed previously embraced the concept of the monarchy, and they did so during the Hyksos era in Lower Egypt.

In a similar fashion, historians also hotly debate the level of Egyptian influence in the court of Saul. The new, emerging government of the United Monarchy of all Israel would have required administrative structures, and the question arises as to where this new Judaean civil service came from and what structures it employed. The evidence points towards the new administration being of Egyptian extract, with some court officials, like Sofer and Mazkir, being identified by some historians as being Egyptians. Other similarities include the elite corps of thirty 'warriors', the use of the Egyptian hieratic numbering system, the use of a court 'day book' and also Solomon's book of Psalms. All of these procedures and structures have been identified as being based upon Egyptian antecedents and they again point towards a long Egyptian heritage within Israelite culture. Of course, there are always dissenting voices to such ideas, and the leading protagonist in this regard has to be Donald Redford:

> Not so long ago a welcome reaction set in against the tendency to imagine Old Testament scripture shot through with an all-pervasive, "Pan-Babylonian" influence. God forbid that a "Pan-Egyptianism" should now take its place! [9]

In other words, don't regard Israelite culture as having any role models on which it was based or drew influence. I get the impression that Redford regards this as intellectual laziness; that a culture can be easily explained in terms of a similar culture when they may, in fact, have been totally independent. But in many respects, this cultural isolationism flies in the face of the known facts. We know that there were regular contacts between Egypt and its surrounding neighbours for at least a thousand years prior to this time, and we also know from the experience of our own era that it is normal, almost mandatory, for smaller nations in the world to ape the superpowers. Egypt and Sumer were the superpowers of the Bronze and Iron Age of the Middle East, and it is inevitable that the surrounding city states would have looked to one or other of these as a role model, wishing to imitate its wealth, influence and power.

I believe that early Israel was primarily looking towards Egypt for its influences, and this favouritism was determined by the historical and family links that still remained between these two nations. Numerous similarities between the people of Lower Egypt and the Israelites have already been highlighted in the books *Jesus* and *Tempest*, but there are perhaps a couple of other similarities that are worth exploring in some detail; the latter of these discussion points will become important when the origins of the word 'Sheba' are explored later in the book.

The first of these similarities involves a mysterious mummy that has languished in the British Museum for a hundred years or more. The mummy is of a high priest who was known as Nesperennub, who died in about 800 BC, just after the era of the Judaean United Monarchy. The oddity about this burial was the strange lump on the mummy's head, which showed up on x-ray images. As nobody could work out what this was, it was decided to give the mummy a CT scan, which is capable of building up a detailed 3-D image of the entire body. [10] However, rather than solving the mystery, the new high-definition images simply served to deepen it, as the object turned out to be a clay bowl. While the new images did manage to sort out what the object was, the problem then became one of finding an explanation for this strange addition to the mummy. Why should an Egyptian priest have been buried with a bowl on his head?

John Taylor, the assistant keeper of antiquities at the British Museum, has declined to speculate on this odd finding, and it is doubtful if anyone with a traditional mind-set would ever be able to fathom out the function and meaning of this peculiar artifact. What is needed here is an insight into the theology of this priest and the accompanying ritual regalia that this belief system demanded. The radical key that can unlock this whole conundrum is that the religious practices of the Judaean United Monarchy were based upon Hyksos-Egyptian observances, because the former were descended from the latter. While this proposal is not acceptable to classical historians, as yet, the proof of a good theory always lies in its predictive powers; and if we are to solve the clay-bowl conundrum, the Hyksos-Israelite theory demands that we look at the later Judaic rituals for guidance as these were the descendants of the original Egyptian rites.

So, can the Hyksos-Israelite theory withstand the archaeological test? Can it explain new artifacts as they come to light? In this case, the answer just has to be in the affirmative. It is fairly obvious that the clay bowl on this mummy's head has been moulded to fit the shape of the priest's skull. In short, what we have here is a Judaic *yarmulke* or skullcap. This priest was being wrapped and mummified so that his remains would last for eternity and no doubt he wanted his *yarmulke* to last for eternity too. I have no doubt that for everyday usage the Egyptian high priests would have worn fabric *yarmulkes*, just as the Pope and all Jews do to this day, but for eternal life nothing but a clay *yarmulke* would have sufficed.

The second of these two new similarities between Egypt and Judaea are the calendrical systems that these two nations employed. The Egyptian calendar was originally based upon the phases of the Moon, and the more familiar Solar calendar did not take over from the Lunar until around the New Kingdom era. The Israelites, being mostly the exiled Hyksos Egyptians, would have already left Egypt before the solar calendar was adopted nationally in Egypt, and it is probably for this reason that the Israelites used (and modern Judaism still uses) the Lunar calendar.

The Hebrew word for the Lunar month was the *yehrah* יִרַח, and this word was only superseded at a much later date by the term *hodesh* חֹדֶשׁ. But the Hebrew word *yehrah* seems rather familiar; would this word be related in any way to the English 'year'? It is currently thought that the English term 'year' was derived from the Germanic term *jaeram*, but personally I suspect that its origins probably go all the way back to Judaea.

But how did an Egypto-Judaean word that denoted a Lunar month become confused with a Saxon name for the Terrestrial year? The answer to this lies once more in Egypt, and the fact that the Lunar month was often described as being a 'year'. When discussing the improbably high reign lengths of the early pre-dynastic kings of Egypt, the historian Manetho says:

> The year I take, however, to be a Lunar one, consisting that is, of 30 days: What we now call a month the Egyptians used formerly to style a year. [M11]

Modern historians tend to discard this account of Manetho but, in contrast, I have come to regard much of his writing as authoritative. The account of Manetho suggests that both the early Egyptians and the early Israelites were observing the orbits of the Moon and counting these as 'years'. But the thirty-day Lunar cycle clearly denotes a Terrestrial month, so what does Manetho mean by the term 'Lunar year'?

In actual fact, there are two Lunar periods that can be observed from the Earth; one is an observation of the Moon relative to the Earth, which is called a Lunar Month, while the other is an observation of the Moon relative to the stars, and this is known as the Lunar year. The Moon, as it traverses its monthly cycle, performs an orbit around the Earth. In the same way that one orbit of the Earth around the Sun is known as a Terrestrial year, one orbit of the Moon around the Earth is known as a Lunar year.

If these early astronomers in Egypt were slightly more advanced than is generally presumed, they could easily have been observing the Lunar year, and these observations may help explain the division of our month into four weeks that consist of seven days each. The normal Lunar month that we observe today, as noted by the changes in the phases of the Moon, lasts for some 29.5 days. Such a period of time might naturally suggest a division of five weeks to the month, with each week consisting of six days. What a 29.5-day cycle does not readily suggest is the modern division into four seven-day weeks, which results in a month consisting of 28 days. It has long been a mystery as to why these periods of time were devised, but the history of Judaism does suggest that this was a very ancient custom as this exact division of seven days to the week is contained in the Old Testament book of Genesis.

However, had these Egypto-Judaic astronomers been noting the Lunar year rather than the Lunar month, then the reason for these divisions to the month and week become more understandable. The Lunar year, defined as the Moon's sidereal year or orbital period, is actually 27.3 days in length. Unlike the Lunar month, this Lunar year would certainly favour a division into four seven-day weeks, and this observation will become more relevant and important in later chapters. What this further infers, however, is that the Hebrew term *yehrah* could well have been the origin of the English word 'year' – not only do these two terms sound very similar, it would now seem that they were both used to denote a year.

This dependence on Lunar cycles that were called 'years' can possibly explain one of the more puzzling aspects of the Biblical account. While the habit of counting reign lengths and life-spans in Lunar years, instead of a Terrestrial years, would certainly make more sense of some of the improbable early Egyptian reign lengths, it would also make a great deal more sense of the enormous life-spans of the early Biblical patriarchs. In both the historical and Biblical accounts, the life-span that is given in the text would have to be divided by thirteen to translate the Lunar years into Terrestrial years. The result, in each case, would be an entirely reasonable time-span.

However, the later accounts of Genesis also contain some intermediate life-spans, which, if divided by thirteen, would result in impossibly short lives for these individuals. But the ever-vigilant historian Manetho has an answer to this conundrum too:

> The most ancient Egyptian kings alleged that their years were lunar years ... whereas the Demigods who succeeded them gave the name *horoi* to years which were three months long. [M12]

In which case, two types of Lunar 'year' were used in these accounts; one that consisted of 28 days, and one that contained 84 days. In other words, the 930 (Lunar) years that Adam was supposed to have lived would need dividing by 13 to become 71.5 Terrestrial years; while the intermediate 162 (Horoi) years of the life of Jared would require a division by roughly 4 to become 40 Terrestrial years. If this explanation for the Lunar year is true, however, it would infer that the Egypto-Judaeans had a very good grasp of celestial mechanics.

Saul

Following the period of the Judges, Judaic history only begins to gel once more into something that can be considered as approaching historical fact with the advent of the reign of King Saul. Although Saul is another monarch who cannot be found in the historical record, his reign, as is narrated in the Bible, has much more substance and a ring of truth to it.

King Saul, and the following two monarchs, King David and King Solomon, presided over what is known as the United Monarchy of Israel.

From the time of the exodus to the coming of the Persians under Nebuchadnezzar, Israel was divided and factional, especially between the northern and southern tribes – Israel and Judah respectively. Only for a brief 100 years or so, under these three relatively powerful kings, was some form of unity maintained. But this consolidation was by no means easily established and Saul, who was primarily a northern ruler from Israel, fought many battles with both external and internal enemies before the kingdom was secured.

Saul was the son of Kish, of the tribe of Benjamin, a family that was considered by Judge Samuel to have had royal pretensions. Although the tribe of Benjamin was nominally allied to the southern Judaean province, Saul was primarily supported by the northern tribes of Israel. Meanwhile, an independent provincial leader known as Jesse, the father of King David, appears to have governed Judaea in the south.

The prime reason for Judge Samuel anointing Saul as king was to unify the tribes of Israel, and to lead them in battle against Nahash, king of the Ammonites. Nahash had come up from 'beyond the Jordan' with a great army and ravaged the southern borders of Israel, terrifying the Gileadites. But the tribes of Israel, under the command of Saul and the guidance of Samuel, came to the aid of the Gileadites and slaughtered a great number of Ammonites, including their king Nahash. They then took their army into the land of the Ammonites and ravaged their borders, which Saul presented as a major triumph for the Israelite tribes.

This little episode will become important in the unfolding story, as I will later show that King Nahash was actually a title for Jesse, the father of King David. It is entirely possible that it was politically unacceptable for the later Judaic scribes to admit that King Saul had killed King David's father, and it may have been for this reason that they used another of Jesse's titles, that of Nahash, to describe him in these sections of the Biblical texts. (See the family tree in the appendix for more details.)

Saul's leadership and reputation, as both monarch and military commander, was to be immediately tested once more when the Philistines, who inhabited the western coastal plain of Palestine, drew together a vast army and pitched it at Michmash. Saul tried to gather the tribes together, but:

> ...some (Israelites) hid themselves in caves, and in dens underground, but the greater part fled into the land beyond Jordan, which belonged to (the Israelite tribes of) Gad and Reuben. [13]

This is perhaps a small clue that the Ammonite nation was not really located to the east of the Jordan, as this particular patch of land seems to have been already inhabited by Israelite tribes. Likewise, if this area were really under Ammonite control, it would have been the last place that an Israelite would have wanted to flee to during a period of danger. The Ammonites were a constant source of aggression and trouble for the Israelites, so why would the Israelites flee from one threat straight into the jaws of another? There is a distinct possibility, as we shall see shortly, that the Ammonites were not living to the east of the Jordan, but to the east of another river entirely – the Nile.

David

The reign of King Saul was punctuated by constant bickering and battles with the Philistines, who inhabited the western fringes of Palestine, and so Saul was forced to maintain a strong military force. He was assisted in this regard by his chief armour-bearer, David. The Bible, it its inimitable way, likes to portray David as being a poor shepherd boy once more, but it later transpires that his family were rather influential Judaeans. One thing that the Bible does make clear, however, is that there was no family relationship between David and King Saul whatsoever; Saul was a Benjamite, whereas David was from the tribe of Judah. Since important dignitaries and army commanders in this era were usually promoted from within the ranks of the ruling family, this assertion makes David's position in the army rather unusual.

Despite David's apparent lack of royal family contacts, he seems to have been aggressively ambitious, and this fact was not lost on King Saul. The king had already been told 'by god' that David would succeed him to the throne of Israel, in preference to his own sons, a vision that may well be confirmation that David had high status despite his lack of royal connections. David's status may well have been derived from his father, Jesse-Nahash, who was obviously influential in Judaea and may also have been a ruler of the Ammonite lands that bordered Egypt. It was this level of support and status that placed David in a position to challenge King Saul for the throne.

The ambitions of David obviously created tensions within the royal court of Israel, and despite David's position of authority within the ruling hierarchy, King Saul made at least two attempts on David's life. But after these attempts failed, Saul became fearful of his own position:

> And Saul cast the javelin; for he said, I will smite David even to the wall with it. And David avoided out of his presence twice. [B15]

And Saul was afraid of David, because the Lord was with him, and was departed from Saul. [B16]

King Saul's assassination attempts had failed and he could see that the gods (the omens) were against him. Perhaps as a token of appeasement, Saul then proposed his daughter in marriage to David, which the latter accepted:

And Saul said to David, Behold my elder daughter Merab, her will I give thee to wife: only be thou valiant for me, and fight the Lord's battles. [B17]

Saul's offer of the hand of his daughter in marriage was designed to gain David's loyalty and his agreement, as an 'army commander', to attack the Philistines, but behind his back Saul was plotting to kill David once more. After a further attempt was made by Saul to spear David with a javelin, David decided it was wise to withdraw into exile for a while. King Saul tried to pursue David and to destroy his camp, in a full military engagement, but David saw the attack coming and escaped into the 'wilderness'. Finding his location once more, King Saul pursued David with 3,000 men and at last the two armies engaged each other. But the forces of David were the stronger of the two on the battlefield, and so Saul had to retire from the field.

Faced with the obvious fact that Saul was now his enemy, David appears to have joined forces with the Philistines, although some of the Philistine commanders were not entirely happy with this arrangement. David fought a great battle with the Amalekites, where he won a great victory and recovered all the spoils that had previously been taken from him. Meanwhile, King Saul faced another campaign against the Philistines, but this battle went very badly for him. The king became surrounded by the enemy and three of his sons, Jonathan, Abinadab and Malchishua, were killed. Saul himself was still surrounded but, as the king of Israel, he did not want to be captured alive:

Then said Saul unto his armour-bearer, "Draw thy sword, and thrust me through; lest these uncircumcised come and thrust me through, and abuse me." But his armour-bearer would not; for he was sore afraid. Therefore Saul took a sword, and fell upon it. [B18]

It is not hard to see in this report a little skulduggery. David was supposed to have been a high-ranking commander within the army of King Saul, and no doubt he still had strong links within this force. Since David desired

King Saul dead, there is a strong possibility that these deaths represented an assassination of the whole Saulite family, including the heirs to the throne.

But this murderous plot had not yet reached its climax. The people of Judaea now crowned David as king of Judaea (the southern province), while the people of Benjamin and Israel crowned Ishbosheth, another of Saul's sons, as king of Israel (the northern province). The land of Israel was divided once more and, for the present, David was only king of the southern state of Judaea. The accounts say that this state of affairs lasted for seven-and-a-half years, until David convened some kind of conference between the warring parties. But the conference was about to become a blood-bath:

> Then there arose and went over by number, twelve of Benjamin, who were loyal to Ishbosheth the son of Saul – and twelve of the servants of David. And (the servants of David) caught every one his fellow by the head, and thrust his sword in his fellow's side; so they fell down together. [B19]

Following the murder of Ishbosheth's highest ranking ministers and courtiers, David then led his followers on a slaughter of the opposition forces and so the rout was nearly complete. But there were still pockets of Israelite resistance and so both Abner, the cousin of Saul, and Ishbosheth, the grandson of Saul, were also dispatched – Ishbosheth being beheaded in his bed. In the end, there were no heirs of Saul left to take the throne, and the tribes of Israel finally assembled to anoint David as king of a united Judaeo-Israelite nation.

As with all these Judaeo-Israelite monarchs, the ancestry of David's family is rather uncertain; nothing is known about him in the historical record and the Biblical accounts are equally lacking in detail. King David is given a fairly simple family lineage that stretches back to the patriarch Judah, but this history lacks detail and it seems impossible to expand upon it. However, later in the book the entire family history of King David and the precise details of who he was in the historical record *will* be given, a feat that is only possible due to a fortuitous agreement between the Biblical and historical records.

However, whoever David was, he must have been either very astute or very powerful, for within just a few years Judaea and Israel were propelled from a backwater of tribal infighting into a major player in the politics and economy of the Near East. Judaeo-Israel was no longer a vassal state; indeed, it now spread its influence and control over neighbouring lands and nations. Judaeo-Israel was no longer poor either, and it somehow even began to accept tribute from other nations; a prerogative normally claimed only by the most powerful and threatening of nations. This tribute eventually enabled the United Monarchy of Judaeo-Israel to construct the Temple of Jerusalem, which is reported to have been fabulously appointed, with tonnes of gold and silver used in its construction. This temple was, of course, the work of King Solomon, but the Bible is at pains to point out that much of the wealth and material for its construction was amassed by King David.

Solomon

Before the great Temple could be constructed, King David was unfortunately confined to his deathbed. As is usual in these times, the succession was not certain by any means and another son of David, Adonijah, the son of Queen Haggith, had already assumed the title of king. Panic set in amongst the other heirs to the throne and Queen Bathsheba, the mother of Prince Solomon, rushed her son in to see the dying King David and pleaded for him to be anointed as king. King David agreed and the priests, Zadok, Nathan and Beniah [who were all either brothers or close relatives of Solomon] were urgently summoned and a hasty coronation was performed. Solomon was now king of all Israel and Judaea.

While King Solomon is yet another famous Biblical figure who is strangely absent from the historical record, the Bible nevertheless reports that Israel in this era had entered a high point in its wealth and power. Perhaps the most telling point is that Israel could now devote an increasing amount of time to cultural pursuits, rather than warfare and tribal infighting. Solomon was not only famed for the building of the great Temple of Jerusalem (the Temple of Solomon), a magnificent royal palace, and several notable fortified cities in Israel; he was perhaps even better known for his wisdom and writing. King Solomon is reputed to have written several books, some of which have been preserved in the Bible – Proverbs, Ecclesiastes, Wisdom of Solomon and the Song of Songs. Whether Solomon was responsible for these books or not, it is apparent that this era represented a high point in the production of Judaeo-Israelite literature.

King Solomon has been considered in some circles to be the archetypal successful monarch, and his wisdom and good justice were legendary. Even today, the coronation of every British monarch is accompanied by a chorus of "Zadok the priest and Nathan, crowned King Solomon". But the obvious question posed by the choice of this anthem is:

does this hymn seek to confer the prestige and wisdom of King Solomon upon the new British monarch, or is this instead a celebration of our monarch's direct 'Judaic' heritage?

But for all his perceived wisdom, even King Solomon had his detractors, and in the Bible he was soundly criticized for taking on too many foreign wives, for being under their influence, and for adopting their strange idolatrous religious practices. These complaints exposed, once more, the fundamental problem that Israel has experienced throughout its entire history – religio-political instability and factional infighting. Not surprisingly, the eventual demise of King Solomon, and the weakening of his strong central control over this region, was to prove to be another turning point in this people's long history.

Following King Solomon, the Israelite monarchy was split between King Rehoboam and King Jeroboam, two minor monarchs who I will later try to show were both sons of King Solomon. Following his coronation, King Rehoboam took the lands of Judah and Benjamin in the south, the traditional inheritance of King David; while King Jeroboam took the lands of Israel in the north, which had been the traditional inheritance of King Saul. The people of Judaea and Israel were divided and factional once .more, with constant battles erupting between the two provinces, and the land was to remain divided until the Persian invasion in the sixth century BC.

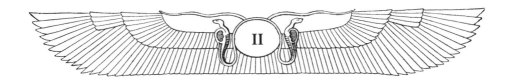

The Nile

The later chapters in this book detail the politics and the geography of the twenty-first and twenty-second dynasties of Egypt, and compare these with the equivalent events in the lands of Judaea and Israel. But on entering this era, the potential researcher is immediately confronted by a morass of names and data that often appear contradictory in their nature. This is not simply true of the Biblical descriptions, which abound in unknown names and localities, but also of the historical archaeology of Lower Egypt. The political landscape of the Egyptian Third Intermediate Period, as it is sometimes known, is based upon particularly threadbare evidence, and so inevitably there has been an amount of padding and guesswork by historians to fill in some of the gaps in our knowledge.

Before discussing some of the core question of this era – questions like, 'who was King Solomon?' – it is probably worthwhile addressing some of these side issues. Some of these questions – like, 'where is Gilead?' – may seem unimportant, but if a pivotal character in the story comes from this town, knowing its exact geographical location can potentially solve many problems. So where, in this case, was Gilead?

While the name of this city or province has eluded translation, the names of the rivers that ran through this area have been preserved more faithfully:

> Sihon king of the Amorites, who dwelt in Heshbon ... which is upon the bank of the river Arnon, and from the middle of the river, and from half Gilead, even unto the river Jabbok, which is the border of the children of Ammon. [B1]

II The Nile

Here we see that the land of Gilead bordered that of Ammon, and the river Jabbok (Yabboq יַבֹּק) probably served as the boundary. The name Jabbok is not in current usage, of course, and so this name is of no immediate help, but the Bible Concordance says of this river that it is:

> A stream which intersects the mountain range of Gilead, and falls into the Jordan on the east about midway between the Sea of Galilee and the Dead Sea. [2]

According to the classical interpretation given above, the river Jabbok has already become a stream, and this is despite the fact that this Hebrew term is usually used to describe a 'torrent' or 'river'. Indeed, if this stream did intersect the Jordan on its eastern side, it would be barely more than a dribble, for the east bank of the Jordan is not exactly known for its high rainfall or water-table.

While the accuracy of this classical interpretation is both bland and completely unverifiable, the alternative interpretation, which can be achieved via a radical translation of this river's name, is much more illuminating. The name Jabbok comes from the Hebrew word *baqaq* בָּקַק meaning 'to empty' or 'to flow out'. Now this repetition of syllables sounded distinctly Egyptian to me, and so the Egyptian dictionary was consulted once more. The dictionary bore out this suspicion, as it stated that the Egyptian word *baqbaq* (*bakbak*) meant 'to flow out' – which is precisely the same pronunciation and meaning as the Hebrew equivalent. This was interesting, for it inferred that this Hebrew term was derived directly from Egyptian sources. But if the name of this river was derived from Egyptian roots, what of the river itself?

The first point of call in this investigation had to be the subsidiary Egyptian meanings for the word *beqbeq*. These related words turned out to be *beq*, *beka-t* and *bekh*, all of which referred in some way to giving birth. In Egyptian terms this made complete sense, because the river Nile was always associated with fertility, and the god of the Nile, Hapi, was generally portrayed with breasts and a pregnant stomach. To the Egyptians, rivers in general could be thought of as 'life-bringing', and the river Nile was especially fecund.

Encouraged by this initial success, I then tried the same technique with the other river mentioned in the previous text, that of Arnon אַרְנוֹן. The Hebrew derivation of this word is *ranan* רָנַן, meaning 'rejoice' or 'joy'; while in a similar fashion the ancient Egyptian version of this same word was *renen-ut* (*ranan-ut*), also meaning 'rejoice' or 'joy'. The term *renen-t* was also giving familiar sub-meanings of 'baby', 'child' or 'harvest'; terms that once more indicated the importance of the river's fertility. In fact, both of these Egyptian words also had additional sub-meanings that suggested 'suckling' or 'breasts full of milk'.

Again, it seemed that I had discovered an exact Egyptian match for the name of an Israelite river. The naming of two adjacent rivers in Palestine with words derived from Egyptian sources was rather setting an interesting precedent – it either inferred a heavy Egyptian influence during the formative years of the Israelite nation or, more provocatively, it suggested that these rivers may have been Egyptian.

Fig 1. *Beqbeq, to flow out.*   *Renen-t, to rejoice.*

The sub-meanings to these names, 'suckling' and 'nursing', did not merely suggest the fertility of these rivers, they also reminded me of the pseudonyms that were used in Egypt as references for the pyramids of Giza. This topic has already been covered in some detail in the book *Tempest*, the results of which indicated that the Giza pyramids were sometimes referred to as 'breasts'. This symbolism was not simply a result of the pyramids' obvious breast-like form, it was also derived from their sacred function as giant gnomons, the shadows of which defined and 'regulated' the seasons and so in turn controlled the flooding of the Nile and the fertility of the land.

The similarity between this regulation of the fertility of the Nile and the word *beq*, meaning 'to give birth', gave me the impression that there was a link to be made between these two words. The more radical of the available possibilities is that the Nile was perhaps being referred to by the name of *Baqaq (Beqbeq)* and, by inference, perhaps the Biblical river Jabbok actually referred to the Nile itself. But this was only supposition; what I needed in order to confirm this suspicion was a much closer link between the word *Beqbeq* and either Egypt or the Nile. Surprisingly enough, the answer to this problem was rather more precise that I could ever have hoped for, as it eventually transpired that one of the original names for Egypt was *Beq (Baq)* 𓃀𓈎𓏏 . In this case, the river *Beqbeq* or *Baqbaq* (Hebrew *Baqaq* בקק) must have been called the 'River of Egypt', a title that just has to refer to the river Nile or one of its branches in the Delta region. But was this so? Did the word *Beq* really refer to the river of Egypt as well as the country itself?

II *The Nile*

Although this evidence was compelling, simply knowing that *Beq* was a name for Egypt was not quite good enough; it would be nice to know what this word originally meant too. Luckily, the precise hieroglyphic spelling of the Egyptian word *Beq* showed some interesting derivations that gave a good indication of what this word actually meant. The first hint of this word's original meaning was the use of the 'tree' determinative glyph, but exactly which type of tree was intended here?

In answer to this, it so happens that the Egyptian name of the olive tree is *baq-t* or *beq-t* 𓏲𓄿𓏏𓆱 , and in addition, this is also a term that was used for the sacred tree of An (On), or Heliopolis. This link with the sacred tree of Heliopolis seems to indicate that *Beq-t* was simply another term for the *Aser-t* tree, which was the sacred tree of *Ap-uat* (Anubis) and Heliopolis that was mentioned in the book *Tempest*. The *Aser-t* tree was identified in the Egyptian dictionary as the tamarisk, but here it appears to be a reference to the olive. This may indicate that there were two types of sacred tree, and the two varieties that are being mentioned in these texts may indicate a reason for their sacredness.

Both of these trees / shrubs are noted for their oil, and the presence of this oil may have had sacred connotations and usage. The evidence for this can be derived from another alternative meaning for the word *beq*. As it happens, the term *beq* also refers to an unguent, specifically an ointment that was made from olive oil; and it was this last meaning that eventually led me to the next name for the land of Egypt, that of *Qebhu* 𓂽𓃀𓏲𓈖 .

Here, then, is another name for the land of Egypt, one that somehow seems vaguely familiar. The reason for this strange familiarity is, of course, that *qeb* is a simple reversal of the word *beq* and, just as their similar spelling might suggest, these two words also have similar meanings. Thus, in addition to being a name for Egypt, we find that *qeb* means 'oil' and 'a tree from which oil is extracted'. Here we can perhaps glimpse the role and importance of these sacred trees once more; it was not necessarily the tree that was important but the oil that it exuded, which could be used in ritual ceremonies. It is well known that the ritual anointing of oil was important in Egypt, especially to prospective monarchs, and that this same ritual has been preserved into the modern era with the anointing of British monarchs. Likewise, the Israelites used to anoint small pyramids with oil, as one of the verses regarding the patriarch Jacob from the book of Genesis demonstrates.

Here, at last, we are closing in on the real meaning of the terms *beq* and *qeb*. It is significant that the word *qeb* refers once more to the breast or nipple, and that this meaning is the same as for the words *beq* and *renen-t*. Once more, the intended reference here is probably to the nourishing waters that were supposed to emanate from between the two main pyramids at Giza. The other spelling of the name *Qebh*, meaning 'Egypt', uses the water-pot-with-running-water determinative glyph 𝕚 , and this determinative has two main meanings. Firstly, it infers a libation, hence the association with anointing and oils. Secondly, it means 'to cool'. It is this latter meaning that is the most widely used derivation for *qeb(h)* and it is mainly used to infer concepts of 'coolness' or 'refreshment'. In addition, however, *qebhu* is also used to describe 'the celestial abyss', 'cool water' or 'the lands flooded by the Nile'.

In this case, I think that the real meaning of this name for the land of Egypt is perfectly clear. The theology of Egypt involved a worship of the great cosmos, a reverence for the intricacies of both the physics and the astronomy of the heavens. The cosmos was seen to be the great void of space, the celestial abyss, plus the myriad of fixed and wandering stars that punctuated this void. In turn, according to the age-old adage 'as above, so below', the celestial abyss was mirrored on the Earth below; and therefore the great serpentine 'river' of the Milky Way was being mirrored on the Earth by the serpentine course of the Nile itself. The words *beq* or *qeb* referred both to the heavens above and also the cool, refreshing and nourishing waters of the Nile below.

If the words *qeb* and *beq* referred to both the heavens and the Nile, it would appear that the land of Egypt was being called the 'Land that looks like Heaven', or as Graham Hancock succinctly put it in the title of his recent book, 'Heaven's Mirror'. Surprisingly enough, this educated guess appears to be correct, and the Egyptian dictionary eventually confirmed that the word *Qebb* ⊿ 𝕝𝕝 was indeed a direct reference to the river Nile. Here, then, we have a very secure translation for the Biblical river *Baqaq* (Jabbok); it was nothing less than a reference to the Egyptian river *Beq* or *Qebb* (*Qabab*), the great river Nile herself.

Notice how both the Biblical and Egyptian names for the Nile have interchangeable consonants, while still retaining the same meaning. The fact that this word can be reversed in exactly the same manner in two different languages must be considered proof positive that these words have the same origins and meanings:

Biblical version	Egyptian version
Jabbok (Qabab-ok)	Qabab
Baqaq	Baqbaq

While the mention of this river represents a minuscule part of the entire Biblical history, this is nevertheless a dramatic reversal of the perceived meaning of some of the Biblical texts; for it is now axiomatic that every reference in the Bible to the river *Baqaq* (Jabbok) may actually be a reference to the river Nile. Unfortunately for this new revision to the Biblical texts, this particular river is only mentioned five times in the Bible; one reference we have already seen, but a similar reference is as follows:

> And they possessed all the coasts of the Amorites, from Arnon even unto Jabbok, and from the wilderness even unto Jordan. [B3]

These were the extents of the possessions of the Israelites at the time of Judge Jephthah and these were being disputed by the Ammonites once more. The traditional interpretation of this verse indicates that the Israelites only held some of the lands around the tributaries of the river Jordan, a miserable patch of land for an entire nation to cultivate. On the other hand, the new, revised translation for the river Jabbok may well be indicating that Israel actually ruled over a vast swathe of land that stretched from two of the branches of the Nile in the Delta lands – from the branches called Arnon and Baqaq (Jabbok) – all the way through the wilderness of the Sinai-Negev desert, and on to the river Jordan. If this were the case, then Israel held a sizeable tract of land at this time and must have been much more powerful than theologians have previously suspected.

This supposition is supported by some of the Biblical campaigns of Joshua, the successor to Moses. Joshua was supposed to have been fighting his way up through Judaea into Israel, at some indeterminate time after the exodus; however, one of the lands he was fighting against was said to be Goshen. But the Bible has already stated in the book of Genesis that the land of Goshen was somewhere in the Nile Delta, and the Egyptologist, Flinders Petrie, has identified Goshen as the ancient city that was once known as Bubastis, which lies just to the north-east of Heliopolis. Once more, there are two possibilities here: either there were two cities called Goshen, one in Israel and one in Egypt, or perhaps some of the cities that Joshua was fighting against during the migration of the Israelites northwards were actually located in the eastern Delta region.

> Joshua took all that land, the hills, and all the south country, and all the land of Goshen, and the valley, and the plain, and the mountain of Israel, and the valley of the same ... Joshua made war a long time with all those kings. There was not a city that made peace with the children of Israel, save the Hivites the inhabitants of Gibeon: all other they took in battle. [B4]

Like all of these verses, the actual location that Joshua was campaigning in could be read in two alternative ways. The Mountain of Israel, for instance, could either refer to the Temple Mount in Jerusalem or to the Great Pyramid at Giza – both are possible. The argument that I shall pursue is that the land of Goshen that was being mentioned here was not in Judaea; instead, it was the alternative location from the book of Genesis that lay in the Nile Delta. This supposition appears to be confirmed when the Bible goes on to say:

> And Saul smote the Amalekites from Havilah until thou comest to Shur, that is over against Egypt. [B5]

In other words, the battle with the Amalekites went all the way down into Egypt. But this statement does not necessarily mean that the battle with the Amalekites finished on the eastern fringes of the Nile Delta. In the Bible, the term 'Egypt' is most frequently used to denote the Theban lands of Upper Egypt, as has been explained many times before. If this were the meaning that was being suggested in this quote, then this battle may not have ended until a location south of Memphis had been reached. But how could such an incursion by Joshua deep into the lands of Egypt be explained? Surely this is just not possible?

The revised geography of these texts is suggesting that instead of Joshua campaigning solely in Israel, he was actually conquering some of the cities that lay in the eastern Delta region at the same time. Having done so, it is entirely possible that the Hyksos-Israelites held onto some of these cities. Just as one of the previous Biblical quotes has suggested, the lands of Israel may have included parts of the eastern Nile Delta in this era. If this was so, then it is entirely possible that some of the later disputes with the Ammonites and Amalekites were conducted in the Delta lands, with subsequent skirmishes breaking out down towards Memphis and perhaps beyond.

This minor alteration to the standard accounts, that the Israelites may have held onto some lands in the north-eastern Delta, places a completely new perspective on the whole import of this era. The previous assertion that the Israelites were defenceless nomads made these suppositions impossible, but the realisation that they were really the Hyksos Shepherd Pharaohs makes the whole scenario rather compelling. The descendants of the Hyksos army could well have taken some lands in the Delta region and then proceeded to threaten some of the weaker New Kingdom Theban pharaohs.

Confirmation of this argument comes from the history of this region. It is a known fact that the Theban stronghold of Pi-Ramesse in the Delta

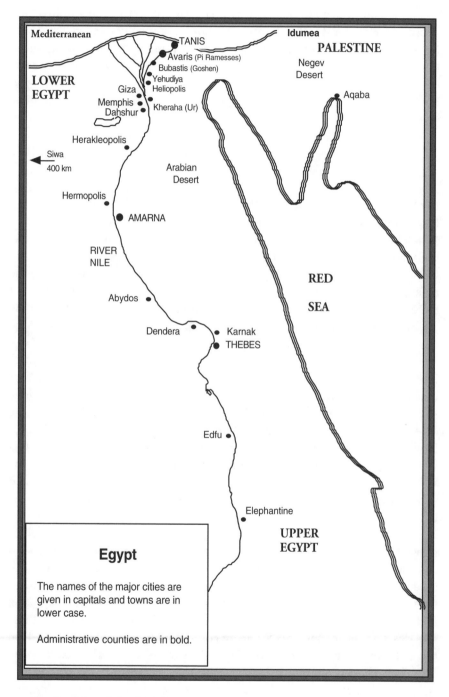

Fig 2. Map of Ancient Egypt.

(previously the city of Avaris) had been wrested from Theban control, at some point in time, by the twenty-first dynasty pharaohs based in Tanis. But who were these northern rebel pharaohs, and when did they actually take control of this region? It will be shown later that this Lower Egyptian dynasty actually had Hyksos-Israelite affiliations and were related to the famous Biblical kings of Judaea. Some of these Biblical reports, about Joshua's battles in the Nile Delta, could have been distant memories of a time when the Hyksos-Israelites regained a foothold of power and influence in the Nile Delta.

This revision of Judaic geography is rather dramatic, and so it must have an equally revolutionary influence on the siting of some of the other towns that are mentioned in the Bible. The town or province of Gilead, for instance, lay on the river Jabbok. But since the river Jabbok has now been identified as a branch of the river Nile in the Nile Delta, then Gilead could not have been located to the east of the river Jordan; it must have resided in the Nile Delta instead. The Bible indicates that both Gilead and a town called Geshur were held by the princesses of Machir (Maachah). Since these princesses and their offspring will all become important characters later in this unfolding story, their possible links with Egypt are particularly illuminating.

Ramesses

A similar conundrum surrounds the possibility of Biblical references to the pharaoh Ramesses II. While the name Ramesses is not explicitly given in the Bible, it is widely known that Ramesses had a sobriquet, or nickname, of Sesey; a name that may, or may not, be present in the Biblical texts.

While most classical historians will stick rigidly to this pronunciation, a few enlightened individuals do recognise that pronunciation can change, especially when crossing from one language to another. One such author, B. S. Isserlin, indicates that the Canaanite consonants 's' and 'th' were amalgamated and adapted into the 'sh' consonant. The even more liberal author, David Rohl, similarly showed that the Egyptian 's' could evolve into the Hebrew 'sh'. In fact, in his book *Legend*, Rohl supplies a long and fascinating list of consonants that have been subtly altered when words were adapted into other cultures and languages. But the Egyptologist, Kenneth Kitchen, strongly disputes Rohl's hypothesis of changing consonants, saying:

> Rohl's attempted equation ... is totally false and ignores what is known of

the linguistic facts. These are that between Egyptian and Hebrew, *s* is always reproduced as *s*, never *sh* – and *sh* as *sh* and never *s*. [6]

Academics are normally so cautious, couching each and every postulation in terms of its degree of possibility; until, that is, they are challenged on a topic. Suddenly, all caution is thrown to the wind and the challenge is deemed to be 'totally false and ignores what is known of the linguistic facts'. The problem is that such intemperate assertions are bound to fall flat on their face; these consonants do indeed change as they are adopted by other languages:

Egyptian	Hebrew	Meaning [7]
Sar	*Shar*	barley (hair of)
Suara (Suala)	*Shul*	chariot equipment
Suabeb	*Shuabeb*	go back
Subi	*Shub*	return
Sirhatta (Silhatta)	*Shelh*	bunches
Shadjiruta	*Suaredeh*	chasm

In addition to these 'exceptions', discovered in a brief perusal of the Egyptian and Hebrew dictionaries, there are any number of words that transpose the 'sh' and 's' within their own language. This is especially so with both Egyptian and Hebrew. This means that even if the word was transliterated correctly into another language, it could still have suffered a transposition either before or after it was adopted by that alternate language. This very point is even spelt out very graphically in a curious extract to be found in the Bible. Regarding the transposition between 's' and 'sh', the Bible says:

> Then said they unto him, Say now S̲hibboleth: and he said S̲ibboleth: for he could not frame to pronounce it right. [B8]

This may sound an odd but innocent enough question to pose, but this Biblical interrogation was apparently a very serious matter indeed. The failure to pronounce the word correctly betrayed the racial origins of the individual, who was then promptly killed. Some 42,000 people from the tribe of Ephraimites are reputed to have answered incorrectly and were subsequently liquidated by the Israelites.

This same question of the correct pronunciation of the word Shibboleth is still enshrined as a central part of the Masonic 'prayer book', and it was through these same associations that this verse also formed the basis of the famous question-and-answer scene between the Templar

Knights in the cult film, *Monty Python and the Holy Grail*. As in the Biblical account, knights that failed to answer the silly questions correctly were liquidated.

Quite obviously, there were differing ways in which the consonants 's' and 'sh' were pronounced in the ancient world, and it was through this same kind of process that David Rohl demonstrated how the Egyptian name Sesey (Ramesses II) could become Sheshey in the Hebrew. Using this same reasoning, Rohl then went on to equate the name 'Sheshey' with the Biblical Shishak, and so to argue that the Biblical pharaoh called Shishak was the famous pharaoh, Ramesses II (Sheshey). While these linguistic corruptions could easily have taken place, I believe that this association between Ramesses II and Shishak is nevertheless a mistake. The Biblical Shishak was, as is more commonly thought, the pharaoh Sheshonq I of the twenty-second dynasty.

Rohl also maintains that the twenty-first and twenty-second dynasties should be viewed as reigning concurrently with the surrounding dynasties, instead of following and leading them sequentially. The evidence for this apparently lies in the fact that these two dynasties are missing from the Apis-bull records in the Serapeum, but again I believe this to be incorrect. I will later demonstrate that these two dynasties were substantially influenced by Hyksos beliefs, and so they would not have wanted to indulge in this particular rite – after all, the primary battle of Moses was *against* these bull worshippers. The twenty-first and twenty-second dynasties were Hyksos sheep (Aries) worshippers, and so it is axiomatic that these dynasties would not be represented at the Serapeum. [9]

Despite this, it seems likely that the pharaoh Ramesses II (Sheshey) *was* named in the Bible after all, but in a very different context. He was probably referred to as one of the three sons of Anaq. These three sons were called Ahiman, Talmai and Sheshai; and the reason that this could be a reference to the pharaoh Ramesses II is that these brothers were known as the three 'giants' who inhabited Canaan. Far from being the three 'giant' sons of Anaq, there is a distinct possibility that these were instead the three 'giant' pharaohs who had caused the Hyksos-Israelites the most grief over the centuries – all of these pharaohs are reputed to have invaded Canaan and therefore ravaged these Hyksos-held lands. The three pharaohs being mentioned here were called Ahmes, Tedjutmes and Sheshey, or, in more common terminology, Ahmose I, Tuthmoses III and Ramesses II.

The Biblical story-line indicates that these three 'giants' were the 'children of Anaq' or 'sons of Anaq', and so the name Anaq is presumed to be that of their father. But it is not implicitly stated in the Bible that Anaq was their father, and so the word Anaq could equally refer to a nation, tribe or cult. The word *anak* עֲנָק means 'neck pendant' or 'amulet' in the Hebrew, and it is perhaps from this identification that we can glimpse the true meaning of this word – there is the distinct possibility that this 'neck pendant' that the Bible was referring to was the Egyptian *Anakh (Anaq)* cross ♀.

The *Anaq* cross was an amulet in the form of a cross with a loop, which was supposed to represent the concepts of 'life' and 'resurrection'. It has been suggested that the shape of the amulet has been taken from the design of an Egyptian sandal-strap, but how a sandal-strap came to represent the concepts of 'life' or 'resurrection' is not fully explained and is equally difficult to comprehend. The truth of the matter is that much of Egyptian symbolism was not simply abstract, however peculiar the glyphs may look; instead, the design of each glyph was firmly based upon real-world events and artifacts. The glyph for 'west' ꝟ is a case in point. The glyph itself may look highly abstract, but in actual fact this glyph was representative of the Sun, the solstice, and the pyramid's causeways and shadows, as was explained in the book *Tempest*.

I believe that the *Anaq* cross was no different in its real-world depiction of the concepts of 'life' and 'resurrection', and that this glyph was actually based upon the design of a mirror. The Egyptian hand-mirror was known as an *anaq* ♀𓅓𓏭, and it took exactly the same form and pronunciation as did the *Anaq* cross ♀, except that the loop of the cross contained a mirror. Rather than the form of the *Anaq* cross being incomprehensibly derived from the toe-loop of a sandal-strap, this representation of 'life' and 'resurrection' came instead from the mirror that was fixed into the cross's loop. When an individual looked into the mirror, the reflection that they saw was not simply regarded as an inanimate picture; it appeared to be a manifestation of another living being. The *Anaq* cross could, therefore, be made to come 'alive' with an exact copy of yourself – it was both 'life' and 'resurrection'.

Coming back to the Biblical tale of the three brothers, they were said to be the 'sons of Anaq'. If these brothers were indeed pharaohs of Egypt, then the Anaq cross would have been a primary symbol of their nation, as it formed a large part of every royal proclamation. Each time the king's name was mentioned on a stele it was followed by the words 'Life, Prosperity, Health!', a trio of concepts that are perhaps more accurately termed as being 'Life, Stability, Contentment'. No doubt this proclamation occurred in real life too, and if a town crier mentioned the king's name, the assembled crowds had to reply in excited unison – "Anaq, Djed, Uas (♀𓊽𓌀)".

The Ramesside pharaohs were particularly fond of the Anaq symbol, which was embodied in the glyph for Maat, whereas the twenty-first dynasty that is about to be studied in depth favoured the Uas and occasionally the Djed glyphs. Although this particular argument is based largely on conjecture, it is likely that these three Biblical 'giants' were actually the three most powerful of the New Kingdom pharaohs, who identified themselves with this talisman that was unique to Egypt and were therefore known as the 'sons of Anaq'.

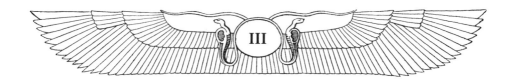

The Queen of Sheba

The first inkling that the two most famous of the kings of Israel, King David and King Solomon, might somehow be related to the Egyptian pharaonic line came to me while researching the history of the Queen of Sheba. During my researches, it transpired that the Queen of Sheba may have been an Egyptian princess; the pharaoh's daughter who, according to the Bible, became betrothed to King Solomon. But this is certainly not the classical interpretation of the history of this infamous queen of the east. Current opinions give two possible locations for the lands and kingdom of Sheba. The Kebra Nagast (the Ethiopian Bible) and some of the Biblical texts place Sheba in the heart of the Ethiopian highlands; while the historical fraternity have instead located her capital in the land of Saba, which lies in modern Yemen.

Just to the south of the great deserts of Saudi Arabia, there lies a small strip of relatively fertile land comprising a small coastal plain and some highlands just inland. The modern name for this area is the Republic of Yemen but two thousand years ago a small section of the highlands, which lie just to the north of modern Aden, was called Saba, and this region was the home of the famous Sabean nation.

It is through the many Arabic legends of the Queen of Sheba that this small nation has become inextricably linked to the story of this famous queen in the minds of classical historians. The Arabic historian, Ibn Ishaq of the eighth century AD, apparently linked the Queen of Sheba to the kings of Himyar, a land that lies immediately to the south of Saba. The stories related by Ibn Ishaq have become so engrained into the legends of this region that when one of the first of the adventurers to investigate this area, Thomas Arnaud, made his first visit in the 1840s, the names of the temples in the ruined cities of Marib and Sirwah were already known as 'Haram

Bilqis'. Since Bilqis is the Arabic name for the Queen of Sheba, the Temples of Saba were already known in this era as the Temples of the Queen of Sheba.

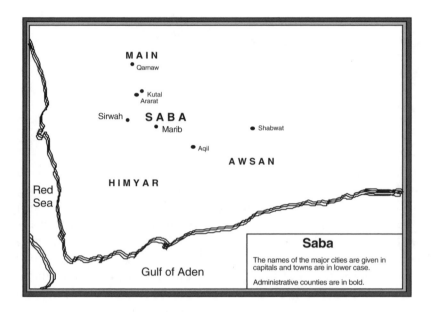

Fig 5. Kingdom of Saba.

As it happens, this association may be true in some respects, but perhaps not quite in the way that historians have assumed. But it is not just the early explorers who have been influenced by these Arabic legends. Alessandro de Maigret, for instance, conducted one of the most recent archaeological explorations in the region and she, too, seems to have taken the legendary bait. Having stated, almost as a fact, that the Biblical nation of Sheba was located in Saba, she then goes on to say that:

> If we are to believe that the (Biblical) account is historically accurate, we must accept that the kingdom of Saba existed in the tenth century BC and this held a monopoly over the incense route (the international trade in spices). [1]

But in continuing her investigation into the history of the region, Maigret completely fails to prove that there was a Sabean kingdom prior to the eighth century BC. In fact, having assessed all the various possible chronologies of the region, she actually settles upon a date for the first king of Saba of 775 BC; a date that is nearly two centuries later than the reign of King Solomon. Despite this abject failure, Maigret never retracts her earlier assumption that the Sabeans were the nation over which the Queen of Sheba ruled. Instead, vague references are made to the possibility of a 'later date for the reign of King Solomon'; that 'later compilers may have incorporated this queen into earlier texts'; or perhaps that this queen was a 'ruler of pre-Sabean nomads in the same region'. Arguing that the Queen of Sheba came from Saba is stretching the realms of credulity, but to indicate that she was also from a rustic, pre-Sabean nomadic society is simply nonsensical.

From the many investigations that my books have explored, it has become apparent to me that the Bible was once a reasonably accurate historical document, whose original manuscripts were contemporary to the eras that were being documented. The assertion by theologians that there was a period of verbal transmission that has garbled these texts is simply untrue. This argument is based upon a complete misunderstanding of the social standing of the people that the Bible documents. These texts were not the history of a few shepherds, they were instead the annals of the pharaohs of Egypt, and if anyone could have afforded to have their family history fully documented it was the Egyptian royalty. The point is that, if it were not for the deliberate amendments by the embarrassed Judaic scribes, I believe that the Bible would have been an authoritative historical document; more so than any of the surviving documents from either Greece or Babylon.

If the Bible was once a historical document, perhaps with a few embellishments and a Hyksos-Israelite political bias, it is entirely possible that many of the accounts that do not contradict Judaic theology can still be taken at face value. While the origins and history of the Queen of Sheba may have been an embarrassment to Judaism – as will be shown later – the fact that she was a wealthy, influential, and powerful monarch was not a particular problem. When the Bible says that the Queen of Sheba came laden with a king's ransom in gold and spices, I see no particular reason to doubt the general thrust of this report. On the other hand, had the Queen of Sheba been a pre-Sabean nomadic princess, arriving in Jerusalem with three worm-eaten camels and a kilo of hashish, I see no reason for the Biblical accounts to elevate her into a monarch of international repute and standing. The failure of historians to answer these issues of chronology and wealth seriously undermines any association between the Yemen and the Queen of Sheba; and all we are left with, in order to substantiate this dubious association between Sheba and Saba, are a few old Arabic legends and a similar name.

III   *The Queen of Sheba*

If this analysis seems to seriously undermine the classical explanations for the history of the Queen of Sheba, and if the location of Ethiopia is equally unlikely as her homeland – as will be shown later – then exactly where did this illustrious queen come from? The first clue that suggested this was a topic worth investigating came from the terms and phraseology that were being used by the Biblical scribes to describe this queen: they seemed to be specifically designed to cover something up. When the history of a very famous and important person is researched, one might expect terms of respect and reverence to be highlighted; instead, what I discovered was that the Biblical descriptions of the Queen of Sheba involved some rather unflattering terms.

Sheba שבא itself simply means the number seven or to swear an oath, but the people of Sheba שבאי also referred to drunkards. Now this term immediately struck a chord with me, because I had already written extensively about a line of Biblical 'drunkards' in the book *Jesus*. The Bible says that the New Testament Jesus was on friendly terms with a number of publicans and drunkards; indeed, some of these people even turned out to be members of his own immediate family. But far from being a simple term of abuse, the reference to 'drunkards' had more complex associations, involving both viticulture and the Roman and Greek gods Bacchus and Dionysus. But the origins of the Old Testament predate the Roman and Greek eras and their gods, so if the Old Testament drunkards were to be associated with a deity it must have been something far older, perhaps something Egyptian. Hence, I began to formulate another idea regarding the origins of the terms 'publican' and 'drunkard', an explanation that was rather more fundamental.

All of the Egyptian words for wine and beer are fairly unique, with little or nothing in the way of puns bar the odd 'vine' or 'grape', which is to be expected. Terms similar to the word 'drunk' were much more illuminating, and they consistently returned equivalents of 'prayer' and 'incantation'. In addition, drunkenness was also to be associated with concepts of 'immersion in water', 'festivals', 'fertility', 'flooding', 'flow of water' and 'waters of the Nile'. The inference was now becoming more clear; the term 'drunk' was possibly linked to some of the religious rituals of Egypt, especially those connected with the Nile floods. But the question was, why should drunkenness be associated with a religious festival?

A clue to the answer to this question can perhaps be glimpsed from the term Sheba שבא itself. In Hebrew, the word *sheba* means to be drunk and, not surprisingly, given the general thrust of these investigations, the word *sheba* also means something very similar in the ancient Egyptian language too, where it means 'to brew beer' or 'to prepare drinks'. But the similar words *sheb* ⬚〰️, *shebu* ⬚〰️ and *sheb-t* ⬚〰️, give us a possible reason for making copious amounts of beer and drinks, as these similar-sounding words mean 'food offerings', 'provisions', 'bread', 'meat' and 'incense'. It seems likely, therefore, that the brewing of beer was in some way involved with the rituals and offerings that took place in the Egyptian temples.

While the Egyptians were obviously using bread and beer in their religious rituals, the main thrust of my trilogy of books on the subject of revisionary religion is that the traditions of Egypt were the foundations upon which Judaism was formed. Accordingly, we find that many centuries later a Judaic leader called Jesus was using bread and wine in his celebration, which is now known as the Last Supper. Many centuries further on again, and we find that Christian festivals still use bread and wine in exactly the same way to celebrate the Eucharist; the Last Supper. In fact, the symbolism of that rite is that the red wine is turned into the actual blood of Jesus, and in a similar manner we find that the Egyptian term *djeshert* ⬚ means 'red drink', 'to get drunk' and even 'blood'. But the term *djeshert* ⬚ has one more meaning in the Egyptian language, and that is the 'Red Crown of Lower Egypt'. I have already used this explanation to show that the Biblical patriarch Esau was a prince of Egypt, but here we also see Jesus using the same symbolism, and so the royal status of Jesus would have been clear to all who had been initiated into these secrets.

Perhaps it can be clearly seen now why Jesus was accused of being friendly with 'publicans' and 'winebibbers', and why a near-relative of his was called Bacchus. A central part of the ancient rituals of the Egyptian priesthood involved the production of bread and beer (wine), and its subsequent ritual offering to the gods. In this case, the Hebrew term Seba (Sheba) referred not simply to the 'land of drunkards', nor to the 'land of bread and beer' (the land of plenty), but instead it referred to the land of 'bread and beer offerings to the gods'. In following these ancient traditions, it is no wonder that the later Judaic priesthood became known as 'publicans' (Bacchus) and were occasionally accused of having a little too much of their own home-brew.

Forgotten land

The Queen of Sheba was quite obviously not some minor queen of a nomadic, pre-Sabean society that inhabited and travelled the lands to the east of the Red Sea, as has been claimed. Instead, the Bible reports that this mysterious queen arrived in Jerusalem in some style:

> And she gave the king a hundred and twenty talents of gold, and spices in
> great abundance, and precious stones: neither was there any such spice as
> the Queen of Sheba gave King Solomon. [B2]

It is often assumed that the talent weighs some 30 kilos, which would have
meant that the Queen of Sheba was bringing some 3.6 tonnes of gold to
King Solomon. The Bible gets carried away in later chapters and boasts of
even larger amounts of precious metals, and so this figure too has to be
doubted. Later in this book I have assumed, from historical precedents,
that these Biblical weights have been inflated tenfold; but even with this
adjustment, the tribute being brought to Jerusalem by this queen was still a
substantial 360 kilos of gold. Perhaps the reason for discounting the
argument that the Queen of Sheba was a pre-Sabean nomad can now be
readily understood.

    While historians still cling desperately to the Sabean myth,
theologians grasp instead at a pseudo-Biblical document for their
explanations. Based upon the texts of the Kebra Nagast and a couple of
Biblical verses, they confidently assert that the land of Sheba was
somewhere in Ethiopia and that the Queen of Sheba was a beautiful dusky
maiden; but there is very little in the way of evidence to support this
notion. Instead of these remote and seemingly exotic locations, the first
century AD historian Josephus, whose testimony has proved rather reliable
in many respects, places the Queen of Sheba in more familiar territory:

> There was then a woman, queen of Egypt and Ethiopia; she was inquisitive
> into philosophy ... When this queen heard of the virtue and prudence of
> Solomon, she had a great mind to see him. [J3]

Here again we can see that Josephus' sources are potentially more
authoritative than those in the current Bible. Josephus presents a much
more sensible and logical argument, which indicates that the Queen of
Sheba actually came from Egypt. The confusion that exists between Egypt
and Ethiopia was probably influenced by the fact that this southern
kingdom was a province of Egypt at the time. It is a bit like saying that the
present British monarch, Queen Elizabeth II, is the Queen of Australia.
While this may be true, it does not infer that Queen Elizabeth was born in
or has lived in Australia, just that she is their monarch. But what of this
assertion by Josephus? And why is this Egyptian connection not trumpeted
quite as vigorously as the Ethiopian and Sabean alternatives? Since
Josephus' account is so plain and obvious, and since this text must have
been read by all the major commentators on this subject, it has to be

suspected that the silence regarding a possible Egyptian connection for the Queen of Sheba is the result of yet more deliberate obfuscation by the religious authorities.

Josephus is reputed to have had access to the original Biblical texts from the ruins of the Temple of Jerusalem, after its destruction by the Romans; texts which were written at least a thousand years before the oldest surviving Torah (Old Testament) manuscript. Josephus, whose material so closely follows, complements and improves upon the Old Testament texts, indicates that the Queen of Sheba came from Egypt. Despite this evidence, however, the religious authorities will ascribe the Queen of Sheba to any and every location on the map, as long as it is not Egypt. But why? Egypt was probably ancient Israel's most dominant neighbour; whether it be trade, diplomacy, marriage or war, Egypt was invariably and constantly involved in the history and destiny of Israel. So why, in this case, can nobody point towards Egypt as being the true homeland of this wealthy queen?

The stock answer to this will be that Egypt was the dominant power in the region, and that it is inconceivable for Egypt to have acted in a subservient manner towards Israel. The Queen of Sheba was a queen (or princess?) who was bringing tribute to Israel, which was politically impossible for the Egyptian royalty in this era. While this is true, to a degree, it is also true that the Bible reports there were many contacts and associations between Egypt and Israel in this same era. It is said, for instance, that relations between Egypt and Israel were so favourable that the pharaoh of Egypt gave Solomon one of his daughters in marriage; although the Bible is not so helpful as to say which pharaoh. In addition, a coalition of the Egyptian and Israelite armies subsequently mounted a joint campaign against the Canaanites in Gezer, and in return for this assistance the pharaoh allowed King Solomon to keep this city:

> And Solomon made a marriage alliance with Pharaoh king of Egypt, and took Pharaoh's daughter, and brought her into the city of David. [B4]

> For Pharaoh king of Egypt had gone up, and taken Gezer, and burnt it with fire ... and given it for a present unto his daughter, Solomon's wife. [B5]

Despite the historical objections, if the Queen of Sheba had been an Egyptian monarch (or princess), it is entirely possible that she could have been giving assistance to Israel in the same way that the pharaoh reputedly did to King Solomon. Taking Josephus at his word, then, it is possible that the land of Sheba could have been located somewhere in Egypt, and I think that further evidence for this assertion can also be seen in the history of the Biblical Jacob. If Jacob were a Hyksos pharaoh, as now seems highly likely, then his homeland would have been Heliopolis and the lands of Lower Egypt. The prophet Isaiah says of the patriarch Jacob, and the lands that he controlled:

> For I am the Lord thy God ... I gave Egypt for thy ransom, Ethiopia and Seba for thee. [B6]

The verse needs reading a few times to see exactly what it is trying to say. Basically, Jacob was involved in a war with his brother, and it looks as though Jacob had to make a political compromise. The text is indicating that Jacob had to give away the lands of Egypt that he held, but he managed to keep control over both Seba (Sheba) and Ethiopia. Since Isaiah mentions both Egypt and Seba in the same sentence, it has often been thought that Seba must therefore be separate from Egypt. But, as we have already seen, the term 'Egypt' in these ancient texts normally refers to Thebes and Upper Egypt, and not to the whole of Egypt. In reality, the land of Seba could have referred to the independent, Hyksos-controlled province of Lower Egypt.

This explanation would make some sense; Jacob was being given Lower Egypt (Seba) and Ethiopia, but he had no control over Upper Egypt, and this explanation concurs with our knowledge of Egyptian history. As is mentioned in many Egyptian texts, the Hyksos pharaohs (the pharaoh Jacoba) presided over an alliance of both Lower Egypt and Ethiopia in their battle against Upper Egypt. In this case, Isaiah was right and Jacob had forfeited Egypt (Thebes and Upper Egypt), but was given the lands of Seba (Avaris, Memphis and Lower Egypt) and Ethiopia.

The Koran seems to confirm this hypothesis. While the Koran does not carry much detail on this era of Judaic history, it says of the land of Sheba that:

> For the natives of Sheba there was indeed a sign in their dwelling place: a garden on their right and a garden on their left ... Pleasant is the land and forgiving is your Lord. But they gave no heed. So we let loose upon them the waters of the dam. [K7]

> I found that she (Sheba) and her subjects worship the Sun instead of god. [K8]

The Koran insists that the land of Sheba was well blessed, with a garden on each side (of the river) and occasional floods, and the people of this land worshipped the Sun. Historians will still insist that this description applies to the people of Saba in Arabia, where the famous Marib dam did break on a few occasions. But although the famous dam and garden of Saba do present us with similar scenes to the Koranical statement, and although the legends of the Queen of Sheba are intimately associated with the Sabeans, the city of Saba is still thought to date from too late an era to be directly associated with the Queen of Sheba. If historians wish to manipulate Saba to fit this description, then it requires the era of King Solomon being re-dated to the fifth or sixth centuries BC. While Alessandro de Maigret did try to hint at some such scenario, to make things fit, this revision delivers yet more problems; the campaigns of the pharaoh Sheshonq I being one in particular. The Bible reports that Sheshonq I (Shishak) was a contemporary of King Solomon's son and that this pharaoh had made a military incursion into Israel; and so if King Solomon were re-dated into the sixth century BC, what happens to the whole of Egyptian chronology?

While the Sabean scenario comes with too many strings attached, there is another, more compelling comparison to be made. Instead of Saba, this description in the Koran more accurately matches the conditions to be found in the land of Egypt. In reality, the Koran is describing the twin 'gardens' that line the east and west banks of the Nile, and the worship of the Sun-god Ra. Seen from this perspective, both the Koran and the book of Isaiah are indicating that Sheba can be seen as a reference to Lower Egypt. But is there any direct evidence to support Josephus' claim that the Queen of Sheba came from this area? Can Josephus really be relied upon to give accurate historical information?

Actually, the Bible appears to confirm Josephus' assertion, and it is a curious wonder that this association has not been highlighted before. The Queen of Sheba went to see King Solomon, and she brought with her a huge treasure of gold, precious stones and spices. It is also reputed that the queen had a son by King Solomon, who was called Menelek. So why did the Queen of Sheba bring all this vast tribute to Israel, and why did she consent to having the king's child? One theory, which is presented by the Koran and which will be explored later, is that this was a peace offering to prevent an attack by a threatening King Solomon. Another possible, and perhaps complementary conclusion, is that the Queen of Sheba was not necessarily a queen at all, but a princess instead, and she was travelling to Jerusalem with a vast treasure (dowry) to marry the most famous of the kings of Judaeo-Israel.

The only drawback to this idea is the implied relative power and influence of King Solomon versus that of Egypt; but as we have already seen, the Bible does indeed record that King Solomon married an Egyptian princess:

III   *The Queen of Sheba*

> And Solomon made a marriage alliance with Pharaoh king of Egypt, and took Pharaoh's daughter, and brought her into the city of David. [B9]

As we have seen, this union resulted in an alliance between the pharaoh and King Solomon, which culminated in a successful joint attack on the Canaanite town of Gezer. This strategic alliance between Israel and Egypt demonstrates the cordial relations that existed between the two countries at this time, a friendship that will be shown later to have been much closer than one might have expected.

However, this whole passage poses a great problem for historians, because the betrothal of an Egyptian princess to a foreign monarch was virtually unheard of throughout Egyptian history. Indeed, there are many historians who will dismiss this Biblical claim as pure propaganda, simply because it is so unprecedented. One Egyptologist says of this event:

> Simply stated, from what is currently known, reigning pharaohs did not marry their daughters to foreigners ... Amenhotep II had said (in reply to a Babylonian king) 'From of old a daughter of the king of the land of Egypt was not given to anyone'. [11]

This may seem like a trivial matter but it nevertheless has reasonably major implications. Under the normal rules of Egyptian royal consanguinity, in order for King Solomon to have married an Egyptian princess he would have had to have been related to this Egyptian pharaoh. The rather surprising proposal that this one, small Biblical verse demands, is that King Solomon must have been a close relative of an Egyptian pharaoh. This is the main concept that shall form the basis of the rest of this investigation, and so the primary task will be to discover in what way King Solomon could have been related to a twenty-first dynasty pharaoh of Egypt.

It is thought that this princess, who was given to Solomon, was the daughter either of the pharaoh known as Siamun, or perhaps Psusennes II; both of whom were of the twenty-first dynasty (c. 990-970 BC). So was this daughter of the pharaoh, who was betrothed to King Solomon, the fabled Queen of Sheba? Has this whole problem been solved in a few pages? Perhaps, but a few pertinent questions remain, and these will lead us on to some yet greater and rather unexpected revelations – the first of these surprises being the precise identity of the father of this princess.

In order to discover this, we need to establish a common chronology between Egypt and Israel in this era, a trail of similarities and comparisons between King Solomon and the Egyptian royalty. If the Queen

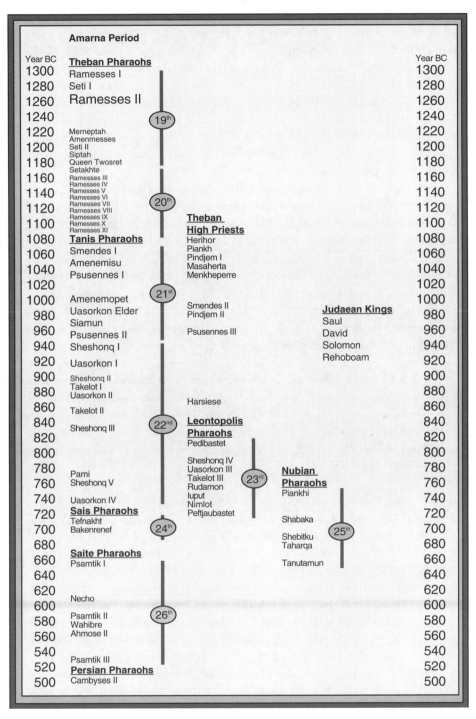

Fig 6.   Classical chronology of the Third Intermediate Period.

of Sheba was really a princess from Egypt, and if King Solomon were somehow related to this same royal line, then we ought to see obvious links and similarities between these two royal houses. The most obvious point of commonality that springs to mind, once more, is the invasion of Israel by the pharaoh Sheshonq I (Shishak), which occurred just after the death of Solomon. While this link is the basis for saying that King Solomon's Egyptian wife was the daughter of the pharaoh Psusennes II, we are really looking for the more subtle and less well-known commonalities here, not major military campaigns.

Despite the continual assertion for the uniqueness of Judaic people and their religion, there are actually some striking parallels to be found between these two nations, as has already been demonstrated. The close similarity between the Biblical book of Proverbs and the ancient Egyptian papyrus known as *Instructions of Amenemopet* is just another good example of this. The book of Proverbs details the life and wisdom (the proverbs) of King Solomon, and it is reputed to have been written by Solomon himself. On the other hand, the *Instructions of Amenemopet* is supposed to date from the Ramesside period of Egypt, or about 1300 BC. The translator of this Egyptian text, Miriam Lichtheim, says of these similarities:

> It can hardly be doubted that the author of Proverbs was acquainted with the Egyptian work and borrowed from it, for in addition to the similarities in thought and expression, Prov 22:20 states: "Have I not written for you thirty sayings of admonition and knowledge?", (which) derives its meaning from the author's acquaintance with the 'thirty' chapters of Amenemopet. [12]

If one takes a look at the book of Proverbs, this verse will invariably say 'excellent' instead of 'thirty', but this is simply a convenient Biblical mistranslation as the Hebrew word *shelowshiym* שְׁלוֹשִׁים can have either of these meanings. It is clear that the Biblical scribes knew of the thirty sayings of Amenemopet and tried valiantly to distance these texts from their hero, King Solomon. After all, how can a monarch be considered to be endowed with divine wisdom if all he did was copy an existing Egyptian text?

What this similarity gives us, though, is a positive cultural link between Egypt of the twenty-first dynasty and King Solomon (c. 960 BC); and it would also appear that much of the primary literature of King Solomon was based upon the literature of Amenemopet. This does not exactly explain how the scribe Amenemopet came to be so knowledgeable that kings plagiarised his work, but later in the book the identity of this scribe will be uncovered and this will greatly clarify the situation.

III The Queen of Sheba

Sabbath

Since it is known that an Egyptian princess travelled to Israel in this era and married King Solomon, it is entirely possible that this princess was the Queen of Sheba. As was previously demonstrated, the word *sheba* שׁבא, was probably taken from the ancient Egyptian word *sheba* ▭◻◻○, meaning 'food offerings' or the 'brewing of beer'. This terminology was indicating that Egypt was the land of plenty and also the land of the 'bread and beer' offerings to the gods. But there is another Egyptian translation of the word *sheba*, and in order to be able to see this meaning a quick look at the underlying Hebrew definition is first required.

The Hebrew word *sheba* שׁבא was partly derived from the word *shebua* שׁבע, meaning a period of seven days and also from the word *shaba* שׁבע, meaning to swear an oath. It is from these two words that the Hebrew word *Shabbath* שׁבת, meaning the Sabbath, or day of rest, was coined. However, this simple association is not accepted by all the authorities in this field:

> Some ancient writers (Theophilus of Antioch and Lactantius) say that the Hebrew word (Sabbath) is derived from *sheba*, meaning seven; but (the) *ayin* (a) is a strong consonant, and this etymology is therefore impossible. [13]

Having fought and lost a battle over the 's' and 'sh' consonants, the authorities now plan to declare war on the 'a' vowel or consonant, or whatever designation one likes to give to this particular letter.

The *ayin* being referred to here is the hard 'a' or *Ah!* at the end of the name *sheba*, which is considered linguistically to be a consonant and not a vowel; and the presence of this letter means that this word should be pronounced as *shebah*. But I think that the experts sometimes get too immersed in the minutiae of their field; they see the leaves and the twigs in incredibly fine detail, but have no concept of the surrounding forest. Whatever the experts may say, according to the Bible Concordance the Hebrew word *sheba* can be spelt with either an *ayin* שׁבע or an *aleph* שׁבא, and so the textual fluidity of this word is confirmed – or perhaps the authorities know better than the very scribes that wrote the Bible!

I had the same kind of discussion recently with a professor who challenged my assertion that the Biblical High Priest Ananias was named after the Jewish High Priest Onias, who was in turn the High Priest of On (the Biblical name for Heliopolis) or An (the Egyptian name for Heliopolis). The succession of these terms, in both profession and pronunciation, seemed clear enough to me, but I was informed that the name On אן began with an *aleph*, and its confusion with an *ayin* was impossible.

> ... this is a matter of established linguistic fact, which rules out the equation you want to make. [14]

Rules and regulations be damned! The fact of the matter is that the *aleph* sounds a bit like an *Oh!*, which is often likened to the cockney 't' in the word bottle (the 't' is missed out and replaced by a guttural sound). In comparison, the *ayin* sounds a bit like a gulping *Ah!*. The trouble with these sounds is that they are incredibly difficult to pronounce if you have not been born into this language, and so as the Egyptian language spread out across the Near East, riding high upon the waves of dispossessed Hyksos refugees, alternative pronunciations were bound to have crept in to the language.

A comparison would be the modern spread of the English language and the resulting German interpretation of the English 'th' (which becomes a 'z'), or perhaps the Chinese interpretation of the English 'r' (which becomes an 'l'). These two cultures find these particular consonants very difficult to pronounce, and no amount of elocution will alter their accent. Equally, the author finds it almost impossible to use the *aleph* consonant, especially when it appears at the beginning of the word. The resulting pathetic attempts at pronouncing the Hebrew word *Oh-n* or the Egyptian *Ah-n*, invariably end up sounding like the English 'On' and 'An'.

The same difficulties can be demonstrated within one culture and even within one small area of that culture. In middle England, the word 'back' is pronounced with a hard 'k' at the end. But one only has to travel a short distance up the road and the burghers of Liverpool pronounce this word as 'bach', with a soft, rolling 'k' that sounds like a Scottish 'loch'. Despite the presence of national and global radio and television over a period of three or more generations, the citizens of Liverpool still acquire their accents from their parents, not the newsreaders on the BBC. Trying to get a Liverpudlian to pronounce 'back' with a hard 'k' is rather like trying to get a German to pronounce the 'th' consonant; in fact, it is almost as difficult as trying to <u>stop</u> a Catalonian, in northeastern Spain, from pronouncing a 'th' in every possible word, whether it is required or not.

If such differences can be found on such small geographical scales, even when the citizens are subjected to the all-pervasive umbrella of the global media, what chance did the words 'On' and 'Sheba' have as they made their way up from Egypt to Judaea and Israel? Indeed, the whole concept of the *ayin* and *aleph* being distinct consonants is dismissible even within the Egyptian language itself. The following is the result of a quick browse though the Egyptian dictionary, looking for similar words using both the *ayin* and *aleph*.

Aleph		Ayin	
Au	violent	*Aua*	violent
Aut	bread offering	*Auait*	fermented drink
Ab	ivory tusk	*Ab*	ivory tusk
Afa	greed	*Afa*	greedy
Am	to swallow	*Am*	to swallow
Am	to understand	*Am*	to understand
Arar	high	*Arar*	to raise up
Aqu	destroy	*Aq*	destroy

The same results can also be found when looking for comparisons between the *ayin* consonant and the '*a*' pseudo-vowel.

Aleph		'a' or 'i'	
Ab	ivory tusk	*Aab*	ivory
Abi	leopard	*Aabi*	leopard
Abeb	wish	*Aab / Ab*	wish
Ab	thirsty	*Ab*	thirsty
Apdj	waterfowl	*Apdj*	goose
Af	food offerings	*Af*	meat, fish, bread
Afu	worm (snake)	*Af*	snake
Ames	sceptre	*Ames*	sceptre
Akhakh	green, blossom	*Akhakh*	green, flourish
Asi	payment	*As*	price
Ash	evening	*Asht-fku*	evening meal
Asher	roast	*Asher*	roast
Aqu	ruin, destruction	*Aqa-t*	ruin, destruction
Aqa	high place	*Aqa*	to be high

There are a small but inescapable number of words that use any or all of the three Egyptian 'a'-type consonants, and to argue that no such transpositions ever take place is fallacious.

It would seem obvious to me that if the line of high priests of Jerusalem who built the temple at On (An) were called Onias; and that after their eviction from On (An), subsequent high priests of Jerusalem were called Ananias; a positive link can be made between the two groups. Likewise, if a festival called a Shabbath (Sabbath) is held every seven days, and the word for the number seven in the same language is called *sheba* (*shabah*), I would consider it obtuse in the extreme to argue that a minor change in one difficult-to-pronounce consonant – from 'ah' to 'a' – negates these two words from being linked.

It is not as if this weekly cycle of six working days and a Sabbath day of rest is a recent Judaic invention; the custom, so we are led to believe, was derived from the working week of god himself, when he supposedly fabricated the Earth from the void. With the Sabbath being descended from such an ancient piece of Judaeo-Hyksos mythology, one might expect that this six-day working week and a Sabbath day of rest was one of the most ancient of religious customs. (Note again the typical change from the letters 'sh' to 's', when moving from the Hebrew word *Shabbath* to the English word Sabbath.)

There are, however, further pointers to indicate that these two words are linked. The Egyptian word *sheba* also refers to various offerings to the gods, as has been demonstrated, and these are the same offerings that an Israelite priest may make to god. Since the Hebrew word Shabbath (Sabbath) is the holy day of Israel, the very day that these offerings were made, there just has to be a direct link between these two words. In which case, the title 'Queen of Sheba' may have been a reference to the queen who officiated at the rituals performed on the holy day of the week (the Queen of the Sabbath). But the Sabbath not only denotes the holy day of the week, it also refers to an oath and a period of seven days, and the reason for these sub-meanings is obvious. Presumably, the Israelite congregation had to assemble in the temple every seven days, on the Sabbath, and renew their oath to god, just as Christians do to this day – hence the three meanings to this word.

Seven

While this explanation for the Hebrew word *sheba* may seem complicated, the Egyptian word *seba (saba)*  appears to have had a similar variety of meanings. Some of these alternatives will become more important as the story in this book unfolds, but the prime import of the Egyptian word *seba* is simply 'door'. But this was no ordinary door, this was the 'Great Door of Heaven', the ancient, secret and sacred portal of communication with the gods. The Egyptian gods were sometimes thought of as Earthly beings, but on other occasions they were envisaged as somewhat ethereal beings that inhabited the cosmos. In order to communicate with these divine beings in the cosmos, this door also had to be a window into the Universe and so, not surprisingly, the word *seba*  also referred to the stars that punctuated this great abyss of heaven. But such a sacred concept and artifact was always going to be a state secret in Egypt, and thus this same word not only referred to the

'Great Door of Heaven', but also to 'wise men', 'teachers', 'education' and 'wisdom'.

Since the word Sheba (*saba*) can refer to concepts of 'seven' and also 'star', researcher Richard Knowles has linked *sheba* with the constellation of Orion. Of all the constellations that comprise seven primary stars, Orion has to be the most prominent, and since the ascension of the deceased pharaoh involved this same constellation, this would also be a suitable place in which to locate a Great Door of Heaven. This same tradition may also have been a part of the symbolism of the Menorahמנרה, the seven-branched candlestick of Judaism. While the symbolism of the Menorah may be complex and manifold, the individual candles can be seen as either seven planets or seven stars. This great candlestick, which is such a central component of traditional Judaism, may be one more facet of the Sheba conundrum. It would seem that the title 'Sheba' may have been a central component of Egypto-Judaic mythology, and so while King Solomon may have been known for his esoteric wisdom, it may be that the Queen of Sheba was equally blessed. [15]

This has been the literary explanation for the word *sheba*, but these Egyptian rituals were not always simply read from a scroll; sometimes they were acted out around the temple precincts, perhaps with priests taking on the roles of the various deities or astronomical bodies. In the book *Tempest*, it was shown that these rituals involved a procession circling around the pyramids. Accordingly, the Hebrew word *sebab* סבב also means to 'walk', to 'circle', to 'compass' or to 'march around'.

If the ancient rituals involved marching around a pyramid, then they would have been firmly linked to the whole issue of 'Giza mythology'. Since the word *seba* (*sheba*) can also refer to the 'Great Door of Heaven', perhaps I should be even more bold and claim that *seba* also referred to the pivoting stone block that once plugged the entrance to the Great Pyramid at Giza. While this may sound like an unjustified assumption, some rather dramatic additional proof in support of this will be given later in the book. As was related in the book *Tempest*, the Biblical Mt Sinai was simply a Judaic term for the Great Pyramid at Giza, and many of the original rituals of the Hyksos-Israelites actually took place upon the Giza plateau. The Biblical link in this explanation is vital, because the Bible places Mt Sinai (the Great Pyramid) at the center-stage of its story. More specifically, the Bible indicates that this sacred 'mountain' had a chamber deep inside it that contained the Israelite god, Yahweh:

> These are the commandments, which the Lord commanded Moses for the children of Israel <u>in</u> mount Sinai. [B16]

If the Hyksos-Israelite god resided inside* the Great Pyramid, then it is of no great surprise that its doorway would have become known as the 'Great Door of Heaven' – the *Saba*. But the linguistics of Egypt are so easy to follow at times that the exact day when this great door was opened can also be stated with some confidence. The obvious supposition, bearing in mind the arguments made so far, is that the opening of the Great Pyramid's door occurred on the seventh day of the week, the Sabbath. In subsequent generations, the *Saba* door donated its name to the holy day of the week, and since this religious holiday occurred every seven days, the same name was also donated to the Hebrew number seven.

This ritual unbolting of the 'Great Door' to the Great Pyramid was obviously a fundamental aspect of the Giza rituals, and accordingly it developed its own unique terminology. The Egyptian word used for unbolting a door, or breaking the seals on a door, was known as *sefekh* 〔glyph〕. But if this ritual opening always occurred on the seventh day, as I have proposed, then one might expect that this word would have absorbed some kind of association with this all-important number seven. Right on cue, a quick search shows that the Egyptian word for 'seven' was also known as *sefekh* 〔glyph〕. In exactly the same way that the Hebrew language has adopted the term for the Great Door (*saba* or *seba* 〔glyphs〕) as its name for the number seven (*saba*), the Egyptian language has adopted the term for unbolting that door (*sefekh*) as its name for the number seven (*sefekh*).

Incidentally, the English word for the number 'seven' has been derived directly from these ancient origins – but on translation into Hebrew, the last letter of 'kh' ך has become confused with and exchanged for the similar-looking letter 'n' ן. In this manner, the Egyptian word *sefekh* became the Hebrew word *sefen* (seven), and so our modern designation for the number seven is directly descended from an Egyptian word.

If the weekly period of seven days were related to the Great Pyramid by this sacred ritual, then the reasons for instituting this seven-day week and the 28-day month are perhaps more understandable. It has already been shown that these two time periods were related to the orbit of the Moon – which may still be true in many respects – but in addition, the Great Pyramid itself is infused with copious amounts of mathematics and metrology. (I have already demonstrated in the book *Thoth* that the 1760-cubit perimeter length of this pyramid is suspiciously the same as the British 1760 yard mile.) In a similar fashion, the 280-cubit height of the Great Pyramid could have been used as a cue for the length of the month.

---

* The RSV Bible translates this as being <u>on</u> Mt Sinai, which is a deliberate mistranslation of the original Hebrew text.

The height of this pyramid, when divided by the favourite Biblical and pyramidal multiple of 40, gives the number seven, which has been used to denote the length of the week. The Egyptians loved to play with numerology, and so this argument for the introduction of the seven-day week and 28-day month is as good as any that I have seen.

If the great entrance door to the Great Pyramid was unbolted and opened on the seventh day, and if the door itself was considered to be the 'Great Door of Heaven' – the divine portal that led into the nether world of the *Djuat*, the land of the gods and the dead – then it is axiomatic that *sefekh*, the Egyptian term for unbolting a door and the number seven, would have become intimately associated with the Egyptian word *seba*, meaning the Great Door of Heaven. The *Seba* 𓂝𓈖𓇳 would have been *s-sefekh* 𓊪𓊪𓆑 (unbolted) on the *Sefekh* 𓊪𓆑 (seventh or *Shabbeth*) day. This is indeed what is found, and in the translation from the Egyptian into Hebrew, the word for the number 'seven' became associated more with *seba* than with *sefekh* – hence the word for 'seven' in Hebrew is *seba*, not *sefekh*.

But the original use of the word *sefekh* 𓊪𓆑 , as a term for unbolting the Great Door, was not entirely lost even within the Hebrew language; and I can confidently assert this because the association of this word with the Great Pyramid was retained in the Biblical book of Ezekiel:

> Behold, therefore I am against thee, and against thy rivers, and I will make the land of Egypt utterly waste and desolate, from the <u>tower of Syene</u> even unto the border of Ethiopia. [B17]

By the era of Ezekiel, the Israelites had been away from Egypt for hundreds of years, and their former homeland had now become the scapegoat for each and every misfortune that the Israelites encountered. This verse is one of many oaths against the newly despised land of Egypt. It may not be immediately apparent what the quote is trying to say, because some daft translator has interpreted the 'tower' as being called Syene. The Gideon Bible has taken this obfuscation one step further by saying that the land was laid waste 'from Migdol to Aswan'! What a tangled web we weave...

The truth of the matter is that the Gideon Bible's city of 'Migdol' was not a town but a 'tower', just as the King James Bible correctly translates – *migdol* מגדל means tower in Hebrew. The problem with the King James' version of this verse is that the word Syene is very badly transliterated into the English. The usual Hebrew pronunciation for this word is actually 'Seven' סון or 'Sheven' שׁון. (Note the mixing of the 's' and 'sh' consonants once more.) The tower in question is, of course, not really the 'Tower of Seven'; it is more correctly translated as the 'Tower of Sefekh' – but the verse is using the Hebrew version of this word, which is 'Seven'. As I mentioned previously, the Hebrew letter 'kh' ך, has simply become confused with and exchanged for the similar-looking letter 'n' ן.

This, however, does not fully explain this verse in the book of Ezekiel. We have still not deciphered which 'tower' in Egypt would have been closely associated with the word *sefekh*, meaning to unbolt a door, and which 'tower' would also be closely identified with the number seven. The answer is not only obvious, but also inescapable – the 'tower' to which Ezekiel was referring was a 'tower' that apparently defined the whole character of the land of Egypt. It was a shibboleth, or symbol, that every enlightened reader was immediately supposed to understand to be a reference to Egypt, and so it is axiomatic that this 'tower' was none other than the Great Pyramid of Giza itself. In reality, Ezekiel was trying to say:

> Behold, therefore I am against Egypt, and against Egypt's rivers, and I will make the land of Egypt utterly waste and desolate, from the <u>Great Pyramid</u> even unto the border of Ethiopia.

If the term *sefekh* referred to the Great Pyramid and if, in turn, the term *seba* was related to the doorway of the Great Pyramid – which is still the largest building on the planet – then the terms *sefekh* and *seba* would have been as Egyptian as apple pie is American. In this case, the name *Seba* (*Sheba*) would have been a positive reference to the land of Lower Egypt and, likewise, the Queen of Sheba is likely to have been a queen or princess of Egypt.

Priestess

Although the threads of this story may have been difficult to follow at times, there are a couple of further twists to this chapter that are quite important. The meaning of the word *sheba* may have referred to this queen in a more specific manner than the meaning of 'door' and 'star' that have just been given. As mentioned earlier, the term *'sheba'* may have been related to the role that this princess played in the rituals performed on the Sabbath days of the Egyptian religion. Her Biblical title was the Queen of Sheba (Malkhah Sheba מלכה־שבע), but she could equally have been called the Daughter of Sheba (Bath-Sheba בת־שבע). The point being made here is that the Hebrew term for daughter is *bath* בת; while in a very similar manner, the holy seventh day of Egypt – the day when the door of the

Great Pyramid was opened – was called the Shab-bath שַׁב-בַּת. (Note the double 'b' emphasis that is always given to the word Shabbath, indicating the possible conjunction of the two words *shab* and *bath*.)

In other words, the title that has been given to this lady is the exact mirror image of the holy day that she most probably officiated at. She was the Bath-Sheba בַּת-שֶׁבַע, while the holy day itself was known as the Shab-Bath שַׁב-בַּת. The link between the rituals of the Sabbath day and the priestess who officiated at those rituals could not have been made any plainer for us – the Queen of Sheba was the Queen of the Sabbath day.

The final point to be made here is the close relationship between this queen and the pyramids. We can see that these Sabbath rituals were intimately associated with the Giza plateau and with the Great Pyramid itself, in which case the Queen of Sheba could easily have been regarded as the Queen of the Pyramid. But since the Bible maintains that the Hyksos-Israelite god actually lived inside the Great Pyramid (Mt Sinai), this same lady could also have been considered to be the Queen of God or the Wife of God.

This latter term is important, for within the twenty-first dynasty of Egypt there arose a very exalted position within the ranking of the royal family, and this was the position of God's Wife. This was a position that was normally assigned to a daughter of the pharaoh and it is often assumed that she had to remain a virgin during her tenure, although she was probably allowed to resign at a later date and allow another princess to assume this position, as we shall see in later chapters. The point about the position of God's Wife is that it was an extremely important position; so much so that the incumbent often inscribed her name within a royal cartouche, a prerogative that was normally reserved only for the king himself. In every respect, therefore, although the God's Wife is not currently thought to have been the wife of the pharaoh, this individual would still have been considered to have been a queen. The God's Wife was not necessarily the wife to the pharaoh, she was instead the consort of the god who lived behind the Great Door, the *sheba* portal. In short, God's Wife was the Queen of Sheba.

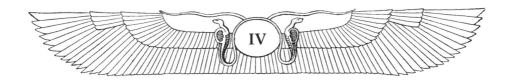

King David

The rather surprising conclusion of the last chapter is that the Queen of Sheba, who was reputed to have travelled to Judaea to see King Solomon, was most probably a queen or princess of Egypt. In a similar fashion, the Bible says that a daughter of one of the Egyptian pharaohs travelled to Judaea to marry King Solomon of Israel. These two stories contain a lot of synergy, and so it is quite possible that this daughter of the pharaoh was actually the Princess of Sheba. But, however compelling this comparison may be, this cannot be the complete answer to the identity of this queen, as the history of the United Monarchy indicates that there may have been another candidate who equally could have been the Queen of Sheba.

To ensure that nothing was missed, this investigation had to start at the beginning of this dynasty, and that meant looking at the family history of King David, the father of King Solomon. The first of many problems that this research generated was that King David married someone called Bathsheba. This did not appear to be the Queen of Sheba, however, as this lady seems to have lived in a whole generation before King Solomon. But now we have a Bathsheba (Bath-Sheba בת־שבע), a title that has already been linked to the Sabbath and the Queen of Sheba, and a separate Queen of Sheba (Malkah-Sheba מלכה־שבא). The obvious question that this raises is: were these two women in any way related? Incidentally, the Hebrew text does hyphenate the name Bathsheba, giving Bath-Sheba.

As has just been explained in the previous chapter, the name Bath-Sheba בת־שבע has been derived from the components *Bath* בת and *Sheba* שבע and these two words are normally taken to mean the Daughter of Sheba. But the word *bath* can mean either 'daughter' or sometimes 'house'. The confusion between these two meanings is based upon the Egyptian words Neb-t Per ⏝𓊹𓉐 and Nesu 𓇓𓏏𓊖, both of which have the dual meanings of 'house' and 'king' or 'queen'. These two seemingly very different meanings have been derived because the 'house' in question was not necessarily the palace itself; instead, it referred to the royal household or the royal family. This type of phraseology is still in use with the modern usage of the phrase 'House of Windsor', which is a formal title that is used in connection with the British royal family. Once more, the term 'house' is being used to denote the entire dynasty rather than their palaces and castles.

If the Hebrew title for Bath-Sheba was being used in the same fashion as the British and Egyptian terms, then the title of this particular wife of King David could also have been referring to the 'House of Sheba'. Since it has already been demonstrated that the term *Sheba* may refer to the land of Egypt, the title 'House of Sheba' could easily be read as a reference to the Egyptian royal family. It would seem that, in addition to King Solomon, King David may have also married a 'pharaoh's daughter'.

Readers who are familiar with the story of Bath-Sheba will perhaps have to suspend their disbelief for a moment, for the family history of this lady does not immediately suggest connections to either royalty or to Egypt. The Bible indicates that Bath-Sheba was originally married to a Judaean army commander, so it might seem highly improbable that she could have been an Egyptian princess; but the reason for Bath-Sheba's strange first marriage will soon become apparent.

The major problem for the whole of this scenario, however, is that marriage into the bloodline of the pharaohs was extremely unusual for the numerous minor potentates, like King David, who inhabited the less prosperous lands around Egypt. As we have already seen, this Biblical account of diplomatic marriages between Israel and Egypt has caused much consternation in the historical world, and there are as many explanations for why this should have happened as there are historians. The following is another possible rationale:

> The marriage of a royal princess (perhaps the daughter of Siamun) to Solomon of Israel is a striking testimony to the reduced prestige of Egypt's rulers on the world stage. At the height of the New Kingdom, pharaohs regularly took to wife the daughters of Near East princes, but refused to permit their own daughters to be married off to foreign rulers. [1]

One marriage into the pharaonic line of Egypt was highly unusual; the possibility that there were two marriages infers that something very strange was going on, and we are probably witnessing another Biblical cover-up. But the problem that is posed by the marriage of Bath-Sheba is even more daunting than usual, for if the princesses of the mighty Egyptian pharaohs never married foreign kings, why should anyone believe that the daughter of a pharaoh had been married off to a mere army commander (Bath-Sheba's first husband)?

The answer lies in the fact that the politics of this era and region are not fully understood. There is a classical habit, inferred in the quotation just given, of separating off the tribes and nations into completely isolated units. But, of course, we know that life is not like this. Europe has had separated tribes and nations for two thousand years or more, and yet the bloodlines of the various royal houses of Europe have mingled and intertwined at every juncture. This has happened not simply during periods of peace and prosperity, but even during the campaigns of the great wars; indeed, it might be suggested that the imperatives for alliances during wartime sometimes produced a flurry of these international diplomatic marriages.

The point being made here is that diplomatic marriages do not only occur between nations of equal status and power, they are also made between related royal individuals. Had the kings of Israel been related to the pharaonic line of Egypt, then the sending of a daughter of the pharaoh to both King David and King Solomon may not be quite so unusual as it might at first seem. In addition, Egypt no longer needs to have had 'reduced prestige on the world stage' in order to have arranged these marriages; in fact, Egypt may well have had increased influence on the world stage but simply felt that giving a daughter to a nephew princeling in Judaea was quite acceptable.

The reason for Bath-Sheba's initial marriage to an 'army commander' was that this individual was actually a royal Judaean prince, and he was also closely related to his bride. The circumstances that allow this to be so will be fully explored in the next chapter.

Ancestry

The brief history of this era, as was explored in chapter I, detailed the life of David up until he became king of all Israel; but this same history sheds very little light upon who this monarch really was. The texts would like us to believe that David was simply a soldier, although when reading between the lines it is readily apparent that he was actually a very important person in his own right. This fact is made abundantly clear in the all-important Biblical genealogies. King Saul may have been a very important person in this region – the first king of all Israel after the great exodus from Egypt –

but when it comes to the history of Israel, the family of King Saul is always sidelined in favour of the family of David. According to the gospel of Matthew, in the New Testament, Jesus was born of the line of Judah and so the ancestors of Jesus were: Judah, Phares, Esrom, Aram, Amnidab, Naasson, Salmon, Boaz, Obed, Jesse, and King David; etc; etc;.

Strangely enough, the gospel of Luke follows this exact same genealogy up until King David, and then diverges. While the gospel of Matthew continues with the list of Judaean kings, indicating that Jesus was descended from King Solomon and his son King Rehoboam etc., the gospel of Luke instead follows a genealogy through the descendants of Nathan, the brother of King Solomon. Not only does Jesus end up with two completely different genealogies in the New Testament, but if Luke was right and Jesus was descended through the line of Nathan, then he was not necessarily the most senior bloodline holder in the first century AD.

One area that these two genealogies do agree on, however, is the list of ancestors up until King David. But the reign of King Saul came immediately before that of David, and yet the names of Saul and his family do not appear in this list whatsoever. Clearly, the family line of King David was considered by many people throughout Judaic history to have been more important than the family of Saul. For this to have been so, King David himself must have been from a royal family – after all, half of the bloodline of Jesus depended on King David's royal connections.

But, if King David was not a simple army commander, and was instead descended from a royal family, then which royal family was this? Was David descended from a purely Judaeo-Israelite family, or were there, as I have previously suggested, strong links to the Egyptian royal dynasties? I think that I already know the answers to these questions, and I think that I already know who King David really was; but since these answers are not directly given to us in the Biblical texts, the resolution of this problem will have to come from a comparison between the attributes of King David and the attributes of another well-known person in this era.

The problem is very similar to the uncertain identity of the New Testament Saul, which was most satisfactorily resolved in the book *Jesus*. It was obvious to me that the name Saul, which was used for the New Testament character known as Paul, was simply a nickname. The majority of Old Testament names are long and complicated, and they are also usually handed down though successive generations, creating a complete confusion of similar names. So, when faced with an unusual name like Saul, it is obvious that one must search for another character with the same attributes and life history, in order to discover the real Saul. In essence, the name Saul was adopted by this character because he liked its royal status and its implied role as an opponent of the family line of King David – but his real name was Josephus (the historian).

The name 'David' presents us with a similar scenario; it is not only very short, it is also absolutely unique in the Bible. These two factors, when taken together, strongly indicate that the name 'David' was a nickname and that King David must therefore have had another full name or title. Like the resolution of the identity of the New Testament Saul, the discovery of the true identity of the Old Testament King David will depend upon a comparison between the life stories and attributes of two very similar individuals. If a sufficient number of connections and similarities between these two individuals can be found, then we will have made a positive identification.

Magen

There are two main claims to fame for King David; phrases and imagery that have come down to us through the centuries and the millennia, and which are probably as familiar to us now as they were nearly three thousand years ago during the reign of this famous king. Nothing can illustrate the power and status of King David better than the continued usage and knowledge of these two household terms in the modern world – the 'Star of David' and the 'City of David'. Having highlighted these two unique terms, which are only ever used in connection with King David, the primary goal of this investigation seems to be self-explanatory: if a member of any royal family can be found, who is strongly associated with both a star and a city, we may well be a long way down the road to resolving the identity of the historical King David.

The first clue, to put us on the right path, can perhaps be seen by remembering that the Egyptian word for 'star' was *seba (saba)* 𓋴𓃀𓇳 ✶ – a word that has endured the millennia and has now taken its place in the English Oxford Dictionary as 'Sabaean', where it still refers to a 'star worshipper'. If the Queen of Sheba could be considered to be the Queen of the Stars, as has already been suggested, then in some respects King David could perhaps be considered to be the King of Stars, or even the King of Sheba. The standard history of this era would have Sheba and David as coming from completely separate countries, but this is perhaps the first clue that points towards these two individuals being related or at least from the same nation – both of them can be seen to be linked to stars.

The traditional Star of David is the familiar, six-pointed star that is created from two interlocking pyramids, one of them inverted. It is still used as the primary symbol of Zionist Judaism and it is also used as the light-blue emblem on the modern flag of Israel. This star is known in the Hebrew language as the Magen David מגן דוד, and despite its ubiquitous modern usage, its history is somewhat uncertain and is often glossed over. Judaic historians like Louis Finkelstein, for instance, can write a thousand-page reference work on Judaic history without even mentioning the Star of David; a fact that has to be peculiar in itself. In some quarters, this symbol is seen to be a recent innovation within Judaism, but although this device was not quite so popular in the past, it became clear from some deeper research that the Star of David was actually an ancient Israelite emblem.

An additional complication is that the six-sided star of modern Judaism was, for many centuries, displayed side by side with the five-sided star, which was in turn known as the 'Seal of Solomon'. But since the five-sided star has been largely demonised and paganised by the Church authorities, it has been almost universally dropped as a symbol – except, of course, for the Pentagon, the military headquarters of the United States.

The term *magen* actually means 'shield' in the Hebrew language, and so it is thought that the Magen David may be related in some way with the shields that were made by King Solomon for his palace in Jerusalem. There is the distinct possibility that these shields were star-shaped and it was from this symbolism that the name of this star became associated with a word meaning 'shield'. The original designs for the Temple of Jerusalem and the royal palace were made by King David, Solomon's father, and so if these shields were indeed star-shaped, this design would probably have been the brainchild of King David:

> And King Solomon made two hundred targets (shields) of beaten gold: six hundred shekels of gold went to one target (shield). And he made three hundred shields of beaten gold; three maneh* (300 shekels) of gold went to one shield: and the king put them in the house of the Forest of Lebanon (Solomon's palace). [B2]

Note here that there were two sets of shields made for the palace of Solomon in Jerusalem. The main difference between these shields was their size, one consisting of 300 *shekels* of gold and the other 600 shekels. The *shekel* was an Israelite unit of weight that appears to have weighed about

---

* The Hebrew weight known as a *maneh* appears to have comprised 100 *shekels* (1kg) in Israel, but only 60 *shekels* (600g) in Babylon. In addition, the monetary value of the *maneh* in Israel was 60 *shekels* – like the peculiar British pound, the *maneh* appears to have measured value (money) as well as weight.

10g, and so it is the rough equivalent of the Egyptian *kite*, which also weighed about 10g. Therefore, the two types of golden shield that were being made for Solomon's palace (or Temple) weighed some 3.0 and 6.0 kilos respectively. If this account can be taken at face value, then King Solomon was using some 2.1 tonnes of gold for these shields alone. Although this figure appears to be very high, it lies well within the total amount of precious metals that were accounted for in the Egyptian records of this era, as we shall see in a later chapter.

The Biblical record then becomes even more unreliable, as it is then noted that King Solomon's annual income was about 20 tonnes of gold and the total amount of precious metals used on the Temple amounted to 3,000 tonnes of gold and 30,000 tonnes of silver. [B3]

The unit of weight being interpreted here is the *talent* כבר, which is normally regarded as weighing 3,000 shekels or 30kg, but this unit of weight (or the numbers of talents specified) just has to be in error. Both the Biblical record and the treasures that are accounted for in the Copper Scroll of the Essene give weights of precious metals that are totally unreasonable. Since the unit of weight being translated as the *talent* is the *kikar* כבר, it might be reasonable to assume that this was an equivalent of the Egyptian *kite*, rather than the *talent*. But such a change would reduce King Solomon's annual income to six-and-a-half kilos of gold, and reduce the total inventories in the treasury to one tonne of gold, which does not sound quite enough. Some alternative accounts from Egyptian history, that will be discussed in the next chapter, suggest that the total amount of gold in Solomon's inventory in this era was 20 tonnes. Making a similar reduction to King Solomon's annual income of gold would result in a figure of 130 kilos, which is a much more realistic figure. Assuming that the numbers given in these accounts were correct, the weight of the *talent* that would achieve this reduction would then be the equivalent of 200g.

Whatever the actual weight of these precious metals, it was obviously regarded in later years as being an obscene amount of wealth to use on a temple or palace. The recoil against this lavish expenditure by King David and King Solomon is to be found in the book of Revelations, where it rather famously says:

> And that no man might buy or sell, save he that had the mark, or the name of the beast, or the number of his name. Here is wisdom. Let him that hath understanding count the number of the beast: for it is the number of a man; and his number is 666. [B4]

This passage has had so many esoteric and prophetic associations attached to it that it has gained a wildly inflated mythical status, but in reality this verse was a simple tirade against wealth and extravagance. In fact, the answer to this strange riddle is that the annual income of King Solomon was 666 *talents* of gold. [B5] Note the comment in this verse about 'here is wisdom', which is a sarcastic reference to the wisdom of Solomon. The author is basically saying, 'if Solomon was so wise, then why did he flaunt his wealth quite so ostentatiously?' Note also that the passage in Revelations goes on to say that a man can only buy or sell with this 'mark' or 'name of the beast' – the 'mark' was obviously a talent of gold, and King Solomon gained another six hundred and sixty-six of them each year.

Whether these reports about Solomon's finances are considered to be reliable or not, the text is clearly pointing towards the lavish appointment of the royal palace at Jerusalem, and a degree of wealth that is probably unrealistic for an Israelite monarch – but just about attainable for an Egyptian one.

The other difference between these two sets of golden shields is that one was called *magen* מגן, while the other was termed *tsinnah* צנה. It would seem likely that the word *magen* is both similar to and derived from the Hebrew word *migdal* מגדל, meaning 'tower'. This can be stated with some confidence, partly because both of these words have sub-meanings of 'protect', and partly because the Greek rendering of *migdal* (meaning 'tower') is *magadan* μαγαδαν, which sounds very much like the Hebrew *magen* (meaning shield). The point of this line of enquiry is that the Hebrew word *migdal*, meaning 'tower', has been directly taken from the Egyptian words *maktar* (*Maktal*) 𓀀𓂝𓏤, or *magardja* (*magaldja*) 𓏏𓆑𓀀, with both words meaning 'tower' or 'protect'. Bear in mind, of course, that in the Egyptian language the term 'tower' was often used as a pseudonym for a pyramid.

This line of enquiry is all rather tentative at present, but it is further reinforced by the other term that was used for these shields, that of *tsinnah* צנה. The Hebrew word *tsinnah* means 'thorn' or 'prickle' and it cannot be a coincidence that the Hebrew word for Mt Sinai סיני has exactly the same meanings. Now the Biblical Mt Sinai has already been identified as being the Great Pyramid, and so the word *tsinnah* (*sinah* or *sinai*) may well be related to the term 'pyramid'. In which case, there are now two translations for the Hebrew terms for 'shield', the *magen* and the *tsinnah*, which may have been derived from loose associations with the Egyptian pyramids, and more evidence for this will be forthcoming shortly.

Both from the Biblical and the literary perspective, it is likely that these shields were used as protective talismans rather than functional shields – even the similar Egyptian word *makatau* 𓀀𓏤𓏤 means a protective talisman. It should also be pointed out that this concept of the star-shaped shield as a protective talisman, rather than a physical shield, is very similar to the way in which stars are used as an emblem in American law enforcement, where each and every officer, vehicle and helicopter is 'protected' by the image of a star. These American emblems may be considered by some to be meaningless symbols, but the 'protective' element of this talisman has nevertheless been reinforced by a number of films that have shown these stars being struck by bullets, thus saving the heroic police officer and simultaneously reinforcing the protective symbolism of this emblem. In a very similar manner, the Israelites used to parade these star-shaped shields in front of the army – they were not being presented as a physical barrier to defend the front line, but as a protective talisman to protect the whole army:

> And the Philistine came on and drew near unto David; and the man that bore the shield went before him. [B6]

It is my assertion that this shield, which formed the vanguard of the Israelite army, was nothing less that two interlocking pyramids made of gold. While that may seem like a bold statement, based on threadbare evidence, there is no escaping the fact that the translations of the words *magen* and *tsinnah* have great synergies with the terms that were used to refer to the pyramids. In addition, the design for the *magan* shield – as we see it today on the flag of Israel – is undoubtedly formed from two pyramids superimposed upon one another (one of them being inverted). It is highly likely, therefore, that this modern Judaic star shape was the very same design that was used for the *magen* shields of David and Solomon in the tenth century BC. The importance of the Great Pyramid within the theology of the Hyksos-Israelites has already been covered in some detail, and now we find that one of the prime symbols of the Judaeo-Israelite religion is the double pyramid – one superimposed upon the other.

Star and city

This may well have been a rather lengthy introduction to the symbology of the Star of David, but the presence of this star and its association with King David is rather important. The task that was set some time ago was to find another royal figure who was intimately associated with both a star and a city; another king who could lay claim to both the Star of David and the City of David. As it happens, there was an Egyptian pharaoh of the twenty-first dynasty called Pasebakhen-nuit, whose name in the hieroglyphic spelling, encompassed both the star ⭐ and the city ⊗ glyphs.

Fig 10. Cartouche of Pasebakhen-nuit.

This initial similarity between these two monarchs is, therefore, quite striking, and so the possibility exists that these monarchs were either related to each other or the same individual. While the latter option might seem like a leap of faith at this point, please bear with me a while longer, for there is a lot more evidence to explore.

The pharaoh Pa-seba-kha-en-nuit, who was called Psusennes II by the Greeks, was the predecessor of the pharaoh Sheshonq I. The latter pharaoh, Sheshonq I, was the pharaoh who was known in the Biblical accounts as Shishak, and it was this pharaoh who was reported to have conquered Jerusalem during the rule of Solomon's son. If the pharaoh known as Sheshonq I ruled at about the same time as the Biblical King Solomon, then it is fairly certain that the pharaoh Psusennes II ruled Egypt at about the same time as King David ruled Judaeo-Israel. If King David is to be associated in any way with King Psusennes II, it would help if they lived in the same era, and that seems to be just the case.

While it may be surprising to see two monarchs of precisely the same era being similarly associated with stars and cities, there are much closer associations to be made between these two monarchs than this. Psusennes II's official title was:

Pa	🐦	meaning	My,
Seba	⭐	meaning	Star,
Kha	👑	meaning	Appears, Rises, Shines,
n or S 〜〜 or —∞—		meaning	His,
Nuit	⊗	meaning	City.

When put together, the complete title becomes something like, 'My Star that Appears in His City'. It is immediately apparent that there is the distinct possibility of deriving shorter sub-titles from this lengthy appellation, which could include 'Star of Psusennes' (my star) or even 'City of Psusennes' (my city). These shorter titles would correspond precisely with the equivalent titles that were attributed to King David. Was this simply coincidence? Was King David simply aping the more powerful monarch from Egypt? Was he related to King Psusennes II? Or, and this is the most provocative of all these suggestions, were these two individuals in reality the same person?

Psusennes II was the last pharaoh of the twenty-first dynasty and he presided over a divided Egypt. The court of Psusennes was based in Tanis, in the eastern Delta lands, and although his name included the formal title of 'King of Upper and Lower Egypt', he effectively ruled only Lower Egypt. In the south, a powerful line of high priests had established themselves in Thebes, and they considered themselves to be the equal of any northern pharaoh; they even took the royal cartouche for their titles, becoming the priest-kings of Upper Egypt.

It cannot be stressed enough, however, how fragmentary the evidence is for the whole of this dynasty. In total there is probably as much information as would cover a few sides of A4, and this meagre data represents an entire dynasty covering some 230 years of the history of both Upper and Lower Egypt.

The information is so sparse that it is not even known if some of the pharaohs and priests of this dynasty actually existed. There is reputed to have been a High Priest Psusennes III of Thebes, who ruled alongside Psusennes II, but many Egyptologists indicate that these two individuals were actually the same person. There was also a pharaoh, now called Uasorkon the Elder, who was mentioned by the historian Manetho, but of whom there had been no evidence until recently. But this new evidence is in itself confusing because it turns out that Uasorkon held the same throne name as Psusennes I – in fact, I will be arguing later that these two pharaohs were the same individual. All in all, the chronology and history of the twenty-first dynasty is a bit of a muddle.

The problem for the historians who are trying to piece together this sector of ancient history is that the confident and wealthy empire of Ramesses II had deteriorated quite quickly. Attacks by the Sea People and subsequent infighting between royal princes had undermined the rule of law and the influence of Egypt's armed forces. The twentieth dynasty of Ramesside kings was weak and ineffectual and the subsequent twenty-first dynasty, which included the pharaohs Uasorkon and Psusennes, saw the nation split in two; a line of priest-kings ruled in Thebes, while an independent line of pharaohs ruled from Tanis in the Delta. It is the evidence from this latter Tanis dynasty that is particularly lacking, and so either this dynasty had become becalmed in the doldrums, or perhaps their history has been deliberately erased from the records by later generations.

The rule of the pharaoh Psusennes II was to prove to be no different; the standard reference book on this era generally gives Psusennes II two lines of text, and yet if this pharaoh were the Biblical King David, he would actually have been a very wealthy and influential monarch.

According to the historical record, the status and power of Egypt did not start to improve until the reign of Psusennes' successor, Sheshonq I. But once more it has to be pointed out that since the data from this era is so fragmentary, this presumed dynamism of Sheshonq I could just be a result of the paucity of inscriptions for his predecessor. The problem that Psusennes II had, in leaving his mark on history, was his lack of control over Thebes. The cities that Psusennes did have control over – Tanis, Bubastis, Avaris, and possibly Memphis – have been thoroughly trashed over the last two millennia or so; but on the other hand, Thebes has remained largely intact. Since the pharaoh Sheshonq I was able to gain control over Thebes, he was able to leave inscriptions in the Temple of Karnak that have lasted into the modern era, and thus we have a reasonable idea of this pharaoh's family connections and achievements.

This lack of data about Psusennes II results in one major drawback in this investigation. The title of this pharaoh states that he was associated with a particular city, but the frustrating consequence of the historical record is that we do not know precisely which city this was. The historian, Peter Clayton, has scribbled 'Thebes?' next to the city glyph in this pharaoh's birth name, but this suggestion is most unlikely. It is reasonably certain that Psusennes II never had control over Thebes because of the apparent lack of inscriptions to him there. The most likely Egyptian options, for the primary city of Psusennes II, would be Memphis or Tanis. But if one were to be really provocative, there is another city that could be associated with this pharaoh. If Psusennes II could be identified with the Israelite King David, then perhaps this city of Psusennes II could be identified as Jerusalem.

It would certainly be a major shake-up for both history and theology to suddenly find out that one of the most famous of the Judaic kings was in fact an Egyptian pharaoh. Many may be tempted to dismiss this suggestion on that basis alone – that is simply too revolutionary to be considered. But, as was discussed in the first chapter, the whole point of historical enquiry is not to get too bogged down in orthodoxy; not to decide upon the outcome before all of the data is uncovered. Only in this fashion can a balanced opinion of the overall picture be obtained. Perhaps I am inured to these drastic revisions of history; perhaps my independent view of theology will allow such revisions without impinging upon any preconceived ideas about who these individuals were. Whatever the case, I think that this is a subject and a line of enquiry that is worth pursuing further, so I shall carry on regardless.

The first question that readers will probably ask is, if Psusennes II is to be compared in any way with King David, how on Earth did the scribes manage to confuse a complicated Egyptian name like Pa-seba-kha-en-nuit (Psusennes II), with the Judaic name, David? The simple answer to this, is that the name David is simply a greatly shortened nickname. But I can confidently predict that the scribes would have wanted to preserve the true identity of who they were writing about, and so this nickname must pertain in some manner to the pharaoh's real name.

The nickname of 'David' was actually based upon the 'star' glyph, which is, as we have already seen, pronounced *seba* – the same *seba* that has already been shown to have been used in the name for the Queen of Sheba. However, *seba* is not the only word in Egyptian that can be used to describe a star, and the one that the scribes were thinking abut when they made the Judaic translation of this name was actually *djuat* ⌐⫐|⁂⟁ . The word *djuat* (*djuait*) not only means 'star'; more specifically, it refers to the 'Morning Star', which is often taken to be a reference to the planet Venus. However, this link between *djuat* and Venus may be misleading: although Venus tends to be a morning 'star', because it lies inside the orbit of the Earth, there were many stars that were observed in the direction of the morning horizon of Egypt. One of the main functions of the astronomical observations of the Heliopolian priests was to track the Earth's rate of precession on its axis. To do this required observing which star and which constellation rose with the Sun at the Vernal Equinox, and thus the term 'Morning Star' could have referred to any of these stars. In fact, the term *djuat* could just have referred to these observations themselves.

The term *djuat* can also have connotations of the 'land of the dead' and a 'pillar of the sky'. This latter meaning is yet another oblique reference to one of the four 'mountains' or 'pillars' that kept the heavens aloft: in other words the *djuat* can be thought of as a pyramid either at Giza or at Dahshur, as has been explained previously. So, like the similar word *seba*, the term *djuat* also has pyramidal connotations and no doubt the 'land of the dead' referred to the necropolis that surrounded the Giza pyramids.

Despite all this talk of stars, the true link between these two monarchs has still not been made, and so in what way does the name of King David relate to the Egyptian name for a morning star? Well, the Hebrew form of the name 'David' is pronounced Daveed דוד and even in this translation it is not difficult to see how this name was derived from the Egyptian original of *Djuat*. But the Hebrew translation, as given in the text books, is not necessarily the original version of this name.

IV *King David*

The name of King David is only given by the three consonants of Daleth, Waw and Daleth, which gives us a name that can be pronounced either as DVD or DUD דוד. As was shown in the previous chapter, the ו consonant can refer either to a 'u' or a 'v' sound, so both of these options must be considered. Since true vowels are not written in Hebrew text, vowels have then to be inserted between these consonants to produce a name, like DaVaD or DaUaD. But if the true pronunciation of the name is unknown then this insertion of vowels is largely based upon guesswork, and if the initial vowel were deleted in this particular case, the resulting name for King David would be either DVaD or DUaD.

Rectifying this error in pronunciation would mean that the real Hebrew name for King David was actually Duad, whereas the Egyptian word for this star was pronounced *djuat*. But the 't' and the 'd' consonants are almost interchangeable within the Egyptian alphabet, and so the words *djuat* and *djuad* could be considered to be almost identical. Only now can the truth of the matter be clearly seen; the Hebrew name Duad, for King David, is the exact equivalent of the Egyptian word *djuat*, meaning the Morning Star, and so King David (King <u>Duad</u>) may well have been related to the Egyptian pharaoh called Psusennes (Pa-<u>djuat</u>-kha-en-nuit).

Incidentally, many of the European languages have used the term Papa for father, a word which was probably derived from the Hyksos pharaoh Popi (Papi). The English language, just to be different, tends to use the term Dad instead. It is possible that this alternative version for father was derived from the short form of David (Duad), which was Dod or Dad דד.

Here, then, we have two apparently separate monarchs, King David and King Psusennes II, who were supposedly ruling separate nations, and yet they share both an association with a star and also the name of that very star – the pharaoh Psusennes II could easily have been called 'Pa Duat' or 'My Star' (David's Star) by the people of Egypt.

Fig 11. The 'Star of David'.

Startling as this discovery may seem, this evidence on its own does not confirm whether King David was actually the same person as Psusennes II, or whether he was just aping his more influential neighbour. If King David were really the same person as a known ruler of Egypt, he must be seen to have other Egyptian attributes and similar family connections.

Having already gained some confidence in making these radical new associations between historical figures, it was not so surprising to me that I quickly found yet more Biblical allusions to the pharaonic line of Egypt. In the book *Tempest*, I made a good case for Esau, the brother of the Biblical Jacob, being a Hyksos prince. The investigation here showed that many of Esau's attributes were associated with 'redness', and that the word 'red' in Egyptian was *djesher* ☒ . The interesting thing about this observation was that the Red Crown of Lower Egypt, the crown of the Hyksos pharaohs, was also called *djesher-t* ☒○◁ . Thus, in order to hint at the connections between the Biblical patriarchs and the royalty of Lower Egypt, many personalities are alluded to in the Biblical texts by their predominant 'redness'. It was for this reason that the first-born sons of Israel were sometimes identified by a scarlet thread on their wrist.

But these allusions do not stop with the much older pre-exodus Biblical texts. During the coronation of King David, we find this same imagery being used once more, and so King David was, for absolutely no apparent reason, said to be red:

> And he sent, and brought (David) in. Now he was ruddy (red), and withal of a beautiful countenance, and goodly to look to. And the Lord said, Arise, anoint him... [B7]

From Adam onwards, the patriarchs of the Bible were known for their strange redness and the unmistakable clue that the scribes were trying to impart – to those who aspired above the plebeian degrees in the craft, to those 'who had ears to hear' – was that King David of Israel was yet another link in the long and illustrious chain of Lower Egyptian Hyksos monarchs.

Daughter

But, interesting as all this information may seem, surely this Egyptian pharaoh cannot be the same as an Israelite king. What about the location in which he lived? What about their language and customs? What about their ancestors and descendants? Surely everything between these two monarchs must, by definition, be completely different? Well, one might like to think so but, after a lengthy investigation, the truth seemed to indicate the complete reverse of these suppositions. This investigation was, by necessity, long and complicated and it forms the bulk of the next chapter; but, just as a small snippet of what was found during that long process, let's take a look at a daughter of King David.

The first thing to note is that there are two separate sources of information in the Bible that detail this era. One is the book of Chronicles, the other is the book of Kings. While these two sources agree in many respects, they also differ on occasions and give slightly different names and family associations. A daughter in one might turn out to be a sister in the other, or a son may become a grandson. Not all of this apparent confusion is due to copying errors or even deliberate obfuscation; some of these differences, I believe, are simply due to the complexity of the family connections that were being reported!

The investigation into Kings and Chronicles eventually threw up a series of ladies with the same name – that of Maachah מעכה. But the first thing I noticed was that everywhere that a Maachah was to be found, there was invariably a lady called Tamar תמר. The Biblical commentators will not admit it, for some strange reason, but it just seemed rather obvious that Tamar and Maachah were two different titles for the same individual. This was at last seen to be true when it was noticed that Absalom, a son of King David, had only one daughter. But the different references in the different Biblical books gave her either the name Maachah or Tamar. Quite obviously, the lone daughter had to be called Maachah Tamar, so the two separate Biblical traditions have each used a different part of her title to identify her. As usual, it was the historian Josephus who came to the rescue and confirmed that my suppositions were correct, and that all of these Tamars and Maachahs were the same people. Josephus says:

> Absalom had three sons and one daughter named Tamar ... who ... was married to David's son Rehoboam. [18]

> Rehoboam married ... a daughter of Absalom by Tamar, whose name was Maachah. [19]

The first quote is saying that Absalom's only daughter was called Tamar, whereas the second is indicating that the same daughter was called Maachah and her mother was called Tamar. The reason for all this confusion is that there was a long line of women within the United Monarchy who were called Maachah Tamar, and it will be shown later that this was quite an important title in this era. Note, however, that through a strange quirk of family intermarriage, which will again be covered later, this daughter of Absalom called Maachah Tamar III מעכה תמר was both a stepdaughter and a granddaughter of King David (work that one out!).

But if the Bible is sometimes confused about who begat whom, then, in a similar fashion, so too is Egyptian history. Take the daughter of

Psusennes II, the pharaoh we have been studying and have already closely linked with King David. His daughter is said, by some historians, to have married the next pharaoh in line, Sheshonq I. But others indicate that she married the next pharaoh but one, the son of Sheshonq I, who was called Osorkon I (Uasorkon I).

So, apart from their complicated and fragmentary family histories, what was the connection between these two daughters? One of these women was born of an Egyptian pharaoh, the other of an Israelite king; so what, if anything, could they possibly have in common? Well, quite a lot as it happens, but we shall start with their names. The full title for the daughter of Psusennes II was Maatkare Mutemhat (Maatkare Mu-Tamhat) 𓇋𓏏𓊨 𓏏𓄿𓏤𓏥 ; whereas the full title of the daughter of King David was Maachah Tamar II (this is another Maachah Tamar to the one just mentioned by Josephus). Surprising as it may seem, both the daughter of the pharaoh Psusennes II and the daughter of King David had precisely the same name; a name which, it has to be pointed out, is quite complex.

Although the fact that these two women shared a common name may raise a few eyebrows, the association does not end there, and the translations of these names raises many additional links and questions.

The name 'Maatkare' actually has a long history in Egypt, and it can be seen that the female pharaoh Hatshepsut, of the eighteenth dynasty, also took this name when she acceded to the throne. But it is not known if she was a 'Maatkare' before she became queen or, indeed, if she was the originator of this title. The syllables that comprise this name are *Maat, ka* and *re*. The term *maat* is denoted by the seated goddess glyph 𓐙 , and it refers to 'truth and justice'; the next syllable has been derived from the two-arms glyph 𓂓 , *ka*, which tends to mean 'soul' or 'name', or perhaps even 'offering' or 'sacrifice'; while the last syllable, *re*, is simply the god-name *Ra* ☉ . Thus there is a variety of possible translations of this name, but all are based upon a common theme of praising the god.

The favourite orthodox interpretation of Maatkare 𓐙𓂓☉ is, 'Truth and Justice are the Soul of Ra', but it could also be translated as 'Maat is the soul of Ra'. The latter interpretation is important as it is suggesting that the goddess Maat was the companion of Ra, which would suggest that she was the role model for the priestesses who were known as 'God's Wife'. As will be demonstrated later, both the Maatkares and the Maachahs were known for being God's Wives, and both were strongly associated with the goddess Maat.

The translation of the name Mu-Tamhat is possibly even more interesting; it is an unusual title that was first used in the twenty-first dynasty. The equivalent tile that was previously used was Mut Neter,

, or God's Mother. Mutemhat (Mu-Tamhat) was a variation on this theme and it was derived from *mut* (*muti*) , meaning 'mother'; *em* meaning 'of'; and *hat* meaning 'front' or 'first'. As an aside, the word *muti* still means 'mother' in the German language. The full meaning of Mu-Temhat now appears to be 'Mother of the Front', with the term 'front' also having connotations of 'breast' – the latter meaning would result in a revised title of 'Mother of the Breast'.

Fig 12.   Maatkare Mu-Tamhat.

In the Egyptian record, this particular lady was also given the title of God's Wife, or Hem-t Neter , and this may explain what the title Mu-Temhat really meant. The peculiar sounding reference to 'Mother of the Breast' may actually have been a reference to the suckling of Horus by Isis. This mother and child symbolism was a favourite theme in this era and it was subsequently taken up by the Christian sect of Judaism, where it was transformed into the more familiar image of the Madonna and Child:

> Several incidents of the wanderings of the Virgin Mary with the Child (Jesus) in Egypt ... reflect scenes in the life of Isis as described in the texts found on the Metternich Stele, and many of the attributes of Isis, the God Mother, the mother of Horus ... are identical with those of Mary the Mother of Christ. [11]

According to these revised translations, however, it is possible that these references to gods and breasts have a deeper symbolism. In some respects the breasts of Isis can be seen to be duplicating the role of the breasts of the Nile-god Hapi: the former nourished the god-child while the latter nourished the lands of Egypt and no doubt made the people 'Happy'.

It was explained in the book *Tempest* that the all-important flooding of the Nile and the nourishment of the soil was supposed to have originated from a well that metaphorically gushed out from between the Giza pyramids: this is because it was the astronomical observations at Giza that appeared to regulate the seasons and so these same pyramids must have appeared to regulate the Nile floods. In turn, the two main pyramids at Giza were shown to be the Twin Peaks, the two breasts out of which the Nile floods originated. As such, these two pyramids were considered to be manifestations of the breasts of both Hapi and Isis.

The peculiar-sounding reference to 'Mother of the Breast' may, therefore, not only refer to the suckling of Horus by Isis, but also pertain to the very important role of a priestess who administered at these pyramid rituals. If so, then the reference to 'Mother of the Breast' would have been another subtle reference to the position of 'Mother of the Pyramids', a position that has already been applied to the Queen of Sheba. Perhaps, in order to complete this symbolism, this post always went to well-endowed ladies!

Fig 13.   Isis and Horus.

Interestingly enough, the mother of the Biblical Jeroboam – who may have been a son of King Solomon – had the very same title; she was called Zeruah צרועה, which means 'full-breasted' in the Hebrew. In fact, there is a distinct possibility that Zeruah may have actually been a Maachah Tamar (Mother of the Breast), and that she was given the nickname of Zeruah (meaning full-breasted) in later Judaic traditions. This suggestion is further reinforced because the name Zeruah not only has breast-like connotations, it also has pyramidal associations too. The name Zeruah is actually pronounced Tseruah צרועה and it not only refers to breasts, it is also based upon the word *tser* צר, meaning 'stone' or 'rock'. There were only two primary breasts made of stone in Egypt, and they stood upon the Giza plateau.

It would appear that the literary evidence is pointing remorselessly and conclusively towards the breasts of the goddess Isis (and Maachah Tamar) being symbolic of the two largest pyramids at Giza. While some readers may dismiss this whole concept as being an embellishment of the ancient texts, presumably based upon the author's personal fetish, nevertheless it would seem that the archaeological record has exactly the same preoccupation. The evidence for this was unearthed by Porter and Moss in 1927, and it demonstrated that the pharaoh Psusennes II [or King David?] had erected a small chapel at Giza, dedicated to 'Isis, the Mistress of the Pyramids'. [12]

When trying to part these ancient veils of intrigue, initiation and enigma, the evidence rarely crystallises quite so clearly as this – here is cast-iron confirmation that the goddess Isis was intimately associated with the pyramids at Giza. As Isis was primarily famed in this era for her role as God's Mother, suckling the infant pharaoh, the symbolism between her breasts and the nourishing effects of the pyramids on the land of Egypt is inescapable. The Great and Second pyramids at Giza were Isis' breasts, hewn out of stone, and no doubt this symbolism was fully reversible.

The same little piece of wordplay was also played out in the New Testament, where the disciple called Peter was also named after a stone. His first name was Petros Πετρος (Peter), which means 'rock', but in order to place another twist to the meaning of this name, Peter was also called Cephas. The English name Cephas is a poor transliteration of the Greek word Khephas κηφας, which was in turn taken from the Hebrew name Khepha כיפא, and both of these words mean 'stone' once more. The reason for this second appellation was highlighted by Adrian Gilbert, who maintained that the Hebrew name Khepha was a direct derivation of the Egyptian pharaonic name Khafre (Khaphra), the supposed builder of the second-largest solid stone pyramid in Egypt. [13]

The reverence that the Judaic faiths, including Christianity and Islam, have for various stones is well known and has been discussed at length in my previous books, but the origins of this reverence have not always been clear. The basing of the Aramaic/Hebrew/Greek term Cephas on the name of a pharaoh who was associated with the massive stone monument known as the Second Pyramid, and the use of that name as a title for the primary disciple of the quasi-Masonic Church of Jesus, may go some way towards explaining those peculiar beliefs.

Having explained the 'petrifying' nature of these Biblical names, the first of these titles, Maachah Tamar [Zeruah] will shortly become associated with the line of Egyptian princesses who were sometimes referred to by the additional title of 'Queens of Sheba'. But if this link is to be made, then the fabled Queen of Sheba would also have to have been known as the Mother of the Breast. Surprisingly enough, this may well be so, and the evidence for this comes from the ancient book known as the Kebra Nagast, the Ethiopian Bible. [KN14]

The Kebra Nagast is a curious document with an uncertain history; the modern transcripts of this book date from the fourteenth century AD, and although some additional New Testament material has obviously been tacked on by later redactors, it is likely that the original text was derived from pre-Christian sources. The main subject that the Kebra Nagast deals with is the visit by the Queen of Sheba to King Solomon in Jerusalem, and in doing so it provides us with valuable material that has remained separate from the Western myths and traditions of this famous queen for up to two thousand years.

It is quite apparent that when George, the patriarch of Alexandria, discovered the Kebra Nagast in the Blue Mosque at Constantinople some time around 1314 AD, he arranged that it should be brought in line with the then current Biblical expectations. It was obviously at this time that this undoubtedly Judaic text became littered with New Testament stories and a few disparaging comments about the Jews being the 'enemies of god'. [KN15]

It was probably at this same time that the Kebra Nagast also had all its references to 'Egypt' changed into 'Ethiopia', and a few very out-of-place comments about 'black faces' were inserted to try and substantiate this otherwise untenable claim to an Ethiopian heritage. That this is a complete falsehood is given away by the paragraph that says the father of the Queen of Sheba and the father of the pharaoh's daughter (who married King Solomon) were exactly the same person. Although the twenty-fifth dynasty Egyptian pharaohs were said to be kings of Nubia (Kush) and were given a darker skin pigmentation in their artistic representations, there were no black pharaohs of Egypt and so the likelihood of the Queen of Sheba being both a pharaoh's daughter and black is extremely unlikely.

While the Kebra Nagast is greatly revered in the land of Ethiopia, and its texts constantly refer to that country and its kings, the earliest copies that have been discovered were actually Egyptian Coptic and Arabic. Wallis Budge suggests that the original text was kept in the Coptic monasteries of Egypt and that they found their way into Ethiopia at a later date: in other words, this may be an Egyptian rather than an Abyssinian document. In which case, it is entirely possible that any references to the 'pagan' lands of Egypt have been altered to make them more acceptable to the Christian sensitivities of the Archbishop George. In order to restore the text into its original state, it is likely that each of the references to 'Ethiopia' should really be changed to 'Egypt', and the evidence that proves this assertion will be shown later.

One of the interesting snippets of information that this new source brings is the apparent veneration of the breast during this very era. Menelek, the son of the Queen of Sheba, was reputed to have said to his father, King Solomon:

> O my Lord, it is impossible for me to leave my country (Sheba) and my mother, for my mother made me to swear by her breasts that I would not remain here (in Jerusalem) but would return to her quickly. [KN16]

Here we see independent evidence indicating that the breasts of the Queen of Sheba were considered to be sacred. Thus, the Queen of Sheba could well have been titled the 'Mother of the Breast' and therefore she may be likewise associated with the Biblical Maachah Tamars, as I have just suggested. But did the mention of these illustrious breasts hold a deeper pyramidal symbolism once more? While the ancient Egyptian artists and sculptors frequently placed great emphasis on the male phallus and the female pubic region, with the latter often receiving a prominent inverted pyramid shape, the breasts do not appear to have been the artist's or sculptor's prime concern. Only in later dynasties do sarcophagi with prominent bare breasts become popular for female burials. The point is, was Menelek swearing by his mother's breasts, or was he swearing by the sacred symbolic 'breasts', the pyramids that his mother officiated at as the high priestess of Sheba?

The latter is the more likely, as even the title for the Kebra Nagast seems to exude echoes of these mammary and pyramidal associations. The name 'Kebra Nagast' is supposed to refer to the 'Glory of Kings', but if the title were influenced more by its Egyptian heritage, the word Nagast may well be derived from *naggat (ur)* – a word that refers not only to the Great Cackler 𓏏𓏏𓅱𓅬𓅭 but also the Twin Breasts 𓏏𓄿𓏏𓄿𓂋. The full title of the Ethiopian Bible may therefore refer to pyramids rather than kings. The book *Tempest* has more details on the pyramidal symbolism of the Great Cackler.

While such suggestions may seem rather esoteric, the term Mu-Tamhat (the Mother of the Front or Breast) may also have had another, more obvious mythical reason for its inception: because this same lady was also known as 'God's Wife'. The pharaohs were considered to be divine beings and so they were often portrayed as being suckled in exactly the same manner as the Horus and Isis imagery. The God's Wife would also have needed to be 'God's Breast' in order to nourish the next generation. But such an exalted position, almost at the same level as the gods themselves, would also have made the God's Wife the First Wife in Egyptian society. It was for this reason that the term *hat* must have inherited a dual meaning, as is so common in the Egyptian language; it not only had connotations to breasts, it also meant the 'front' or 'first', and so the incumbent to this office was also known as the First Wife.

A similar title was also given to the female pharaoh Hatshepsut. It has already been shown that Hatshepsut took the throne name of Maatkare, but is also seems that she held a birth name that alluded to her leading position among the women of the royal court. Although she was not quite God's Wife, she was nevertheless named Hatshepsut, a title that is normally translated as meaning 'Foremost of the Royal Ladies'. The later equivalent title, Mu-Tamhat or First Wife, was quite obviously the descendant of a very ancient title that has been handed down from dynasty to dynasty. Not surprisingly, in the circumstances, this is the very same title that is still given to the wife of the president of the United States.

In order to complete this modern symbolism, the Treasury of Egypt, which received all incoming tribute from foreign nations and allocated the goods and treasures that were required for all state occasions, was known as the White House. This name for the Treasury was a very ancient tradition that went right back to the very beginning of our knowledge of Egyptian literature, and it survived right into the era of the Tanite pharaohs. Since the White House was run by the priesthood and the position of God's Wife was one of the highest ranks within the priesthood, it is not beyond the realms of possibility that the First Wife was involved in occasional duties at the White House.

The evidence uncovered so far demonstrates that the similarity between the names of the two royal daughters of the pharaoh Psusennes II and King David was quite striking; but on further investigation, it would seem that these names may have been even closer than I have just shown. The original spelling of the name of the daughter of Psusennes II was probably not Maatkare, but Maakare instead. The first syllable of this name has often been assumed to have been *maat*, but this assumption is unjustified as the word *maa* is just as suitable. *Maa*, like *maat*, means 'truth' and 'integrity', but it also means an 'offering' or 'sacrifice'. The orthodox text books are divided on this matter, with about half using the name Maatkare and the other half, including Breasted and Gardiner, preferring the shorter form, Maakare. The link that is being forged between Egyptian and Biblical history at this point, and the fact that the Bible emphatically uses the shorter version of the name, strongly points towards this being the correct pronunciation. In which case, the comparison between these two names is now: Egyptian, Maakare Mu-Tamhat; Biblical, Maachah Tamar.

If the pronunciation of the historical name, Maakare, now seems to be more like that given in the Bible, it is also possible that the original Biblical pronunciation, Maachah, was substantially more like the historical rendering than it at first seems. The Biblical rendering of this name, in the English translation, is consistently given as Maachah. However, the Hebrew version gives the central consonant a hard 'k' instead of the softer 'ch' and so the name was originally pronounced as Maakhah מעכה in the Torah. In this case, the historical version of this name was pronounced Maakare, while the Biblical version was pronounced Maakhah. While the pronunciation of these 'two' ladies' titles now seems to be very close indeed, not surprisingly perhaps, the functions and duties of these two titles may also have been direct equivalents, as will be explained in the next chapter.

Having found such a precise correlation between the Biblical and historical records, we are now in a position to list the first of many such equivalencies. The two members of the Egyptian royal family that appear to have been mentioned in the Biblical texts so far, are:

Egyptian name	**Judaean name**
Djuad (Psusennes II)	Duaid (King David)
and his daughter	and his daughter
Maakare Mu-Tamhat	Maakhah Tamar

Here, then, is the rather startling result that I found when I started to look at the family history of these two monarchs. Two separate dynasties in two separate countries, who nevertheless seem to be identical in many respects. The evidence that these two royal dynasties were linked in some manner is becoming overwhelming.

The conservative historian may eventually be persuaded that there were some family links between these two royal houses and that the same names were often used in both of them. The more radical and provocative position to take, however, is that King Psusennes II of Lower Egypt marched into Judaea to assist his Israelite cousins and allies in a common struggle against the Philistines. But, after some political machinations and a bloody coup against the ruling House of Saul, Psusennes II was eventually crowned King David of Israel, and presided over a united Egypto-Judaean-Israelite empire. Although this possibility may seem dramatic and unprecedented, it is the latter option that this book will pursue with some vigour – and not without good reason.

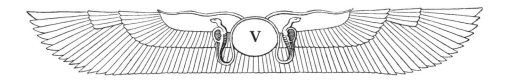

Psusennes

Once again, an investigation into the history of a very famous Israelite leader appears to have turned up evidence pointing towards an identification with a pharaoh of Egypt. While I might have been amazed, when writing the book *Jesus*, to have turned up a line of Israelite pharaohs in the seventeenth century BC (the Hyksos-Israelites), it has to be remembered that this line of kings reigned a very long time ago so it would not be quite so surprising that their true history and status were lost to us. The kings that were known as Psusennes II and King David, however, lie within the bounds of recent history, in Biblical terms. If King David were actually a pharaoh of Egypt, who had conquered Palestine and was eventually crowned as king of Judaea and Israel, then it is unlikely that this information could have been lost from this well-documented section of the Bible. The fact that no mention is made of David's Egyptian background means that there must have been some deliberate editing of the Bible once more.

Looking deeper into the texts, however, some hints of this Egyptian heritage can be glimpsed. Perhaps the first thing to note is that the feats and legacies of both King David and his son, King Solomon, are improbably impressive. The book of Kings indicates that these Judaean monarchs possessed some 1,400 chariots, 12,000 horses and some 4,000 stalls to house them. Even allowing for the usual Biblical exaggeration, the figures seem inordinately large. Nevertheless, the archaeology of the region, far from disproving these figures, seems to confirm them.

Impressive fortifications were apparently constructed in many Israeli cities, including Gezer and Megiddo. At Megiddo alone, excavators discovered some 450 well-built stalls for horses. It would only take another eight garrison cities of this size to equal the Biblical equine totals. So was this the kind of standing army that the local Israelite monarch, King David, required to police the boundaries of Israel? Historical opinion is divided on this matter, with the majority of commentators indicating that this association is 'problematic'. The strata indicates that this building phase is linked to the United Monarchy, but the economy of Judaea and Israel is unlikely to have supported such extravagance.

Most historians agree that it would be rather nice if such grand building programmes could be off-loaded onto an Egyptian pharaoh, but Tuthmoses III and Ramesses II were both too far in the past, and Sheshonq I (the Biblical Shishak) is not thought to have stayed long enough to have been associated with these Israelite citadels. The much more radical possibility that this new scenario highlights is that perhaps these were the kind of fortifications and army that were required by the Egyptian pharaoh Psusennes II, to guard the frontiers of his entire Egypto-Israelite empire. Although there is no record of Psusennes II entering Palestine, since this pharaoh's history can be reviewed in just two lines of text, perhaps this omission is not too surprising. If Psusennes II were the Biblical King David, however, the evidence for his campaigns in Israel would be undeniable, and the mystery surrounding the source of the resources that would have been required to build Megiddo would be fully explained. As an aside, a cartouche of the pharaoh Sheshonq I was unearthed at Megiddo, a discovery that will become more important in chapter VII.

The distinct possibility exists that some scribal sleight of hand has been used to completely divorce King David from his Egyptian heritage, and to produce an entirely Judaeo-Israelite king for domestic consumption in this region. Hence, the mighty Egyptian pharaoh, Psusennes II, who was invited into Judaea by his Hyksos-descended relatives and allies, has been turned into a completely Jewish hero. Somehow, this deceit has been maintained for nearly three thousand years, while all along the trail that would lead back to this identification has been clearly visible for all to see. Once more, the question has to be asked as to how so many theologians and historians have missed these vital clues, and once more the answer must be that none of them wanted to see them. To notice the evidence would be theologically troubling; to mention it in public would be professional and economic suicide.

But if King David were actually a pseudonym for Psusennes II, and if Judaea and Israel were ruled by an Egyptian king and government during the United Monarchy, then why is there no evidence for an Egyptian 'occupation' in this era of Israelite history? Actually, there is a reasonable amount of material that points towards an Egyptian controlling influence in the land, but very little is made of it because it is not 'Israelite' material. Paul Ash lists the Israelite cities in which archaeologists have made discoveries of Egyptian artifacts that originated from this specific era of Israelite history. These include:

> Galilee, Dan, Hazor, Sharon, Achziv, Awam, Dor, Zeror, Jerishe, Megiddo, Beth-Shan, Shechem, Ashdod, Ekron, Yurzah, Sharuhen, Zuweyid, Shephelah, Lachish, Arad, Halif, Yattir, Quadeirat, Quasile, Beth-Shan, Beth-Shemesh and Ajjul. [1]

Ash himself does not think that these finds are significant, but bearing in mind the general paucity of any material and artifacts from ancient Israel, such a spread of finds, which are all connected with the twenty-first and twenty-second dynasties, must indicate the presence of substantial trade and political contacts with Egypt. Admittedly, most of these items are only small trinkets and scarabs connected with burials, plus one or two larger, luxury items such as vessels and goblets. But the archaeology here is hampered by the complete lack of finds from the capital city of Jerusalem. This major city would have been the hub of any Egyptian royal dynasty controlling Israel, but the tombs and burial grounds of Jerusalem have all been stripped bare in previous eras, and so this vital source of evidence is denied to us.

It is also possible that many of these finds have been mis-identified. One of the recurring themes in these excavations are scarabs of Tuthmoses III, but these scarabs were incorporated into United Monarchy burials. The reasoning for the burial of these scarabs, which were already some 500 years old by the time they were interred, is unconvincing. A more likely interpretation is that these were actually scarabs of the High Priest Menkheperre, a twenty-first dynasty high priest who happened to share the same name as the throne name that was given to Tuthmoses III. As is demonstrated in the appendix, Menkheperre had an incredibly long period in office and so he is likely to have issued commemorative scarabs to mark this achievement. This was also an era in which the high priests of Thebes were emboldened enough to use the royal cartouche on occasions, as did Menkheperre, hence the modern confusion between a strange 'pharaoh' called Menkheperre and the presumed links to a much earlier pharaoh, Tuthmoses III.

In short, the current archaeological material and artifacts from Palestine do not preclude or prevent the proposed concept of occupying Egyptian forces, which were present during the rule of the pharaoh Psusennes II [King David]. Indeed, this scenario may actually explain a worrying aspect of this era. Never mind the 'lack' of Egyptian artifacts, one of the major problems with the archaeological evidence in this area, and era, is the complete lack of evidence for any of these Israelite monarchs. Here are the most famous, influential and powerful monarchs in all of Judaic history, and not one inscription has been found bearing their name – now this is a situation that just has to be considered peculiar. Suddenly, the Egyptian solution has some distinct benefits, for it solves this little puzzle completely. In fact, there are many inscriptions of King David, and even one or two that have been recovered from excavations in the Levant; it's just that the name mentioned on these artifacts is Psusennes II.

If this Egyptian scenario is true, however, it is highly likely that the Biblical scribes have indulged in some textual as well as nominative revisions. But knowing that this editing has taken place might be a distinct advantage in the continuing investigation, as we now know the favourite way of covering up the names of the individuals involved. The pharaohs of Egypt were given a name at their birth, but upon their coronation they took on the full five names of the royal titulary: the Horus, Nebti, Golden Horus Throne and Birth names. In the case of the name 'David', the scribe has simply taken one component of the birth name, Pa-<u>djuat</u>-kha-en-nuit (Pa-<u>seba</u>-kha-en-nuit or Psusennes), and used this as a short nickname. Hence we find the very unusual name of Duad or David in the Bible.

On the other hand, the much lesser-known daughter of King David, Maakare Mu-Tamhat, was allowed to keep her name virtually intact. No doubt the scribes never dreamed that a future class of professional historians would inspect every crumbling papyrus, fraying mummy wrapping and remote corner of the Temple of Karnak, and eventually come across her name. Where this particular lady does come to great prominence in the Biblical texts, however, her name *is* shortened to a nickname once more, as we shall see later.

This same process may also be seen at work in the name of King David. The immediate family history of King David is not so certain as the Bible likes to portray and although the texts confidently say that David's father was Jesse (Yeshay יַשַׁי), when the sons of Jesse get together, David is often not among them. Due to many such uncertainties in the Bible, it is entirely possible that David was actually descended from Obed instead of Jesse, and in the family tree in the appendix, I have highlighted both possibilities. The upshot of this is that there is another family name that frequently crops up, and was probably of the same generation and family as King David – that of Shebaniah. There is a possibility that we can see, in this name, the full title of Psusennes II.

The standard birth name of Psusennes II was Pa-seba-kha-en-nuit, and there is a possibility that the syllables the scribes extracted from this name were:

V *Psusennes*

Pa-	seba-	kha-	en-	nuit
	Sheb-		an-	niah

The scribes may have been of the opinion that where the individual or their current role was not so important in the text, they could be given nearly all of their full title. So, when all the sons of Jesse and Obed are mentioned together, the name Shebaniah may be written instead and nobody is any the wiser; but where the king is mentioned, the scribes resort to the nickname of David once more.

So will the knowledge of this selective shortening of royal titles into nicknames deliver any other revelations? What about David's ancestors, for instance; who were they? One of the major problems mentioned previously was the lack of an Egyptian heritage for King David, but can any progress be made with this new technique? Is it possible that further Egyptian revelations can be discovered among the names of David's relations and relatives?

The first thing to note is that the people of Judaea had different allegiances to those held by the people of Israel, and so the princes that the Judaeans looked towards as leaders were not necessarily Israelite as such; in fact, they were not necessarily Judaean either! It should be remembered that the land of Judaea was to be the area most heavily influenced by Hyksos culture during their invasion of Palestine at the time of the exodus. As the Hyksos-Israelite tribes left Lower Egypt and spread out across Palestine, their beliefs and customs were to be continually diluted as the tribes moved northwards. The result was that the southern tribe of Judah (Judaea) remained faithful to the Hyksos ideals, whereas many of the Israelite tribes to the north indulged in alternative gods and allegiances.

It is perhaps for this reason that the royal names given in the Biblical genealogy of Jesus start with the patriarch Judah, the son of Jacob. If anything, the royal line of Israel should have been passed down through the patriarchs Joseph or Benjamin, who were the sons of the chief wife of Jacob. But, presumably because of their position in the south of Palestine and their strong Hyksos-Egyptian allegiances, the royal line seems to have flowed through the patriarch Judah instead.

From the patriarch Judah (one of the twelve sons of Jacob by a lesser wife) the royal line then passed through Pharez, Hezron, Ram, Amminadab, Nahshon, Salmon, Boaz, Obed, Jesse, and finally to King David and King Solomon. Note once more that the royal house of Saul, who was a Benjamite, has been completely bypassed in this genealogy. This is probably one of the main reasons for the tribal infighting that dogged

Israel for the next thousand years or so. The bloodline was supposed to have passed through the patriarch Benjamin, and presumably on to King Saul, but the complete assassination of this royal family had effectively left a Judaean monarchy in control of Israel.

Like most of the individuals to be found in the Bible, none of these ancestors of King David appear anywhere in the historical record of Israel and, apart from what the Bible has to say about them, nobody has any idea of who these people were or what they were famous for. Actually, I do not think that this position is either credible or true at all, as several of these names can be found in the historical record – if people dare look at all. Even a brief glance at the pharaonic history of Herodotus would set a researcher onto the right road. Herodotus mentions in his *Histories* that there was a pharaoh called Pheron, who reigned before Ramesses:

> On the death of Sesostris, his son Pheron, the priests said, mounted the throne. He took no warlike expeditions; being struck with blindness. [H2]

But while the Biblical Pharez sounds very similar to Herodotus' pharaoh called Pheron, the accounts of Herodotus have to be taken with a degree of caution – he even has the pharaoh Cheops (Khufu) following the reign of Ramesses. The much more reliable reports of the historian Manetho make no mention of any pharaoh called Pharez or Pheron, but perhaps his accounts can show us what this word really means. The point is that there are various blanks in the king-lists of Manetho, and there is just one such blank for the twentieth dynasty, which preceded the dynasty of Psusennes II. For this whole dynasty, Manetho just says 'twelve kings of Diospolis', and gives the total reign length of all the twelve kings together. This twentieth dynasty consisted of the less influential Ramesside pharaohs who had very short reign lengths. The word that Manetho used for 'king' in his account of the twentieth dynasty was basileuo (βασιλευω), but the Greeks could just as easily have said pharao (Φαραω) and the Bible could have said pharaoh פרעה.

This, I believe, was the reason for starting the family tree of King David with the name Pharez פרץ. Neither the Egyptian record nor the Biblical record could remember who these particular pharaohs were, so they just inserted the word 'pharaoh' into the text. But we are not simply dependeant on the Greek or Hebrew languages for the word pharaoh; it was also used in Egypt itself, to describe both the royal family and the king in particular. The name they actually used was *per-aa* , and this word could also be taken literally to mean 'house'. As has already been explained, *per-aa* was not simply a term used for the king, but it more often than not referred to the entire royal family as a complete unit – the 'firm' or 'company' as the British monarchy sometimes style themselves.

There is a strong possibility that the first name on the list of King David's ancestors, that of Pharez, was simply a corruption of the Egyptian term *per-aa*. The solution to this particular problem would also solve another perennial Biblical puzzle. One of the reasons for placing the Biblical exodus in the Ramesside period of the thirteenth century BC is that there are not enough generations to take the Biblical family much further back than that. But if the name Pharez simply refers to the generic term 'pharaoh', then the total length of the Biblical chronology is no longer a problem and the roots of this family can be taken back as far as one wishes. It would seem that the Bible has done exactly the same as Manetho, and where it found a great break in the list of Israelite 'kings' (pharaohs), it simply inserted the name 'Pharez'.

Pharaonic line

Perhaps I should be excused for continually pushing the theory of a 'line of Israelite pharaohs' when there seems to be not very much evidence in favour of it at the moment, but that is simply because I know the evidence that is about to be unearthed. The point is that the rest of the list of the ancestors of King David matches up very nicely with the known names of the pharaohs of the twenty-first dynasty.

Biblical leaders	Historical pharaohs
Pharez,	Per-aa
Ezron (Hezron),	Ramesses
Ram,	Ramesses
Amminadab,	Amen-Nesbanebdjed (Smendes)
Nahshon,	Nemneshu (Amenemnisu)
Salmon,	Siamun
Boaz,	B-uasorkon
Obed,	Amenemopet
Jesse,	Harsiese
David,	Psusennes II

Some of the entries in this list are quite obviously equivalents of each other, while some of the others look less convincing. For the latter entries perhaps some extra explanations are required, and these are listed overleaf. In the following list, the top line in each case represents the Biblical pronunciation (B), while the lower line is the historical equivalent (H):

B	Ez- -ron,
H	Esses- -ram (Ramesses X),
B	Ram,
H	Ram- -esses (Ramesses XI),
B	Ammin- -nad -dab,
H	Amen- -nes -ba -neb -djed,
B	... Nah- -shon,
H	Amenem -ne -shu
B	S- -almon,
H	Si- -amun,
B	B- -oaz,
H	B- -uas- -orkon,
B	... Obed,
H	Amenem- -opet,
B	Jesse,
H	Harsiese,
B	David (Duat),
H	Psusennes (Pa-djuat-khaen-nuit).

I think that readers will have to agree that there is a substantially good agreement between these two separate lines of 'kings', and if these links and similarities are taken to be true, then many of the Biblical leaders – including King David and perhaps even King Solomon – may have been pharaohs of Egypt. This family tree, which starts with the names of two of the Ramesside pharaohs from the previous dynasty, would also explain why the pharaoh Psusennes I [or II] often linked his name with that of a Ramesses. While it is not known which Ramesses was being referred to, the title of Ramesses-Psusennes must have been coined because one of the Ramesside pharaohs was a direct ancestor of Psusennes II [King David].

Although the previous list is reasonably self-explanatory, perhaps some further clarification and explanations are required for some of these names:

a. For the name Amenemne<u>sh</u>u, I have used a 'sh' instead of an 's'. I think that this is justifiable as not only are the 's' and 'sh' often interchangeable in Egyptian, but also if the *su* plant glyph ⚘ has flowers ⚘, it is invariably pronounced as *shu*. The *shu* syllable then equates very nicely with the suffix of the name Nah-shon.

b. For the pharaoh traditionally called Oasorkon I have substituted the name Uasorkon, as the rope glyph 𓍯 is actually pronounced as *ua*. The common modern spelling with an 'o' was probably influenced by Manetho's Greek spelling of Osochor. A more recent Masonic usage of this word will be explored later, and this will confirm the validity of the *ua* version.

   The reason for the addition of the letter 'b' in the Biblical version of this name can be seen on the inscriptions in the eastern temple of Uasorkon at Tanis. Here, the name Uasorkon is often preceded by the sealed-jar glyph 𓎢 , which has the phonetic value of *bas*. Including this glyph in the name would either result in the name Bas-uasorkon or perhaps Buasorkon, a name that is easily shortened to Buas or Boaz.

c. I have changed the name Amenemope into Amenemopet because the final glyph being used here is the 'harem' glyph 𓉐 . This glyph, which is more likely to be a concubine's fan than a building, as is often claimed, is actually pronounced as *opet*. This is undoubtedly the true pronunciation of this name, although only one classical account that I have seen has used it. The extent of the similarity between the truncated name *Opet* and the Biblical Obed does not need labouring.

It seems to be an inescapable fact that the people of Judah, in southern Israel, were not looking to the Israelite line of royalty for their leaders, nor to their own family of domestic Judaean leaders; they were looking instead to the land of Lower Egypt and to the new line of 'Hyksos' pharaohs who seem to have re-established themselves in Tanis. Nominally at least, the Judaeans must have considered themselves to be associated with, and a part of, the dominions of Lower Egypt; and this was especially so during the reigns of the twenty-first dynasty pharaohs, who seemed to have distinctly Hyksos tendencies.

   What these allegiances to Lower Egypt by the Judaean clan have left us with is nothing less than a line of Tanite pharaohs listed in the Bible. This royal family history finally results in a pharaoh known in the classical record as Psusennes II, who was crowned King of Judaea and finally King of Israel, and he was considered by many in southern Israel to be the rightful Israelite king as well as a rightful Egyptian pharaoh.

   One of the prime reasons for the founding of the Egyptian Exploration Society in London in 1882 was to discover archaeological evidence that would confirm the Biblical texts. How that esteemed organisation has managed to miss all this synergy (and that which will follow shortly) between the historical and Biblical records is quite baffling

– one has to suspect that the evidence they found was not exactly the evidence they expected, and so their investigations were quietly discontinued or concealed.

It has to be noted, however, that the synergy that has just been discovered between the Biblical patriarchs and the historical king-lists of Egypt has been achieved at the expense of a few alterations in the order of succession. In comparison, the established historical order of the twenty-first dynasty is as follows. The proper Egyptian name is given first, with the more commonly used name (often taken from the Greek pronunciation) following in brackets:

Egyptian name	Greek equivalent
(Amen) Nesbanebdjet	(Smendes I)
Amenemnisu	(Amenemnisu)
Pasebakhaennuit I	(Psusennes I)
Amenemopet	(Amenemope)
Uasorkon	(Osorkon the Elder)
Saamun	(Siamun)
Pasebakhaennuit II	(Psusennes II) [King David]

It is true that the Biblical order of secession is slightly different from this, but there is no degree of certainty that the historical king-list is any more authoritative than the Bible's. The chronology of Egypt that is used to this very day was based upon the king-lists of the historian Manetho. While it may be a correct assumption that Manetho had access to many records that are not extant today, and that his list of pharaohs represents a good overview of the Egyptian royal succession, it would be extremely misguided to say that Manetho has delivered to us the absolute truth. It is clear from even a brief glance that there are many gaps in his record, and that the names of the pharaohs have been transcribed from Greek documents with many of the names having been grossly distorted in the process and in some cases they are barely recognisable.

Subsequent to the discovery of Manetho's lists, many dockets and documents have come to light during the major archaeological excavations of the nineteenth and twentieth centuries AD. These records have confirmed the historical existence of these particular pharaohs and they have added greatly to our knowledge of the pronunciation of their titles, but these same records have shed very little light upon the family relationships, the royal succession, and the precise chronology of this era. Indeed, some of the pharaohs of this dynasty are simply known from the occasional cartouche, so no confirmation of their reign is possible. This lack of data has forced Egyptologists to lean rather heavily on the claims being made by Manetho, with there being little or no way of confirming or refuting his assertions. As Donald Redford says:

> Because of the drastic reduction in the number of written sources for the 21st through 24th Dynasties, it becomes substantially more difficult ... to describe in specific detail the culture of Egypt during the Tanite or Libyan hegemony. [3]

This is perhaps greatly understating the problem; the classical king-list of the twenty-first dynasty, which is used today, is essentially that of Manetho's with one or two embellishments. The column on the left of the following table is taken from the records of Manetho, while the one on the right is the modern list of the twenty-first dynasty. It should be noted that, apart from one simple swap of adjacent kings (denoted *), the modern list is completely faithful to the original. Again, the more commonly used names are given in brackets:

Manetho's list	Modern list
Smendes	(Amen) Nesbanebdjet (Smendes I)
Psusennes I	Amenemnisu*
Nephercheres (Nefer-amen)	Pasebakhaennuit I (Psusennes I)*
Amenophthis	Amenemopet (Amenemope)
Osochor	Uasorkon (Osorkon the Elder)
Psinaches (Psin-amun)	Saamun (Siamun)
Psusennes II	Pasebakhaennuit II (Psusennes II) [King David]

Perhaps a brief explanation for the Greek derivations of these Egyptian names is also necessary here:

a. Smendes (Nesbanebdjet):
It is said that Manetho's derivation of 'Smendes' was not arrived at though distorting the syllables sban-djet, derived from the name Amen-Nesbanebdjet, but instead from the Greek name Mendes. It is thought that the pharaoh Nesbanebdjet was primarily based in a town called Djede in the Nile Delta, which the Greeks called Mendes. However, this does not explain why the high priest of Thebes should also be called Smendes, and the suspicion has to be that the name Smendes was indeed a poor corruption of Nesbanebdjet.

The name of the town may have been derived from the pharaoh and not *vice versa*, a possibility that may have further implications later in this investigation. In the circumstances, I think that the Biblical version of this name, Ammin-naddab, which has been taken from the following underlined syllables of the name <u>Amen</u>-Nesba<u>nebdjet</u>, is a much better derivative.

b. Nefercheres (Amenemnisu):

The Greek reference to Nefer<u>cheres</u> has used the Hebrew word *Cheres* (חרם *Khe-res*), meaning 'the Sun', instead of using one of the more familiar Egyptian names for the Sun-god, like Amen, Aton or Ra. When rectifying this Hebrewised translation back into the Egyptian original, Nefer-<u>cheres</u> would become Nefer-Ra. What the Greeks have done, therefore, is to use this pharaoh's throne name of Nefer-Ka-Ra, and shorten it to Nefer-Ra (Nefer-Cheres).

The Biblical king-list has focused instead upon this king's birth name, so the historical name Amenemnisu (Ame-Nem<u>nisu</u>) has become <u>Nahshon</u>. Once again, the Biblical version is equally as good a transliteration as the Greek.

c. Psinaches (Siamun):

The reference to Psina<u>ches</u> has again used the Hebrew word *Cheres* for the Egyptian Amun (Amen). Substituting Amun for Cheres on this occasion would turn Psina<u>ches</u> into pSin-<u>amun</u>, which is very close to the Egyptian rendering of Siamun (Sa-amun). Again, the Biblical version of Salmon is equally satisfactory.

Although Egyptologists are more than happy to equate these barstardised Greek names with the Egyptian originals, the fact of the matter is that the Biblical versions of these names are often much closer to the Egyptian originals, as the three previous examples demonstrate. Pronunciation aside, the main problem with the classical chronology is that it was written in the third century BC and derived from a Greek list that was probably no older than the start of the Ptolemaic period of Egypt, which began in the fourth century BC. When listing the pharaohs of the twenty-first dynasty, Manetho's data may therefore have been some six hundred years out of date. On the other hand, the Biblical list of these same pharaohs may well have been compiled at a much earlier date, and there is always the possibility that it was compiled contemporaneously.

Both theologians and historians would dispute that possibility, and the reason for the traditional assumption that the early Biblical accounts were only transcribed into written records at a very late date is largely based upon the erroneous view that the Biblical patriarchs were simple shepherds. Quite simply, shepherds do not make written accounts of their lives in the fifteenth century BC. However, the fact that these 'shepherds' were actually the Shepherd Kings of Egypt (the Hyksos pharaohs) changes that view entirely – it is entirely possible that the Hyksos pharaohs left Egypt with a complete library of written records and a scribal class capable of maintaining and updating those records.

While there is general agreement among theologians and historians that the books of Genesis and Exodus were written long after the events they recorded, the academic view of the later United Monarchy is more divided. Judaic historians will take the entire books of Kings and Chronicles as faithful guides to the events of that era, while many historians attempt to enforce upon them the same reasoning that has just been given for the books of Genesis and Exodus. Despite the United Monarchy supposedly being a powerful monarchy and a functioning royal household complete with royal scribes, it is simply assumed by some historians that no contemporary records of this era were taken. Donald Redford, for instance, says of these Biblical records:

> The current fashion of treating the sources at face value as documents written up in a large part during the court of Solomon arises from a misplaced desire to rehabilitate the faith and underline it with any arguments, however fallacious.

> And so the succession document, the great J-epic ... can be credited to the literary activity of Solomon's court ... It is difficult to decide whether it is worthwhile to attempt a rebuttal of such irrelevant arguments...[4]

Worthwhile or not, Redford eventually does attempt a rebuttal and the examples he gives are illuminating, although perhaps not in the way that he originally intended. One example that Redford gives for the 'obvious' late date for the writing of the Biblical accounts of Kings and Chronicles is the inference that kingship was already of 'considerable antiquity'. The kingship had only just been adopted in Israel, so why should the Bible talk of royalty in such mature terms? The answer, according to Redford, is that these accounts were written long after the United Monarchy had ended, perhaps during the Babylonian exile. But the true answer, of course, is that the monarchy that the Bible was referring to was the long-established Egyptian Hyksos monarchy. Since the Israelites were the Hyksos, they had already experienced a thousand years or more of life under a monarchy, and only a relatively short period under the rule of the Judges.

Another example Redford gives for the late writing of these

accounts is the mention of 'sophisticated siege techniques' for assaulting cities, which were supposedly not available in early Israel. But only a few pages later on, Redford indicates that the Egyptians already had these same siege techniques in the Ramesside era – indeed, Psusennes I [II] was known from his tomb artifacts as 'The Seizer of Cities'. Once again, if King David was a pseudonym for Psusennes II, then the mention of sophisticated siege techniques is to be expected. Rather than being unfamiliar with this form of warfare, it was actually their stock-in-trade.[5]

Again, Redford mentions the curious fact that 'iron picks and axes' are mentioned in these Biblical texts as if they were common in Judaea. But in Egyptian terms, the Iron Age began with the twenty-second dynasty of Sheshonq I, the next pharaoh in line after Psusennes II. The mention of many iron implements in a Hyksos-Israelite document is therefore natural.

Redford is also concerned about the size of the army that King David's rebel son had at his command, and the number of casualties that were inflicted in this battle. But if the pharaoh Psusennes II had been forced to put down an insurrection, which had been masterminded by one of his sons as the Bible infers, then the sizes of the armies involved in this conflict are likely to have been immense.

Finally, Redford is also unhappy about a Cushite runner who was employed by this same Israelite army, which is apparently more likely to fit a much later period in Israelite history. Again, this ignores both the long-standing Hyksos treaty with the Nubians (Cushites) and also the fact that Moses married a Nubian queen and brought a Nubian retinue with him to Lower Egypt.

In short, most of the arguments against an early date for the composition of the Judaic Torah can be easily nullified if a heavy Egyptian influence is presumed within the royalty and administration of the Judaeo-Israelite nation. In fact, had there been such Egyptian influences, it would have been a certainty that such records and documents would have been composed during the life of the United Monarchy. But, due to the climate, periodic warfare and constant religious strife in the region, little or none of this original information has survived; consequently, we are now solely dependent on the many copies of copies that represent the modern Biblical record.

It is likely that the Torah was composed from a great sheaf of ancient texts that had been taken to Babylon by the Judaic priesthood during the second exile, and it was there that the odd mention of 'camels' and 'money' was inserted into the text. But the bulk of the Torah, including all the complex genealogies, could easily have been taken from ancient contemporaneous documents.

V Psusennes

In fact, many of the peculiar alterations to the names of these famous kings, such as Psusennes and Sheshonq, may have been deliberate. During the Babylonian exile, Egypt had become a pariah state for the Israelites, so any admission to an Egyptian history or the presence of Egyptian pharaohs within the Israelite royal family was deemed to be impossible. By all available means, the identities of these people had to be altered, and so an alternative, pan-Judaic ancestry was devised, inserted and maintained in these texts.

But rather than fabricate the whole story, the scribes simply distorted a few royal names here and there, and likewise they distorted the names of the cities and states that they were associated with. The result was a wholly Israelite narration resting on substantially Egyptian foundations, and it was done in such a manner that one or two of the chief priests could still follow the original story-line. The priesthood could wax lyrical about 'David' and his battles with the 'Ammonites', and only the inner circle of high priests would comprehend the true image of a pharaoh of Tanis battling with elements of the Theban army.

Psusennes I

There is one obvious difference between the historical king-list devised by Manetho and the Biblical king-lists that have just been discovered. Manetho has included two pharaohs with the name Psusennes, and these have been absorbed into the classical history of Egypt and labelled as Psusennes I & II. On the other hand, the Bible only has one entry for a King David. But which of these king-lists is correct, Manetho or the Bible? Was there only one Psusennes or two?

One of the main historical arguments about this pharaoh called Psusennes I, revolves around the relative reign lengths of this and the following pharaoh, Amenemopet (Obed). Manetho gives a long reign for Psusennes I (46 yrs) and a short reign for Amenemopet (9 yrs), which makes Psusennes I a relatively important character in this dynasty. However, Egyptologists may have found a 'year 49' docket for the pharaoh Amenemopet. The suspicion is that Manetho's nine years for Amenemopet (Obed) was a corruption of his true reign length of forty-nine years. But, in turn, Egyptologists are of the opinion that the reign length of Psusennes I would then have to be shortened in order to compensate for these extra years for Amenemopet. In which case, it is entirely possible that the reign of Psusennes I was relatively short and that this pharaoh was not so important as was previously thought.

V   Psusennes

Perhaps the main thing that really stands out from these arguments, however, is how fluid the history of this dynasty really is; a few manipulations here and there, and suddenly the complete chronology has been changed.

The problem that Egyptologists are trying to grapple with is that the records of Thebes have survived, while the records of Tanis have not. The pharaohs of the twenty-first dynasty were based in Tanis, where the relatively damp climate and successive military invasions have not been kind to the ancient records, and so we have very little data mentioning the Tanite reign lengths and family relationships. On the other hand, the equivalent high priests of this dynasty were based in Thebes, and so a fairly good record of their history has survived. This one-sided view of Egyptian history wouldn't be quite so bad if it were not for the fact that the high priests of Thebes invariably mention the northern pharaohs that they nominally served under or even the year number of the king's reign, but not both. The records left by the high priests at Thebes tended to say something like "High Priest Pinujem did this in year 34": the inscription gives the name of the high priest and the year of the Tanite pharaoh's reign, but not his name.

The resulting jigsaw puzzle is to sort out which high priest served under which pharaoh, and simultaneously to discover which reign length belongs to which pharaoh. For example, a text or docket that mentions a high reign length is often taken to be referring to the pharaoh Psusennes I, because he was the only king in this dynasty who was thought to have had such a long reign. But if Amenemopet (Obed) actually had this long reign instead, then perhaps this high priest was really referring to Amenemopet instead. But there again, two of the surviving lists of Manetho give a long reign (35 yrs) for Psusennes II, so perhaps this text was referring to the last pharaoh of this dynasty. The possible permutations and muddles that this data can generate are endless.

The primary confusion for us, however, is between the two pharaohs known as Psusennes (I & II). If the reign of Psusennes I was actually quite short and the reign of Psusennes II was in reality quite long, then many of the former's exploits may actually be referring to the latter – Psusennes II [King David]. Had it not been for the assertion by Manetho that there was a Psusennes I following on from the pharaoh Smendes, I am quite sure that a good argument could have been made showing that all of these references and data actually refer to Psusennes II instead. I have attempted this feat myself and the very interesting results to this are contained in the appendix.

The effect of this manipulation is to eliminate the pharaoh

Psusennes I completely, and he is replaced instead by a shadowy Theban high priest called Psusennes III, who may have been confused with the equally elusive Uasorkon the Elder, as both these characters had the same (throne) names. In this case, Manetho's assertion that there was a pharaoh called Psusennes I may have been the result of a confusion with High Priest Psusennes III and a similarly named pharaoh called Uasorkon. This would explain one of the prime oddities about this phantom pharaoh Psusennes I:

> Extremely curious is the fact that at Tanis Psusennes I often uses the epithet 'High Priest of Amen Re', and once ... describes himself as 'Great of Monuments in Ipet-eswe', i.e. at Karnak. [6]

Gardiner is confused by a pharaoh from Tanis, in Lower Egypt, who is describing himself in terms that pertain to a high priest of Karnak in Thebes, in Upper Egypt. But the Biblical chronology completely eliminates this 'extremely curious' titulary of Psusennes I by turning this 'pharaoh' into a high priest of either Thebes or Memphis. The problem, along with the pharaoh, has now evaporated, and Gardiner need not have been so concerned. The two chronologies, both Biblical and orthodox – including the all-important high priests who served each pharaoh – are as follows:

Established chronology

Pharaoh	High Priest
Smendes (Nesba<u>nebdjed</u>)	Pinedjem
[Amminadab]	Masaharta / Pinedjem I
	Menkheperre / Pinedjem I
Amenem<u>nisu</u> [Nahshon]	Menkheperre / Pinedjem I
Psusennes I	Menkheperre / Pinedjem I
	HP Smendes
Amenem<u>opet</u> [Obed]	HP Smendes
	Pinedjem II
<u>B-Uas</u>orkon [Boaz]	Pinedjem II
Siamun [Salmon]	Pinedjem II
	HP Psusennes III
Psusennes II [David]	HP Psusennes III

V Psusennes

Biblical chronology:

Pharaoh	High Priest
Smendes / Nesbanebdjed	Pinedjem I
[Amminadab]	Masaharta / Pinedjem I
	Menkheperre / Pinedjem I
Amenemnisu [Nahshon]	Menkheperre / Pinedjem I
Siamun [Salmon]	Menkheperre / Pinedjem I
	HP Psusennes III
B-Uasorkon [Boaz]	Menkheperre
Amenemopet [Obed]	Pinedjem II
	HP Smendes
Psusennes II [David]	HP Smendes

The complete reasoning for all of these amendments, including a list of all the textual evidence that underpins these claims, is given in the appendix; although it has to be said that the arguments and data there are rather complex.

The main result of this transfer from the Manetho to the Biblical chronology is the swapping of Salmon and Obed and the deletion of Psusennes I from the list completely. So is this justified? Can this comparatively famous and supposedly long-lived pharaoh of this dynasty really have been a figment of every historian's imagination? Perhaps another king-list will assist in deciding this matter. The following is a king-list that has been extracted from the annals of the Memphis priesthood, and instead of being later translations out of Greek records, this list is thought to have been contemporaneous to the era in question:

Tanis Pharaoh	High Priest of Memphis
Amenemnisu	Asha-khet A
Akheperre - Setepenamun	Pipi A
(Psusennes I ?)	
Psusennes I	Harsiese
Psusennes I	Pipi B
(Siamun)	Asha-khet B
(Psusennes II)	Asha-khet B
(Psusennes II)	Ankhefensekhmet A
(Sheshonq I)	Shedsunefertem

(Names in brackets are taken from other documents.)

V *Psusennes*

The problem with this chronology is that the name Akheperre Setepenamun is normally taken to be a reference to the pharaoh called Psusennes I, as these are his prenomens. But this identification throws up some anomalies in this list. Firstly, there is the question of why Psusennes I should have been known by his prenomens (Akheperre Setepenamun) and then by his birth name (Psusennes I) in the same list; the change in terminology seems peculiar. Secondly, this list positively places Amenemnisu [Nahshon] before Psusennes I, and for many other reasons historians would like him to have reigned afterwards, just as Manetho claims.

However, these problems can be overcome if it is assumed that the name Akheperre Setepenamun referred not to Psusennes I, but to Uasorkon the Elder instead – as the latter shared the same prenomens. Uasorkon the Elder seems to have been an elusive character in the historical record, but that may simply be due to all his references being classified as belonging to Psusennes I. While this possibility is mentioned in passing by historians, it is quickly dismissed as it throws up a whole host of chronological problems. It assumes too long a reign for Psusennes II, and more importantly it takes away the need for a Psusennes I. As Kenneth Kitchen says:

> The most important result of this interpretation is that the Berlin (Memphis) genealogy ... would not actually mention Psusennes I at all. [7]

Having dealt such a mortal blow to the classical chronology's dependence on a Psusennes I, this interpretation was hastily forgotten. However, while this interpretation of the Memphis priest-lists may clash with the classical chronology, the same is not true of the Biblical chronology. Since the Biblical king-list has dumped the pharaoh Psusennes I completely, the result is that the Memphis chronology agrees perfectly with the Biblical chronology:

Tanis Pharaoh	High Priest of Memphis
Amenemnisu	Asha-khet A
(Siamun)	Asha-khet A
Akheperre - Setepenamun	Pipi A
(Uasorkon E)	
Psusennes II	Harsiese
Psusennes II	Pipi B
(Psusennes II)	Asha-khet B
(Psusennes II)	Ankhefensekhmet A
(Sheshonq I)	Shedsunefertem

(Names in brackets are taken from other documents.)

V Psusennes

The important thing to note from this whole exercise, however, is that had historians been given the Biblical chronology to work from instead of Manetho's king-lists, it would seem that the available archaeological evidence would have fully supported that chronology. Neither of these two chronologies can therefore be absolutely proven by using the extremely limited data available to historians, although I myself can see distinct advantages to the Biblical chronology. At present, therefore, the matter cannot be resolved one way or the other and no doubt this topic will continue to be debated *ad nauseum*.

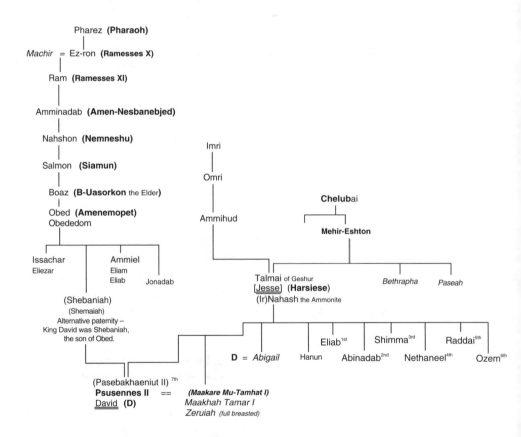

Fig 14. Ancestors of Psusennes/David.

One vital aspect to note about the Biblical king-list, which has already been mentioned, is that it does not necessarily indicate a family lineage. The list itself is a list of pharaohs, and the many 'begats' in the Biblical record may simply infer a royal secession rather than a family bloodline. This is important as the historical accounts seem to indicate that there was a break in the succession after Psusennes II [King David], and that the pharaoh Sheshonq came from separate (but closely related?) line. The Biblical history also indicates a break in the line, but it may well place the break after the patriarch Obed [Amenemopet], where it may be indicating that the family patriarch known as Jesse was of a separate bloodline (with Jesse's daughter becoming the chief wife of King David). The latter would agree with the historical record, which seems to place the high priest of Memphis, called Harsiese [Jesse], in a separate family. The family lineage in both of these accounts would then look something like this:

Historical	Biblical
Smendes (<u>Amen</u>-Nesba<u>nebdjed</u>)	Amminadab
Amenem<u>nishu</u>	Nashon
Psusennes I	...
Amenem<u>opet</u> (Amenemope)	Salmon
<u>B-Uas</u>orkon (Osorkon the Elder)	Boaz
Saamun (<u>Siamun</u>)	Obed
...	**break**
...	Jesse
...	continuation from line of Obed:
Psusennes II (Djuad)	David (chief wife from Jesse)
break	...
Sheshonq I	Solomon??

But who was the Jesse that the Bible says came between Obed and David, and why was he so easily taken out of this list? Although the sons of the Biblical Obed עוֹבֵד were relatively numerous, apart from the separate mention in the Biblical king-list, there is no explicit mention of a son called Jesse.

Jesse's other Biblical name is Nahash נָחָשׁ, and this is known because the daughters of Nahash, Abigail and Zeruiah, were the same as the daughters of Jesse. Even the Biblical Concordance admits this possibility, and although the characters Jesse and Nahash are normally listed separately, when it comes to the mention of the daughters, Abigail and Zeruiah, both Jesse and Nahash are suddenly listed together as being the same person. But Nahash was said to be an Ammonite, and if this nationality does in fact refer to the god Amun and the people of Thebes, as has been suggested, then Jesse may well have been an Ammonite high priest. Once more, the Biblical and historical records are in close agreement, as the latter indicates that Harsiese was a high priest of Memphis, as is mentioned in the Memphis king-list. [8]

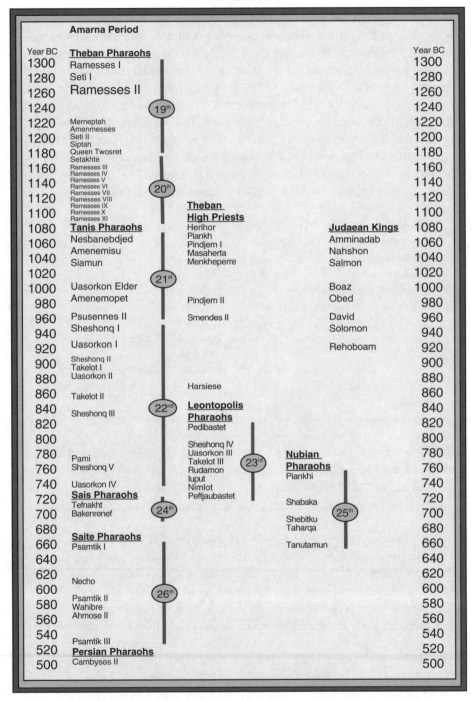

Fig 15.   New chronology of the Third Intermediate Period.

The reason for the additional name of Nahash for Jesse is not given, but the Bible Concordance gives the derivation of *nahash* נחש as meaning 'serpent'. This, I believe, is only half the story and the true derivation of this name should be *nahash* נחש, meaning 'divination' or 'enchantment'. The reason I think this to be so is twofold. Firstly, snakes were closely associated with both enchantment and the priesthood in this era, and thus we can see that the Egyptian priests who opposed Moses during the exodus were making their 'enchantments' through the use of such snakes. Secondly, the Egyptian word *nahas* 𓆓𓏤𓈖𓏛 not only refers to someone from the south (Sudan), which will become important later, it also means 'to recite incantations', which was another conspicuous role of a priest in this era. In this case, Jesse was most likely to have been a high priest from the south (Memphis or Thebes).

If Jesse-Nahash was an Ammonite, then so too must have been Maakhah Tamar I, the first chief wife of King David, as she was the daughter of Jesse-Nahash. In fact, Jesse-Nahash was also the father of two more of King David's wives, who were known as Abigail and Zeruiah. The mention of the term Ammonite, and the obvious inference to the city of Thebes or Memphis, would also make Maakhah Tamar I a 'southerner', and this term will become important later in the story. But it is always possible that these two characters did not hail from quite as far south as I have previously suggested. Another alternative title for Jesse-Nahash is given in the Bible as 'Talmai of Geshur'. It has to be noted that if Jesse were synonymous with High Priest Harsiese of Memphis, then the city of Memphis lay right next door to the Giza plateau.

Wife

Like most of the Biblical patriarchs, King David had many wives, but only one or two were of sufficient social stature and of the correct lineage to become the chief wife. David was to have two chief wives and presumably the first of these was demoted from her position after she had passed childbearing age. The first of these chief wives was called Maakhah Tamar I, exactly the same name that has already been linked to the Queen of Sheba. This was most probably not the famous queen of the south herself as the latter went to visit King Solomon, not King David; in fact, this particular Maakhah Tamar was most probably Sheba's mother.

Despite the bloodline of the chief wife being all-important within the Judaeo-Egyptian royalty, the Biblical ancestry of this particular chief wife of King David is rather obscure. She was said to have been the daughter of someone called Talmai:

And the third (son of David, was called) Absalom the son of Maachah the daughter of Talmai king of Geshur. [B9]

The only problem with this identification is that both Talmai and Geshur are very obscure references in the Bible. Neither of these names is used very often and when they are used, the family histories and the locations are not given, so the family history of Maakhah Tamar remained a mystery for quite some time. A minor breakthrough was made when it was noticed that Absalom, who was a son of King David, fled to this same 'king' called Talmai:

But Absalom fled, and went to Talmai, the son of Ammihud, king of Geshur. [B11]

The reason for Absalom's flight will be covered later; the more important thing here is that we can now see that 'king' Talmai was the son of Ammihud. Another single Biblical reference then links Ammihud to Omri, Imri and Bani, and it is from this point that we can confidently link this family all the way back to Pharez, as can be seen in the family tree below. Although these links are so obscure that the Biblical Concordance makes no mention of this family history, it is as certain as anything in the Bible can be that Maakhah Tamar I, the first chief wife of King David, was descended from Pharez and from the line attributed to Judah.

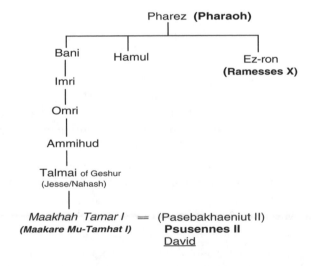

Fig 16. Family tree of Maakhah Tamar.

Now, the chronology of Jesse's family is on slightly firmer ground, as this is a part of the family history of King David that has already been covered in some detail. Pharez was the Biblical patriarch whose name refers to the generic term 'pharaoh'; in which case, the bloodline of this particular Maakhah Tamar (I) was suitably important and royal because her family was descended from the pharaohs of Egypt.

Maakhah Tamar I will be shown later to have been the mother of the Queen of Sheba, as mentioned previously, and yet the New Testament writers refer to the Queen of Sheba as the 'Queen of the South', a fact that again points towards Maakhah Tamar I being a southern princess. These southern origins may allude towards a possible reason for King David's choice of chief wife: he may have wished to make a diplomatic alliance between Upper Egypt and his expanding empire in Lower Egypt. It is entirely possible that King David [Psusennes II] wanted to secure his southern borders with a treaty and a diplomatic royal marriage, in order to be able to concentrate on his impending campaigns in Palestine.

Uriah

If the family history of David that has been described thus far may seem complex, this has only been the tip of the iceberg. The new ingredient to thicken this already gelatinous plot is the famous incident surrounding the death of Uriah. The Bible describes Uriah as being a senior army commander serving under King David – but King David fell in love with Uriah's wife, and made her pregnant. This state of affairs was a bit embarrassing for David so he gave Uriah leave to go home, in order that his indiscretion would not be discovered. But Uriah conformed to the military tradition of not having conjugal relations while on active service and did not sleep with his wife.

Knowing that the king's little indiscretion would be discovered in the near future, a plot was hatched to dispose of Uriah. The answer to King David's problems was to send Uriah into the thick of the battle, so that he would be killed. The scheme worked as planned and with Uriah out of the way, David was able to marry Uriah's wife, Bathsheba.

This is the rather folksy tale as described in the Bible, but it is obvious that Uriah must have been a much more important character than the Bible implies, and the whole incident just has to have been more serious and complicated than this. Had Uriah merely been an army commander, he would hardly have dared mention the king's indiscretions. Had he been foolhardy enough to say something, he would probably have been paid off by the king or murdered for his troubles, with barely a trace of royal guilt or embarrassment – this was not an era in which to be disputing the wisdom and actions of a monarch.

Likewise, this same tale infers that Bathsheba must also have been much more important than is implied, as it was through Bathsheba that the later King Solomon was born. While King David had a string of proper wives plus a complete harem of busty belles to choose from, he nevertheless appears to have made Bathsheba his chief wife – allowing her to replace the previous chief wife, Maakhah Tamar I. There was no possibility of Bathsheba's son, Solomon, becoming king without her being the chief wife, and there was no possibility of Bathsheba becoming the chief wife of the king if she was not a senior royal princess.

Rather than being a trivial indiscretion with a plebeian, this pregnancy and 'execution' must have been a major diplomatic incident in the royal court, as the repercussions continued to rumble on for some time. Instead of the death of Uriah swiftly resolving this issue, King David was taunted by the priesthood, and a snippet of this discontent has rippled through both the Bible and Koran. The Koran chose to chastise David's actions in the form of a parable:

> My brother here has ninety ewes, but I have only one ewe. He demanded that I should entrust it to him, and got the better of me in the dispute. (King) David replied: He has certainly wronged you in seeking to add another (sheep) to his (large) flock. [K12]

King David has, of course, been deceived by this tale of the two brothers. In actual fact, the shepherd with ninety ewes was a reference to David and his many wives, while the additional ewe that he was trying to steal was Bathsheba, the wife of Uriah. Note, however, that the Koranical story makes these two shepherds brothers instead of neighbours; this is the first clue that David and Uriah were actually related.

The next clue to the royal status of this 'army commander' can be seen in the Egyptian translation of Uriah. The name was actually derived from the word *ur* or *uraa* ![hieroglyph], meaning 'great man', 'prince', or even 'king'. This was the main problem that King David faced; the lady that he had just deflowered was the wife of a prince, and this was sure to ruffle a few feathers within the royal court. But the question is, which prince was the cuckold? The evidence is there in the Bible for all to see, but the scribes have certainly tried their best to conceal it.

One of the sons of David was called Absalom and, although he was the king's favourite son, he had had a troubled past. Absalom had already killed one of his brothers in a fit of jealous rage, due to the following circumstances. Tamar, the sister of Absalom, had been raped by her stepbrother Amnon; but Absalom was furious about this and killed Amnon in retribution. For this crime Absalom suffered the wrath of his father, King David, and so Absalom was forced into exile in Egypt. On returning to Israel after an unspecified time away, Absalom found that he had lost his favoured status and was being shunned by King David; it is even possible that he had been advised that he had forfeited his position as prince regent. In frustration at this, Absalom became the leader of an insurrection against the king, his father:

> But Absalom sent spies throughout all the tribes of Israel, saying, As soon as ye hear the sound of the trumpet, then ye shall say, Absalom reigns in Hebron. [B13]

> And Absalom sent for Ahithophel the Gilonite, David's counsellor. And the conspiracy was strong; for the people increased continually with Absalom. [B14]

Absalom was trying to usurp the power and the throne of King David and, favourite son or not, this was unacceptable to the king. But the insurrection was initially successful and Absalom chased King David out of Jerusalem and was hailed as king; he even dared enter the king's harem, which was seen to be the final snub to the authority of his father. There was no escape for Absalom now: he would either be anointed as king or be killed as a traitor to the realm. Royalty constantly engaged in political games like this, but more often than not the stakes in these games were very high indeed.

Eventually, a truce was made and the armies representing the two monarchs met in the fields of Gilead to discuss the situation. Note here that the site of the coming battle was Gilead, which has already been equated in chapter II with a location in the Nile Delta. If Absalom had, as previously suspected, fled to [Upper] Egypt for support, this would be a logical site for the confrontation. As usual, the Bible plays down this event as a meeting between servants: in fact, it almost sounds like a picnic on the plains of Gilead. But it is the historian Josephus who shows us the real truth once more, as he describes instead a major military confrontation between the prince and the king:

> Absalom got together a great army of the Hebrews ... David resolved not to tarry until Absalom attacked him ... (and) put his army into battle array over ... in the Great Plain. Upon joining battle, both sides showed great

actions with their hands and boldness ... Now David's men were the conquerors, so they followed the others as they fled away through the forests and valleys. [J15]

Despite the seriousness of the confrontation, the ever-astute King David still apparently showed nothing but fatherly concern for the welfare of his wayward son, Absalom:

> And the king commanded ... Deal gently for my sake with ... Absalom. And all the people heard when the king gave all the captains charge concerning Absalom. [B16]

Yet, during the battle, Absalom somehow got himself hung by the neck in an oak tree and died! As may be expected, King David flung himself to the floor and wailed in grief at this 'unexpected' tragedy, but meanwhile, according to Josephus, David's army commander, Joab, trust a spear three times through the heart of Absalom's corpse, just to make sure. Once more, David showed himself to be a cunning and ruthless monarch who would stop at nothing to maintain his position and rule.

The way in which King David learned of the death of his son is also a small Biblical conundrum, which has been debated in many a book on Israel. The strange aspect about this was that there were two runners who were sent to the palace with this information; one was the son of Zadok and the other was called Cushi רשׁי. The debate centers on the question of why King David should be using a Cushite (Ethiopian) runner, as these were not supposed to have been introduced in this region until a later date.

This new theory of an Egyptian King David (Psusennes II) rather turns this question on its head, for it is unlikely that this character called Cushi was a lowly runner. The information being delivered to the king was of national importance and possibly a state secret, so the second runner sent back to the king was the son of Zadok, who was a very important person in his own right. So who, in this case, was the first runner, Cushi? Was he a low-ranking runner, or someone more important and trustworthy?

From the Egyptian perspective the answer to this is rather obvious, for the Egyptian army commander was often a high priest of Thebes; this would have been the high priest Smendes II during the reign of King David [Psusennes II]. While it is claimed that High Priest Smendes II was a Theban pontiff, who might be presumed to be an enemy of the Tanis regime, it is an established fact that the pharaohs Psusennes II and Sheshonq I began the process of installing their sons into the Theban priesthood and aristocracy. Since High Priest Smendes II donated a pair of bracelets to the burial of King Psusennes II, he is likely to have been a supporter or a relative of the Tanis kings. [17]

So how does this information fit in with the Biblical claim that there was a Cushite dignitary (runner) in the Judaean army? Well, the high priest had various titles and duties other than plain priest, including the important position of vizier, the second most important office in the land. One other title, which appears to have been more traditional than functional, was that of 'King's Son of Cush'. The Egyptian term for this title is *A-keshti* ⌐▭⌐ , which happens to be identical to the Biblical name, Cushi. This new interpretation of Biblical history infers that it was King David's ally, High Priest Smendes II, who was entrusted with the details of Absalom's death.

Repetition

Having discussed the death of Absalom at some length, there now appear to be two very similar stories during the reign of King David. One story concerns Absalom and the other concerns Uriah, and both of these individuals were executed during a military engagement on the orders of King David. As usual, the question that has to be asked is: are these two stories the same? Even a brief overview of the details will confirm the similarity between the two stories, and the suspicion has to be that they arrived on the Biblical compiler's desk from two different sources. Since the different versions of these events used different names, both were included in the Bible; but this inclusion has proved a thorny problem for theologians ever since, for the ramifications of the combined tale are formidable. The gist of the two tales is as follows:

    a. King David had an illicit liaison with Uriah's wife, Bathsheba. Uriah was then killed in battle.

    b. A son of King David raped his half-sister, Maakhah Tamar II, who was also Absalom's full-sister. Absalom was then killed in a battle.

While these brief details seem to be vaguely similar, are there any more similarities between these two stories? We have already seen, of course, that the name Uriah was most probably just a title, and that in the Egyptian it means 'prince'. In a similar fashion, Absalom, the son of David, was also a prince. But this is not quite the convincing evidence I was looking for; the link between these two episodes needs to be much closer than this. In fact, the evidence is there in the Bible, but one really has to search to find it.

The truth only came to light when it was noticed that the Hebrew suffixes of *iah* יה and *iel* אל are interchangeable: they both mean god. *El (iel)* is a shortened version of *Ayil* איל, while *iah* is the shortened version of *Yahweh* יהוה and both are routinely used in the Torah to denote the name of god. Incidentally, *Ayil* is also the Hebrew word for a 'ram', so the association between the Israelite god *El (iel)* and the Hyksos Shepherds is being made perfectly clear once more.

This similarity between these god-names means that the army commander called Uriah could equally have been called Uriel, with both of these names meaning 'Light of God' in the Hebrew translation, or 'Prince of God' in the Egyptian. Suitably equipped with this knowledge I searched the Bible once more, but the search was nearly fruitless. The trouble is that some diligent scribe has been through the entire Bible, searching for any references to the name Uriel and making sure they were all changed to something less incriminating. But there is just one quote, throughout all of the Biblical texts, where they have missed a solitary reference. This sentence says:

> Now in the eighteenth year of king Jeroboam, began Abijah to reign over Judah. He reigned three years in Jerusalem. His mother's name also was Michaiah (Maakhah) the daughter of <u>Uriel</u> of Gibeah. [B18]

The verse is indicating that someone called Uriel of Gibeah had a daughter called Michaiah, and her son was King Abijah, the grandson of Solomon. So who was this Uriel? Well, a quick glance at the Biblical Concordance does not shed much light on the problem, because it just says "Uriel was the maternal grandfather of Abijah".

The fact that the Concordance will write a sentence like that, without giving Uriel's real name, indicates that theologians are quite prepared to be economical with the truth in order to cover up an embarrassment. Unfortunately for the scribe that missed this passage, and for the theologians who created the Biblical Concordance, the maternal grandfather of Abijah is rather well known: it was none other than Absalom (Abishalom). The quote above is from Chronicles, but just in case this is not sufficient evidence for us, the following passage is from the book of Kings, and it is a direct copy of the sentence above – except that we now have the real name of Uriel:

> Now in the eighteenth year of king Jeroboam ... reigned Abijam over Judah.

Three years reigned he in Jerusalem. And his mother's name was Maakhah, the daughter of <u>Abishalom</u>. [B19]

Despite the blatant Biblical deceit, it is abundantly clear that Uriel was none other than Absalom, the son of King David. But remember that Uriel and Uriah can be exactly the same name. Since Uriah is only mentioned in the book of Samuel and Uriel is only mentioned in the book of Chronicles, it is more than likely that the two scribes who wrote these books were simply using a different god-name suffix for Ur; one chose the god-name of *iel* giving Ur<u>iel</u> and the other scribe chose *iah* giving Ur<u>iah</u>. If this was so, then Absalom would have been called both Uriel אוריאל and Uriah אוריה. In which case, the 'army commander' called Uriah-Uriel was, in fact, prince Absalom; and so two story-lines that were described previously have become significantly closer together, both in their characters and their content:

a. King David 'raped' Absalom's <u>wife</u>, Bathsheba. Absalom was then killed in battle.

b. The son of King David raped Absalom's <u>sister</u>, Maakhah Tamar II. Absalom was then killed in a battle.

The fact that both the sister and the wife of Absalom were raped (or seduced) is easily explained by the usual Egyptian practice of a pharaonic prince marrying his sister, which is probably what happened in this case. This was the reason that Absalom was so upset by the 'rape' of Maakhah Tamar; it was not only his sister who had been molested, but his sister-wife. It was for this crime that Absalom had killed Amnon, his half-brother.

As usual, it was Josephus who came to the rescue and confirmed that my reading between the lines was correct and that Absalom had indeed married his sister. Josephus says of the wife of Absalom, the mother of Maakhah Tamar III:

Rehoboam married ... a daughter of Absalom by Tamar, whose name was Maakhah. [J21]

What the text is trying to say, in its rather quaint equine language, is that Rehoboam married Maakhah, who was the daughter of Absalom and Tamar. Therefore, the wife of Absalom *was* Maakhah Tamar II, his sister, and in addition, this also infers that the full titles of both mother and daughter would have been Maakhah Tamar. There are now three Maakhah Tamars in this tale, so perhaps it is worth listing them for clarity:

Maakhah Tamar I   The first chief wife of King David,
                    the mother of both Absalom and Maakhah Tamar II.

Maakhah Tamar II   The sister-wife of Absalom,
                    the mother of Maakhah Tamar III.

Maakhah Tamar III   The wife of King Rehoboam, the son of King Solomon.

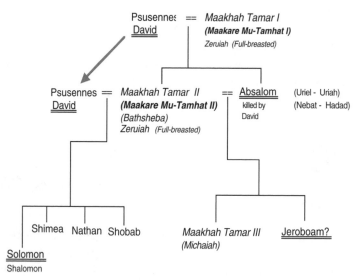

Fig 17.   Family tree of Absalom.

As has already been discussed in chapter IV, the name Maakhah Tamar was in fact a title, and in the Egyptian she was known as Maakare Mu-Tamhat. Since this was only a title, it is not surprising that we see a succession of wives called Tamar, and it would seem that David, Absalom and Rehoboam all married someone called Maakhah Tamar. But this Egyptian title invariably went with the similar title of God's Wife, *Hemet Netjer* 𓎛𓏏𓊹 , who was supposed to be the virgin wife of the gods. However, since this title was held by a number of mothers who appear to have had a succession of children, it seems likely that the virginal God's Wife was either not quite so virginal, or perhaps she was eventually married off to a prince and another virgin princess was found to fill the vacancy.

This additional title means that Maakhah Tamar II, the sister-wife of Absalom, must have been the virginal God's Wife at some point in time. This is why Maakhah Tamar II was also described as being a virgin; the virgin that Amnon had raped. Since Maakhah Tamar II was not simply an

Israelite but also an Egyptian princess, her response to this tragedy was typically Egyptian:

> And Tamar put ashes on her head, and rent her garment of divers colours that was on her, and laid her hand on her head, and went on crying. [B22]

The act of putting ashes and a hand on the head was not only typically Egyptian, it was especially typical of the Amarna regime of the pharaoh Akhenaton. In the book *Jesus*, I identified Akhenaton with the brother of the Biblical Moses, and if this were so then one would expect there to be numerous similarities between the people of Amarna and the Hyksos-Israelites. The act of mourning in Amarna was graphically displayed on many of their wall scenes and in one such scene Nefertiti, the chief wife of Akhenaton, is shown in precisely the same pose as was being adopted by the Biblical princess, Maakhah Tamar II.

There is no historical explanation as to why placing ashes on the head was considered to be an expression of grief in Egypt, but the Biblical account of the exodus may give one possible reason. The Bible graphically explains that one of the plagues that fell on the lands of Egypt was an ash-fall, and Moses claimed that he had caused this to happen by throwing ash from a furnace up into the sky.

Fig 18.   Expressions of grief, with ashes being placed on the head.

In more rational terms, in the book *Tempest*, I have already linked this ash-fall over Egypt to the eruption of the volcano at Thera (Santorini). It is further explained that this ash-fall caused a great lamentation throughout Egypt, and the result of all this grief was to be a civil war that ended in the exodus of the Hyksos-Israelites. Considering the despair and anguish that this ash-fall caused, not only while the ash was falling but also during the civil unrest in its aftermath, it is not too surprising that ash being placed on the head became a symbol of grieving. Similarly, since this event was primarily recorded as being an act of the Israelite god, it is again not too surprising that both the Amarna and the Tanis regimes, in particular, should have used this symbolism.

Since the God's Wife (Maakhah Tamar II) was supposed to have been married to (or the wife of) the god Amun, it is entirely possible that the character called 'Amnon' who raped Maakhah Tamar II was actually Amun (Amon) the god, rather than Amnon the half-brother of Absalom: the point being that the blame for the rape of Maakhah Tamar II appears to have been off-loaded onto a third party (a god) while the blame should, in reality, lie elsewhere.

There is a very strange parallel to this Biblical tale of the rape of the virgin, Maakhah Tamar II, which was discovered when the mummy of one of the Egyptian Maakare Mu-Tamhats was examined. This Maakare Mu-Tamhat was supposed to have held the title of 'God's Wife', and Egyptologists have always assumed that this position was always held by a physical virgin, as has been mentioned previously. However, when this mummy was opened, investigators discovered:

> ... a 'secondary mummy', held to be an infant at whose birth Maakare might have died, and leading to much romantic speculation as to whether the God's Wife had had an indiscreet liaison. [23]

Like the rape of the Biblical Maakhah Tamar II, the real person on whom this tale was based was also thought to have had an 'indiscreet liaison'. However, the 'secondary mummy' turned out not to be that of a young child; instead, it was the remains of a small baboon. While the burial of animals with dignitaries is not unheard of in Egypt, it is not exactly that common either; so why was this done? Was this a domestic pet, as has been suggested, which was sent into the afterlife along with its owner? Or was this perhaps a jolly jape by the officials at the mortuary who, knowing the story of the rape of Maakhah Tamar II [Maakare Mu-Tamhat] by the 'gods', placed a child of the gods (a baboon representing Thoth) in with the mummy? Whatever the case, the resulting mythology of this event is surprisingly similar to the Biblical story-line.

While this speculation is interesting, the Bible offers us another possible perspective on the true role of God's Wife. The title of the Maakhah Tamars is given in the Torah as being *gebiyrah* גבירה, a term that needs further explanation. The literal interpretation of this name is 'queen', but it can also mean 'Queen Mother'. It is from the latter interpretation that the meaning can also be expanded to infer the formal title 'Great Lady'. The Queen Mother, often being the elder royal, was not only 'great' in terms of her status, but also in her age and wisdom. [24]

But there is another possible meaning to this name that no Jewish historian would ever contemplate, so it will not be found within a modern historical treatise on the Israelite nation. The Hebrew name Adhon אדני literally means 'god', but because the Israelite god is a singular being, the word has no female form. Due to this lack of a female form for the god's name, the female equivalent is taken to be *gebiyrah* גבירה, and this was the name given to the Biblical Maakhah Tamars. In this case, the meaning of the title *gebiyrah* may be even more specific that has been hitherto thought. Since this title is said by theologians to be the female counterpart to the name of god, and since it also means 'queen', the term may actually mean 'God's Queen' or, almost by definition, 'God's Wife'. While the point hardly needs labouring, this does mean that Maakare Mu-Tamhat's formal Egyptian title was 'God's Wife', and Maakhah Tamar II's formal Judaean title was also 'God's Wife'.

It does appear that this title was only used in respect of the Maakhah Tamars when they had already become mothers of the next king – in other words, they only became *gebiyrah* when their son had been crowned king. This has been traditionally thought to infer that the previous king, the *gebiyrah's* husband, was dead. The Judaic historian Roland de Vaux certainly indicates that this was true of Bathsheba, the mother of Solomon, after the death of her second husband, King David. So was the 'God's Wife' supposed to have been a virginal princess or a widowed queen?

Firstly, the Judaean interpretation may not have applied to a royal family that used the co-regency technique – the previous king may not have been dead, but in retirement instead. Secondly, the Egyptian texts may have been written retrospectively, and the individual may have been called the Queen Mother (God's Wife) in hindsight. This same retrospective reporting often happened to the British royal family's late Queen Mother, who was often called the Queen Mother even during documentaries about her youth. Thus, to a future generation of historians, it might appear that the British Queen Mother was given this title even when she was a young girl.

Whatever the case, the possibility that God's Wife was also a

Queen Mother significantly alters the historical perspective. The post of God's Wife is thought to have originated in the New Kingdom era, and it was conferred upon the mother of the 'Great Royal Wife'. The 'Great Royal Wife' was the queen, and so her mother would naturally have been the Queen Mother. However, conventional wisdom has decreed that Ramesses VI, in the twentieth dynasty, conferred the title upon his daughter, and from then on the title was given to a virginal daughter of the pharaoh. The Bible, however, is indicating that the title of God's Wife was being applied during the twenty-first dynasty, in exactly the same manner as it was supposed to have been at the beginning of the New Kingdom. The God's Wife was still the Queen Mother.

The title would actually make more sense if it was applied in this way. Like the New Testament Jesus, the pharaohs of Egypt were supposed to have been sired by the gods. If god was the 'father' of the pharaoh, then in order for the pharaoh to be a legitimate child, the pharaoh's mother must have been 'married' to this god. The new pharaoh's mother was, therefore, known as 'God's Wife'. The reason for the historian's confusion with young princesses and virginity is based upon a misconception (if the pun is excused) of the term 'virgin', and an inability to equate Egyptian and Biblical history.

Firstly, the God's Wife appears to have been 'unmarried' in the historical records, because she was probably barred from marrying again after the death of her husband, the pharaoh. Secondly, the fact that the God's Wife was called a 'virgin' did not imply either youth or physical virginity. Instead, this term was simply a theological gloss that was designed to confirm to the ignorant population that the god had the primary role in siring the infant prince. In effect, the biological necessities of the pharaoh's seed were being sidelined by the priesthood, while the role of the god's impregnation was being highlighted. This explanation may seem like idle speculation, but it is not; it is based upon a well-known event.

According to the revised Biblical history outlined in this Egypto-theological trilogy, the line of King David was pharaonic. This line was classically supposed to have 'terminated' with the birth of the Biblical Jesus, who was of the line of David. The infant Jesus was, therefore, the *last of the pharaohs,* and so here was yet another Egypto-Judaean king who was born of a 'virgin' mother. Mary, the mother of Jesus, was the mother of the crowned king of Israel, and therefore she was called the 'virgin'. Yet this fable about Mary's virginity has created speculation out of all proportion to the simple realities of this title.

If this virginity of Mary had been simply based upon this ancient tradition, which had been maintained within the upper echelons of the Israelite royalty, then Mary the 'virgin' should also have been given the title of God's Wife. Despite the two or so changes in language that have taken place between the New Testament princesses and their Egyptian ancestors, I think that this can be seen to be true. Mary, the mother of Jesus, was visited by an 'angel' who informs Mary that she will give birth to a prince of the gods:

> And the angel answered and said unto her, The Holy Ghost shall come upon thee ... that holy thing which shall be born of thee shall be called the Son of God. [B25]

This is the prophecy that Mary will be pregnant with Jesus, a prince of the gods. Mary was supposed not to have believed this prophecy, and so she replied:

> And Mary said, Behold the <u>handmaiden of the Lord</u>; be it unto me according to thy word. [B26]

In this sentence, Mary calls herself the 'handmaiden of god'. In this Greek text, the term being used for handmaiden is *doule* (δουλη); but the ancient Egyptian term for handmaiden was *hem-t* 𓍑𓂝𓏛, and it is from this term that we can glimpse the original title that was being conferred upon Mary by the 'angel'. In the Egyptian, the title 'God's Wife' was known as Hem-t Neter 𓊹𓍑𓂝𓏛, and so this title could just as easily have been translated as 'Handmaiden of God'. Like the Maakhah Tamars of the Old Testament and the Maakare Mu-Tamhats from Egyptian history, it would appear that Mary was both 'Virgin' and 'God's Wife'.

Historians have mused for centuries over whether the title of God's Wife demanded strict celibacy, but clearly that was not the case. Although this latter 'virgin' lived some 900 years after the reign of the Maakhah Tamars of the Old Testament, it is known that the Jews have attempted to rigidly enforce religious orthodoxy, so Mary's title may well have been representative of the position of the Maakhah Tamars. The evidence that Mary's new title presents us with demonstrates that the 'virginal' God's Wife did not have to remain celibate for her whole life; after all, Mary herself had at least seven children.

In addition to being God's Wife, the prime duty of the wife of the pharaoh was to perpetuate the dynasty with children from the bloodline. But the princes of the pharaoh were destined to become gods themselves on accession to the throne, and so the very act of giving birth changed the title of 'God's Wife' into 'God's Mother'. This new title was a particular favourite of the twenty-second dynasty:

> It is of no coincidence that the prominent role played by high-ranking women in religious cults in the 21st dynasty was often in connection with child-gods ... Among their many titles, these ladies were ... 'divine mothers', of these gods and (this era) marks the early stages in the growth of emphasis on the mother-child relationship in Egyptian religion. [27]

In other words, 'God's Wife' had now gained another title – she had become 'God's Mother'. As has already been explained, this symbolism was graphically depicted in the popular imagery of the time by the goddess Isis suckling her son Horus on her knee. When translated into Earthly symbolism, the equivalent imagery that would have been presented to the populous was of the pharaoh's Chief Wife (the God's Wife) suckling the royal prince, and this latter imagery was particularly popular during the twenty-second dynasty.

Once more, this same imagery is to be found in the later Christian traditions, where the primary icon of this new religion was the Madonna and Child. Quite obviously, the Madonna and Child symbolism is an exact duplication of the Isis and Horus iconography. To add to her many titles, Mary now had one more of great significance. She was not only the Virgin and the Handmaiden of God, she was also the Madonna, the 'Holy Mary, Mother of God'.

Fig 19. Isis and Horus – Madonna and Child.

But there is one other of aspect of the birth of Jesus that contains very similar parallels to those that have just been aired, for the Egyptian princesses called Maakare Mu-Tamhat had one more priestly role and title: that of Divine Adoratrice or, as Kenneth Kitchen likes to pronounce it, Divine Adoratrix. The term 'Adoratrix' is derived from the duties of a priestess whose role was to worship the deity, but having said that, I am not entirely certain that this is the correct translation for this particular title. The Egyptian form for this title was actually Djuat Neter 𓇳𓏤𓆑𓊹 , and the word *djuat* can mean either 'worship' or 'adoration', which is the traditional interpretation; but, perhaps more importantly, this same word can also mean 'star'.

Instead of suggesting the role of a chief worshipper of the gods, this title could, in fact, have been referring to the title 'Star of the Gods'. This title would then have direct parallels to the title of 'Queen of Sheba', which can also be translated as 'Queen of the Stars'. As we shall see in a later chapter, the Queen of Sheba held all of the titles that have been traditionally associated with Mary, and so these two women would have held exactly the same roles within their respective societies.

This new designation gives a further parallel with the Biblical accounts that is just as striking as anything covered so far. While the title 'Maakare Mu-Tamhat' can now be seen to be associated with stars, so too was Mary, the mother of Jesus. In the New Testament accounts, Mary was not only known as the Virgin, she was also closely associated with a star as well:

> ... and, lo, the star, which they saw in the east, went before them, till it came and stood over where the young child was. [B28]

The traditional view is that this 'star' was somehow associated with the infant Jesus, but now it would seem that it was actually a coded reference to Mary herself. Indeed, as King David was also associated with a star, perhaps mother and child were to be linked to this star imagery.

The exact star that was intended by the Biblical scribes has long been a topic of debate. As has already been demonstrated, the Egyptian term *djuat* refers to an eastern or morning star and so for this reason it is sometimes said to refer to the planet Venus. Being one of the inner planets, Venus can only be seen in quadrants of the sky that are close to the Sun; ie, in the morning or evening.

However, an alternative explanation is that both the *djuat* and the Nativity star were cunningly devised to conceal the truth, which is that the Biblical 'star' was rather closer than one might expect. The whole of the Giza observations revolved around observing which constellations rose with the Sun in the morning sky. If this were the tradition that the Biblical scribes were trying to describe, then the mysterious 'star' in the east, which rose up in the sky and stood over this 'miraculous' birth, may have been nothing more than our Sun.

The equating of Mary with this eastern 'star', rather than Jesus, is further supported by the later traditions of the fringe Churches, which held legends detailing the subsequent fate of Jesus' family. One of these apocryphal tales, already covered in the book *Thoth*, is that a Mary (either the mother or the wife of Jesus) travelled to France in a small boat.

This story is graphically presented in the windows of the Templar church known as Eglise St-Croix, in Bordeaux. The interesting thing about this stained-glass tableau is that the name of this boat is said to be the 'Mari Stella'. This name, I understood at the time, translated into the English as 'Sea Star', from the Latin *marinus* meaning 'sea'. While this would be a sensible maritime-sounding name for any seagoing vessel, it is not the only translation that one could place on 'Mari Stella' – it could also be taken to mean 'Maria Star', or 'The Star of Mary'.*

In this case, Mary could have been identified with a star in exactly the same way as the Maakare Mu-Tamhats were. Thus, the full title of Mary, the mother of Jesus, would have been ⌇⌇⌇ ⌇⌇⌇ ✶ (*Hemet Netjer & Djuat Netjer*) in the Egyptian; while the English equivalents to this would have been 'God's Wife' & 'God's Star'. The Egyptian heritage of Mary, the mother of Jesus, could not be made any more plain than this.

However, this association between Mary and a star can be taken one stage further. Again, the argument has already been made that Jesus was himself of royal stock, a prince of Egypt in exile who was eventually crowned King of the Jews. But if that were so, then his mother would have been either a princess or a queen. The strong link between Mary and a star means that she too could be considered to be a 'Queen of the Stars', or a 'Queen of Sheba'. This link between the title 'Queen of Sheba' and Mary is also supported by a passage in the Kebra Nagast, which says:

> Now there was a law in that country of Ethiopia that (only) a woman should reign, and that she must be a virgin who has never known a man. [KN29]

While the text was referring to the Queen of Sheba, it may not have been discussing a monarch as such, but instead the position of God's Wife. Like the Maakhah Tamars and the 'virgin' Mary, it would seem that the Queen of Sheba also had to be a 'virgin' in order to hold her high office. This is another of the many pieces of evidence that points towards the position of God's Wife being held by a succession of important Biblical ladies all the way through to the New Testament, and it also supports the notion that the Queen of Sheba was one of the many Maakhah Tamars that appear in the Bible.

---

* Incidentally, the reason why the name Maria can be confused with marinus, meaning 'sea', is that Jesus was born under the precessional sign of Pisces and his astrological symbol was the fish. Mary was inheriting that same symbolism and donating it to the Latin lexicon. See the book *Jesus* for details.

V Psusennes

The title 'Star of Mary' is interesting from another perspective too, for this same title was used in a very mysterious incident in much more recent times. The name of the boat in which Mary was supposed to have travelled was the 'Mari Stella'; but the term 'star' being used here was derived from the Egyptian word *djuat* ⌒⫐⧹✶ , and while *djuat* can mean 'star', it can also refer to the heavens in general. If this latter meaning was intended, then instead of using the Latin word *stella* for 'star', one could more accurately use the Latin word *caelestis* meaning 'heaven'. Had this been done at any stage, the resulting name of this sacred boat would have been changed to the Mari Celeste. This was not only the name of Galileo's daughter, it was also the name of another rather famous and mysterious ship.

The Mary Celeste (with an Anglicised spelling) was reputed to have been a 280-tonne brig, built in Nova Scotia in 1860. Originally called 'Amazon', she was apparently renamed 'Mary Celeste' after a refit in 1870. The fateful voyage took place in November 1872, when the ship is said to have set sail from New York bound for Genoa in Italy with a cargo of alcohol. Tradition has it that the ship was found utterly deserted, but still sailing on towards her intended destination. But how much of this famous tale is fact and how much is fiction?

The truth of the matter is that much of this story was actually based upon a story written by Sir Arthur Conan Doyle, the author of the Sherlock Holmes mysteries, in 1884. It was Doyle who subtly changed the name of the vessel to the 'Marie Celeste', but how much more of this story is more fiction than fact? Had the story been completely fabricated by Doyle, it would most certainly have been a dramatic and effective method of highlighting and promoting the fact that a Biblical Mary, either the mother or the wife of Jesus, sailed away to Europe after the fall of Jerusalem in AD 70. Tradition has it that this Biblical Mary sailed on the Marie Stella (Mary Celeste) to southern France, whereas in comparison the mysterious Mary (Marie) Celeste was bound for Genoa, which is situated on the border between Italy and southern France.

Bearing in mind the almost total lack of historical data regarding this fabled voyage, it is difficult not to conclude that Doyle has simply recreated the voyage of the Biblical Mary in order to preserve this event in the national psyche; although why he chose to revolve the story around the drama of an abandoned ship is another mystery. Perhaps the abandonment reflected the refusal of the Catholic Church to acknowledge the existence of Mary's family, but there again, perhaps it is unwise to add speculation to an already speculative argument.

V Psusennes

Tower

While it would appear that the mother of Jesus was following in these ancient Egyptian traditions, there is another section of New Testament evidence that again points towards Egypt, but it is not quite so speculative as the sea voyages of the two Marys. If, as it seems, Jesus' mother bore titles that had very strong links with the Maakhah Tamars of the United Monarchy, then so too has the next Mary in line, Mary Magdalene. This Mary has already been identified in the book *Jesus* as being both the sister and the wife of Jesus, and if this was so, it would only be natural that she would have followed in her mother's footsteps by being the next Mother of God, the next Queen of Sheba.

Mary Magdalene has been given some bad press in the Bible, and this was probably due to a strong priestly desire to distance her from Jesus – it was too embarrassing to admit that she was Jesus' wife, let alone contemplate the possibility that she was his sister too. But some of this bad press may actually have been derived from a subtle and deliberate mistranslation of a particular verse in the gospel of Luke:

> And certain women, which had been healed of evil spirits and infirmities, Mary called <u>Magdalene</u>, out of whom went <u>seven</u> devils. [B31]

But this is not the only possible translation of this verse; it could also be taken to read:

> And a certain woman who had worshipped blinding (strong) winds, Mary, named (after the) *Seven Tower* out of which went god (winds).

The word for 'healed' (theraputae θεραπευω) can mean 'worshipped' and the term for 'evil spirits' (ponerous pneuma πονηρος πνευμα) could easily become 'blinding winds'. The reason for Mary, in her guise as a much later 'Queen of Sheba', being associated with whirlwinds (the *jinn* of the Koran) will be given later. The term for 'devils' (daemons δαιμονιον) can be a reference to 'god' or even the *jinn* whirlwinds once more – in fact, the latter are still called dust-devils to this day.

More important, however, is the fact that Mary Magdalene can be seen as being associated with both a tower and the number seven. The name Magdalene (Μαγδαληνη) can be literally translated from the Greek as meaning 'tower' and, as we have already seen, this association between the terms 'tower' and 'seven' is present in a famous Biblical quotation:

> Behold, therefore I am against thee, and against thy rivers, and I will make the land of Egypt utterly waste and desolate, from the <u>Tower of Seven</u> even unto the border of Ethiopia. [B32]

Just to review the explanations from chapter III, both of these words have been directly transliterated out of the original Egyptian: the Magdalene 'tower' has been taken from the Egyptian word *maktal* or *magdjal* ⟨hieroglyphs⟩ meaning 'tower', while the number seven has been derived from the Egyptian word *sefekh* ⟨hieroglyphs⟩ meaning 'seven'.

So, Ezekiel's 'Tower of Seven' is none other than the Egyptian '*Magdal* of *Sefekh*', the same title that is now being associated with Mary Magdalene. The Tower of Sefekh was historically seen to be a prime symbol of Egypt and because of this notoriety it has already been identified with the Great Pyramid (the Great Tower) of Egypt. The number seven is also translatable as Sheba, as this is one of the prime Hebrew meanings for this word.

Once more, the links between the family of Jesus and the Hyksos veneration of the Giza pyramids are clear to see. The title of Magdalene, which was given to the sister-wife of Jesus, appears to have had pyramidal connotations that have already been linked to the position of God's Wife, and in turn these lead on to stellar connotations that were linked to the term *sheba*. Just like her mother, Mary, the younger Mary Magdalene was one more in the long line of Maakhah Tamars, one of the Queens of Sheba.

Indeed, these two New Testament Marys did not just hold the same titles as the Old Testament Maakhah Tamars, it is entirely possible that the Greek name Mary was directly derived from the Hebrew name Maakhah.

In the Hebrew, the name Maakhah was spelt מעכה. Although the spelling was probably the same in the original Aramaic script from which the formal square Hebrew script was derived, the Aramaic characters that were used looked more like מעדה. It is entirely possible that later scribes could have mistaken the letter ך 'k' in this word for the very similar-looking letter ר 'r'. In fact, the letter ך 'k' in the older Aramaic script had a slightly hooked tail that looks a little like a ב, but so too did the Aramaic ר 'r' and to the untrained eye these two letters look absolutely identical. [33] Incidentally, the modern Hebrew consonants כ and ך both refer to the letter 'k', which means that the exact same confusion could have occurred in both the ancient and the modern scripts.

While it is true that the scribes being employed on these important works would have been professionals who were familiar with the Aramaic script and all its foibles, it is also a fact that they were probably copying older texts that were getting a bit battered and frayed. In addition, these were not computer-designed and laser-printed texts, in which every letter is perfectly formed; they were handwritten parchments that probably employed a fraying quill on an uneven surface, using ink of an unpredictable quality. Under the circumstances, it is not surprising that mistakes were occasionally made, and this particular transcription error would have resulted in the name Maakhah מעכה being turned into the name Maarah מערה. It so happens that the name Maarah, or Marah, was the original root Hebrew spelling of the Greek name Miriam or Mary. The progression of this name through the generations following the United Monarchy is as follows:

𓈖𓊬𓂀	Maakare
מעכה	Maakhah
מעדה	Maakhah
מערה	Maarah
מרה	Marah
מרי	Maria
Μαρια	Maria
Mary	Mary

This quick detour into the New Testament has proved to be quite fruitful, and so here is the final piece in this particular jigsaw puzzle that proves these New Testament Marys were the holders of a long and illustrious Egyptian heritage. These influential women, who inadvertently and unintentionally founded the new sect of Christianity, not only held the original titles of the Egyptian royalty, they also had the very same name that had been originally used by Queen Hatshepsut-Maakare in the early years of the New Kingdom. This same name had been handed down through the generations; it had endured the many centuries; it had passed through at least two changes of language; it had withstood the deliberate modifications of the Biblical scribes; and yet despite all this, the name still bore glimmers of the original Egyptian pronunciation. More importantly, perhaps, is the fact that the meaning of this title was also clearly understood by the Church of Jesus and James in the first century AD. It was only the ignorant manipulations of the New Testament Saul that came close to breaking a link in the chain and ending this historic custom.

This has been such a long diversion from the original arguments that perhaps a summary is required at this point. This investigation has shown that the two New Testament Marys, were given no less than five titles, which were the exact counterparts of those used by both the Israelite and Egyptian royalty. The later Mary was titled the Tower of Sheba (seven), while her mother was known as the Virgin, the Handmaiden of God, the Mother of God and also the Star (Sheba) of God. In holding these many titles, the New Testament Marys were upholding a long and illustrious heritage that stretched back to the beginnings of the Egyptian New Kingdom, into the sixteenth century BC and perhaps far beyond this. As I have speculated previously, the family of Jesus were true heirs to the pharaonic crown of Lower Egypt.

Guilty

So where does this investigation leave us in the search for the guilty party for the rape of Maakhah Tamar II, the sister-wife of Absalom? From the perspective of the Biblical account of this episode, I think that the case for royal involvement in this affair is now overwhelming. The rape of the 'virginal' Maakhah Tamar II by someone called Amnon just has to be a coded reference to Maakhah Tamar's position as the virginal God's Wife of Ammon, and it is entirely possible she was *supposed* to have been raped by this god.

Such a contrivance by the Egyptio-Israelite priesthood might be understandable, as conjugal relations between the god and his wife were expected. But this sexual union between god and his Earthly spouse may have been modified into something more saucy due to foreign influences on this religion: because the rape of a goddess by a god was a long-standing theme of Canaanite theology. Since the Canaanite gods were substantially the same as the Israelite ones, some cross-fertilisation of these beliefs into the Hykso-Judaic culture was almost inevitable:

> ... the rape of Anath by Baal formed a standing theme in Canaanite mythology, in spite of the fact that she was at the same time regularly called a 'virgin'. Anath is represented as a naked woman astride a stallion, brandishing her lance. [34]

The latter episode was probably re-enacted by Lady Godiva in Coventry, England, in the eleventh century AD. The '*iva*' in this lady's name refers to a feminine suffix meaning 'to have the nature of'; in which case this semi-mythical lady's name means 'Lady with the nature of God' or 'Goddess' for short.

In Canaanite terms, however, the fact that the 'virginal' goddess, Anath, was regularly raped by the god Baal supports the assertions that have already been made regarding the role of 'God's Wife'. Although she was regarded as a virgin, the God's Wife *was* supposed to have been ravished by the deity and borne god's children.

This argument is again supported by the translation of the Biblical patriarch Joseph's name in the book *Tempest*, and once more the deity would have been involved in this sexual act. This translation showed that Joseph's Egyptian name, *Sothom Fanuch,* could be read as 'Creation by Fornication', which probably referred to the Egyptian creation myth involving the phallus of the god Atum. Joseph himself was the high priest of Heliopolis, and so if there were any rituals involving the God's Wife at this temple, Joseph would certainly have been involved. Joseph's title, 'Creation by Fornication', suggests that the role of God's Wife involved a re-enactment of this stimulation of Atum's phallus, but it is not known if this ceremony involved physical as well as ritual duties.

While this translation of Joseph's title may have seemed unsubstantiated at the time, the fact that the Maakhah Tamars worshipped these fertility deities and took part in these very rituals is explicitly and graphically stated in the Bible. It is said that Maakhah Tamar III worshipped an idol, which is not in itself very illuminating:

> And also Maachah his mother, even her he removed from being queen, because she had made an idol in a grove; and Asa destroyed her idol, and burnt it by the brook Kidron. [B35]

While the King James' translation in the Bible is functionally accurate, it is also highly (and deliberately) misleading. The original Hebrew scribes were not much more forthcoming with this particular verse, and they deliberately mistranslated the word 'idol' as *miph-letseth* מפלצת, meaning a 'terrible thing'. What they have done, of course, is indulge in the usual Egyptian habit of deliberate obfuscation through inventive wordplay. The original text was written as *maphli-leytsanutha* מפליא ליצנותא, which has a similar pronunciation but a very different meaning.

If the answer to the Hebrew version of this mystery is ultimately resolvable, it is rather remiss of the King James Bible to omit the proper translation. No doubt their scholars were intimately familiar with the Hebrew language and all its nuances, so why did they choose to turn a blind eye to this peculiar word that they eventually transcribed as 'idol'? The Vulgate Bible gives the reader a little more information, but it still manages to translate the 'idol' as a *priapus*, which is all very well if your Latin is up to scratch but it is still (deliberately) unintelligible to the masses.

Just to add to these oblique references in archaic languages, Rabbi Solomon Jarchi indicates that this same 'idol' was an *ad instar membri virilis.*

V *Psusennes*

Note that every time something interesting or embarrassing comes to light in the Bible, the Church authorities instantly resort to the classical languages, which is a deliberate ploy designed to confuse the proletariat. But this is not good enough. If the account was worthy of being placed in the Holy Bible – which is supposed to be the 'word of god' – it is certainly worthy of being taught to the common people. So what, then, is the answer to this muddle? With my Latin being as rusty as it is, I turned instead to the trusty Biblical commentary by Adam Clarke, only to be faced with yet more obfuscation:

> What the Roman *priapus* was I need not tell the learned reader; and as to the unlearned, it would not profit him to know. [36]

This is a statement that clearly demonstrates the contempt that the religious elite have for their followers – the common man is apparently not equipped either linguistically or morally to deal with such arcane secrets. This same reaction also shows the acute embarrassment that the Church feels in regard to the events and actions of its most famous ancestors. What the Church wants to present to us is a model family and an unblemished, superior morality; what the Bible consistently shows us, however, is the nitty-gritty of human existence.

As to the truth of this particular matter, the term *priapus* gave me the first clue. Perhaps Mr Clarke was unaware, but Priapus was not a Roman. He was instead a Greek godlet who was born from a union between the promiscuous goddess of love, Aphrodite, and the god of viticulture and debauchery, Dionysus. Poor Priapus was primarily known for an unfortunate enlargement of a certain piece of his anatomy, and the Romans obviously picked up on this affliction and coined the word *priapus*. Perhaps the alternative word, *virilius* (virile), gives the obvious clue as to what is being debated here, but it still took a Latin dictionary to confirm that my suspicions were correct. It would appear that the idol made by Maakhah Tamar III, was an erect penis.

Here we have the wife of one of the heroes of Judaism, Islam and Christianity, and she was caught in the act of worshipping (or masturbating) an erect penis. I am still not sure if the Church is more embarrassed by the term **erect penis**, or by the fact that Maakhah Tamar III was apparently worshipping what is normally considered to be a fertility deity – perhaps the embarrassment is caused by a combination of the two. On reflection, I think that the whole concept of penile embarrassment has been fostered by a seismic shift in the theology of Judaism. The fundamental problem here is not one of morality; instead, this evidence

131

calls into question the precise nature of the religion that was being worshipped in Israel during the tenth century BC.

A quick review of the evidence that has already been presented in this trilogy may illustrate the true heritage of the theology of Judaeo-Christianity. As was explained in the book *Tempest*, the title of the patriarch Joseph – 'Creation by Fornication' – was most probably based upon the ancient Egyptian creation myth of Atum, which invoked several generations of divine sexual union in order to produce the visible Universe. In Egypt, this ritual revolved around the phallic Benben tower which used to reside in the Temple of Heliopolis.

This monument and the resulting cult of the 'round-tower' or minaret were discussed at length in the book *Jesus*. In this book, the assertion was made that these prominent towers – which can be seen across a wide swathe of land from the Hindu Kush through the Mediterranean and on to Ireland – were originally constructed as religious monuments that mimicked the Benben tower of Heliopolis, which was itself a representation of the phallus of the Egyptian god Atum. It is apparent from this near-universal mimicry, that the belief systems of Egypt have infused themselves into many cultures around the world; and here, in the Biblical book of Chronicles, those very same rites and rituals can be seen being performed in the royal court of King Solomon.

This new light that is being thrown onto this ancient embarrassment may actually make this whole incident more understandable. In the ancient Egyptian funerary texts, known as the Book of the Dead, one of the chapters shows the worship of a pair of obelisks; indeed, the worship of these monolithic towers was a well-known aspect of Egyptian theology. The precise function of the obelisk is not fully understood but the traditions that surround the god Atum must be an obvious clue. The suspicion has to be that, like the round-tower, the obelisk was a phallic symbol, and this is confirmed by the original name for an obelisk, *tekhen* 🔯, which can also mean a 'bodily emission'. The required link between an obelisk, a phallus and a bodily emission does not need labouring. But this symbolism gives the distinct possibility that Maakhah Tamar III was not worshipping an erect penis as such; she was simply taking part in the established Egyptian ceremonies involving the veneration of an obelisk – an artifact that happened to be representative of a divine phallus.

I had initially presumed that the Biblical Joseph's title, as just discussed, must have represented the solitary role of the self-masturbation of the god Atum. But now it seems that there may have been a goddess to assist in this re-enactment of the moment of creation with the divine erection. Maakhah Tamar III's use of this same phallus as an idol simply serves to confirm her status as God's Wife, and it simultaneously confirms that the duties of this rank involved some kind of re-enactment of her duties as god's consort.

In Egyptian terms, the 'Hand of God' was not envisaged as the divine wrath of a fierce deity, as the Bible often describes it; instead, it referred to the hand that stimulated the phallus of Atum. Although this was supposed to have been Atum's own hand, because the hand was performing a 'feminine' action it was always considered to be a feminine article. It is said of these rituals that:

> Both Atum and his hand were therefore portrayed as a divine couple on coffins of the First Intermediate Period. (Later), the title 'God's Hand' was adopted by the Theban priestesses (who were) supposedly married to the god Amun. [37]

The inference from this quotation is that the addition of a female assistant for Atum was primarily a Theban innovation from the New Kingdom era. The same Theban priesthood also adapted and incorporated Atum into their state god Amun. The timeless theology of Egypt had just been subtly changed and the resulting coupling was no longer just Atum and his hand – the ritual now involved Amun and the hand of his divine consort *Hem-t Neter* ⌐⌐, or God's Wife. Perhaps the reason for Mary being titled the 'Handmaiden of God' (God's Wife) is a little clearer now – indeed, it is not beyond the realms of possibility that the English translation of 'handmaiden' was deliberately chosen to reflect these ritual duties.

This may also explain a strange aspect of Egyptian archaeology that has remained forgotten and unanswered for over a century. When Queen Hatshepsut's mortuary temple at Deir el-Bahri was excavated in the nineteenth century, a great collection of wooden erect penises were discovered. But the era of their discovery was not conducive to debate about their role or function, so they were simply packed away in a basement of the British Museum and forgotten about.

The reason that these artifacts are pertinent to these explanations is that Queen Hatshepsut was also known as a Maakare (Maakhah Tamar), a 'Handmaiden of God'. Since Queen Hatshepsut must have been famed for her role as the queen that caressed Atum's phallus, it would appear that the people of Egypt flocked to her magnificent temple with their penis offerings – in the hope that their ritual entombment there would ensure either personal fertility, or perhaps the wider fertility of the land and country.

This same modification to the ancient rituals of Atum, by the addition and assistance of the priestess who was known as God's Wife, may also explain the term 'Virgin' that was applied to this same priestess. It has been assumed by Egyptologists that this title inferred life-long physical virginity, but as that now seems highly unlikely, why should this term have achieved such prominence? The answer may lie in the fact that this priestess' masturbation of Atum did not directly involve copulation and so it would seem logical that she could theoretically remain a virgin. But while the god Atum could demonstrate his fertility and reproduce himself through masturbation, this was not possible for humans, so to demonstrate the god's fertility in human terms required God's Wife to have sexual intercourse and produce a child (of the gods). But this was human not divine copulation, and so the God's Wife was still a theological virgin.

The strange and unfathomable dichotomy that lies at the heart of Christian beliefs is that while Mary was obviously not a virgin in physical terms, she was still regarded as a perpetual virgin because the god Atum did not require sexual intercourse to reproduce. Canaanite lore seems to have followed these same basic principles, and so the goddess Anath was also supposed to have remained a 'virgin' despite her continual ravishment by Baal.

The evidence from the New Testament seems to show that the revised liturgy of Egypt involved God's Wife bearing god's children and becoming the Mother of God. In which case, the 'rape' of Maakhah Tamar II may well have been a normal component of this ritual marriage, where the god had to take the predominant role in the conjugal relations between a king and queen, in order to ensure that the resulting prince was a son of the gods. Just as Mary managed to remain a 'virgin' despite having been ravished by god, Maakhah Tamar II also managed to remain a virginal God's Wife despite the rape by Amon (Amun).

If this ritual was a normal component of these Egypto-Judaean myths, through which the king and queen were said to produce their royal sons and daughters, then the guilty party in this 'rape' of Maakhah Tamar II was not just the god but also the husband. But since Absalom, the husband of Maakhah Tamar II, was so enraged by this rape, the evidence must point towards another member of this royal family as being the guilty party – King David. There are two strands of evidence that make this assumption a near certainty.

Firstly, it is said that King David had already done almost exactly the same thing in order to gain the hand of Abigail in marriage. Secondly, although the rape of Maakhah Tamar II indicates that the guilty party was the god Amun, this is not the only record of this incident that we have, and the second version presents a slightly different story. It has already been demonstrated that Absalom was also called Uriah, and in this second version of the same story it most definitely *was* King David who seduced Bathsheba, the wife of Uriah-Absalom. Since it has already been shown that Bathsheba was Maakhah Tamar II, it must have been King David who performed this act of seduction or rape. In which case, the two stories that we have been following become identical:

a. King David raped Uriah-Absalom's sister-wife, Bathsheba-Maakhah Tamar II. Uriah-Absalom was then killed in a battle.

b. King David raped Uriah-Absalom's sister-wife, Bathsheba-Maakhah Tamar II. Uriah-Absalom was then killed in a battle.

Now the need for some deft sleight of hand by the Biblical scribes is plain to see. Under the identity of Bathsheba, King David had merely seduced an army commander's wife. But in the guise of Maakhah Tamar II, King David had not only seduced his son's wife, who was a princess, he had also seduced his own daughter. The true story of the 'rape' of Maakhah Tamar II therefore involved King David 'forcing' his own daughter.

As I have said many times before, there was nothing so very strange or abhorrent about King David having this kind of incestuous marriage union; in pharaonic terms, the marriage to a sister or a daughter was not only normal, it was almost a duty – for the bloodline ran in the female line and the ancient traditions demanded that the pharaoh had to maintain this bloodline. For the later Judaic scribes, however, the marriage of King David to his daughter would have caused the scribes to suffer a few palpitations, and so the name of Prince Absalom had to be changed to Uriah-Uriel in order to disguise this fact.

However, there was more to this story than a simple incestuous marriage. Maakhah Tamar II was already married to her brother, Absalom-Uriah and, as is to be expected, this prince was outraged by his father's indiscretion with his sister-wife. It was no doubt for this reason that prince Absalom led a rebellion against his father, which eventually resulted in Absalom's own death. King David then proceeded to marry his daughter, Maakhah Tamar II, the widow of Absalom, and undoubtedly this kind of indiscretion *would* have raised an eyebrow or two within the royal court, even in this era.

But this was not the only problem for the later Biblical scribes to sort out. King David had already married Maakhah Tamar I, the mother of both Absalom and Maakhah Tamar II. If the Biblical texts had said that King David had married another Maakhah Tamar, their deceit would probably have been obvious once more. It was for this reason that the name of the wife of Uriah-Absalom was changed from Maakhah Tamar II to Bathsheba. But, as has already been explained, the term 'Bath-Sheba' simply means the 'Daughter of Sheba', and this is just another way of saying the 'Queen of Sheba' – in which case, King David was marrying a Queen of Sheba. The relationship between this queen and the later and more famous Queen of Sheba who visited King Solomon will be explained later.

There is one more piece of evidence that can confirm this complex scenario. The Bible tries to claim that Uriah and Bathsheba were nothing to do with Absalom and Maakhah Tamar II. However, when King David took Bathsheba for his wife, their first child was called Solomon, and yet this choice of name would be more easily explainable if Bathsheba was the widow of the late Absalom. The names Absalom (Ab-shalowm אבי-שלום) and Solomon (Shalomoh שלמה) are not only substantially the same, they are also both derived from the same root word, *shalom* (shalowm שלום), which is the Hebrew greeting meaning 'peace'.

In addition to this similarity, the name Absalom was also derived from the Egyptian loan word *sharem (shalem)* [hieroglyphs], which has exactly the same meanings of 'peace' and 'greeting' as the Hebrew word *shalom*. But if the entire name 'Ab-Salom' was based upon Egyptian antecedents, then the prefix of *Ab* [hieroglyphs] would mean 'wisdom' in the Egyptian. The later King Solomon was, of course, noted for his great wisdom, and in this regard he can be seen to be inheriting the same name, titles and attributes of his much older stepbrother, Ab-Salom, who was killed in battle by his father, King David.

In other words, King David had just killed his son and heir, called Absalom (Ab-Salom, meaning Solomon the Wise); but after marrying Absalom's wife, Maakhah Tamar II (Bathsheba), their first child together was called Solomon, who became known as Solomon the Wise. This much younger Prince Solomon became the new son and heir to the throne of King David, and he was quite obviously a replacement for the late Absalom. All of which tends to support the assertion that Bathsheba was Maakhah Tamar II and Absalom was Uriah. Such a tangled web of intrigue was certainly worth the scribe's odd name change or two, in order to conceal the truth about the marital complexities within the royal court.

Here we have an ancient tale of intrigue in a royal court, but this was not simply the minor intrigues of a Judaeo-Israelite dynasty; this was a major conspiracy within the palace of an Egyptian pharaoh, Psusennes II. While the archaeological records of Israel remain strangely silent about these events, the annals of Upper Egypt abound with artifacts and texts, and so the possibility exists that this unfortunate prince, Absalom, may be visible in the historical record. The Bible maintains that after the 'rape' of Maakhah Tamar II and the murder of Amnon, Absalom-Uriah fled to his grandfather Talmai:

> But Absalom fled, and went to Talmai, the son of Ammihud, king of Geshur. And (King) David mourned for his son every day. [B38]

The case has already been made that Maakhah Tamar II's family came from either Thebes or Memphis, so it is entirely possible that Absalom-Uriah was fleeing to Upper Egypt. But Absalom-Uriah was still a favourite son of King David [Psusennes II] and so it is not beyond the realms of possibility that this son was found a position in the priesthood of Thebes.

In the historical record of Thebes we find just such a person. His name was Iuapet, he was high priest of Amun and, like Absalom-Uriah, he was also an army general. The interesting thing about Iuapet is that he also bore the title Uriha-t ⟨glyphs⟩ , a name that bears more than a passing resemblance to the Biblical name for Absalom – that of Uriah. More interesting still is that this title uses the lion glyph ⟨glyph⟩ for the syllable *ha-t*. New Kingdom hieroglyphs did not use the letter 'l', but later in Egyptian history the recumbent lion was adapted to spell out this letter that was missing from the Egyptian alphabet. Had the lion glyph in the name Uriha-t been read as an 'l' instead of the syllable *ha-t*, then this same name would have become Uriel. This usage of the lion glyph again explains the two forms of pronunciation, but from an Egyptian instead of Biblical perspective; thus, this particular high priest of Amun in Thebes bears both of the names of Absalom.

Unfortunately, the historical record, from the Bubastite Gate at Karnak, shows this character to have been the son of Sheshonq I rather than Psusennes II [King David]. However, despite this apparent generation gap in the historical record, this link between Iuapet and Uriel-Uriah is still interesting enough.

While the precise Egyptian identity of prince Absalom still hangs in the balance for the moment, the next task is to discover exactly who the succeeding pharaoh to Psusennes II of Tanis really was. In the Egyptian record he was known as Sheshonq I, the first pharaoh of the twenty-second dynasty, while in the Bible he was sometimes called Shishak – but who exactly was this pharaoh?

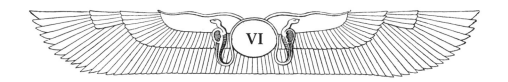

Mashuash

The Egyptian twenty-second dynasty is classically termed as being a new line of Libyan kings, whose ancestors arrived from the north-western regions of Africa and superseded the dynasty of Psusennes II [King David], and they are supposed to be distinguishable from the native Egyptian population by their distinctive foreign names. The first of these kings to come to power in Tanis, the capital of Lower Egypt, was the pharaoh Sheshonq I, who was known in the Bible as the pharaoh Shishak. Conversely, Sheshonq I was known to the priesthood in Thebes by the title of 'Great Chief of the Meshwesh', with the latter part of the title often being shortened simply to 'Ma'. So, was the pharaoh Sheshonq I really a Libyan monarch who had taken over the Delta lands? Was the entire twenty-second dynasty composed of foreign tribes who had invaded from the west? And if so, what did this title of 'Meshwesh' really mean?

The answer to the first question may be a qualified 'yes'. In the book *Jesus*, I traced both the migrations of the Hyksos-Israelites, who had been expelled from Egypt during the reign of the Theban pharaoh Ahmose I, and also the later and smaller migrations of the religious 'lepers', who were led by the charismatic pharaoh Akhenaton. Manetho states that the bulk of the refugees from both these exoduses fled into Canaan/Palestine. While this was probably so, it is also highly likely that some of these refugees took to boats and fled to new lands that were much further afield – to the western Mediterranean and perhaps beyond.

I then rather speculatively guestimated that the rise in the western Mediterranean of the alliance of nations, known to history as the 'Sea

People', and their dramatic military thrust into the civilised strongholds of Mycenae Greece and Egypt, may have been motivated by exiled Hyksos-Israelite leaders who wanted to regain control of their ancestral lands. Using a combination of Hyksos exiles and a host of these local mercenaries (or newly acquired loyal subjects), this bold attack by the Sea People very nearly succeeded in overthrowing all of Egypt.

There were successive waves of these attacks by the Sea People upon Egypt, lasting for a century or more, and they began during the reign of Seti I. In fact, the first of these attacks came not from the Sea People as such, but from the Shasu tribes who inhabited parts of Palestine:

> Although the Shasu ... had always been a thorn in Pharaoh's side, they burst with especially grievous force just before the beginning of the nineteenth dynasty across the Arabah and into the Negev and northern Sinai, cutting off Egypt's coastal route. [1]

The history of the Shasu nation will be explored later but, in short, these people were probably elements of the exiled Hyksos, who were now living in Judaea and may have held a few strongholds in the northeastern Nile Delta.

Although the Shasu were a 'thorn in pharaoh's side', the most successful invasions came not from these Hyksos exiles acting alone, but from the rather peculiar Sea People alliance. The most devastating of these attacks occurred during the later reign of Ramesses III. An assorted confederacy of tribes – known as the Asbuta, Hasa, Labu, Karkisa, Shardana, Daanu, Tyrenoi, Shekelesh (Equash?), Peleset, Tjekru and of course the Meshwesh nations – gathered in the valley of the Aamurru for an assault on Egypt. Many of these tribes, or at least their leaders, may well have had Hyksos-Israelite ancestries. In the book *Jesus*, I have previously identified the tribe of the Aamurru of Palestine and the Shardana of Sardinia with the Hyksos-Israelite exiles; while evidence that will be presented later shows that the Meshwesh and the Dannu were also descendants of these Semitic exiles.

Although the planning involved in organising a coalition of forces from across the whole of the Mediterranean was a logistical triumph unsurpassed in this early era, the invasion itself was not entirely successful and Ramesses III was able to lick his wounds, re-group and write an account of these battles. This 'victory' proclamation, which was inscribed into the walls of the mortuary temple at Medinet Habu, says of this assault:

> A camp was established at one location within Aamurru, ... On they came, with fire prepared at their front, faces towards Egypt. Their main (forces)

were the Peleset, the Tjekru, the Shekelesh, the Daanu, the Uashosh, and the lands all united. They laid their hands on countries as far as the circuit of the Earth, their hearts trusting and confident: "Our plans will succeed".[2]

According to the Egyptian record, Ramesses III shook off these attacks with a stunning victory at Djahy. But in all reality, this 'victory' was probably nothing more than a facade, a pretence that fooled nobody except the Theban Egyptians. Accordingly, Ramesses III also records that:

> I settled them (the Sea Peoples) in fortresses, confined through my name. Their draftees were numerous approaching hundreds of thousands, and I supplied them all by tax with clothing and provisions (paid for) against the treasury (and) the granaries each year.[3]

I get the impression that Donald Redford sees this statement in terms of a prisoner-of-war camp, with the dejected losers of the conflict being given alms to make them feel more comfortable. Personally, I see the total reverse of this concept. This was not an era in which wars were fought by the rules of the Geneva Convention; normally, the victor in these ancient conflicts either took vast tributes as recompense, or placed the able-bodied into slavery and killed the rest.

The fact that the Sea People were receiving supplies from Ramesses III shows that they were in a position of relative strength here. The truth of the situation is that the Sea People were probably extracting tributes from Ramesses III – the 'clothing and provisions' – in order to stop them making further attacks on the Theban-held lands in the south. Ramesses may have been boasting of victory, but he may have done little more than stop the invaders at the apex of the Nile Delta. What is more, he stopped the invaders as much by a promise of wealth and tribute as by military might.

Ammon

Although the victory proclamation is a record dating from the beginning of the twentieth dynasty, I think the foundations of the twenty-first dynasty can be clearly seen in these accounts. I have been arguing for some time now that the twenty-first dynasty, which ended with the pharaoh Psusennes II [King David], had a substantial Hyksos content. This Judaeo-Hyksos bias was the reason for the alliance between Tanis and Jerusalem, and for the acceptability of a unified Egypto-Judaean nation under the rule of the pharaoh Psusennes II.

VI *Mashuash*

This attack upon Ramesses III was a major battle that was fought by a mixed coalition of Sea People and Hyksos-Israelites, working under the names Shasu and Aamurru, which was launched from a base that was situated in Canaan, the Biblical Judaea. As such, this attack on Egypt would have been of great interest to the Judaeans and Israelites, and so it is highly likely that an account of this battle would have been included within the Biblical texts. This possibility has perhaps not even been considered before, but if this confederacy of Sea People was organised and controlled by the exiled princes of Hyksos-Israelites, then the twelve tribes of Israel would have had a vested interest in the success of this invasion. Indeed, they may have organised the whole campaign in the first place.

There are two military campaigns within the account of Judges that could be interpreted as being attacks on the Upper Egyptians by the Sea People alliance. The first of these is an attack by the judge Gideon upon the Midianites. The account of this battle, which was inscribed upon the walls of the temple at Medinet Habu by Ramesses III, states that the Sea People advanced on the Theban forces with 'fire prepared at their front', as one of the previous quotations demonstrates. The Bible is in complete agreement with this, and states that as the Israelite confederacy advanced upon the Midianites:

> (Gideon) placed trumpets and empty jars in the hands of all of (the soldiers), with torches inside ... the three companies blew the trumpets and broke the jars. Grasping the torches in their left hands and holding in their right hands the trumpets. [B4]

As is usual, the Bible manages to fill in all of the missing details from the Upper Egyptian account of this battle. According to the Biblical version, the strategy of the Sea People was to creep up on the Upper Egyptians with trumpets, and burning torches hidden in pots; at the appointed time, the pots were smashed to reveal the torches and the trumpets were blown. The strategy was so successful because this was an unexpected night attack on a slumbering army camp. The Upper Egyptian army would have been awoken from their tents by the commotion of the trumpets, and suddenly presented with a line of torches surrounding their camp; not only would this spectacle have been completely mesmerising, it would also have had the effect of multiplying the size of the attacking forces in the minds of the defenders.

The surprise and confusion that Gideon's strategy created ensured that the victory for the Judaeo-Israelites over the forces of Ramesses III was complete. Some of Ramesses III's forces did, of course, escape the carnage, and they even managed to take some captives with them. The survivor's accounts of this battle were then inscribed upon the walls at Medinet Habu, and these scenes give us further confirmation of the nationality of these Sea People. It is often stated in text books that the Sea People were spiky-haired warriors from the western Mediterranean, and some of the captives do indeed appear in this fashion; but there are many more of these captives who wear beards and long side-locks of hair. Quite obviously, these captives are conforming to the traditional styles adopted by the Judaeans, which are still worn by orthodox Jews to this day; and so the account of Gideon's battle in Judges is detailing exactly the same military engagement as is inscribed on the walls of Ramesses III's temple at Medinet Habu.

The second possible candidate for a Biblical version of these attacks on Egypt is again to be found within the account of Judges.

> And it was so, that when the children of Ammon made war against Israel, the elders of Gilead went to fetch Jephthah out of the land of Tob. [B5]

Here we see that the 'children of Ammon' עמון were threatening the lands of Judaea and Israel, and so – in a similar fashion to the Sea People alliance – a confederacy of Judaean tribes was being assembled in order to counter this threat. The whole thrust of the book *Jesus* was that the Hyksos dispute was basically theological; the Hyksos monotheists of Abraham and Akhenaton versus the Theban Amun (Amen) worshippers and their multiplicity of gods. In this case, the reference to the 'children of Ammon' attacking Judaea could easily be equated with the (Theban) Egyptians launching raids upon Israel.

According to the Biblical texts, however, the attack of the Ammonites was not only checked and reversed, the Israelites actually won another great victory:

> So Jephthah passed over unto the children of Ammon to fight against them ... And he smote them from Aroer, even till thou come to Minnith, even twenty cities, and unto the plain of the vineyards, with a very great slaughter. Thus the children of Ammon were subdued before the children of Israel. [B6]

That the Israelites could have defeated the Egyptians in battle on so many occasions may have seemed illogical to the classical perspective, and perhaps this was another of the many reasons for distancing the Ammonites and Midianites from the land of Egypt. But had the Israelites been the exiled Hyksos and their army, and had they attacked Egypt as part of a united confederacy, it is likely that they could have inflicted grievous losses on the Egyptian army, just as the annals of Ramesses III seem to imply.

While Ramesses III tried to boost public morale with claims of victory, the subsequent history of Egypt shows that both the nation and the southern kingship were grievously wounded. During the twentieth dynasty that followed the reign of Ramesses III, there were reputed to have been eight Ramesside pharaohs in just eighty years. Not only was the Theban monarchy unstable, so too was the economy. The northern Theban capital of Avaris became abandoned and it would appear that even the wealthy capital city of Thebes itself fared no better:

> ... excavations have shown that the population (of Thebes) suddenly declined at the beginning of the twenty-first dynasty, and large sectors of the city were abandoned. By year 48 of the Tanite king Psusennes I ... the temple of Amun was dilapidated... [7]

The classical inference is that as the power of Thebes declined, the Tanite pharaohs were then able to fill the political, economic and monarchal void that had been created. Personally, I think that there was a more direct causal influence than this. The Theban influence and power actually declined because of the debilitating attacks by the Sea People, who were being organised by the pre-Tanite leaders. Eventually, the later generations of Tanite leaders were able to declare themselves to be kings, and to take the throne of Lower Egypt by force and establish the twenty-first dynasty.

I have just suggested that the attacks by the Sea People were connected somehow with the Biblical accounts in the book of Judges. While this Biblical account of the gathering of the tribes does sound very much like the historically documented confederacy of Sea People, theologians would heartily disagree with this argument because it is clearly stated in the earlier book of Joshua that the land of Ammon actually lay to the east of the Jordan.

> Now these are the kings of the land, which the children of Israel smote, and possessed their land on the other side of the Jordan toward the rising of the sun, from the river Arnon unto mount Hermon, and all the plain on the east ....

> Sihon king of the Amorites, who dwelt in Heshbon, and ruled from Aroer, which is upon the bank of the river Arnon, and from the middle of the river, and from half Gilead, even unto the river Jabbok, which is the border of the children of Ammon. [B8]

It was Moses who had fought this earlier battle against the neighbours of the Ammonites during the great exodus, and it was apparently this battle that precipitated the conflict that is being discussed. The Ammonites were claiming that the Israelites had dispossessed their lands during the exodus, a claim that the Israelites denied.

Since, in this Biblical verse, the land of Ammon appears to have been firmly located to the east of the river Jordan, there appears to be little scope for any associations with the Egyptians. However, because of this eastern location for the land of Ammon, historians and theologians alike have been forced to give the Biblical exodus a rather tortuous route to arrive in Palestine from the south east – across the river Jordan. The more logical route out of Egypt would have been straight up along the coast of the Mediterranean and into Jerusalem, cutting weeks of the journey-time. So why do the Biblical texts indicate that the Israelites took such a peculiar route, and how can this situation be resolved?

The answer lies in the rivers. It is said that the land of Ammon lay on the river Beqbeq (Jabbok), which has already been identified with the river Nile. In this case, we may have to look south-west rather than east for the lands of Ammon. But if Ammon lay close to the river Nile, how did the scribes manage to muddle up the directions quite so comprehensively? How did south-west become east? Personally, I think that there has been a fortuitous (for the clergy) mistranslation of the Hebrew text at this point, and the answer lies in the phrase 'towards the rising Sun'.

It may well be that the text once said, in the original Egyptian, 'towards *Beqa*', as the ancient Egyptian word *beqa* means 'the sunrise'. But, as we have already seen, the word *Beq* also means the land of Egypt . In which case, the Biblical scribes were not necessarily wrong at all; it is only our perceptions and prejudices that are in error. It is quite possible that the original text, as just quoted, was supposed to be read as:

> Now these are the kings of the land, which the children of Israel smote, and possessed their land on the other side of the river toward Egypt, from the (branch of the) river Nile unto mount Hermon, and all the plain on the east.

This new interpretation means that during the great exodus, Moses had attacked and taken some of the eastern Delta lands of the Nile and all of the plain of the Sinai desert to the east. During the exodus, Moses was trying to exit Egypt with some 500,000 soldiers and civilians, so it was well within his power to devastate much of north-eastern Egypt. Although Egypt is often spoken of in terms of a completely homogeneous population, there

145

had always been various allegiances and city states that formed the individual components of the greater nation state. What appears to have happened is that Moses decimated one of these states in the Nile Delta and took possession of their city.

There is the distinct possibility that the later account in the book of Judges – regarding a renewal of these same hostilities between Israel and Ammon – may well have been the same event as the Sea People invasion that was inscribed upon the walls at Medinet Habu. However, if this was so, we now have an alternative, complementary and rather comprehensive account of the precursors and negotiations prior to this battle with the Sea People, and also an alternative account of its final resolution.

The Biblical account suggests that Ammon [Upper Egypt] was being rather bellicose and threatening Israel. The newly appointed Israelite leader, Jephthah, sent an emissary to the Ammonite king [the Upper Egyptian pharaoh] asking why he was so upset. The king [pharaoh] replied that during the exodus, the Israelites had attacked the Ammonite people and destroyed their cities, and he was looking for restitution. Jephthah denied this, claiming that the Israelites had destroyed the lands of Sihon and Amor (now identified as the lands to the east of the Nile), but that they had not attacked the Ammonites. The Israelite leader, Jephthah, also challenged the king to explain why he had allowed the Israelites to live in 'Aroer and her towns, and in all the cities that are along by the coasts of Arnon' for some three hundred years, but had only now got upset about it and demanded a restitution of these lands.

Is this possible? Were small pockets of Hyksos-Israelites still left over from the exodus and living in some of the fortified cities in the Nile Delta? The history of this era and this area is not entirely clear, as the records and cities have largely been destroyed, but some intelligent guesses are still possible. The mention of Israelite cities by the coast makes it appear that the portion of the river Arnon (a branch of the Nile) that the Hyksos-Israelites had managed to hold on to, lay in the far north of the Nile Delta, somewhere along the Mediterranean coast. While this is interesting, there are a couple of other facets of the late New Kingdom era that may support this interpretation.

The original capital of the Hyksos-Israelites was at Avaris and they would also have maintained control of Heliopolis, Memphis and much of Middle Egypt. But it is certain that the Hyksos-Israelites were ejected from all these cities at the time of the great exodus. Avaris was eventually taken over by the Ramesside pharaohs, who rebuilt the ruined city and called it Pi-Ramesse after their most famous ruler. It was from Pi-Ramesse that the Biblical exodus was supposed to have begun and, of course, this assertion is correct because Pi-Ramesse was the same city as Avaris. The only aspect of this exodus story that the Bible got wrong was the name of the city and, by inference, the era of the exodus.

Subsequent to the Ramesside era, however, a new city to the north of Avaris/Pi-Ramesse began to rise, a city that was eventually to become the capital of the pharaohs of the twenty-first and twenty-second dynasties –Tanis. This city had probably been used by the confederation of Sea People to launch their raids upon Pi-Ramesse and other Theban-held towns in the Delta. These raids were eventually successful and Pi-Ramesse was eventually abandoned by the Upper Egyptians at the end of the Ramesside period. The twenty-first dynasty pharaohs at Tanis then used this former capital city as a quarry, from which building material was taken to construct new monuments in Tanis. With Pi-Ramesse having been abandoned by the Theban military, it is a little peculiar that the Tanite pharaohs did not just re-occupy the city instead of pillaging it. The reason normally cited for this is that the river that served this city was beginning to silt up, which is a plausible enough suggestion. But it is also possible that the northern pharaoh's hold over this region was uncertain during the early part of this dynasty and that Pi-Ramesse was still not considered to be a safe enough location for a capital city.

The other question that remains unanswered is how the city of Tanis was founded. Was it an isolated Hyksos-Israelite stronghold that had been established way back in the era of Abraham? Or was it instead the city of the Ammonites, who were annihilated by the army of Moses? The evidence that has been given so far would point towards the latter interpretation. The inference is that this battle against the Ammonites occurred during the early part of the exodus journey, rather than at the end; so, instead of the Ammonites being located to the east of the Jordan, as the Bible tries to suggest, this siege was actually staged in the north-eastern Nile Delta.

In comparison with the standard Biblical interpretations, the only additional inference that is being suggested by this argument is that, in addition to defeating and occupying most of the lands of Canaan, the Hyksos-Israelites also held onto a few cities in the far north-east of the Nile Delta. This may well have been the origin of the twenty-first dynasty's fortified capital city of Tanis and it has to be noted that this city was located in the far north-eastern quadrant of the Nile Delta; indeed, it is not too far from the Mediterranean coast.

That the Israelites may have held onto a strip of land in the north-east of the Nile Delta can perhaps be glimpsed in the excavations that have been undertaken there. From the name Tel el Yehudiyeh, to the 'Pits of

Joseph', to the account of the 'Mound of the Jews', the history of this small region in the Nile Delta seems to be infused with Judaic influences. The fortified town of Tel el Yehudiyeh was also thought, by Flinders Petrie, to have been the location where the high priest of Jerusalem, Simon Onias, came to build his new 'Temple of Jerusalem'. The traditional explanations for the region are at a loss to explain why a Jewish high priest would want to build a Jewish temple in the Nile Delta. But if these lands had been traditionally Israelite, this would explain the situation to great satisfaction.

Flinders Petrie even goes as far as to speculate that the ground plan of the site of Onias' temple at Yehudiyeh mimics the layout of Jerusalem itself. He may well be right about this, but the people who built this temple actually lived some four hundred years before Simon Onias and they were actually the ancestors of the Sabean nation, as I will relate later.

Star City

If the Hyksos-Israelites had managed to hold onto a small strip of the Nile Delta during the exodus, and if this was the basis of the Tanis monarchy's power in this region, then it is axiomatic that the city of Tanis should have Hyksos aspects and traits. An obvious piece of evidence for this, which links the city of Tanis to both the Hyksos and to these Biblical accounts, is contained in one of the original names for the city of Tanis – the Egyptian capital of the pharaoh Psusennes II was once known as Khet-Seba-Thar.

Fig 20.   City of Tanis.

This name was derived from three separate elements. The first of these, *khet* ⌂✎, has connotations of 'terrace' and 'stairway', with the latter meaning also inferring a stairway to Osiris. While not wishing to seem obsessive about the connections with the Great Pyramid, it also has to be noted that *khet* can also mean a measurement of forty cubits and the number forty has already been closely associated with this pyramid. The second element, *seba (sheba)* ⎍, has obvious links to the Biblical accounts of the United Monarchy. While it is unlikely that the famous queen herself could have originated from Tanis, both the queen's and the city's names could have had the same source. In the Egyptian, the name *seba (sheba)* means 'door' or 'gateway to heaven', and I have already tentatively associated this 'great door' with the swinging entrance stone that once graced the northern face of this same pyramid. Finally, the third element is *thar* 𓈖𓂋𓏏𓊖 , which simply means 'protection' or 'fortress'.

The original name for Tanis would therefore equate to something like 'Stairway to the Door of the Fortress'. This functional description may simply refer to the design of the fortified city of Tanis, as it is known that Tanis was surrounded by a particularly substantial mud-brick wall measuring some 430 x 370 meters. Egyptian cities in general were not known for their elaborate fortifications, so if any city in Egypt could be called a fortress, it was Tanis. While this interpretation may seem satisfactory, it is not necessarily the complete answer. The Egyptians were known to be the most pious nation in the then known world and if the meaning of a capital city had to have any rationale, it is most likely to have been theological rather than secular.

I have already tried to point this discussion in the direction of Giza, and the word *thar* does this once more in a rather compelling manner. *Thar* also refers to either 'body armour' or a 'shield', and this word has been picked up and used in the Hebrew language as *sharyan* שריך, meaning 'body armour'. The fact that this word can mean 'shield' as well as 'fortress' is quite interesting, for it invokes images of the numerous golden shields that Solomon had commissioned for his palace in Jerusalem. The design used for Solomon's shields was the six-pointed Magen David, the Star of David, and if this was the desired meaning for the word *Thar*, then the meaning of the name for the city of Tanis may well be radically altered.

Since the design for the Magen David was based upon the outline of two interlocking pyramids, this alternative translation would infer that the door *(sheba)* in question was indeed related to the pyramids, and that the *Thar* 'fortress' was perhaps the Great Pyramid itself. Since much of the writing from Egypt can be read on many levels, the secondary meaning of Khet-Sheba-Thar, the city of Tanis, would then be the 'Stairway to the Door of the Pyramid'. The determinative being used for the name of this town, the three-hills glyph, would seem to confirm this. The orthodox opinion is that this glyph denotes something foreign, but the city of Tanis lies in the Nile Delta; and even if historians see the Tanite Meshwesh tribes as being 'foreign', they were hardly likely to have described themselves as being foreign. The alternative translation of the three-hills glyph, that it refers to the three pyramids of Giza, not only makes more sense, it also confirms the assumptions that have just been made.

This brings us to an alternative meaning for the word *Khet*. Instead of referring to 'steps', the word can also mean 'seal'. This alternative translation is interesting, because rather than this word describing the steps leading to a door, it could actually have referred to the seal on the door of the Great Pyramid. But this may not be describing a clay seal on the door of the Great Pyramid itself, even if one existed; instead, it could be referring to the seal (the instrument) that stamped the seal – the 'seal' of the people of Tanis themselves.

A direct comparison to this might be the Great Seal of the American people, which is a physical stamp that was once used for sealing and authenticating important government documents. While America may be a predominantly white, western, Judaeo-Christian country, this seal of America has nevertheless been designed with a curious combination of Egyptian imagery. As everyone now seems to know, the Great Seal's design incorporates an unfinished pyramid with a Masonic all-seeing eye superimposed upon it, and this same design was incorporated into the layout of the one dollar bill by Vice-President Henry Wallace (the eye is probably a representation of Ra). Since the design of this seal shows an unfinished pyramid, the general assumption is that this is a representation of the Great Pyramid at Giza.

Perhaps the reason for leading this argument towards Giza and the pyramids can now be understood, because the original name for the city of Tanis may be invoking a strikingly similar scenario to the American example just given. The name for this city may well have meant something like the 'Great Seal for the Door of the Great Pyramid'. This new rendition of the name is no longer referring to the pyramid itself, but to the Great Seal that was once used for sealing the Great Pyramid's entrance, and was subsequently used for administrative purposes within the city of Tanis. Like the American example, the design that it impressed into the wet-clay seal probably included an image of the Great Pyramid.

This new and rather radical interpretation for the name of the city of Tanis may also explain why the five-sided partner of the Star of David was known as the Seal of Solomon. King David was not the only monarch to have choosen a design for his administration's seal, and while it would seem that King Solomon chose the five-sided star for his Great Seal, the seal of King David may have incorporated the pyramid and a six-sided star. In fact, there is evidence that the Magen David (the Star of David) is still an important symbol in the modern world, and not just within Judaism, as this symbol still forms a major part of the imagery and symbolism of Masonry; which is why it has been carved into HRH the Duke of Kent's throne in the Masonic Grand Temple in London.

VI *Mashuash*

Meshwesh

The investigation so far has indicated that the Meshwesh (Ma) ancestors of the pharaoh Sheshonq I (Shishak) may well have been of Libyan origins. The slight amendment to the standard interpretation of this dynasty is that these Libyans may simply have been returning exiled Hyksos-Israelites. Sheshonq I may have been one of the first in a very long and distinguished line of Israelite diaspora, one of the first Zionists. Although this amendment may seem radical, it may actually explain a few long-standing problems for Egyptologists.

It has always been something of a mystery as to why the Meshwesh twenty-second dynasty of Sheshonq I became so thoroughly Egyptianised so quickly. Aside from the seemingly strange names and the deep antipathy with Thebes, there would be no way of distinguishing the Sheshonqs from any other line of pharaohs. It would also explain their particular brand of Egyptian theology; Alan Gardiner says of this idiosyncrasy:

> Great stress is laid upon his (Amen's) ... uniqueness and his inscrutable nature ... use being made of the play on words between his god-name Amen and the verb *amen* 'to be hidden'. The existence of other deities is ignored rather than denied, and there was no persecution of them as in the Aten period.

> It would be interesting if we could confidently diagnose the reasons for the over-exaltation of the mighty Theban deity. [9]

Diagnose it we can, for the answer being championed in this chapter, in terms of a returning exiled Hyksos royalty, explains every aspect of these problems. The returning exiles were practising the traditional Hyksos-Israelite form of worship, which laid stress on the unique and hidden nature of the one and only god. But, with these people having been through the tragedy of civil war and exile twice before, under the leadership of the pharaohs Jacoba [Jacob] and Akhenaton [Aaron], they were not about to make the same mistakes again. Thus, the Meshwesh were more than happy to leave an orthodox gloss on the surface of their religion by calling their deity 'Amen', while subtly amending the attributes of this Theban state god to suit their own brand of Hyksos theology.

Another element of Meshwesh culture, which was supposed to show their foreign origins, was the single feather that they wore in their headdress. Donald Redford says of this adornment:

> The (Meshwesh) stubbornly preserved titles in the Libyan tongue ... and to the end of their tenure of power in Egypt (they) preserved the barbaric feather insignia as headgear. [10]

Why Redford should have such an aversion to the simple feather, I cannot quite understand. The Royal Fusiliers of the British Army still use this single feather insignia to this very day. While this organisation may be a component in a professional fighting force, does this feather insignia imply that the Fusiliers are 'barbarous'?

In fact, far from being a symbol of 'barbarism', the feather insignia of the Meshwesh was most probably a representation of the goddess Maat. It so happens that the prime element of the Maat goddess glyph 𓐙 is the single feather, and Maat can even be represented by the feather alone 𓆄 . Rather than showing their 'pagan' heritage, the wearing of the single feather may have identified each and every member of the Meshwesh nation with the concepts of truth and justice. Since many of the generals who control the British Army have Masonic leanings, it would not be too surprising to find that the Royal Fusiliers' feather insignia is similarly based upon the concept of Maat.

The evidence for this comes from the history of King David and King Solomon. As we have already seen, the Maakhah Tamars were important priestesses and queens of the United Monarchy, and in turn this same United Monarchy will shortly be shown to have been closely associated with the Meshwesh tribes. But the Egyptian alter-egos of the Maakhah Tamars were the Maakare Mu-Tamhats and, as we have seen before, the term 'Maakare' can be split into the syllables Maat-Ka-Ra 𓐙𓂓𓇳 , meaning 'Maat is the Soul of Ra'; or, if the term *maat* is translated into the English, we can then derive 'Truth and Justice are the Soul of Ra'. In other words, the Maakhah Tamars were closely associated with the goddess Maat, just as the Meshwesh may have been.

But there may have been more to this Maat symbolism than is currently thought. The proverbs of King Solomon were thought to represent 'wisdom', but in essence most of these proverbs simply give advice that is rather similar to a modern secular treatise on common law. In many respects, Solomon's 'wisdom' was the direct equivalent of our notion of truth and justice. In other words, as researcher Richard Knowles pointed out to me, the Biblical concept of 'wisdom' and the Egyptian concept of 'Maat' are almost identical to each other. This is further confirmed by the book in the Biblical Apocrypha known as the Wisdom of Solomon, which states:

Her I loved and sought out from my youth,
And I sought to take her for my bride,
And I became enamoured by her beauty,
She glorifies her noble birth in that it is given her to live with god,
And the sovereign Lord of all loved her,
For she is initiated into the knowledge of god,
But if riches are a desired possession in life,
What is richer than wisdom? [B11]

She knows the things of old and divines the things to come,
She understands subtleties of speech and meanings of esoteric sayings,
She foresees signs and wonders and issues of seasons and times,
Because of her I shall have glory among the multitudes,
Because of her I shall have immortality,
All things that are either secret or manifest I learned,
For she that is the artificer of all things taught to me, even wisdom. [B12]

Like many of the Biblical monologues, this rather pleasing verse can be read on many levels. The text is not only speaking of wisdom, it is also referring to one of Solomon's wives, who will be shown in a later chapter to have been Maakhah Tamar II. Since 'wisdom' is being explained in female terms, and since the divisions between 'wisdom' and 'wife' are being deliberately blurred in this verse, it would seem that Solomon's devoted wife, Maakhah Tamar II [Maakare Mu-Tamhat II], was also a prime source of Solomon's great wisdom. The clue that the wife being referred to here was indeed a Maakhah Tamar is given in line four, which says that 'it is given (for) her to live with god'. This is an unmistakable allusion to the position of God's Wife, who, by definition, *must* have 'lived' with god.

As the concepts of 'wisdom' and 'truth and justice' can also be blurred in much the same manner, the clear inference is that Queen Maakhah Tamar (Maatkare Mu-Tamhat) was regarded as an Earthly manifestation of the Egyptian goddess Maat – which is why her name incorporated the Maat glyph . Indeed, this same verse can also be seen to be referring to Maat herself, rather than the wife of King Solomon, and this deliberate ambiguity, which is being generated between Maat the goddess and Maat the Maakhah Tamars, demonstrates how important the priestly role and duties of the Maakhah Tamars was considered.

Another point that shouldn't be overlooked is the unlikely source of all these details. The fact that a Judaean book of King Solomon was discussing, in great detail, the attributes of the Egyptian goddess Maat, shows once more how closely associated the United Monarchy was with

Egyptian culture. But this is just what one would expect to find if King David had indeed been the Egyptian pharaoh Psusennes II.

However, this verse also shows us how much emphasis the United Monarchy placed on the veneration of Maat. If the Meshwesh tribes were actually the ancestors of this United Monarchy, as will shortly be shown to great satisfaction, it should be abundantly clear by now that the Meshwesh feather was nothing more than a symbol of Maat. Rather than demonstrating how 'foreign' and 'barbarous' these people were, the feather symbolism that this nation was using actually demonstrates how deeply integrated into Egyptian culture they really were, and how sophisticated and wise they were attempting to be.

Having shown that the Meshwesh were infused with Egyptian culture and quite possibly Egyptian themselves, this just leaves us with the supposedly 'peculiar' names that were adopted by the Tanis royalty during this 'Libyan' dynasty. The obvious questions are: what did these names really mean, and were they really so foreign?

The first name to look at, I suppose, is the title 'Meshwesh' itself. Egyptologists have probably glossed over this name, not thinking it worthwhile translating. As an 'obviously' foreign name, which had connotations of reeds and marshes and was no doubt poorly transliterated from the Libyan into hieroglyphs for domestic consumption, it would have no intrinsic meaning in Egyptian anyway. But this is not necessarily so. If the Meshwesh had been led by returning exiled Egyptian princes, it is entirely possible that they still spoke an old-fashioned form of Egyptian. Even if they had already lost the Egyptian language for everyday usage, they may well have retained it for ceremonial functions and for important titles and names. In short, the title 'Meshwesh' may well have a real meaning in the Egyptian language.

The first thing to note is that the name 'Meshwesh' can also be pronounced as Mashuasha 𓈖𓏏𓆑𓈖𓏏𓅱𓀀 , and the word is literally taken to mean a 'Libyan tribe'. Secondly, there is the separation of the two primary syllables, with the name 'Mashuash' often being shortened to 'Ma'. This dislocation may well signify a natural break in this word, where two sub-units are joined together – *Ma* and *Shuash*.

When looking at possible translations for these syllables, it can be seen that the syllable *Ma* has several meanings, and a case could be made for each of them. A couple of the permutations are 'by means of' and 'grant me', but the most likely is perhaps *Ma* meaning 'come', a term that also has a strong association with the idea of travel. This option is possibly confirmed by the meaning of the word *Masha* 𓈖𓂝 , which also means 'travel' or 'go'.

VI *Mashuash*

The true meaning of the syllable *shuash* is perhaps easier to define, and the word was most probably based upon two very similar concepts. The first of these is the name *Shasu* 𓈗𓃀𓂝𓂻𓀭, which is a reference to the Shasu tribes in Judaea, and this nation can be further identified with the word *shasiu* 𓈗𓃀𓄿, which again has connotations of 'travel'. Both this term and this tribe itself will shortly be explored in much more detail. The second word to be identified with *shuash* is the name *Uasheshu* 𓂝𓃀𓈖𓀭, which again refers to a 'foreign' people and has vague connotations of walking.

Fig 21. Mashuash.

These translations seem to show that the Mashuash were a nation who were proud to be known as nomads (gypsies) and who also used the 'marshlands' glyph at the beginning of their title. The full title of the Mashuash may well, in this case, have meant something like 'foreign travelling nation who lived in the Delta lands'. But the 'foreignness' of these people may be more presumed than real. To historians, the Mashuash and Shasu were foreign tribes because they appeared to originate from Syria and Libya, but if these people were actually Hyksos diaspora, then they would not have been quite so foreign after all. If this were the case, their title could be reduced from 'foreign travelling nation' to 'travelling nation'.

While the reference to 'travelling' may infer a nomadic lifestyle, it is a known fact that these same people actually lived in great fortified cities and, apart from a presumed immigration into Egypt from elsewhere, they appeared to be far from nomadic. The reason for this conundrum may well be that the notion of 'travelling', which was being highlighted by this name, was actually a reference to the Hyksos ritual circling of the pyramids, as discussed in the book *Tempest*. The fact that these same people had fled Egypt in the great exodus and survived these great migrations would have doubly reinforced this gypsy identity, so that it became one of their primary symbols.

It is from these very same ethnic roots and expressions that modern Gypsies are supposed to have originated. Classical encyclopaedias will say that the Gypsy people are from Indo-European stock and they trace their roots back no further than a location somewhere in Persia in the tenth century AD. This information is primarily derived from linguistic comparisons, as the Gypsies speak an Indo-European language that is related to Sanskrit. However, Gypsy mythology has a very different explanation for their ancestry. The term 'Gypsy' is reputed to have been derived from the word Egyptian, and since the Gypsies are still famed for being a travelling nation, they too would have originally been known as an 'Egyptian travelling nation', much as the Shasu and Mashuash were.

While this semi-mythical history of the Gypsies may seem fanciful, there may be some strands of evidence that support it. The first of these comes from the historian Manetho, who relates a tale of a pharaoh and his brother:

> Armais, also called Dannus ... was banished from Egypt and, fleeing from his brother Aegyptus, he arrived in Greece, and, seizing Argos, he ruled the Argives. [M13]

The name for the country of Egypt is said, by Manetho, to have been derived from this pharaoh called Aegyptus, who he seems to identifiy with Ramesses II. However, the precise identity of this brother of Ramesses II, called Armais (Dannus), is not known. As Armais was said to have ruled after Akhenaton and to have preceded the reign of Ramesses II, in the book *Jesus* I provisionally identified Armais with Seti I; mainly because Seti I was likely to have been related to Ramesses II. Conversely, many historians have taken the view that Armais was the pharaoh Horemheb, as the name Armais is sometimes spelt as Harmais; but there is little else to back up this assertion.

Having looked at the problem more closely, however, it would seem that Manetho has amalgamated the reigns of Ramesses II and Seti I into one individual, which means that it is unlikely that Armais was Seti I. But if Armais was not Seti I, and if he was not Horemheb, who was he?

The most likely, albeit radical, explanation is that Manetho's pharaoh called Armais was actually the Amarna pharaoh who was known as Ay. Although this suggestion may initially seem unlikely, in actual fact the two names are rather close equivalents of each other. Manetho calls this pharaoh who fled to Greece Armais – whereas the throne name of the pharaoh Ay was actually Irmaa-t or Armai-t  . The two names, Armais and Armait, are sufficiently close in pronunciation to warrant further investigation.

In fact, this rather radical suggestion is further supported by the equivalent Phoenician myths that describe this very same story. These Phoenician tales indicate that the goddess Io went to Egypt and her descendants ruled Egypt for four generations. But for some unspecified reason, no doubt involving some kind of political conflict, many of the fourth generation fled from Egypt. Agenor went to rule Phoenicia, Belos ruled Mesopotamia, Danaus (Dannus) ruled Argos while Aegyptus remained in Egypt. This is obviously the same story that Manetho has repeated in his king-list of Egypt, but the added details allow us to further pinpoint the source of this story. [14]

The fact that this family were supposed to have travelled to Egypt, ruled the country for four generations, and then left to become kings of other countries is a simple repetition of the Biblical books of Genesis and Exodus. It was Joseph who descended into Egypt, whose descendants ruled Egypt (as viziers) for about four generations, and who were then expelled from the country on the second of the two exoduses from Egypt. But, since I have already identified this second Biblical exodus as being something to do with the Amarna regime of Akhenaton, then the princes or pharaohs who were expelled from Egypt must have been something to do with the Amarna regime. Once more, the likelihood is that Dannus was actually Ay. However, the additional data from the Phoenician myths allows us to further speculate on the identities of the other brothers who fled Egypt – was Agenor Akhenaton, for instance?

This connection between the pharaoh known as Dannus and the Amarna regime would actually make a lot of sense because it was this same Dannu tribe from Greece who joined the Sea People in the raids upon Egypt in the twelfth century BC. The Greeks would not have had any particular grudge against Egypt, but if they were under the command of the descendants of Ay (Dannus), they would most certainly have had good reason to despise the Ammonite Egyptians. The Ammonite Egyptians, under Horemheb and Seti I, had destroyed the entire Amarna regime and no doubt slaughtered a number of their family, so the chance of paying back the compliment (with interest) would have been very satisfying – even if the revenge took six or so generations to organise and execute.

The most radical part of this new identification, however, is the inferred relationship between the Amarna regime and the nineteenth dynasty of the Ramesside pharaohs. Manetho states that Ay (Armais-Dannus) was the brother of Ramesses II, whereas the classical chronology would suggest that there was a complete regime change in Egypt at this time, and that the Ramesside pharaohs were descended from a completely different family line. But that, of course, is not how royal dynasties operate, and there is absolutely no historical evidence to support this assertion. Within the greatly extended family of the Amarna dynasty, there would have been any number of royal cousins who would have fought for the throne if it became available. While I do not think that Ramesses II and Ay could have been brothers, it is entirely possible that a close relative of Ay decided that they had never supported the religious reforms of Akhenaton and organised a military coup against the Amarna regime.

It should also be pointed out that the chronology of Manetho deviates considerably from the accepted chronology during this era, so the precise identification of Aegyptus with Ramesses II is by no means certain. Essentially, Manetho has inserted another Ramesses and Amenophis into the tail end of the eighteenth dynasty, as the following table demonstrates:

Classical chronology	Manetho's chronology
18th dynasty	**18th dynasty**
Amarna Regime	Amarna Regime
Ay (Armait)	Armais (Dannus)
Horemheb	
	Ramesses (The Great)
	Amenophis
19th dynasty	**19th dynasty**
Ramesses I	Sethos
Seti I	Ramesses
Ramesses II (The Great)	Ammenenephthes
Merneptah	Ramesses
Ammenenemnes	Ammenenemnes
Seti II	
Siptah	
Twosret	Thuoris

Although the Ramesside dynasty is generally portrayed as being wholly separate from the earlier Amarna dynasty, it is an established fact that one of the primary founders of this dynasty, Seti I, came from Avaris – the former Hyksos capital in the Nile Delta. It is inconceivable that a pharaoh from Avaris did not have some element of Hyksos blood and sympathies. While the theological dispute that raged during this era may have split this Hyksos family down the middle, this does not mean that Ay and Ramesses II could not have been closely related to them.

This story by Manetho would have a tribe of exiled Egyptians ruling parts of Greece, and presumably having a monarch who was called Ay (Armais-Dannus), who was the brother of Aegyptus. In which case, there would have been a strong link between the name Aegyptus (Egypt) and this region. It happens that the Kebra Nagast relates a story that the king of this region (Greece-Constantinople) in the tenth century BC wrote to

King Solomon and asked for a son who could marry his daughter. The peculiar thing about this later story is that this king was said to be the king of 'Rom' or 'Rome'. Surprisingly enough, the other name that is perhaps even more strongly connected to the Gypsy nation is that of Rom or Romany. Therefore, the ancient texts, which predate the emergence of the modern Gypsy nation by some 2,000 years, connect the names Gypsy and Rom to a people or monarchy on the European / Asian borders. Could the descendants of the pharaoh Ay be the modern Gypsies?

The answer may lie in the very name of these people. While the name Gypsy is reputed to have been derived from the pharaoh Aegyptus, the name Rom does not appear to have a direct ancestry. The Gypsy language is supposed to have been derived from Sanskrit, but in fact the name Rom is more likely to have originated from Egypt. In the Gypsy language the name Rom simply means the 'people', the nation of Gypsies. It so happens that the Egyptians used exactly the same phraseology; they described themselves as the 'people' while all other tribes were just 'foreigners'. Surprisingly enough, the name the Egyptians used to describe themselves was *Romu* ⌒🐦𓀀 , meaning 'people' or 'mankind'. Complicated and convoluted as the history of this title may seem, it would appear that the Gypsy nation has inherited both of its titles directly from Egypt – these people were known as the Aegyptians and the Romians.

Khasu - Shasu

So much for the history of modern Gypsies, but what of the other ancient nomads, the Mashuash? We have already seen a strong linguistic link between this nation of foreign nomads, the Mashuash, and the concept of a travelling nation. But this same formula could also apply to other groups of nomads like the Aperu, who have often been equated with the 'Hebrew'. The Aperu are thought to have been 'foreign stonemasons', but they are also linked to the Egyptian word *ap* meaning 'journey'. Likewise, we have also just discussed the Semite *Shasu* nomads from Palestine, a name that also means 'to travel' once more.

It is also worth noting that the Shasu can be spelt using the 'three-hills' glyph ⌒⌒ and the 'stone-door' glyph 🔲 . The three-hills glyph has already been equated with both the Hyksos and the three pyramids at Giza, while the stone-door glyph will become important in later chapters. As will be explained later, the stone-door glyph is also an oblique reference to Giza, but strangely enough this glyph is still used today in Masonic ceremonies.

VI Mashuash

Here we have three groups of nomads – the Mashuash, the Aperu and the Shasu – who are all linked to the concept of travel. One of these groups, the Mashuash, is thought to have arrived from the west; while the other two, the Shasu and the Aperu, are thought to have originated in the east. The reason that the latter are thought to have come from the east is due to their presumed Semite ancestry.

Note how the title of the nomadic Mashuash, the name of the pharaoh Sheshonq I, and the name for the nomadic Shasu are all quite similar in their spelling and pronunciation. Since the pharaoh Sheshonq I was supposed to have been from the Libyan tribes of nomadic Mashuash, why should his name look suspiciously like that of a tribe of Semitic nomads from the east, who were called the Shasu? The reason for this, I believe, is that the Mashuash leaders and kings (including the pharaoh Sheshonq I) were not of Libyan extract at all. While they could have been the leaders of a Libyan invasion using Libyan mercenaries, they were themselves of Semite, Shasu ancestry; and who were in turn the exiled Hyksos nation from Egypt.

Wallis Budge, the renowned Egyptologist, is in agreement with this and he confidently equates the Shasu directly with the Hyksos people living in the east of Egypt. [15] Budge does not give his full reasoning for this association, but Flinders Petrie gives a compelling rationale. Petrie noted that the traditional name for the Hyksos was *Hyk Khasut*, meaning 'Kings of the Foreign Lands', or 'Kings of the Mountains'; a term that has already been interpreted in the book *Tempest* as meaning 'Kings of the Pyramids'. When these names were translated, at a later date, into the Semitic and Greek languages, many errors and differences were introduced into the pronunciation and some of these linguistic anomalies are a recurring theme running throughout this book. Petrie says of one such common alteration, which effects the word *khasut*:

> (The consonant) *'kh'* became *'sh'* in later times, and so passed into the Greek *'s'* – as already noted in the instance of Khufu = Souphis [Sufis] – so the Khasut would read Sasut or Sasu. [16]

Petrie could also have noted many more illustrations of transpositions between 'sh' and 'kh' from within the Egyptian language alone, the following being just a few examples of this modification:

Sekhes	Shesh	move quickly
Sekher	Sheser	plans, designs
Sekhmu	Shesmu	judge, chief

Since the consonant 'kh' can become 'sh', the name k̲hasut can become *Shasut* (Shasu). The term *Hyk* had also been dropped by this nation, because the term *Hyk* means 'king' and these tribes had abandoned the concept of kingship for a number of generations. The Bible is quite clear in saying that there was a long period of the 'Judges' before another monarch, King Saul, was eventually asked to lead the Israelite people. Thus, the Hyk-Khasut (Greek Hyk-Sos) people of the seventeenth century BC had become the Shasu (Greek Sos) of the tenth century BC. Incidentally, the 'u' at the end of the word Shasu simply indicates a plural, and since there was more than one person in the Sos (Sas) nation, the proper pronunciation was Shosu or Shasu.

As can be seen, both Petrie and Budge directly equate the Shasu with the Hyksos; they were the same people who had simply been displaced from their homeland and were now living somewhere in Israel or Judaea. It is for this reason that the term Shasu is most often used in the eighteenth dynasty, with only a few references going back into the fifteenth dynasty. Since the name Shasu was simply another term for the Hyksos, it is likely that the original association with nomads would have been no more than an occasional reference to the journeys that were undertaken during the Hyksos religious processions that took place at Giza and Dahshur. During the eighteenth dynasty, however, this 'nomadic' term would have been greatly enhanced by the great exodus out of Egypt by the Hyksos-Israelites (the Shasu) that occurred at the beginning of this dynasty. The Shasu could now be derided by the Theban priesthood, not only for their strange processional celebrations at Giza, but also for their great nomadic exodus to Jerusalem.

This derision was further enhanced by another title that the Hyksos-Israelites-Shasu had used to describe themselves: the Shepherds. The term had been coined because the Hyksos priests had observed the movements of the stars and noticed that the constellation of Aries had become dominant in the dawn skies of the Vernal Equinox. But the title was a double-edged sword because now the Theban priesthood could mock the Hyksos (the Shasu) for being uneducated Bedu tribesmen (nomadic shepherds) who had fled to Jerusalem.

In fact, all of the aspects and attributes of the Hyksos belief system could now be ridiculed; it was open season on the Shasu people. Accordingly, nearly every one of the Egyptian terms pertaining to the Hyksos people, their culture and belief systems have been twisted into equivalent words that are full of hate and vitriol. The Hyksos-Israelite diaspora had become the loathed, mocked and persecuted nation, a situation that seems to have been perpetuated into the modern era.

The location of the Shasu people, as given in the *Soleb* and *Amarah* lists, strongly supports this argument for the Shasu having Hyksos as well as Semite origins. They were supposed to have lived in Seir, Laban, Samath and Werber. [17] These place names are distinctly Biblical, with Seir being the location of Mt Sinai and Laban being the brother-in-law of Isaac. But the original location of Seir and Mt Sinai, as explained in the book *Tempest*, was in reality the Giza plateau – a location that was sacred to the Hyksos. An even closer link between the Shasu and the Israelites, however, is again to be found in the *Soleb* list. The document goes on to name something called 'Yehew in the land of Shasu'. [18]

Even Donald Redford is forced to acknowledge the possible link between the 'location' of Yehew and the Israelite god Yahweh (Yaheweh). But there is a problem here. If the Shasu were Israelites, and if the name Shasu ⸢𓈗𓏏𓇋𓂝𓈖𓀀⸣ has a similar spelling to that of the pharaoh Sheshonq ⸢𓈙𓈖𓈙𓈖𓐝⸣ and the Mashuash ⸢𓌳𓈙𓍯𓂝𓈙𓈖𓀀𓀭⸣; and if the pharaoh Sheshonq I was a leader of the Mashuash tribe; then shouldn't the Mashuash be a Semitic people? But if the Mashuash were Semitic (Israelites), then how could they also be Libyan? The answer to this has already been given – the Libyan leaders were in actual fact the Hyksos-Israelite diaspora, the exiled renegade Semites from the civil war against Ahmose I.

The proof of this, which links the Hyksos, Shasu and the Mashuash nations all together, is to be found in the Egyptian Museum in Cairo. One of the greatest finds in Egyptian exploration was the discovery of the royal tombs at Tanis. The only problem with this dramatic discovery, however, was the timing – it occurred right at the start of the Second World War and so the impact of this exciting news was submerged under the events of the unfolding political crisis in Europe.

Despite this, the finds were definitely worth exploring, and the untouched and intact tomb of King Psusennes (I or II) was eventually uncovered. In among the chambers there were also the remains of the burial of the pharaoh Sheshonq (I or II), and his magnificent silver hawk-headed sarcophagus. Of the many smaller funerary items that were recovered, the one of particular interest in this investigation was that of the solar barque pectoral, made from gold and lapis lazuli, which was placed upon the chest of the mummy. The plaque was inscribed with an inscription that reads:

> Amun-Ra-Horakhty travels the heavens every day to protect the great chief of the Mashuash. [19]

The most interesting aspect of this inscription is that the term Mashuash has been shortened into Ma, and the glyph being used to denote this is the 'throw-stick' 〗 . But the throw-stick was the glyph that was used to denote the Aamu, who were the citizens of the city of Avaris and who were in turn the Hyksos. These people were probably known as the Aam, but just as in the case of the Shasu, a plural glyph 'u' has been added on the end.

The term Aamu was exclusively used as the common name for the Hyksos, and while writing the book *Tempest* I speculated that the Aamu had inherited this name because of its association with the sub-meaning of 'shepherd'. But, since the Egyptians loved to invent multiple puns in their convoluted language, there is another word that is equally suitable as a source for this title. The word *amm* 〖 〗 also refers to the date-palm, and excavations at the cities of Bubastis and Tanis, which closely straddle the location for the city of Avaris, have been found to be littered with the finest granite date-palm columns that have been discovered in all of Egypt. The 'Aamu' would therefore have been a fitting title for the citizens of these northern Delta towns, and one of these towns may also have been known as the City of Palm Trees, as we shall see later.

But how have the throw-stick or date-palm been confused with the Mashuash? The answer to this question comes down to the escapades of the inventive scribes once more. The throw-stick and date-palm were both pronounced as *aam* but, just like the words *beq* and *qeb*, the scribes have simply turned this syllable around and produced *maa* – a word which still manages to mean 'date-palm'. In fact, the positive association between the throw-stick and the title 'Mashuash' may actually call into question the whole idea that this particular glyph was ever pronounced as *aam*. It may well be that the Aamu people were more often referred to as the Maau.

This pronunciation would make a great deal more sense that the orthodox version, and for one very good reason. The traditional thinking has always been that this glyph was a throw-stick 〗 . But, having already noticed that the three-hills glyph ⌒⌒ was a representation of the three Giza pyramids, it also struck me that the throw-stick glyph 〗 was a precise representation of the Great Pyramid's causeway, which used to have exactly the same kink in it. Since the throw-stick was often placed on top of the three-hills glyph ⌒⌒ , this association between the throw-stick and the pyramid causeway was graphically confirmed. But this argument can be taken one stage further because the throw-stick is no longer being called *aam*, it is *maa* instead.

One of the chief roles of the Great Pyramid's causeway was the observation of the Sun's shadow at sunrise and sunset. The position of the sunrise, or the position of the pyramid's shadow relative to the causeway, determined both the month and the season of the year. In effect, one of the prime uses of the Great Pyramid was as a gigantic gnomon, and the role of the priesthood was to observe the Sun's shadow as it crossed the length of the causeway. However, if the causeway was such an intimate part of these observations, then surely its name should reflect that role? This is exactly correct, but the connection cannot be made with the *aam* pronunciation, only with the *maa* version. The word *maa* has one clearly predominant meaning, and that is 'watch' or 'see'. If the *aam* throw-stick had sometimes been pronounced as *maa*, then its new subsidiary meanings would include 'to watch' or 'a place to keep watch'. Both of these meanings would precisely suit the function of the Great Pyramid's causeway as an astronomical marker that required daily observations.

In the book *Tempest*, I laid out the arguments for the Hyksos leaders being both the Kings or Guardians *(hyk)* of the Giza plateau. This is what the name Hyk-Sos meant; it could be translated either as 'Kings of the Pyramids', or 'Guardians of Giza'. But it would now appear that the pronunciation and meaning for the other main title for the Hyksos people, that of Aamu, was slightly wrong. They were not the Aamu, they were the Maau, the people who made astronomical observations on the Giza plateau. This new pronunciation and meaning for the Maau is highly satisfactory because it is complementary to the explanations given for the title Hyk-Sos – the Hyksos were indeed the 'Watchers over the Plateau'. This argument is perhaps confirmed by one final meaning for the word *Maau*, which is 'he who keeps a lookout on a fort'. It would be difficult to find a more accurate description of the rituals that were maintained by the Hyksos priesthood at their Giza observatory.

Throughout these explanations for the term Mashuash, there is one element that has not been satisfactorily explained, and that is the meaning of the syllable *Ma*. The original name for the Hyksos is known to have been the Hyk-Khasut, meaning the 'Kings of the Pyramids'. On occasions, however, this name could be modified by the inclusion of the name that was used to denote the citizens of the Hyksos capital of Avaris, Aamu, which resulted in the compound name Aamu-Khasut. But some subtle alterations were subsequently made to this name over the years:

a. As already explained, the word Khasut was changed to Shasut or Shasu, as the people emigrated northwards and were influenced by other languages.

b. The title for the citizens of Avaris, Aamu, was either changed to or had always been pronounced as Maau.

The result of these two simple changes was that the traditional title of Aamu-Khasut had become Maau-Shasu. From this root word the scribes then derived the word Maashashu or Mashuash. Therefore, the name that these people used to denote themselves had altered only slightly over the centuries, even if the pronunciation seemed to be quite different. They had once been the 'Kings of the Pyramids', but they were now known as the 'Watchers of the Pyramids' or even the 'Watchers of the Processions'. Here is the true derivation for the name for the Mashuash nation of Sheshonq I and the twenty-second dynasty, and it is an explanation that clearly shows that the apparently 'foreign' name of the Mashuash people was originally based upon a Hyksos-Egyptian heritage.

Osorkon

The other pharaonic name from the twenty-second dynasty, which is often considered to be of Libyan origins, is that of Osorkon (Uasorkon). It is not readily explained why this name should be considered to be foreign in nature, although this assumption may be based upon the Uashosh nation who were a member of the Sea People confederacy. Whatever the reasoning, I do not think that this is the case at all. In my opinion, the name was derived directly from the god Osiris, and nothing could be more Egyptian than the name of Osiris.

Fig 22.   Cartouche of Uasorkon.

The basic spelling of Uasorkon is that of ⟨glyphs⟩, and the first three glyphs in the name spell the word *uasar*. Whilst the spelling is not quite the same, one of the most common of names for Osiris was Uasar ⟨glyphs⟩. While the spelling may be different, there may nevertheless be a reason for this. The twenty-second dynasty were heavily influenced by the thoughts of the Hyksos, and one of the prime tenets of Hyksos-Israelite beliefs was monotheism – the worship of one, supreme god.

While the naming of the pharaoh Uasorkon was to use the god-name Osiris, the court officials who pontificated upon these matters decided to incorporate into this name the concept of a single, omnipotent god who was nevertheless still called Osiris. The result was that the spelling now used the ⸢glyph⸣ glyphs, which together are pronounced as *uas*. The latter glyph is said to represent a 'razor', but it was, as we shall see later, an image of a stone plug that concealed a passageway. The similar-looking ⸢glyph⸣ glyph was based upon this same concept, but probably included a bolt on this 'door'. This 'door and bolt' glyph was pronounced as *ua*, and its prime meaning is said to be 'one', 'single', 'alone' or even 'the one and only god'. This glyph was also used in a similarly pronounced name of Osiris, Ua ⸢glyph⸣ , and this latter reference is again suggesting a single god. In which case, the *ua* in Uasorkon could well have been a reference to a solitary manifestation of Osiris.

This idea is supported by another spelling of the pharaonic name Uasorkon ⸢glyphs⸣ , which also utilises the 'throne' glyph. But this was not simply any royal throne – this was supposed to have been the 'throne of Osiris'. It looks as though this 'throne of Osiris' glyph may have been used as a determinative for the name of Uasorkon, and the evidence for this can be seen in a name for Osiris that appears to mimic this determinative-type usage ⸢glyphs⸣ . The other glyph that was sometimes included in the cartouche for Uasorkon was the jar glyph *bas* ⸢glyph⸣ . This glyph not only produces the Biblical pronunciation of B-Uasorkon [Boaz], it also refers to the cat-headed goddess, Bastt ⸢glyphs⸣ , who was popular in the north-eastern Delta region, and to the leopard-skin tunic that was worn by the high priests of Egypt.

This inclusion of the Egyptian god-names Bastt and Osiris into the name B-Uasorkon shows that this 'foreign' twenty-second dynasty pharaoh was using distinctly Egyptian terminology and titles. A later chapter will quite conclusively confirm this by explaining the precise nature of this 'Osiris door' glyph in Masonic terminology, and this comprehensive explanation will demonstrate very close links to Egypt indeed.

King Solomon

The close links between the Judaean monarchs of this era and the Egyptian royal line have already been made in no uncertain terms, and if King Solomon were a son of King David, these links should continue unabated. Since King David was none other than the pharaoh Psusennes II, then, despite the paucity of historical data for this era, this son of his called Solomon should also be visible in the historical record. So who was this celebrated King Solomon? Perhaps the first thing to note about this monarch is that his fabled wealth again outstrips the capabilities of a purely indigenous Israelite monarch:

> So King Solomon exceeded all the kings of the earth for riches and for wisdom. [B1]

> In the days of King Solomon, gold was as common as bronze, and silver as lead, and bronze and lead and iron were abundant as the grass of the fields and the reeds of the desert ... and god gave unto him glory, and riches, and wisdom, and grace in such abundance that there was none like unto him among his predecessors... [KN2]

At their first reading, these statements might be taken as pure Biblical propaganda, as it seems impossible that an Israelite king could aspire to such wealth. How could the king of a minor province like Judaea-Israel exceed the riches of the great civilisations of Persia and Egypt? While these matters may seem unanswerable in pure Biblical terms, the texts continue unabashed:

VII King Solomon

> And King Solomon made a navy of ships in Eziongeber, which is beside Eloth, on the shore of the Red Sea, in the land of Edom. [B3]

It would appear that King Solomon not only had a substantial royal court, untold wealth, a fabulous palace, a richly adorned temple and a large number of wives and concubines; it seems he had a navy, too. Josephus then continues to add that this navy went on an expedition, looking for trade:

> (Solomon) commanded them to carry all sorts of merchandise into the remotest of nations, by the sale of which a great quantity of silver, gold, ivory, Ethiopians and apes were brought to the king; and they finished their voyage, going and returning in three years time. [J4]

This story is actually based upon a historical event that was narrated by Herodotus. Herodotus says that it was the pharaoh Necho, son of Psammetichus, who assembled a fleet of ships on the Red Sea and sent them off on a voyage of discovery and trade:

> Necho ... sent to sea a number of ships manned by Phoenicians, with orders to make for the Pillars of Hercules. They took their departure from Egypt by the (Red) Sea and so sailed into the southern ocean ... two years went by, and it was not until the third year that they doubled the Pillars of Hercules and made good their voyage home. [H5]

While one may scoff at the idea of the Egyptians rounding the South African cape and returning via Gibraltar, it is certain that this did indeed happen in this early era. The proof for this lies in the strange tale that the Sun always lay on the sailors' right hand – a tall story that Herodotus both recounts and simultaneously scorns. But, of course, this account is reasonably true. The Egyptian adventurers were travelling clockwise around Africa, and so the midday Sun will be on their right-hand side (to the north) while travelling around South Africa, and it will also be on their right-hand side (to the south) while travelling through the Mediterranean. It is fortunate, in this case, that Herodotus included so many myths and tales in his *Histories*, as this particular sailors' yarn conclusively proves that the Egyptians had indeed circumnavigated Africa.

The Biblical and historical accounts of this voyage are obviously the same, but this leaves us with a dilemma because the eras are not. Herodotus indicates that the pharaoh concerned was Psammetichus, whereas the Bible and Josephus indicate that it was King Solomon. As Herodotus' chronology is so notoriously unreliable, it may well be that he has mistaken Psammetichus for Psusennes (Pasebakhaen-nuit) [King David], the father of King Solomon. Whatever the truth of this matter, the main point to be made is that the same event is being ascribed to both an Egyptian Pharaoh and a Biblical king of Israel. Once more, the only inference that can be derived from this is that these Biblical kings were, in fact, pharaohs of Egypt.

Under the classical interpretation of theology and history, these grandiose claims by the Biblical texts, of power, wealth, influence and superior armed forces, appear to be nothing more than court bravado. But, on the other hand, if Solomon were really the son of the pharaoh Psusennes II, then all of this could easily have been true. These statements are the first piece in a long line of evidence that demonstrates that King Solomon was not simply a minor royal of the pharaoh Psusennes II's extended royal family; instead, he was most probably the next reigning monarch of Lower Egypt and Judaea.

As an Egyptian prince, King Solomon is sure to have been educated at the royal college of Heliopolis, and to have been instructed in all the arcane knowledge of this ancient, pyramid-building empire – and this can be seen to be so from a quick comparison with the New Testament accounts. Solomon was not only the son of King David [Psusennes II], he was also reputed to have been a direct ancestor of the New Testament Jesus. I have already shown that Jesus' titles and actions demonstrated that he was not a simple carpenter, but instead a prince of Egypt and a theological Mason. Like the pharaoh Akhenaton, who reigned long before him, the Biblical Jesus was apparently educated at Heliopolis, and both of these princes became architects. It is known that Akhenaton held the title of 'Chief Architect', and the title held by Jesus, which demonstrates that he held the same symbolic position, is *tekton* τεκτων, from whence the word 'archi*tect*' was derived.

King Solomon was also reputed to have been a Mason and the scribes have demonstrated King Solomon's association with the craft in the very same terms that were used to describe Jesus' position. During the construction of the Temple of Jerusalem, it is said that:

> And (King Solomon) showed the workmen the measurement and the weight ... and he told the workers in metal how to use the hammer, and the drill and the chisel, and he showed the stonemasons the angle and the circle and the surface (measure). [KN6]

Although the senior degrees of ritual Masonry once held within their cabal the secrets of secular architecture (plus the foundations of science, medicine, mathematics and astronomy), it is nevertheless unlikely that King Solomon was such a skilled artisan himself – but the allusion to the ritual craft is clear to those who can follow the rather unsubtle code.

The foundation of Masonic lore, as the lower-degree brothers are informed, was based upon the construction of the Temple of Jerusalem by Hirom of Tyre, and so much of Masonry is naturally infused with building terminology. Here is that very event, the building of the Temple of Jerusalem, and King Solomon is being portrayed as its Chief Architect, the founder of the ritual craft. The scribe who wrote this particular passage was simply stating that King Solomon was the Masonic Grand Master during this era; and since this post has been traditionally bequeathed upon the senior members of the royalty, it is not too surprising to find that the current Grand Master of the British contingent is H.R.H. the Duke of Kent, the grandson of King George V. Of course, the traditions of masonry go back much further than King Solomon and the Temple of Jerusalem, but these additional revelations are only taught by degrees.

Solomon

The name 'Solomon' is given in the Hebrew as being Shalomoh שלמה, which is apparently based upon the word *shalom* שלם (שלמ), and while this word literally means 'peace' or 'contentment', it is most often used as a formal greeting. In its turn, the word *shalom* is supposed to be based upon the word *sha'al* שאל, meaning 'salute' or 'sue for mercy'.

As is usual, however, these Hebrew words have a longer history than might be expected. The word *shalom* is actually based upon the ancient Egyptian word *sharem (sharema)* 𓈙𓄿𓂋𓅓𓀀, which means 'peace' and 'contentment' or to 'greet', 'salute' or 'sue for mercy' – the two words are identical in meaning. Remember that the Egyptian language did not have a letter 'l', so the equivalent Hebrew words have often transliterated the Egyptian 'r' as an 'l'. The result of this modification is that there is a direct transliteration between the two languages, and the Egyptian word *sharema*, meaning 'greeting', has become the Hebrew word *Shalomoh (shalema)*, which also means 'greeting'.

Interestingly enough, the Egyptian word *sharema* 𓈙𓄿𓂋𓅓𓀀 is rather similar to the word Masuash 𓈙𓅓𓂋𓈙𓅓𓀀 spelt backwards, and it also has pretty much the same spelling as was used for the pharaoh Sheshonq I, 𓈙𓅓𓈙𓅓𓈖 . Since the word *sharema* has the same meaning and spelling as the name for King Solomon, and since the word *sharema* now seems to have many similarities to the name that was used for the pharaoh Sheshonq I, this has to be a first indication that the pharaoh Sheshonq I was directly related in some way to King Solomon. Like King David before him, it is looking likely that the Israelite King Solomon was nothing less than another Egyptian pharaoh.

Fig 25.   Cartouche of Sheshonq.

The Egyptian word *sharema* is also very similar to the name *Sharedjina* , which is an Egyptian term that was used for the natives of Sardinia, and this title is clearly the ancient origin of the name for this island. The attacks on Egypt by the Sea People were primarily organised by the Mashuash, as we have seen in the last chapter, but a significant contingent of these invaders was also drawn from the Shardana (Sharedjina). This may seem like a curious location for a nation who decided to take on the might of Egypt, but in the book *Jesus*, I indicated that the primary Mediterranean bases for the exiled Hyksos-Israelites were, in fact, the islands of Sardinia and possibly the Balearic islands; both of these being locations in which the enigmatic *nuraghi* towers were built. Thus, although the native populations of these islands would have had no grudge against the Egyptians, their new leaders most certainly would have had.

We now have two homelands for the contingents that comprised the Sea People confederation – Libya and Sardinia – whose people were known as the Mashuash and Shardana respectively, and yet these names are both very similar to the name of Sheshonq I. While historians have made this same association in order to show the 'foreign' nature of the Sheshonq dynasty, it is now being made to show the Hyksos affiliations of these Sea People.

These same two locations are also strongly reminiscent of the history of the Phoenicians. In a very similar fashion, the Phoenicians, who I also closely link with these exiled Semitic tribes, had their main western Mediterranean bases in Sardinia and Carthage on the North African coast. The ancient city of Carthage is actually in modern Tunisia, but this whole area originally came under the umbrella title of Libya. Therefore, the estates and possessions of the Phoenicians exactly mirror those of the

Shardana and the Mashuash Sea People. Not surprisingly, it was Phoenician sailors who were said to have crewed King Solomon's navy.

Wisdom

Armed with this additional background information on the nature of the twenty-second dynasty, it is possible that the meaning of King Sheshonq I's name can now be seen and understood.

The letter 'n' in Sheshonq is often left out, indicating that it may be of less importance, a preposition perhaps. In fact, a suitable word would be *n* ⁓⁓⁓ , meaning 'because' or 'of'. Likewise, the last letter 'q' often has an 'a' added, which would give *qa* ◁🦅 , meaning 'exalted' or perhaps even 'royal' or 'prince'. Since it is now likely that Sheshonq(a) was a Hyksos pharaoh, this suffix to his name may have the same meaning as the suffix in the title of the Hyksos kings themselves. The true pronunciation of the first syllable in Hyk-sos is either *Heq* or *Heqa* 𓏲◁🦅 , which means 'prince' or 'king'.

The bulk of the name Sheshonq consists of the syllable *shesh*, and some of the possible translations of this word have already been covered in some detail. But the best option for *shesh*, in Biblical terms, has to be that of *sesh* ⟨⟩ , *seshit* ⟨⟩ or *sesha* ⟨⟩ , meaning 'wisdom', 'secret' or 'mystery'. The antelope determinative infers being skilled in prayer, so it is obvious that this wisdom was based on sacred or esoteric secrets. It is here that we can see the strongest links yet between King Solomon and King Sheshonq I because Solomon was also known for his wisdom, which was mentioned on no less than fourteen occasions in the Bible.

> And all the earth sought to Solomon, to hear his wisdom, which God had put in his heart. [B7]

In a similar refrain, the full translation of the name for Sheshonq I has now become 'Exalted for Wisdom' or even 'King of Wisdom'. But what was this great esoteric learning of King Solomon-Sheshonq? Why were foreign monarchs supposed to have travelled across the known world to hear the wisdom of Solomon?

> And there came of all people to hear the wisdom of Solomon, from all kings of the Earth, which had heard of his wisdom. [B8]

> And when the Queen of Sheba had seen the wisdom of Solomon, and the house that he had built... [B9]

While the inference of these verses may seem obvious, King Solomon-Sheshonq may not have been known just for his wisdom. While the Egyptian title of Sheshonq(a) could have been rewritten as 'Sesha-n-Qa' ⌐⌐⌐ meaning 'Exalted for Wisdom', it could also have been derived from the words 'Shasu-n-Qa' 𓈖 , which would infer 'King of (the) Travellers' – with the term for the 'prince' or 'king' *(qaa)* also having connotations of a high place or mountain. In reality, if both the 'travelling' and the 'wisdom' referred to the circling rituals at Giza (the mountain), then these two translations are actually complementary. Note again how the name Sheshonq(a), which is traditionally regarded as being peculiarly Libyan in origin, appears to have been closely related to the nomadic and Semitic Shasu tribes, and how this 'foreign' name seems to be eminently meaningful in an Egyptian context.

This meaning, which has been teased out of the name Sheshonq, can also be verified from the Biblical texts. Like the pharaoh Sheshonq I, King Solomon himself was also a king who was noted for his great wisdom, and who was also noted for his love of preaching from high places; the latter being something that is mentioned on numerous occasions in the Bible:

> For Solomon had made a brazen scaffold, of five cubits long, and five cubits broad, and three cubits high, and had set it in the midst of the court: and upon it he stood, and kneeled down upon his knees before all the congregation of Israel, and spread forth his hands toward heaven. [B11]

Compare this Biblical description of King Solomon giving a sermon from his 'high place' with his arms stretched out towards heaven, and the hieroglyph of the word *qaa* , meaning 'exalted', 'king' or 'high place'. Rather than being an eyewitness account of Solomon giving a speech to the assembled priesthood, it is almost as if the Biblical scribe was simply attempting to describe the hieroglyph itself. Undoubtedly, all of this is yet more evidence that the names for Solomon and Sheshonq(a) were closely related and that they may actually have been the same person.

This great wisdom of Solomon was also noted by King Hirom (Hiram) of Tyre, and according to Josephus these two monarchs exchanged letters and puzzles:

> ...the main bond of friendship between them was their passion for learning. They used to send each other problems to solve; in these Solomon showed the greater proficiency, as, in general, he was the cleverer of the two. [J12]

VII *King Solomon*

This period of peace, stability and friendship between Hirom and Solomon resulted in Solomon's request for raw materials from Lebanon, mainly cedar wood from the mountains for the building of his great Temple and palace at Jerusalem. In fact, so much timber was used during their construction that the palace became known as the 'Forest of Lebanon'. From the descriptions of the temple, it would appear that it was designed around substantial stone footings, and upper courses consisting of a timber framework with stone in fill. The resulting hall may well have looked very similar to the many Elizabethan timber-frame houses that can still be seen on some of the fine English country estates.

While the tradition of Lebanon supplying cedar to Israel is not greatly featured in ancient literature, the supply to Egypt was a regular event. The *Report of Wenamun* tells of a journey from Thebes to Lebanon to collect wood for the construction of the barque of Amun, during the reign of the twenty-first dynasty king Smendes I (Nesbanebdjed-Amminadab). Egypt was divided at this time, and it seems that Wenamun had to stop off at Tanis to get the blessing of the northern king, Smendes I, before continuing his journey. Unfortunately, it would appear that the expedition had not been financed properly and Wenamun was rebuffed by Tjekerbaal, the prince of Byblos.

> 'I have come in quest of timber for the great noble bark of Amen-Re. What your father did and the father of your father did, you too will do it.' He said to me: 'True they did it. If you pay me for doing it, I will do it. My ancestors carried out this business after Pharaoh had sent me six ships laden with the goods of Egypt, and they had been unloaded into the storehouses. You, what have you brought for me?' [13]

It would seem that the wealth of Thebes was not so great as in the past, and it appears that Wenamun had only brought a statue of Amun to Lebanon and he was hoping that the command of the god Amun (the statue) would induce the Byblos prince to supply the wood. Tjekerbaal was unimpressed and a promise of payment had to be made before the logs were cut. The goods for trade, which seem to have come from Smendes I and not Thebes, were not terribly impressive: five jars (one golden), four jars of silver, ten garments, 500 mats, 500 ox-hides, 500 ropes, 20 sacks of lentils and 30 baskets of fish. As the prince of Byblos said:

> Look, the business my fathers did in the past, I have done it, although you did not do for me what your fathers did for mine. Look, the last of your timber has arrived and is ready. [14]

VII *King Solomon*

Wenamun had managed to complete his trade with not much more than a few baubles and the faded reputation of another Egyptian era. Times must have been tough in Byblos, because the Biblical account indicates that King Solomon had this exact same problem a few generations later; with what should he pay the Lebanese for their fine cedar wood? The plaintive cry from Solomon to Hirom, king of Tyre, sounds remarkably familiar:

> And Solomon sent to Huram (sic) the king of Tyre, saying, As thou didst deal with David my father, and didst send him cedars to build him a house to dwell therein, even so deal with me. [B15]

The monarchs of Lebanon were dealing with King Solomon in exactly the same manner that they had traditionally done with the pharaohs of Egypt. Indeed, if it were not for the different dates that are traditionally ascribed to these two accounts, the *Report of Wenamun* could easily be mistaken for this Biblical text. If this similarity was due instead to the traditional bartering that these traders regularly engaged in, then the whole episode sounds like the petty bartering of any Eastern bazaar. In fact, the Egyptian phrase for 'doing business in the Syrian tongue' eventually became another word for 'haggle'. [16]

'How can you offer such a miserable sum? Have you no respect for the honour of my mother?', might be the reply to your offer – even though the price is three times what the product is really worth. But once the haggling is finished, a payment of some sort is required in any trade, and the solution for King Solomon was to send Hirom some agricultural produce:

> And Solomon gave Hiram (sic) twenty thousand measures of wheat for food to his household, and twenty measures of pure oil: thus gave Solomon to Hiram year by year. [B17]

But Israel was not noted for being blessed with a regular surplus in wheat or oil in this era and the usual source of wheat would have been Egypt, so this detail once more hints at an Egyptian source of wealth for this trade. But this tribute was still not enough payment for the amounts of timber that Hirom (Hiram) was supplying for the Temple and palace at Jerusalem, and so Hirom was also given some cities in northern Israel:

> Now Hiram the king of Tyre had furnished Solomon with cedar trees and fir trees, and with gold ... then king Solomon gave Hiram twenty cities in the land of Galilee. [B18]

Is this the kind of trade that a king would willingly make? To give away a part of his kingdom to pay for some raw materials? Much more likely is the possibility that this king was occupying this land and making decisions in the manner of a third-party administrator. Since Solomon [as the pharaoh Sheshonq I] was largely supported by the southern tribes of Judah and Benjamin, the loss of a few northern cities in Israel would hardly have mattered to him.

The Bible indicates that these northern cities were only taken over by the Judaean royal family during the reign of King David [Psusennes II], whereas the historical record indicates that it was Sheshonq I [King Solomon] who led these campaigns into the northern province of Israel. The campaign records, which were inscribed upon the walls of the Temple of Amun in Karnak, show that Sheshonq I [Solomon] took over control of many Israelite towns. Although many of these names are no longer legible, those that remain show that Sheshonq I controlled: [B19]

Egyptian	Hebrew	Egyptian	Hebrew
Rubaty	Rabbith	Taanaka	Taanach
Shanma	Shunen	Batyshaner	Bethshean
Ruhaaba	Rehob	Hapuruem	Hapharaim
Mehanem	Machanaim	Kebiana	Gibeon
Battyhua	Bethhoron	Ayuruen	Ajalon
Yudh-meruk	Kingdom of Judah	Pahukhrw-Aabaram	Field of Abraham

It may well be that the Karnak inscriptions are a little misleading here. King David [Psusennes II] may well have been the pharaoh who invaded and conquered the lands of Judaea and Israel, just as Josephus and the Biblical texts describe, but since he was not in full control of the city of Thebes he was unable to record this fact there. Josephus says of these campaigns by King David [Psusennes II]:

> David was hereby enraged and began the siege of Jerusalem ... intending by the taking of this place, to demonstrate his power ... so he took the lower city by force... [J20]

Although the Biblical texts like to imply that King David simply succeeded to the Israelite monarchy on the death of King Saul, Josephus is equally adamant that King David had to mount a major military campaign in the region to secure his rule there. Like most conquerors of new lands, King David then imposed a census on the people of Judaea and Israel, which revealed populations of 400,000 and 900,000 respectively. The purpose of this census was to impose that other common element of a successful

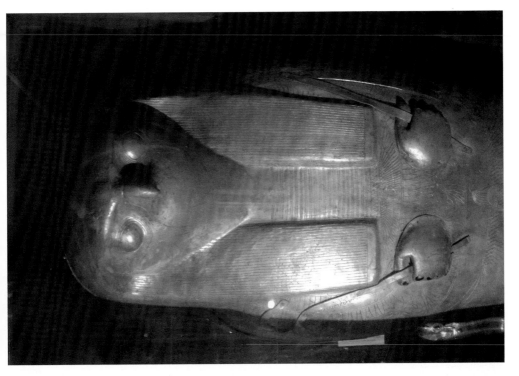

Plate 1. The beautifully engraved and uniquely styled solid silver outer sarcophagus of King Solomon.

Plate 2. The wooden inner coffin of King Solomon. Again, this design shows the close associations that were being made with Horus, the falcon-headed god of Egypt.

Plate 3. The solid silver inner coffin of King David, fabricated in the traditional Egyptian style.

Plate 4. The solid gold death-masks of King David (left) and his father Obed (right). Note the dramatic leap in quality between the two masks, which strongly indicates that a new artisan with superior skills and technology had been employed by King David.

Plate 5. Solid gold plates and bowls from the tomb of Joab, King David's army commander.

Plate 6. Gold ladle from the tomb of King David.

Plate 7. Golden bowl from the tomb of King David.

Plate 8. Golden vase from the tomb of King David.

Plate 9. Sarcophagus of Maakhah Tamar, the daughter-wife of King David who became immortalised in later traditions as the Queen of Sheba.

Plate 10. A megalithic statue discovered at Bubastis. The similarity between this statue and the sarcophagus of Maakhah Tamar, and its dedication to the son of King Solomon, strongly indicates that this was a statue of the Queen of Sheba.

Plate 11. The face of the Queen of Sheba.

Plate 12. The Great Temple that lay at the heart of the City of David, which may have become known in later generations as the Temple of Solomon. From the number of pink granite palmiform columns in this temple, the city may also have been known in the Bible as the 'City of Palms'.

Plate 13. The eastern temple in the City of David. Note, once more, the beautiful design and craftsmanship involved in the fabrication of these palmiform granite columns.

Plate 14. The tomb complex of the United Monarchy in the City of David. The tombs of King David and King Solomon are on the left.

Plate 15. The much ruined shrine of the Queen of Sheba at Karnak, Luxor.

Plate 16. The mummy of Nesperennub at the British Museum, London – note the pottery Yarmulke or skullcap. (Picture courtesy of SGI/British Museum.)

Plate 17. The Bubastite Gate at Karnak, commissioned by King Solomon. The design of this entrance-gate was modelled upon the design of the Temple of Solomon, and it indicates that the pillars of Jachin and Boaz in Solomon's temple may well have had a similar phallic design.

Plate 18. The campaigns of Sheshonq-Solomon, which are inscribed upon an outer-wall near the Bubastite Gate at the Temple of Karnak.

Plate 19. An inscription detailing the battle between Ramesses III and the Israelite/Sea-People alliance, that has been carved upon the walls of the temple of Ramesses III at Medinet Habu, Luxor.

Plate 20. Captives taken by Ramesses III during the battle with the Israelites/Sea-People alliance. Note that the captives wear standard Israelite dress, including beards and side-locks of hair.

Plate 21. The valley in which lies some of King Solomon's Mines.

Plate 22. One of the two sluicegates that controlled the waters in the Marib Dam, Saba. Note the style of the masonry and the expert finish of the entire construction.

Plate 23. The entrance-gate to the Temple of Awwam, which lies across the river from the city of Marib and was dedicated to Maakhah Tamar – the Queen of Sheba.

Plate 24. A group of modern Gypsy travellers in traditional waggons.

Plate 25. One of the palmiform pillars from the eastern temple at Tanis.

Plate 26. The pyramidal tomb of 'Zechariah', which lies just outside the walls of Old Jerusalem, (courtesy Adrian Gilbert).

Plate 27. The Egyptian papyrus detailing the *Instructions of Amenemopet*, which was copied into King Solomon's book of *Proverbs* in the Bible.

Plate 28. An image of the Judaic Menorah, the seven-branched candelabra that once lay in the Temple of Solomon. This carving was discovered in the Great Temple at Tanis, in the Nile Delta.

military campaign, a poll tax. Each adult, or more likely each working man, was required to pay half a shekel to god – which no doubt went towards the cost of building the Temple of Jerusalem. In each and every respect, King David [Psusennes II] was acting like the true conqueror of Judaea and Israel. [121]

It is likely, therefore, that the campaign lists, which were inscribed in the Temple of Karnak by Sheshonq I [King Solomon], were mainly listing the military campaigns of his father, Psusennes II [King David]. It was for this reason that King Solomon had dominion over so many towns and villages in Israel that he could afford to give some away to Hirom of Tyre as payment for the timbers of cedar. According to Josephus, however, King Hirom inspected these cities in Israel and rejected them, and so they gained the name 'Cabul', meaning 'those that do not please'. [122]

Since all the available precious metals in Lower Egypt and Judaea were being used to decorate the Temple of Jerusalem, the balance in dues that King Solomon still owed to King Hirom was therefore paid in a slightly unusual manner:

> It is said that Solomon, the sovereign of Jerusalem, sent riddles to Hirom and asked for others from him, on the understanding that the one who failed to solve then should pay a sum of money to him that succeeded. [123]

It was Solomon who triumphed in this battle of wits, and so the timbers for the Temple of Jerusalem and the great Palace of Solomon were eventually paid for. Interestingly enough, the term being used for 'sovereign' in the account of Josephus was *tyrannus* (τυραννος), which means tyrant. While *tyrannus* can indeed mean sovereign, it also has obvious connotations of an oppressive despot, so it is highly probable that not all of Israel was in favour of King Solomon's rule. Had Solomon been the pharaoh Sheshonq I (Shishak), whose rule over Israel would have been primarily supported by the southern tribes of Judah and Benjamin, and underpinned by the Egyptian army, this situation would have been extremely likely.

While the concept of Sheshonq I (Shishak שׁישׁק) being supported by these southern tribes in Judaea may in itself sound radical, there were many similarities and connections between these two peoples that make this proposal a distinct possibility. One good illustration of this is that the name Shishak appears to have been quite familiar to the Judaeans of this era. One of the descendants of Benjamin was called Shashaq שׁשׁק, which is as close as one can come to the Hebrew name for the pharaoh Shiyshaq שׁישׁק. Then there is the strange case of the royal scribes. The chief royal scribe during the reign of King David was called Shavsha

שׁישׁא, while the chief scribe during the reign of Solomon was known as Shiyshah שׁישׁא.

Within both Egyptian and Israelite societies, the majority of the senior posts in the administration went to members of the extended royal family. This same tradition infers that the name Shishak was not just simply known within the tribes of Benjamin and Judah, but that it was actually used by the senior-ranking members of the royal family. At the very least, this familiarity with the name Shishak shows that there were high-level affiliations between the court of Solomon and the Mashuash people, who were supposed to have been the ancestors of the pharaoh Sheshonq I (Shishak). But that is the most conservative of positions and, personally, I believe that it is unlikely that these Mashuash influences would have occurred in this fashion if Solomon was not a pseudonym for Shishak.

Further links to the Egyptian royalty can be glimpsed in the many Biblical references indicating that Solomon was being supplied with materials from Egypt. If the texts can be relied upon, the Bible is not even indicating in these passages that Solomon was trading with Egypt; it sounds much more like he was requisitioning supplies from his homeland. So, in order to maintain his campaigns in the Levant:

> Solomon had horses brought out of Egypt, and linen yarn: the king's merchants received the linen yarn at a price. [B24]

Solomon was not only acting like an Egyptian monarch in demanding that horses be brought from Egypt, the construction of his Temple has distinct Egyptian overtones too. The building of this great Temple at Jerusalem, with the timbers being supplied from Lebanon, was perhaps the greatest and most memorable of achievements during the reign of King Solomon. This was indeed a mighty edifice and its design not only drew heavily on the layout of the great northern Egyptian temples at Tanis and Heliopolis, but also upon those at Karnak in the south. Although it was a wooden construction, unlike the great stone temples of Egypt, the execution of the work was in every way the equal of those southern temples. There were literally tonnes of brass used for the pillars and baths; the door hinges and the lavish ornamentations were all made in silver and gold; and the mighty state throne was made of ivory covered in gold. It was a stupendous and lavish edifice and King Solomon was rightly proud of his achievements.

What, then, of the equally mighty pharaoh Sheshonq I? If this Egyptian monarch were simply a pseudonym for King Solomon (or *vice versa*), would he not be similarly famed for creating a fine temple?

VII *King Solomon*

Surprising as it may seem, Sheshonq I was indeed famed for commissioning a new temple, and so the similarities between these two monarchs continue unabated. In fact, Sheshonq I indicates that he commissioned many new temples:

> Thou hast begun to make monuments in Southern Heliopolis, Northern Heliopolis, and in every city ... thereof for the sole god of its district. [25]

There was, however, one main temple to which Sheshonq's energies were directed – the Temple of a Million Years. Like the Temple of Solomon, this edifice was also extravagantly covered in precious metals:

> Thou hast made my temple of millions of years, ... of electrum, wherein I (...). Thy heart is satisfied over (...). Thou hast (...) more than any king of them all. [26]

In order to create his monuments, the pharaoh Sheshonq I had to open up a new stone quarry, so that the stone for this magnificent temple could be hewn:

> (Sheshonq I) made the opening of the new quarry, as a beginning of the work ... [27]

Since I maintain that Sheshonq I was simply another name for King Solomon, it is likely that the latter monarch would also have needed to open a new quarry – despite the new Temple of Jerusalem being largely constructed of wood. Accordingly, King Solomon gave exactly the same orders to his people in Jerusalem:

> And Solomon had threescore and ten thousand that bear burdens, and fourscore thousand hewers in the mountains. And the king commanded, and they brought great stones, costly stones, and hewed stones, to lay the foundation of the house. [B28]

The real question, which could answer many of the problems that these similarities pose, is where was Sheshonq I's new temple constructed? The traditional interpretations of the Egyptian historical texts say that this temple, which was commissioned by Sheshonq I, was either in Karnak in Upper Egypt, or perhaps in Memphis in Lower Egypt. Certainly, a temple in Thebes was mentioned on the stele at the Silsileh quarry, and it is fairly certain that this was a reference to the additions that

Sheshonq I made to the Temple of Karnak – with a large court and side-gate being constructed.

While it is reasonably certain that Sheshonq I was responsible for the addition of this large forecourt, the Bubastite Gate – upon which the main inscriptions of Sheshonq I and his descendants were made – is an unimpressive and hasty addition to a side-wall of this same court. Presumably, since the court and its pylon were never completed, Sheshonq I needed a completed section of walling on which to record the triumphs of his reign. The Bubastite Gate was to be that small strip of fresh parchment, upon which the artisans could inscribe these details.

However, if Sheshonq I had also boasted of commissioning a new 'Temple of a Million Years', would this really have been a reference to this insignificant side-gate? I think not. This fact can be seen in the Silsileh stele itself, for when the chief architect of the Temple of Karnak referred to this new project, he called it a 'pylon' and a 'jubilee-court', with the word for pylon graphically illustrating the shape of a pylon ⌷⌷ . There was no mention on the stele of any 'temple' and certainly not of one important enough to be called the 'Temple of a Million Years'.

The classical interpretation for the location of this new Temple of Sheshonq, which can still be seen in some reference books, just has to be suspect. The mention of a Temple of a Million Years has to be in addition to any references to the Temple of Karnak. As Kenneth Kitchen points out, the text in block D part c of the Bubastite Gate inscription seems to indicate that this temple was located at Memphis.

Hiram of Tyre

While the location of this new temple is still uncertain, the name of the temple's chief designer, who worked under Sheshonq I, may give us some clues as to its location. The historical texts, taken from the Silsileh quarry, say:

> His majesty decreed that command be given to the house of Harakhte, chief of works of the Lord of the Two Lands, Haremsaf, triumphant, to conduct every work (...) the choicest (stone?) of Silsileh, to make very great monuments for the house of his august father, Ammon-Re, lord of Thebes. There returned in safety to the southern city (Thebes), to the place where his majesty was, the ... chief of works in House of Kheperhezre Setepenre (Sheshonq I) in Thebes ... Haremsaf, triumphant. He said, All that thou didst say has come to pass, O my good Lord; none sleeping at night nor slumbering by day, but building the eternal work without ceasing.[29]

Here we can see that the chief architect and engineer of Sheshonq I, who worked upon the Karnak project, was a man called Haremsaf (Hiramsaf). But in what way does the name Haremsaf give us any clues to the location of this Temple of a Million Years? The answer to this question lies in the Bible once more, and the identity of the chief architect who worked for King Solomon. The Bible says of this man:

> And King Solomon sent and fetched <u>Hiram</u> out of Tyre. He was a widow's son of the tribe of Naphtali, and his father was a man of Tyre, a worker in brass: and he was filled with wisdom, and understanding, and cunning to work all works in brass. And he came to King Solomon, and wrought all his work. For he cast two pillars of brass... [B31]

So the Biblical architect of the Temple of Solomon was called Hiram, while the historical architect of the Temple of Sheshonq I was called Hiram(saf). Rather surprisingly, the architects who supervised the construction of these 'two' new temples, which were commissioned by 'different' monarchs, had the same name in both the historical and the Biblical accounts. The only discrepancy here is that the Bible says that Hiram came from the city of Tyre in the Lebanon, whereas Hiramsaf most probably came from Upper Egypt.

It should be noted, however, that there were actually two Hirams in the Bible; one was said to be a king of Tyre in Lebanon, while the other was the chief architect, who just happened to come from the same 'city' as the king. The reason for this confusion in names and cities is based on a little mistranslation and the fact that these two individuals called Hiram were actually related.

The name Harem (Hiram) was a known royal/priestly title in Egypt, it being used by the pharaoh Haremheb and also by Haremkhet, the high priest and son of the twenty-fifth dynasty pharaoh, Shebitku. In this case, it is more than likely that Hiram of Tyre originally came from Egypt, so why does the Bible maintain that the chief architect of King Solomon, Hiram, came from Lebanon? The answer to this lies in a little (deliberate?) mistranslation of the Biblical texts, which may take a while to fully explain.

King Solomon was bartering with King Hiram חירם of Tyre about the export of cedar wood to Israel. However, when the construction of the Temple of Jerusalem commenced, it was another Hiram of Tyre, who was skilled in architecture and metallurgy, who oversaw the building of the Temple. Just to make this point – about there being two people who were called Hiram – absolutely clear, Adam Clarke, the renowned theologian, says of the architect from Tyre who was called Hiram:

> This (Hiram) was not the Tyrian king, mentioned before, but a very
> intelligent coppersmith, of Jewish extraction by his mother's side, who was
> probably married to a Tyrian. [32]

As this architect called Hiram happens to be a Masonic as well as a Biblical
hero, the popular Masonic authors, Robert Lomas and Christopher Knight,
wrote an entire thesis on his life. But in this book, which was entitled *The
Hiram Key*, these authors say of this chief architect to King Solomon:

> Neither of us had ever heard of such a person (Hiram) and no version of the
> Bible that we have come across makes any mention of an architect for
> Solomon's Temple ... We, like all Freemasons of our acquaintance, accept the
> Masonic hero (Hiram) despite knowing that he was not recorded as being
> involved in the creation of Solomon's Temple. [33]

Perhaps the answer to this astounding statement is to distribute a Bible and
a pair of spectacles to each Masonic lodge, and then perhaps the more
secular brothers would know something about their belief system.

Hiram of Tyre, the chief architect of King Solomon who built the
great pillars at the Temple of Jerusalem, was and is mentioned in every
Bible that has ever been printed, just as Adam Clarke has rightly pointed
out. The fact that the Masonic hero was actually called Hiram-Abif is not an
excuse for this blunder either, as the Biblical Hiram was also called Hiram
Abif (Atif). The evidence for this assertion comes from an alternative copy
of the Biblical verse that has just been quoted, this time from the book of
Chronicles:

> And now I have sent a cunning man, endued with understanding, of
> <u>Huram (Hiram) my father's</u>. The son of a woman of the daughters of Dan,
> and his father was a man of Tyre, skilful to work in gold, and in silver, in
> brass... [B34]

The book of Chronicles generally follows the book of Kings reasonably
well, but the two texts have obviously arrived on the Biblical compiler's
desk from different sources, as there are often differences in detail between
the two. Here is a good example of just such a difference. The change in
spelling here is not an issue, as the book of Chronicles calls both the king of
Tyre and the architect from Tyre, Huram. But although the verse in
Chronicles is almost the same as the version from Kings, the first line is a
little confusing; what does it mean by 'my father's'? My father's what,
exactly? The question is, was this revised sentence a mistake, or was it a

literal translation that holds the clue to a deeper understanding of the text? The above verse was taken from the King James Bible, but the RSV Bible has noticed the inconsistency in this sentence's meaning, and adjusted the text accordingly; it says instead:

> I have sent a skilled man, endued with understanding, Huramabi. [B35]

Personally, I don't think this version is much more illuminating than the King James' offering. The RSV Bible has just taken the Hebrew word *abi* אבי, meaning 'my father', and tacked it onto the end of the name Hiram, giving Huram-abi (Hiram-abi) חירם-אבי. Funnily enough, this is actually the answer to this problem, although it does not look like it yet.

The true name for this person was indeed Hiram-abi, but the phrase should not be translated as 'of Huram my father's'; instead, it should be read as 'Hiram is my father'. The first piece of evidence in favour of this new translation comes from the Egyptian name for the chief architect of Sheshonq I, who was called Haremsaf 𓅃 𓃮 ⸺ . The three elements of this name are:

𓅃	Heru (Hira)	the falcon-god, Horus
𓃮	m	like, from, is
⸺	f (or *atif*)	father*

* This word is generally spelt and pronounced as *itif* 𓇋𓏏𓆑 , the spelling here is just using a shortened form of the word. The missing 's' or 'sa' from Hiramsaf is an alternative version based upon a similar translation, as will be explained shortly.

The resulting name of this chief architect, in the Egyptian language, was either pronounced as Hiram-f or Hiram Atif. As can be seen, the meaning (and the spelling) of this name is, therefore, virtually the same in both the Hebrew and the Egyptian languages:

Hebrew	**Egyptian**
Hiram-Abi	Hiram Atif
Hiram is my father	Hiram is my father

The traditional translation of the Egyptian name Hiram Saf, instead of Hiram Atif, is rather similar in meaning to the one that has just been given. From the single 'f' glyph ⸺ , rather than reading the short form of *atif*, historians have instead inferred a short form of the word *saf*, meaning 'boy', which is a common suffix to many Egyptian names. The resulting classical name for this chief architect would then mean 'Hiram's boy' or 'the son of Hiram' – a term not unlike the American preference for names like 'Jones Jnr', or the Scottish 'Mac' and the Irish 'O' prefixes, which mean 'son of' and 'descendant of' respectively. Needless to say, these two titles – Hiram-Saf, meaning 'the son of Hiram', and Hiram Atif, meaning 'Hiram is my father' – ultimately mean exactly the same thing. But the fact that the latter translation of the ⤸ glyph is the more precise of the two will be confirmed shortly from both Biblical and Masonic sources.

This same type of suffix was used in the names Osarseph (Osiris-saf) and Peteseph (Ptah-saf) in the works of Manetho, individuals who were identified as being the Biblical patriarchs Moses and Joseph respectively. In each case the title was prefixed by a god-name, Osiris or Ptah, so that the full titles of these Biblical patriarchs were the 'Son of Osiris' and 'Son of Ptah' respectively. Both the Biblical and the historical versions of Hiram's name were following in this same ancient tradition, and the real title of this chief architect from Thebes (or Tyre) was Hira-m-Atif (Hiru-m-Atif), which means 'Horus is my father', or even 'son of Horus'.

I have already asserted that Hiram Atif was the true pronunciation of this name, rather than the classical offering of Hiram Saf, and the compelling evidence for this can be gleaned from Masonic lore. This same Hiram, who built the Temple of Solomon, happens to be the primary hero of the Masonic world, where he is known as Hiram Abif. This alternative source gives us yet another version for the pronunciation of this name, and while this new version clears up a few questions, it also clearly demonstrates how little secular Masons know of their true heritage.

The Masonic traditions from this era appear to have corrupted the Egyptian word *atif,* meaning 'father', into the title 'Abif'; and presumably the Hebrew spelling for the word 'father' *(abi)* played a major part in this alteration. Having done so, however, these same Masonic traditions have somehow managed to retain that Egyptian viper glyph ⤸ 'f', and thus substantially preserve the original spelling and pronunciation of the Egyptian word *atif* ⟨⟩ . But having preserved the spelling so diligently, these same Masonic traditions seem to have forgotten that this word means 'father'. In complete contrast, however, the Biblical scribes have managed to drop the 'f' in *atif,* creating the title 'Abi', but they have nevertheless preserved the original meaning of 'father'. The elements of the Masonic compound name are as follows:

True meaning	Egyptian	Hebrew	Masonic
Horus	Hiru	Hira	Hira
is	m	m	m
(my) father	Atif	Abi	Abif

The Biblical version of this same name has been re-translated as 'Hiram is my father', with the true meaning of the word *'hiram'* being lost somewhere in the translation. But if the truth about this name's heritage were known and admitted by theologians, it should really be read as 'Horus is my father'. Quite obviously, the translator of this text did not understand (or did not want to understand) what the Egyptian word Hira (Heru) meant, and so this name has been slightly modified by the inclusion of the 'm' glyph 𓅓 , resulting in the garbled compound name 'Hira<u>m</u>'. Nevertheless, the essence and spelling of this name remains remarkably untouched by the passing millennia.

This confluence in both pronunciation and meaning clearly demonstrates that the Biblical architect called Hiram had an Egyptian heritage; and so once again these two architects called Hiram should be regarded as being the same individual.

The only discrepancy that remains between the Biblical and historical Hiram Atifs is that the Bible says he came from Tyre in the Lebanon, whereas the stele at Silsileh infers that he came from Upper Egypt. The answer to this little problem is equally lateral, and comes from an unexpected source. The answer is actually given to us by Herodotus, but somehow I don't even think that Herodotus knew what he was talking about here. I rather get the impression that Herodotus was a rather gullible tourist who believed everything that he was told, while the Egyptian priesthood were rolling on the floor with mirth every time he turned his back. They were probably vying with each other to tell the Greek barbarian the most lurid (and coded) of stories.

Herodotus mentions that in this era the Tyreans had a large presence in the city of Memphis, which is located just to the south of Giza. The pharaohs that Herodotus mentions are Pheron and Proteus, whom Herodotus has somehow managed to squeeze in between a Seti and a Ramesses. Never mind the mention of Seti, because Herodotus' chronology is notoriously wayward; the important thing is that this event occurred in the era of a pharaoh called Pheron, who was the first in the list of Biblical pharaohs in this era, as discussed in chapter IV. Herodotus goes on to say that:

> There is a sacred precinct (temple) of this pharaoh in Memphis, which is very beautiful, richly adorned, situated south of the great temple of

Hephaestus. Phoenicians from the city of Tyre dwell all round this precinct, and the whole place is known by the name of 'the Camp of the Tyreans'. [H36]

If he did but know it, Herodotus was talking in Biblical parables here. In the New Testament, a number of luminaries, from Peter to Jesus, were known as 'rocks' or 'stones'. In a similar fashion, the reference here to the city of Tyre has nothing to do with a city in the Levant and everything to do with rocks. The reason for this is that the Hebrew name for the city of Tyre is Tsor (צור or צר) and it so happens that this word also means 'rock' or 'stone'. (Like Gibraltar, Tyre was known as the 'Rock'.) The 'Camp of the Tyreans' was nothing more than a poor allusion to the position of Architect (the esoteric, Masonic variety) and so this passage is simply saying that a group with Hyksos-type Masonic allegiances inhabited Memphis in this era. This is exactly correct, and this is why the Masonic Architect hero, Hiram Atif, was so closely linked with this era and these events.

However, this group of people were not simply priests and administrators. The esoteric Architects of this era were equally skilled and useful in the real world of manufacturing and construction, because they held within their tightknit group the secrets of astronomy, alchemy, geometry and mathematics. In which case, it is not so surprising that one of the highest-ranking Architects of this era also held the profession of a secular architect and was a skilled coppersmith, capable of casting the bronze pillars of Jachin and Boaz.

Since the Hebrew word *tyre (tsor)* צור means 'rock', the 'city of Tyre' where Hiram Atif was supposed to have come from probably had nothing whatsoever to do with the city of Tyre in the Lebanon and everything to do with the quarry in which this architect worked. When the Bible says that 'Hiram's father was a man of Tyre', it is really meaning that 'Hiram's father was a worker in stone'. Likewise, when the Biblical texts indicate that 'King Solomon fetched Hiram out of Tyre', this should really be interpreted as 'King Solomon fetched Hiram out of the stone quarries': all of which makes perfect sense for an architect, whose primary working material was stone and whose records and genealogy are still preserved in the quarries of Upper Egypt.

In fact, there may have even been another layer to this obfuscation in this Biblical report because, although the city of Tyre in Lebanon was known in the Hebrew as Tsor צור, in the Egyptian it was actually known as Tchar 𓄿𓃀𓂋𓊖 . But there was another city that was equally famous in this era, and that was the city of Thar 𓅱𓂋𓊖 , which was the name for the city of Tanis, the original capital of the twenty-first dynasty and the United Monarchy. In fact, it was not unusual for the 𓅱 and the 𓄿𓃀

glyphs to be confused and become interchangeable, so there was plenty of scope for confusion, deliberate or otherwise, between these two names and these two cities. Indeed the later Hebrew translation of the word *tsor* (Tyre) as 'rock' may well have been derived from the Egyptian word *thar* 𓌃𓈖𓉐, which means 'castle' or 'fortress'. Tanis, the capital city of this Hyksos-Israelite nation was, by necessity, a fortress and doubtless similar fortress cities like Tyre picked up this same appellation.

Although the island city of Tyre was a historical reality, there is no evidence in the historical record that a King Hiram of Tyre ever existed. A perfectly reasonable reason for this may be that, since the term 'Tyre' may actually refer to a quarry or even the city of Tanis, the elder 'king' Hiram may actually have been an architect (Architect) who resided in Tanis. This elder Hiram was called 'Melek Hiram' חירם מלך, which has been translated as 'King Hiram', but the term *melek* was also used in a later Biblical text to denote a prince, so it is entirely possible that this King Hiram of Tyre was actually a Prince Hiram of Tanis. If this were so, it is more than likely that he would have been a son of King David. It is also possible that this Prince Hiram was actually the father of the later chief architect called Hiram Atif, who cast the two great bronze pillars and finished off the construction of the Temple. If so, then both of these characters followed the same exalted position of Mason and Architect, and they would therefore have been the son and grandson of King David.

Further evidence for this comes from the genealogy of the chief architects of Egypt, a complete list of names that covers the period from the time of Ramesses II through to the reign of the pharaoh Darius II, and which was inscribed upon a rock in the quarry at Wadi Hammamat. This chronology does indeed indicate that there were two architects called Hiram (Atif), who were both chief architects of the pharaoh Sheshonq I; but rather than being father and son, this document indicates that they were actually father and grandson. The fact that these quarries and inscriptions are located to the east of Thebes would also tend to suggest that the elder King or Prince Hiram was closely associated with Thebes, as well as Tanis.

The other historical document that mentions Hiram Atif, which was left in the stone quarries of Silsileh, indicates that Hiram was sent there by Sheshonq I to cut stones for the Temple of Karnak. The Biblical and historical texts then agree with each other, and take this written history one stage further by saying that Hiram Atif was subsequently called out of these quarries by royal command and sent away to build another temple. According to the historical text, Hiram Atif's new commission was Sheshonq's Temple of a Million Years in Memphis (?), whereas the Biblical texts insist that his task was actually to build Solomon's great temple at Jerusalem. The decision as to which of these locations is correct will have to wait for a while.

But Hiram was not just a stonemason, he was also an accomplished artisan who was equally skilled in metalworking, with bronze being his speciality. The links that have been forged in the orthodox explanations of this era, between the chief architect called Hiram Atif and the city of Tyre, were reinforced by the knowledge that the metalworking skills of the Philistines, who inhabited the west coast of the Levant to the south of Phoenicia, were thought to be of high quality; and so the idea of Hiram being from the western Levant was not at all far-fetched. However, this was not the only region in this era that produced high-quality smiths. The metalworking of Egyptian artisans, particularly those of the twenty-first and twenty-second dynasties, was of an even higher standard than that of the Philistines, as historians are equally ready to admit:

> Perhaps the most lasting contribution of the (21st & 22nd dynasties) to the arts and crafts lay in the field of metalworking. The silver coffins of kings Psusennes [II] and Sheshonq [I] and the wide range of gold and silver vessels and jewellery from the Tanite royal tombs testify to the continued expertise of Egyptian metalworkers ... Of greater significance was the huge expansion of the range and technical excellence of metal sculpture that occurred during this period ... the major part in bronze. [37]

If Solomon were indeed the pharaoh Sheshonq I, as now seems extremely likely, then who would he have turned to for the casting of his great bronze pillars of Jachin and Boaz at his new temple? Would he have chosen a Phoenician from Tyre, or a member of the Egyptian royalty who was probably closely related to his own family in some manner? Bearing in mind the new nationality that has been attributed to King Solomon [Sheshonq I] and the undoubted quality of the Egyptian artificer's work, which nation would have been the king's first choice? Tyre or Egypt?

The question is, of course, rhetorical. But the result of commissioning this new chief architect demonstrates that he and his artisans were generations ahead of their Tanis rivals in both technology and expertise. Despite it being commissioned by a king, the gold death-mask of the pharaoh Amenemopet was a very basic piece of workmanship; but then there was a sudden revolution in the smithies of Lower Egypt and the death-mask and sarcophagi of Psusennes [II] and Sheshonq [I] were truly spectacular artifacts. The inescapable conclusion is that this revolution in metalworking resulted from the arrival of Hiram Atif (Abif) of Tyre and his fellow artisans, and that they were indeed 'skilful in gold and in silver and in brass'. But this observation appears to conflict with the previous translation of the city of 'Tyre' being closely associated with Tanis, so does it invalidate this translation? The equivocal answer is that I don't think so, because this 'Prince of Tanis' called Hiram may have spent a great deal of his life in his mother's home city of Thebes, and this possibility will be discussed in the next chapter.

Incidentally, since the silver sarcophagus of Sheshonq [I] was made in the image of a falcon, and since the name of the Biblical Hiram Atif means 'The Falcon-god Horus is My Father', yet another link can be seen between these two architects. As this falcon-headed sarcophagus is rather unique for an Egyptian monarch, one cannot help feeling that this was not Sheshonq [I]'s sarcophagus. As will be shown in the next chapter, the funerary arrangements of Sheshonq [I] [King Solomon] were a hurried affair that had all the hallmarks of a re-burial, perhaps because the original tomb of King Solomon in Jerusalem was not available any more.

This spectacular, silver, falcon-headed sarcophagus would have been far more suitable as the last resting place of the chief architect Hiram Atif, who was known as the 'Son of Horus'. It is entirely possible that, during the hurried re-burial of Sheshonq [I], the chief administrators of the necropolis requisitioned Hiram's sarcophagus. The cartouches on this coffin confirm that this was Sheshonq's [Solomon's] burial, but these titles and names could easily have been added at the last minute by any competent smith. The reason for this possible exchange of sarcophagus is a story in itself, which will be fully explored in the next chapter.

The identification of the Biblical chief architect Hiram Atif as being the chief architect of Sheshonq I, who was also known as Hiram Atif, is looking increasingly certain. But it is not only the epigraphic evidence from the quarry at Silsileh that points towards an Egyptian master-craftsman being employed for the foundry work at the Temple of Jerusalem – the archaeological evidence points in that direction too. Beno Rothenberg conducted an investigation of the copper works at Timnah, just north of Elat. The conclusions from this dig were that these mines and smelting works were run by Egyptians from the fourteenth to the twelfth centuries BC, a period during which the Israelites must have been in Palestine. It is further said that:

> ... a more interesting question is whether the short period of operations which took place in the tenth century had anything to do with the Israelites ... Rothenberg (originally) agreed that the mining and smelting took place at Timnah at the behest of Solomon ... However, Rothenberg now assumes that

the late phase was due to the initiative of the twenty-second dynasty, probably in the wake of Sheshonq's invasion. [38]

The problem for Rothenberg was that the Biblical history of this era required substantial amounts of bronze (a copper-tin alloy), whereas the archaeological data incongruously presents us with evidence of Egyptian copper smelting in Israelite-held locations. So, were these smelting works Judaean or Egyptian? The evidence is equivocal, hence the vacillation in Rothenberg's explanations. The simple, if lateral, answer to this problem is that Solomon's empire was substantially Egyptian, as was the ancestry of King Solomon himself. In this case, the assumption that the metalworking at Timnah was conducted by Egyptians during the reign of Sheshonq I, and the Biblical requirement for this metal to be used at Solomon's temple in Jerusalem, are two sides of the same coin. Once more, the data can be greatly simplified if Sheshonq I and King Solomon were actually the same individual.

While the evidence that has been gathered so far seems to conclusively point towards this metalworking at the Temple of Solomon being organised and designed by the Egyptian chief architect known as Hiram Atif, there is yet more evidence to demonstrate that this argument is one hundred percent true. When discussing the Egyptian name of Hiram Atif, I have deliberately withheld the full spelling of this name. In reality, the name Hiram Atif was written as ![glyphs], and the extra element that is now included in this name is a *djed* pillar. The result of this extra glyph is that the name now becomes:

![glyph]	Heru (Hira)	the falcon-god, Horus
![glyph]	m	is
![glyph]	djed	pillar*
![glyph]	atif	father

* The single stroke after the djed pillar means that the pillar itself is being referred to, rather than the syllable *'djed'*, in which case the pronunciation of the name Hiram Atif remains unchanged.

The single stroke after the *djed* pillar is indicating that it is the real *djed* pillar that is intended by this glyph, not any subsidiary meanings, and the reason for this is given in the Bible. Amazingly enough, the Biblical accounts credit Hiram Atif with the construction of the two great bronze pillars at the Temple of Solomon, while the historical account now directly associates Hiram Atif with the *djed* pillar.

Doubtless, for this association to have been included in this name, these petroglyphs at the Wadi Hammamat quarry were only inscribed when each chief architect retired or died – just as Christian priests do in their churches to this day. Since Hiram Atif was famed for his work on the two great pillars at the Temple of Jerusalem, his epitaph in this genealogy became 'Hiram Atif of the Djed Pillar'.

Fig 26.   Hiram Atif (djed), the chief architect of the Temple of Solomon.

Not only is this another certain indication that these two Hiram Atifs, from the Biblical and historical records, were one and the same, it is also a good indication as to what the two pillars of Jachin and Boaz really looked like. In the clearest possible terms, the evidence is demonstrating that the two pillars that stood at the entrance to the Temple of Solomon were two giant *djed* pillars. The primary meaning of the *djed* pillars was 'stability', and this inferred the stability both of the nation and also of the monarchy that ruled that nation.

It is entirely possible that the two pillars constructed at the Bubastite Gate in Karnak were intended to be copies of the two pillars that graced the Temple of Solomon. If this is so, then the design of these pillars may give a further insight into the symbology of the *djed* pillar. The pillars on the Bubastite Gate are said to be representations of 'closed lotus flowers', and this design is a common feature of Egyptian temples. It is entirely possible, however, that since much of Egyptian theology was concerned with fertility and copulation, this design instead represents a male phallus. The 'stability' element of the *djed* pillar would then infer the stability of the monarchy and population that is generated by fathering the next generation. Much to the embarrassment of theologians, it is entirely possible that the gateway to the Temple of Solomon was originally held aloft by two giant penises.

As a summary of this rather important section, perhaps it is worth recalling the many similarities that have been unearthed between these two architects who were called Hiram:

a. Both architects were called Hiram Atif.
b. Both names contained a suffix meaning 'father'.
c. Both worked as chief architects to the king.

d. Both of these kings are known to have reigned at exactly the same time.
e. Both architects were called away to build a temple for the king.
f. Both had an elder relative of the same name.
g. Both were associated with stones or a quarry (Tyre).
h. Both were associated with pillars.

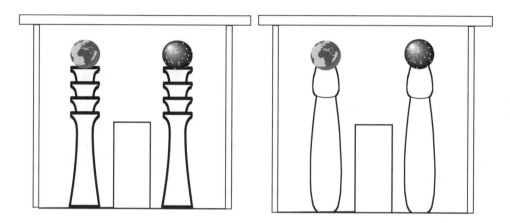

Fig 27.   Two possibilities for the entrance to the Temple of Jerusalem.

Here, then, is the real history of the Masonic hero Hiram Abif (Hiram Atif), delivered straight from the historical and Biblical texts in unprecedented detail. The paucity of this type of information from secular Masonic sources, and the poor quality of that information, demonstrates how little the lower grades of this organisation know of this era and these events. Christopher Knight and Robert Lomas, who are both Masons, wrote an entire book trying to prove that the Hyksos were an evil race and that the Masonic hero, Hiram Abif (Hiram Atif), was the pharaoh Seqenenre Tao II of the seventeenth dynasty. [39]

Even at the time, I thought that this explanation was a bit odd, but the passing years have simply added to my puzzlement. The foundation of this new history is that Masonic and Judaic influences have all sprung from Hyksos beliefs and rituals, and yet Seqenenre Tao II was a Theban pharaoh who was attempting to throw the Hyksos out of Egypt. In addition, the era of Seqenenre's reign lies some five hundred before the building of Solomon's Temple and so there is no way, by any stretch of the imagination, that Seqenenre can be linked to this era and the life of Hiram Atif. In essence, some Masons know so little of their organisation's history that they revile the very people who laid the foundations of their belief system, and hero-worship the kings who nearly destroyed them!

Having said all that, the manner of Seqenenre's death does appear to be significant, as this mummy displays exactly the same three wounds that Masonic lore ascribes to Hiram Atif. If a comparison between this mummy and the Masonic hero Hiram Atif is to be made in any way, then this cannot have been the mummy of Seqenenre Tao II. But how does one go about completely re-identifying a mummy to another era without stretching credulity to its limits?

The answer is simple, for the mummy of Seqenenre Tao II was discovered in the Deir el Bahri cache, which was discovered just behind the magnificent mortuary temple of Hatshepsut near Thebes. This gathering of some forty-one New Kingdom mummies was assembled by the Theban priesthood during the period of tomb-robbing in the twenty-first dynasty. Since the majority of these mummies had been completely stripped of their finery and titles, there is no way of identifying them apart from the tags that the priesthood had pinned to their corpses. But with so many mummies lying around with no identification on them, what if the priesthood had mixed one or two of them up prior to writing these tags? This problem has, of course, already been identified, and there has long been a suspicion amongst some Egyptologists that one or two of these mummies were mis-identified by the priests when they hurriedly re-interred them in the tomb at Deir el Bahri.

If the wounds on this particular mummy bear a striking resemblance to those that were ascribed to Hiram Atif, a character from the twenty-first or twenty-second dynasty, then perhaps this is not the mummy of Seqenenre Tao II – perhaps they are the remains of Hiram Atif instead. But if this was the mummy of Hiram Atif, then who exactly was he and how did such a character become interred in a royal and priestly tomb? In addition, why should the Masonic world revere an architect called Hiram Atif rather than one of the really important characters of this era, like King David or King Solomon? The answer to this is that Hiram Atif was actually a prince, as has already been suggested, but Hiram Atif was a prince who had fallen from grace at the royal court of Tanis. It was primarily for this reason that Hiram Atif was so brutally killed, and this may also be the reason for his sarcophagus being usurped by King Solomon [Sheshonq I], but the identification of exactly which prince was called Hiram Atif will have to wait until the next chapter, as more details on the family of King Solomon are required first.

The true history of these historical events is much more believable and understandable than any of the previous explanations that have been attempted over the years and decades. This Masonic hero, Hiram Atif, was not a nebulous figure derived from dubious folklore and mythology; he was not a citizen of Tyre; and he was most certainly not a Theban pharaoh of the seventeenth dynasty. Instead, Hiram, the chief architect of King Solomon, who supervised the construction of Temple of Jerusalem and cast its great bronze pillars, was actually the chief architect of the pharaohs Psusennes II and Sheshonq I, who supervised the construction of the Temple of a Million Years. Not only was the genealogy of this famous chief architect inscribed onto the cliff-face of Wadi Hammamat, but his sarcophagus and mummy may well lie in the Cairo museum, as we shall see later.

Temple of Ptah

Has enough information now been extracted from these texts to decide which account is telling the truth, with regard to the location of Sheshonq's temple? Was it located in Jerusalem or Memphis? The historical account, as inscribed upon the walls of the temple at Karnak, says that Sheshonq's 'Temple of a Million Years' was built in Het-Ka-Ptah. This is known to be a reference to the Lower Egyptian city of Memphis, and by inference the main temple in this city was probably dedicated to the god Ptah. This would appear to be firm evidence in favour of a location at Memphis, and in some respects this location would actually make some sense. The city of Memphis, which lay on the west bank of the Nile between Saqqara and Dahshur, had been the second most important town controlled by the Hyksos nation and at one time they had a great temple there, which was called the Mansion of Ptah. If the Mashuash people of the twenty-second dynasty, under the reign of Sheshonq I, were descended from the Hyksos-Israelites, then Memphis would have been both a logical and a historic place on which the new Temple of a Million Years should be built – if they had control over this region, of course.

As usual, however, there is an equally plausible alternative argument. As refered to previously, Manetho mentions that one of the Biblical patriarchs was called Peterseph (Son of Ptah). Like the Hyksos, it would seem that the Biblical patriarchs were also associated with the cult of Ptah. After the Hyksos-Israelite exodus from Egypt, a significant number of the Hyksos people would have been based in Judaea, and no doubt they were still practising the same belief systems in this new and strange land. What could be more natural than for these people to ask their new leader, Sheshonq I [King Solomon] to create their own Ptah temple for them in their new capital city of Jerusalem? So could the records have been misinterpreted? Could Sheshonq's new temple, the 'Temple of a Million Years', not have been built in Het-Ka-Ptah (Memphis), but in Jerusalem instead?

The evidence in favour of the latter option comes from the name that Sheshonq I chose for his temple, which has an enduring synergy with the temple of Jerusalem. Sheshonq decreed that this would be a 'Temple of a Million Years', a 'Temple of Eternity'; which it evidently was not, wherever it was built. Like the temples in Memphis, the Bible indicates that the Temple of Solomon only lasted a few hundred years until the coming of the Persians, under the command of King Nebuchadnezzar, to Israel in around 600 BC. The Jerusalem temple was destroyed during this campaign, but all hope was not lost and a replacement was quickly made in the sixth century. This intermediate temple is largely forgotten about, as it is reputed to have been a pale shadow of the former temple. The construction of the temple of Jerusalem that is regarded as the true Second Temple was not begun until 23 BC, under the reign of Herod the Great. But the Second Temple had an even more perilous existence and it, too, was destroyed, this time by the Romans in AD 70. But the hope of the Jews throughout the ages is that when their Messiah finally arrives he will oversee the divine and miraculous building of the Third Temple, which will be known by divine command as the Temple of Eternity. Sheshonq I desired a Temple of a Million Years, whereas the Jews have long prayed for a Temple of Eternity.

The hopes and desires for Sheshonq's new temple therefore display some distinct similarities with the Biblical record. But the deciding factor, which indicated most clearly that Sheshonq's new temple was probably built in Jerusalem and not Memphis, was to be the comparison between the Hebrew and Egyptian names for this temple. In the Egyptian texts, taken from the Temple of Karnak, the temple of Sheshonq I was said to be located at Het-Ka-Ptah ⌷⌷⌷⌷⌷ , and this name seems to firmly link it to Memphis as already mentioned. While the name Het-Ka-Ptah is generally taken to be a reference to the city of Memphis, the precise translation of the name – the 'Temple of the Image of Ptah' or the 'Temple of the Spirit of Ptah' – shows that this was actually the name of the *temple* at Memphis – not the city itself. But Memphis was not the only city to have a temple with this name, and the site of this alternative temple may actually be given in the Bible.

The Biblical name for the Temple of Solomon was sometimes given as the 'House of the Lord' (Bayith Yahweh בית יהוה), but occasionally it was said to be the 'Temple of the Lord' (Heykal Yahweh היכל יהוה). Amazingly enough, the Hebrew term being used for the word 'temple' was nothing less than *heykal* היכל, which is exactly the same as the Egyptian version. The Egyptian term for this temple was inscribed as *Het-Ka*, while the Hebrew term was written as *Hey-Kar* (the Hebrew letter 'l' being derived from an Egyptian 'r', as is usual). The only thing that appears to have changed within these two, entirely separate accounts is the name of the deity to which this temple was dedicated. The Memphis temple was said to be dedicated to Ptah (Het-Ka-Ptah), while the Jerusalem temple was dedicated to Yahweh (Het-Ka-Yahweh) – but I think that the explanations given in the book *Tempest* cover all the reasons for this change in name for the deity.

Fig 28.   Temple of Jerusalem.

The annals of the Mashuash, as have been inscribed upon the Bubastite Gate at the Temple of Karnak, said that Sheshonq I had constructed his Temple of a Million Years at a location known as Het-Ka-(Ptah). While this word can normally be taken to be the Egyptian name for the temple in the city of Memphis, it can now be seen that the Jerusalem Temple was also called Het-Ka-(Yahweh). In which case, the location given in the Karnak text was not wrong, as such, just a little confusing to later historians. Sheshonq did build a temple at Het-Ka, but this was probably a reference to the citadel at the new Judaean capital city of Jerusalem (Yireh-Shalam ירָאה-שׁלם).

There is an interesting addendum to this interpretation, which can give some confirmation that Het-Ka-Ptah did indeed refer to the Temple of Solomon. According to the Amarna Letters, which were found in Akhenaton's city of Amarna, a Canaanite merchant described this temple as the Hi-Khu-Ptah, or the 'Khu Chapel of Ptah'. Although this reference was some four hundred years before the reign of King Solomon, it was after the date for the Hyksos-Israelite exodus, so the Hyksos-Israelites would have been in Jerusalem at this time and they would definitely have required and constructed some kind of temple for their rituals.

The reference to the Hi-Khu-Ptah may be important in this investigation, as it possibly gives us yet another image that demonstrates what this temple of Ptah in Jerusalem looked like. Although the letter was written in cuneiform text, the Egyptian word that was being used on this occasion was *Khu*. [41]

While it may be argued that this change in pronunciation was just a mistake, I feel that the evidence points towards a nickname being used for this temple. As mistakes go, it is rather convenient that the word *Khu* means 'palace', 'high place', 'heaven' and 'evening', all of which could be considered to be the attributes derived from the evening celebrations at the Temple. In addition, the *Ku* glyph is formed from a very graphic glyph that looks like this:

Fig 29.   The Ku Portico.

The glyph clearly shows two cylindrical columns at the front of a large building or temple, and I have no doubt that this was the logic that lay behind this particular pun.

It so happens that this is the exact same form that is taken by the Bubastite Gate – as can be seen in plate 17 – which was commissioned as an addition to the Temple of Karnak by Sheshonq I [King Solomon]. It is also the exact same design that was used for the Temple of Solomon in Jerusalem, as is graphically described in the Bible. The Bible account even names these two cylindrical pillars as Jachin and Boaz, and two replicas of these pillars are to be found on the entrance to the Grand Masonic Lodge in Holborn, London. The fact that the Bubastite Gate at Karnak – built by Sheshonq I – mirrors so closely the design of the Temple of Jerusalem – built by King Solomon – clearly demonstrates once more that these two monarchs were one and the same person.

Sacred city

While it may be surprising that a direct comparison can be made between the Hebrew name for the Temple of Solomon and the Egyptian name of the Memphis Temple, it may be equally startling that a similar argument can be made in regard to the Hebrew name for the actual mount upon which the Temple was built, which is known as Moriyah מריה. But before the answer to this interesting conundrum can be seen, there first has to be a slight digression into the rituals and religious significance of these temples. In the book *Tempest*, I tried to show that the primary ritual site for the

Hyksos-Israelites in Egypt was actually the Giza plateau, and that the pyramids themselves played a large role in the ceremonies and liturgy of these people. The term Moriyah once more confirms this suspicion of links to Egypt and the Giza plateau, when in the book of Genesis god is reputed to have said to Abraham:

> And he (god) said, Take now thy son, thine only son Isaac, whom thou lovest, and get thee into the land of Moriah; and offer him there for a burnt offering upon one of the mountains which I will tell thee of. [B42]

According to the orthodox interpretation, Abraham was supposed to have been in Palestine at the time, having a little disagreement with a local king called Abimalech over his seizure of a 'well'. The standoff having been resolved, god then orders Abraham to go to the 'land of Moriah'. Since Moriah is the name of the Temple Mount in Jerusalem, it has always been thought that Abraham went back to this city. But he did not. Abraham was a Hyksos pharaoh and he was most probably resident in Avaris in the Nile Delta, so he went back not to Moriah but instead to Mori ⟨glyph⟩ , which was one of the ancient Egyptian names for Egypt. The fact that this 'well' was called Beersheba בְּאֵר שֶׁבַע, and the name *sheba* has been so closely linked to Egypt, only serves to reinforce this argument.

Fig 30.   Mori – Egypt.

Actually, this name for Egypt is a little more specific than one might expect, for the term *Mor* (*Mer*) ⟨glyph⟩ actually means 'pyramid', and so Abraham was going back to the land of the pyramids. The suspicion has to be that the 'mountain' that Abraham was going to sacrifice his son upon was actually a pyramid at Giza. Likewise, the 'well' that Abraham was arguing over was most probably the mythical source of the Nile, which was reputed to have sprung from between the pyramids at Giza.

In all likelihood, it was at Giza that Abraham was about to sacrifice his son Isaac, until god conveniently stepped in and provided a ram for Abraham to sacrifice instead. Abraham then named this 'mountain', which resided in the land of Moriah, 'Yahweh-Yireh' (יְהוָה יִרְאֶה), which means the mountain that 'god sees'. Alternatively, the RSV Bible says that this phrase means 'the lord will provide', but the Biblical concordance agrees with the King James version of the Bible, and as a confirmation of this interpretation the Hebrew word *yireh* does mean 'to see'. The King James Bible seems to indicate that this phrase means 'god can be seen at', but it is equally likely that it means 'god can see from'.

Although this location has again been classically attributed to Mount Moriah in Jerusalem, the Egyptian translation would suggest otherwise. The Hebrew word *yireh* (also *ra-ah* ראה) was derived from the Egyptian word *ir-ra (yirah)* ⌒⌒⊙ , meaning the 'Eye of Ra', or 'Ra Sees'. As already explained, the pyramids of Egypt were Sun temples, and the association between the god Ra and the pyramids was very strong indeed. In fact, most of the pyramids contained the glyphs of the two eyes of Ra on the pyramidion – right on the summit of the pyramid – looking down on the assembled priests and crowds below. In which case, the Hebrew phrase Yahweh-Yireh, meaning 'god sees', is identical in both pronunciation and meaning to the Egyptian word Ir-Ra. Just as in the name for the Het-Ka-Ptah temple, the only thing to have changed here is the name of the god being invoked.

This same explanation can also be used to refine the definition of the word Moriah, the name for the Temple Mount in Jerusalem. The Bible concordance indicates that the word Moriah was again based upon this same word *yireh* (*ra-ah*), meaning 'god sees'. In which case, when Abraham renamed Mount Moriah with the phrase 'Yahweh Yireh', he was not really giving the mount a new name, he was just confirming its existing name – Mor-ra-ah ⌒⌒⊙ . In the Egyptian translation, the full name of Moriah would translate as the 'Pyramid-of-Ra-Sees'. As Giza is the primary pyramid site in Egypt, it is entirely likely that both Moriah and Yireh refer to the Great Pyramid at Giza. But does this mean that the Temple Mount mentioned in the Bible was actually at Giza?

> Then Solomon began to build the house of the Lord at Jerusalem in Mount Moriah, where the Lord appeared unto David his father. [B43]

Actually, I think not. The whole point that was being made in the book *Tempest* was that the Hyksos-Israelites took with them on their exodus not only their families and their personal belongings, they also took with them their language, their liturgy and their rituals. What they were looking for in their new 'promised land' was a replacement Giza plateau, and they found it at a town called Jerusalem where the craggy plateau closely resembled the location of their primary ancestral temple on the Giza plateau.

The whole point about the pillar symbolism of the Tabernacle, and the subsequent pillar symbolism of the Temple of Solomon, was that it mimicked the pyramids in their role as the four pillars of heaven, the great pillars that held the skies aloft. In this case, the symbolism of the Jerusalem temple was now complete. The name of the temple was the Heykal Yahweh (Hey-Kar-Yahweh), and it sat upon the plateau of Moriah (Mori). In other words, the Temple of Solomon was known as the 'Temple of the Image (Spirit) of Yahweh', and it stood upon a rocky crag known as the 'Pyramid that Ra Sees (from)'. The fundamental rationale for the building of the Temple was that it was a substitute for the lost temples and pyramids in Egypt, and so the design, nomenclature and the liturgy of the Israelite priesthood followed the Hyksos originals as closely as possible.

Strangely enough, even the name for Jerusalem itself can be seen to follow this very same argument. The name for Jerusalem has been derived from the Hebrew words Yireh-Shalam (שלם יראה). The first section of this name is said to be derived from *yarah*, meaning either to 'teach' or to 'shoot arrows', while the second part is from *shalam*, meaning 'peace' or 'payment'. This would mean that the name chosen for the city of Jerusalem could either mean 'teach peace' or 'shoot arrows for payment'; as might be expected, it is the former version that has been chosen by the Biblical concordance. Interestingly enough, the word *shalam* has connotations not only of 'peace' but also of 'payment' and 'settlement', and so the name chosen for Jerusalem has distinct echoes of the enormous tribute that was given to the Hyksos-Israelites as an inducement for them to leave Egypt on the exodus. The terms of the settlement between Ahmose I and the Hyksos did involve tribute and it did result in a short period of peace, and it may have been because of this event that the words became inextricably linked.

However, if this were so, the full name for the capital city of Judaea does not sound quite right; it would now mean 'teach a settlement' or 'teach a tribute'. But there is an obvious alternative to this interpretation because the first word of 'Jerusalem', *yarah* יראה, is spelt in exactly the same way as the word *yireh* יראה that has just been discussed, which means 'to see' in the Hebrew. In the Egyptian translation, however, the word *ir-ra (yirah)* is more explicit – it means 'Ra sees'. If this were the true origin of the name for Jerusalem, then the entire city would be aping the terminology of both the Giza plateau and the Hyksos nation. The name would now mean 'Ra Sees Peace', 'Ra Sees the Tribute', or even 'Ra Sees the Settlement'. In which case, the hopes and wishes of the founding fathers of this city can be clearly seen; they not only wanted a replica of the Giza plateau in their land, they also wanted the settlement with Thebes to maintain the peace, after centuries of civil war. While their hopes may have been genuine, the reality was to be three thousand years of war and strife.

VII *King Solomon*

Wisdom

The likely outcome of all this is that the temple designed by Sheshonq I was not built at Memphis at all, but is more likely to have been located at Jerusalem instead. This Temple of a Million Years, whose construction is mentioned on the walls of the Temple of Karnak, must, therefore, be the same as the Temple of Solomon. This has to be another historical exclusive – a first-hand account of the building of the Temple of Solomon.

Once more, this gives us strong evidence that Sheshonq I was none other than Solomon himself – but if this was so, then we ought to be able to find some further similarities between the reign of King Solomon and the parallel reign of Sheshonq I. In fact, there are some additional and striking similarities and these can be seen when comparing the Biblical book of Proverbs with the ancient Egyptian papyrus known as *Instructions of Amenemope*.

Solomon, as we have already seen, was known for his wisdom, and the Biblical book of Proverbs is the document that details some of this great wisdom. The book of Proverbs was reputedly written by King Solomon himself – through divine revelation, of course – and this manuscript was set down in the form of a long list of sayings or proverbs. Being proverbial, the sayings themselves are largely allegorical and can be read on many levels, which can make their true meaning obscure. In the Hebrew, these sayings are known as the *Meshalim,* and they were originally designed to be far more than just gems of wisdom and items of general interest. Instead, the word for 'proverbs' originally meant:

> ... the Hebrew *meshalim* (מִשְׁלִים), (means) to rule or govern, (it) signifies a set or collection of weighty, wise, and therefore authoritative, sayings, whereby a man's whole conduct, civil and religious, is to be governed. [44]

In other words, the book of Proverbs was the civil law of the land. As politics were inseparable from theology in this era, the courts of the land would judge a dispute according to the holy law – represented by the original laws of Moses and now the supplementary laws of King Solomon.

The constitution of Egypt was organised in a similar fashion, and there are many cases of civil disputes being judged by the priesthood, who in turn consulted the gods for their wisdom and judgement. One of the standard methods of conducting a trial in Egypt involved communing with the gods and allowing the deity to determine the truth. The god was able to communicate its answers via a nod of the head:

O my good Lord; there is a matter (to discuss), shall I recount it? The great god nodded exceedingly, exceedingly... [45]

The court then proceeds with a series of questions, which elicit nods of affirmation as appropriate from the god and determine the outcome of the judgement. Note that this method of communing with the god is the same as I deduced in the book *Tempest* – it involved copious amounts of nodding, which is a method of communicating with the gods that is still practised today by orthodox Jews and Muslims.

It would seem that in both Egyptian and Judaean societies, civil law was ultimately governed by divine wisdom, and the judgements of these gods eventually became collated into a set of written laws. While this may seem to be a natural process that need not infer any contact between the two nations, the resulting written texts are rather too similar to each other for this process to be considered coincidental.

The Egyptian equivalent of the book of Proverbs, the *Instructions of Amenemope*, is thought to date from the Ramesside period, or about 1300 BC, and it is set out as thirty chapters of sayings. But why have historians decided upon the Ramesside period? As is often the case with these works, we no longer have access to the original documents and the texts that have survived are copies of copies that date from a much later period. Since there is no date or monarch mentioned in this text, the original date of its composition becomes a matter of conjecture. The best guess at present is the Ramesside period, and while some of the information contained in the *Instructions* may have had a very long history prior to their inclusion in this text, there is a more logical author for this work than a Ramesside scribe. Having traced this Biblical line of pharaohs through King David [Psusennes II] and on to King Solomon [Sheshonq I], and since King Solomon was reputedly the author of a very similar set of 'instructions' or 'proverbs', then shouldn't the true author be linked to this Tanite royal line in some way?

The obvious answer is that the author of the *Instructions of Amenemope* was most probably the grandfather of King Solomon, who has now been identified as the pharaoh Amenemopet [Obed]. This suggestion develops a nice symmetry, as the Bible's Proverbs were attributed to King Solomon, while the *Instructions of Amenemope(t)* can now be associated with Obed [King Amenemopet]. The only trouble with this identification is that the scribe known as Amenemopet was not a king; instead, the text indicates that he was both overseer of the grain and chief scribe to the pharaoh. The former of these two titles was the same honour that was held by the Biblical patriarch Joseph who, in addition, was also the chief vizier to the pharaoh.

As the position of vizier might be considered to be the equivalent of a modern prime minister, this shows that the humble 'scribe' called Amenemopet must have been an important court official and probably held the highest rank in the Egyptian court, as did the Biblical Joseph himself.

The latter of these titles, that of chief scribe, further indicates that Amenemopet not only held high office, but was probably related to his namesake, the pharaoh Amenemopet. When the historian Manetho talks of a scribe and prophet in the New Kingdom era, he is said to be Amenophis who worked under the pharaoh Amenophis. The Biblical King Solomon has just been identified as the pharaoh Sheshonq I (Shishak), but the chief scribe who worked under King Solomon (Shishak) was known as Shiysah שׁישׁא. It would seem more than likely that the exalted position of chief vizier or scribe was often chosen from the immediate family of the king; perhaps it was a post that was even given to the princes of the land – at the very least, it is apparent that the scribe often bore the same name as the king.

Alternatively, the scribe might have been called Smith, but he nevertheless signed his work in the name of the king because this was an official document from the royal court. This is rather like the methods that are adopted by prestigious firms of Solicitors in London. A solicitor working for 'M. C. Bloggs & Co', in the City of London, will often sign their letters as 'Yours Sincerely, M C Bloggs', even though their own name is John Smith. Even in the modern era, the scribe will often take the name of his/her patron or employer.

If this were the tradition in Egypt, as the evidence appears to suggest, then the most likely era for the compilation of the *Instructions of Amenemopet* is during the reign of King Amenemopet himself. Since the Biblical book of Proverbs was important enough to be ascribed to King Solomon, should not the book of *Instructions* be equally important? The final piece of evidence to show that these *Instructions* – a title that can also be translated as *'Proverbs'* – were composed by somebody who was related to the Biblical kings of the United Monarchy is their uncanny similarity to the book of Proverbs. Some of the similarities between the two texts are as follows:

Instructions	Proverbs
Chap 1	Verse 22:17
Give your ears, hear the sayings,	Bow down thine ear, and hear the words of the wise,
Give your heart to understand them	and apply thine heart unto my knowledge.

Note: The modern translations of both *Instructions* and *Proverbs* have re-translated 'heart' as 'mind'. This interpretation has come about because the Egyptians believed the mind was in the heart, but it is interesting to see that the original Hebrew maintained this same concept. This issue will be important in the continuing story of Hiram Atif in the next chapter.

Chap 2	Verse 22:2
Beware of robbing a wretch	Rob not the poor,
Or of attacking a cripple	Neither oppress the afflicted in the gate:

Note: The infirm and old used to gather at the gate of the Temple to beg for alms, as they still do at the gates of Russian churches.

Chap 30	Verse 22:20
Look to these 30 chapters	Have not I written to thee thirty things
They inform, they educate	in counsels and knowledge,
They are the foremost of all books	That I might make thee know the certainty of the words of truth
They make the ignorant wise	That thou might answer the words of truth to them that send unto thee?

Note: The book of Proverbs will invariably say 'excellent' instead of 'thirty' but this is simply a deliberate mistranslation, as is discussed below.

Chap 30	Verse 22:29
As for the scribe who is experienced in his office	Seest thou a man diligent in his business?
He is found worthy to be a courtier he shall stand before kings;	he shall not stand before mean men.

Note: This last quote is an indication of the rank and status of Amenemopet, the scribe. If he was diligent in his work he would be able to 'stand before kings', but was this as a valued courtier or was it instead as a prince of the realm? Perhaps, if the scribe was extremely dedicated, he would be chosen by his father as heir to the throne.

These are a few of the many similarities between *Instructions* and *Proverbs* and, at the very least, it can be seen that the two sets of proverbs are based upon the same original material. But all the evidence points towards the Egyptian *Instructions* being older than Biblical *Proverbs* and so for all his perceived wisdom, King Solomon [Sheshonq I] was only copying and expanding upon established Egyptian material. The translator of *Instructions*, Miriam Lichtheim, says of this similarity between the two texts:

> It can hardly be doubted that the author of Proverbs was acquainted with the Egyptian work and borrowed from it, for in addition to the similarities in thought and expression ... verse 22:20 states: "Have I not written for you

<u>thirty</u> sayings of (advice) and knowledge?". (This) derives its meaning from the author's acquaintance with the 'thirty' chapters of Amenemope.[46]

When this quotation is referenced in the Bible, the book of Proverbs will invariably say 'excellent sayings' instead of 'thirty sayings'; this, however, must be a deliberate mistranslation. The Hebrew word being used here is *shelowshiym* שְׁלוֹשִׁים, and this can have either of these meanings – 'excellent' or 'thirty'. It would seem that the thirty chapters of *Instructions* arrived at the Biblical compiler's desk from a specific source, as all these sayings have been grouped together in chapter 22 of Proverbs. Submerged as they are in this position, it is possible that the English translator saw little reason to believe that there were just 30 sayings and so this translation seemed rather obscure. The preferable option, under the circumstances, seemed to be the linked word 'excellent'; and so the 'thirty sayings' became the 'excellent sayings'.

Having said that, this is the only time in the Bible that the word *shelowshiym* has been translated in this fashion. This same word is used 163 times in the Bible as the number 'thirty' and 15 times as a 'captain' (the captain of the thirty elders), but it is only translated the once as meaning 'excellent'. In addition, the fact that King Solomon was supposed to have composed 3,000 sayings shows that the Biblical scribes knew of the 30 sayings – the inflation from 30 to 3,000 was simply a clumsy attempt by the same scribes to show that King Solomon had the wisdom of a hundred Amenemopets: all of which goes to show that the English translation represents yet another deliberate attempt to cover-up the embarrassing truth.

What this similarity between these two sets of proverbs provides, is a positive link between the pharaoh Amenemopet of the twenty-first dynasty (c. 980 BC) and King Solomon (c. 960 BC). It was once thought that this textual similarity was based upon some simple cultural links, with one scribe borrowing the material of another, but now we can see that these links run far deeper than this. King Solomon had access to a complete copy of the *Instructions*, and he included them within the royal court's book of judgements because they were a part of his family's own history and heritage. In which case, the Biblical Book of Proverbs represents nothing less than the civil law of Egypt, devised by the pharaoh Amenemopet [Obed] and transcribed into the Torah by the pharaoh Sheshonq I [King Solomon].

Sheshonq

The previous chapter has uncovered a lot of interesting evidence that appears to demonstrate that King Solomon was the pharaoh Sheshonq I. But before jumping to any conclusions, there is also the little matter of the different family histories of these two monarchs to consider. In what manner do the complex family relationships of King Solomon equate with the equivalent relationships for Sheshonq I?

The first piece of evidence in this regard concerns the chief wife of King Solomon. While Solomon is reputed to have had dozens of wives, the wife that bore the next king of Judaea was called Naamah נעמה. When looking at the historical record, however, the chief wife of Sheshonq I is known to have been called Karama(t). But if King Solomon is to be identified with the pharaoh Sheshonq I, then it is likely that these two women would have to have been the same individual – and yet their names do not look particularly similar.

While that may be true in the English translation, it is not quite so true in the Hebrew. The name Naamah is spelt נעמה in the Hebrew script, and it would only take a minor slip of the pen to produce כעמה instead. This is the same type of transcription error that was highlighted previously, and in the original Aramaic the 'n', 'k' and 'r' all looked very similar. In fact the hooked tail on the later Hebrew כ character is a passable imitation of the original Aramaic form for all three of these consonants.

While these two Hebrew words above may look identical, the former is pronounced as Naamah, while the latter is pronounced as Kaamah. This, then, is the first piece of the family jigsaw puzzle that will slowly be assembled to confirm that Solomon was indeed Sheshonq I –

both of these monarch's chief wives had the same name; it was pronounced as Karama in the original Egyptian and as Kaamah in the Hebrew translation.*

The second piece of the puzzle concerns another wife (or daughter) of King Solomon [Sheshonq I], but the historical record here is a little confused. The respected authorities in this field – Breasted, Gardiner and Kitchen – indicate that a lady by the title of Maakare Mu-Tamhat married Uasorkon I, the son of Sheshonq I. On the other hand, Peter Clayton argues that this same Maakare married Sheshonq I himself, and not his son. I am not sure whether this difference is due to the confusing nature of some of these documents, or whether Clayton has some more recent information unavailable to the other, more venerable, historians. Whatever the case, the Biblical record indicates that both arguments are correct.

Firstly, it is worth reminding ourselves that there were four Maakhah Tamars in the Bible, which have been labelled I - IV, as we saw in chapter V:

Maakhah Tamar I,   the daughter of Jesse; the first chief wife of King David.
Maakhah Tamar II,   the daughter of Maakhah Tamar I and King David. **
Maakhah Tamar III,   the daughter of Maakhah Tamar II and Absalom.
Maakhah Tamar IV,   the daughter of Maakhah Tamar III and Rehoboam.

** Maakhah Tamar II was also known as Bathsheba or the Queen of Sheba, and she became the sister-wife of Absalom.

Turning instead to the historical record, this says that Princess Maakare Mu-Tamhat was the daughter of Psusennes II [King David], and this seems to fit in very well with the Biblical account as King David also had a daughter called Maakhah Tamar (II). While the historical and Biblical records seem to agree about the birth of Maakhah Tamar II, her marriage presents a bit of a conundrum.

The majority of the reference books indicate that this Maakare Mu-Tamhat married the son of Sheshonq I, who was a pharaoh by the name of Uasorkon I (Osorkon I). In like fashion, the Biblical record says that a Maakhah Tamar married the son of King Solomon, who was a king called Rehoboam. In both cases, a lady called Maakare Mu-Tamhat [Maakhah Tamar] married the son of Solomon-Sheshonq – but in the Biblical record this was Maakhah Tamar III, not Maakhah Tamar II.

Is it in any way 'cheating' to assume a change in the generations in this fashion? Not a bit. As it happens, the younger lady – Maakhah

* It is perhaps worth noting that the syllables in the name Karamaa(t) could be reversed to produce Maatkare, although the Egyptian spelling is different.

Tamar III – was, due to the complexities of King David's marriages, also his granddaughter. So, in each case, a daughter (or granddaughter) of King David [Psusennes II], called Maakhah Tamar, married this monarch's grandson (the son of Solomon-Sheshonq).

However, in *Chronicle of the Pharaohs*, Peter Clayton claimed that Maakare Mu-Tamhat married Sheshonq I, instead of his son. But this is rather contradictory to the other reference books, so how can both of these claims be correct? The answer is, in Biblical terms, that there was more than one Maakhah Tamar; but which of these queens was available to marry King Solomon? The first wife of King David would have been too old to be a candidate, while the granddaughter has already been married off to the son of Solomon, so the only Maakhah Tamar who would have been available to 'marry' King Solomon was the widowed (second) chief wife of King David, Maakhah Tamar II (Bathsheba). While the explanation that solves this problem may present a family history that seems a little bizarre, as will be explained later, it may also solve one of the greatest mysteries in the Bible – exactly who the Queen of Sheba was.

The Queen of Sheba was the 'Queen of the South' who came to visit King Solomon, the son of David, and she was reputed to have borne him a son called Menelek. In the Hebrew, the name 'Menelek' is simply a generic name for 'king', which was derived from the word *melek* מלך, meaning 'king'. But the original meaning of the name 'Menelek' was not supposed to refer to a king as such; instead, it was supposed to refer to the 'son of a wise man'. Once more, the Egyptian version of this title shows us how this meaning may have been achieved.

Since the Egyptians did not have the 'l' consonant, the original Egyptian rendition of *menelek* must have been spelt *menerekh*. The basis of the name may therefore have been the words *meni* 𓏠𓈖𓀭 and *rekh* 𓂋𓐍, meaning 'Image of Wisdom', with the term *meni* having distinctly royal overtones. The traditional interpretation indicates that the name Menelek refers to the 'son of a wise man', which in this case would have been the 'son of Solomon'. But the text from the Kebra Nagast places a very deliberate and obvious emphasis on the son of King Solomon being so identical to his father that everyone confuses the two. It is entirely possible that this was done because the scribes knew the original meaning of this title and were indulging themselves in the traditional delights of wordplay, so the translation 'Image of Wisdom' is probably more correct.

In Ethiopian literature, the title that was given to Menelek has been changed to Aebna Hakim, a name that is likely to have been of Egyptian extraction once more. The term *Ab* or *Ib* 𓋏𓎡𓏛 means either 'wisdom' or 'image'; the word *na* 〰〰⌇ means 'belonging to'; while the word *Heq* ⌇⊿⌇ means 'ruler' or 'king', and is a part of the title used for the line of Hyksos kings. The resulting title, Aeb-na Hakim, could therefore be translated as 'Image of the King', or even 'Wisdom of the King', either or both being suitable interpretations. Thus, in the Egyptian, the titles Menelek and Abna Hakim have virtually the same meaning.

Sheba

As we have already seen, one of the many wives of King David was called Bathsheba, and her real name has now been resolved as Maakhah Tamar II. It has also been demonstrated that the title 'Bathsheba' is the direct equivalent of the title 'Queen of Sheba'. In a similar fashion, the Hebrew name for the Queen of Sheba is 'Malkah Sheba' מלכה שבא, and the first element in this name strongly echoes the title 'Maakhah' that was held by the Maakhah Tamars. While the many similarities between these two titles could have been coincidental, and borne by two separate women, I personally believe that Bathsheba (Maakhah Tamar II) was the Queen of Sheba herself. But can this be proven?

Maakhah Tamar II was the daughter of Psusennes II [King David], who had become her father's second chief wife on the retirement or death of her namesake mother. Although Bath-Sheba was descended from the Lower Egyptian royal family of Psusennes II, she was also an independent princess who probably had strong maternal links through Makhaah Tamar I, her mother, that went back to the priest-kings of Thebes. With this complementary, but independent, power base in Upper Egypt, both Bath-Sheba and her mother could have afforded to be independent women with their own court officials, finances, politics and policies. As marriages go, the relationship between King David and Bath-Sheba (Maakhah Tamar II) could well have been stormy and confrontational, and the Kebra Nagast in particular makes a great play of Bath-Sheba trying to subvert the theology of the king. The marriage was probably typical of many a royal union: it was a strategic alliance between nations that demanded the two leaders occasionally shared the same bed.

The fact that the Queen of Sheba (Bath-Sheba) was married to King David, her father, may also shed more light on why she was known as the Queen of Sheba. Thus far, I have been content to call Egypt 'Sheba' simply because of the associations between the term *seba* (*sheba*), the stars, and the astronomy rites and rituals that were performed on the Giza plateau. The only trouble with this association is that the word Sheba is not really a known name for Egypt, or the Giza plateau for that matter, and so this correlation is by no means proven. But there is another reference to the term *sheba* that is directly linked with this queen and may have been the true origin of this title.

The Egyptian name for King David was Psusennes II, or more accurately Padjuat-khaennuit ⌐▭⌐𓂋𓃭☆𓂝⊗ . It was from the star glyph in this name ☆ , which can be pronounced as *djuat* ⌐🏺𓃾☆ , that this king's nickname of Duad or David was derived. Since the *djuat* was a star that was closely associated with this particular pharaoh, the common phrase for this glyph became the 'Star of Duad' or the 'Star of David'. In turn, since Maakhah Tamar II was married to King David [Psusennes II] she would naturally have picked up the same associations, and she is likely to have been called the 'Queen of King Duad' or the 'Queen of King David'.

But there is another, more common way of pronouncing this particular pharaoh's name in the modern reference manuals, and that is Paseba-khaennuit ⌐▭⌐𓃾☆𓂝⊗ . All that has happened here is that the star glyph ☆ has been translated as being the word *seba* (*sheba*) ⌐⌐𓆓☆ , which also means 'star'. If this had also been the fashion in ancient times, then King David could also have been known as King Sheba. This alteration would, of course, have had a corresponding effect on the title that was given to Maakhah Tamar II, and instead of being known as the 'Queen of King David', she would quite naturally have been called the 'Queen of King Sheba', or perhaps the 'Queen of Sheba' for short.

That the queen may have picked up the title of the king would naturally explain another of this queen's possible titles. It was noted in a previous chapter that the Queen of Sheba had also been known as Bathsheba. The name Bath-Sheba בת-שבע simply means the 'Daughter of Sheba', and since Maakhah Tamar II was the daughter of King David (King Sheba) this title is absolutely correct. But Maakhah Tamar II eventually married her father, the king, after the tragic death of her first husband, Prince Absalom. This marriage had a consequential effect on Maakhah Tamar II's title, and so the 'Daughter of Sheba' (Bath-Sheba) had now become the 'Queen of Sheba' (Malkah-Sheba). This explanation not only explains why Maakhah Tamar II was given two titles, it also gives us greater confidence in identifying the true Queen of Sheba. There was only one of the many Maakhah Tamars who was both the daughter (Hebrew: *bath*) and the wife or queen (Hebrew: *malkah*) of King David [King Sheba], and that was Maakhah Tamar II.

But the texts say that the Queen of Sheba was supposed to have visited King Solomon, not King David, so how does this new theory solve this little puzzle? The main point here is that Maakhah Tamar II, the Queen of Sheba, was not only the wife of King David but also the very young mother of King Solomon. She must have retired to Egypt after the death of King David, as she disappears from the Biblical record at this point in time. But when she later visited her most famous son, who was by now the king of all Israel (and Lower Egypt), she was still known by her previous formal title of the Queen of Sheba. This would explain the great status that the Biblical texts attached to this monarch; she was, after all, both the king's mother and also the widow of the most powerful of all the monarchs in that era.

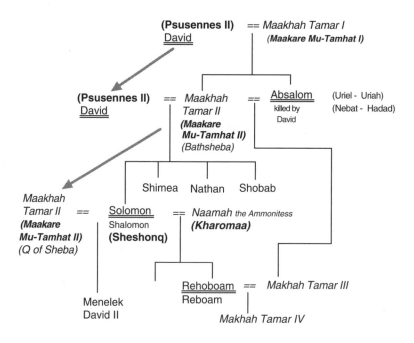

Fig 35.   The family tree of the Queen of Sheba.

That the Bible has subtly changed the name of this queen at this point in the texts is quite understandable; in fact, it was almost compulsory. While the queen may naturally have changed her title because of her marriage to King David, there was an additional complication for the scribes that may have accelerated this process. The problem was the strong and persistent court rumours that the Queen of Sheba may have had conjugal relations with King Solomon, who was her son, and while this kind of activity may have been acceptable in King Solomon's day, it most certainly was not in the era in which these texts were being collated. By necessity, the names

Bathsheba and Maakhah Tamar II had to be subtly different from the name of the more famous queen of the south, and so the 'Daughter of Sheba' (Bath-Sheba) became the 'Queen of Sheba' (Malkah Sheba).

That the wife of King David would naturally have been known as the Queen of Sheba is probably indisputable, but was this wife really Maakhah Tamar II? For confirmation we need to turn to the Kebra Nagast, the Ethiopian Bible, once more. The evidence lies in a passage that states that the merchant from the land of Sheba, who had informed the great Queen of the South of the wealth and wisdom of King Solomon, was called Tamarin:

> And there was a certain wise man .. whose name was Tamarin ... related to the Queen (about) all the wisdom of Solomon, how he administered judgement and did what was just, and how he ordered his table and how he made feasts and how he taught wisdom... KN1

First of all, it is worth noting that this man was a Sheban merchant who owned seventy-three ships and was supplying King Solomon with gold, ebony and precious stones for the construction of his Temple. While Ethiopia may have been synonymous with the supply of spices, the amount and types of goods that this merchant was dealing in is more likely to suggest that the trade was with Egypt. The name of this merchant is suspiciously familiar, too. Tamarin, in the Egyptian, could well be translated as Tamar-in, with the word *in* 𓈖 𓂝𓏭 meaning 'merchant' or 'imports'. If this were the case, then this person's name could have been interpreted as the 'Merchant of Tamar', a title that defines both his trade and the royal patron that he worked for. Therefore, this verse from the Kebra Nagast strongly links the Maakhah Tamars with the Queen of Sheba once more.

That the Queen of Sheba should be so besotted by this merchant's long and detailed tales of the court of King Solomon, as the Kebra Nagast relates, seems highly unlikely – unless, of course, the southern queen was King Solomon's mother. Any mother would have been rapt with awe at the tales of her illustrious son, and she would have requested them to be told and retold daily, just as the story in the Kebra Nagast relates.

Another rather surprising, but eminently satisfactory, piece of evidence that supports and confirms these connections between the Queen of Sheba and the Biblical Maakhah Tamar is the Arabic name for the Queen of Sheba. In Arabia, this legendary queen was known as Balkis; but, as is usual, this alternative name may have been based on an Egyptian original. If the Queen of Sheba were Bathsheba and if, in turn, Bathsheba were

Maakhah Tamar II, then the Queen of Sheba would have been the princess who was raped by Amnon, her brother. But this 'rape' has already been explained in terms of an affair with King David, and Maakhah Tamar performing the usual ritual duties between God's Wife and her divine spouse.

As it happens, the name Balkis can be formed from the Egyptian words *Bal* and *Kis*. *Bal* (*Bar*) turns out to be the Egyptian name for the god Baal 𓃀𓂝𓏤𓀭 , and it was also used as a common Semitic name for 'lord'. The Egyptian word *Kis* 𓂧 , on the other hand, is the ancient Egyptian term for rape. The surprising result of this translation is that the Arabic name for the Queen of Sheba, Bal-kis, can be interpreted to mean 'Raped by God'. Such a title would have been quite fitting for Bathsheba – alias Maakhah Tamar II, the wife of King David who was raped by the gods.

On initial reading, such a title may sound like something that has been devised by a royal detractor, to mock the position of the queen. Just as King David was mocked for stealing Bathsheba from her husband (Prince Absalom), so the queen herself may have been mocked for allowing this to happen. Alternatively, this title may have been a simple reference to the ritual relations between God's Wife and the deity. The exalted position of God's Wife presupposed that Bathsheba (the Queen of Sheba) would have conjugal relations with god as it was a condition of her high office, so the name Bal-kis may actually have been delivered with awe and respect. After all, how many women in the world could boast of being quite so intimate with god?

Pharaoh's daughter

Once more, the evidence is distinctly in favour of the Queen of Sheba being none other than Maakhah Tamar II. In the historical record, however, the Biblical Maakhah Tamar II is to be identified with the daughter of Psusennes II [David], who was known as Maakare Mu-Tamhat. Thus, the following women were all the same individual:

> Queen of Sheba
> Bathsheba
> Maakhah Tamar II
> Maakare Mu-Tamhat II

But there is one more individual who could be placed into this nominative melting pot; one who may answer a few more of the Bible's conundrums. The lady in question is known only as 'pharaoh's daughter':

> And Solomon made a marriage alliance with Pharaoh king of Egypt, and took Pharaoh's daughter, and brought her into the city of David. [B2]

As usual, when the Bible has something embarrassing to hide, it deliberately fails to provide all of the required data. The obvious problem here is that if the Queen of Sheba was an Egyptian princess, as I have suggested, then by definition she would also have been a pharaoh's daughter. As was mentioned in a previous chapter, this would suggest that the 'pharaoh's daughter' being referred to in this passage was the Queen of Sheba herself.

   The problem for the Biblical scribes here was twofold. Firstly, they would not have wanted the public to know that the Queen of Sheba was Egyptian. Secondly, they most certainly would not have wanted anyone to know that the pharaoh, the father of this unnamed lady, was actually King David. These would have been knotty problems indeed, and the simplest method of dealing with them was to delete the names of the pharaoh and his daughter.

   All of this has been hinted at before, but the reason for reiterating this Biblical sleight of hand is that the Kebra Nagast appears to positively confirm that this was the truth of the matter – that this pharaoh's daughter was both the Queen of Sheba and Maakhah Tamar II. The first passage to look at is the account that states that the city of Gezer (Gaza) was given to the pharaoh's daughter as a present:

> For Pharaoh king of Egypt had gone up, and taken Gezer, and burnt it with fire, and slain the Canaanites that dwelt in the city, and given it for a present unto his daughter, Solomon's wife. [B3]

Here, the city of Gezer (Gaza) is being given by the pharaoh of Egypt to his daughter, who happens to be King Solomon's wife. This 'daughter of the pharaoh' is the same one that was taken to the City of David in the previous passage to the one above. The Kebra Nagast, however, has a different variation on this very same tale:

> And they halted by Gaza, the city of the mother of the king, which Solomon the king had given to the queen of Ethiopia when she came to him. [KN4]

There are a number of discrepancies between the above quotation and the Biblical version, but the material can be confusing and probably needs further explanation:

a. The phrases 'mother of the king' and 'queen of Ethiopia' in this verse both refer to the Queen of Sheba – the king that the Queen of Sheba was the mother to, was her son Menelek. Her son had travelled back to Jerusalem in order to be anointed as king of 'Ethiopia' by King Solomon, his father, and so the Queen of Sheba was now the 'mother of the king'. Just why the citizens of Ethiopia would want their future king anointed by an Israelite monarch is not explained; but the alternative scenario, of an Egyptian pharaoh [Solomon] anointing his son as co-regent of Upper Egypt, makes a great deal more sense.

The major point about this quote, however, is the ownership of the city of Gaza. The Biblical version of this event says that the city of Gaza was given to the unnamed lady who was known simply as 'pharaoh's daughter'. On the other hand, the Kebra Nagast suggests that Gaza was given to the Queen of Sheba. Once more, the clear inference of this dual ownership of Gaza is that the Queen of Sheba was the 'pharaoh's daughter' who married King Solomon, just as I have suggested.

b. The other point to be made about these quotes also concerns the city of Gaza. The Biblical verse says that a conveniently unnamed pharaoh gave this city to his daughter, while the Kebra Nagast says that *King Solomon* gave this city to his wife. Once more, both these texts are substantially correct, but the Egyptian pharaoh in question was probably King David rather than King Solomon.

The Bible indicates that 'pharaoh' gave this city to his daughter, but in another passage the Bible also says that it was King David who destroyed this city. It is extremely likely, therefore, that the pharaoh in question was actually King David [Psusennes II] and the daughter who received this present was Maakhah Tamar II [Maakare Mu-Tamhat II], who was in turn the Queen of Sheba and who did indeed 'marry' King Solomon.

These little snippets of information about the city of Gaza were most probably deemed to be unimportant by the scribes and so they evaded the censor's quill. Besides, the complete set of deductions that have just been made can only be observed if the two texts are placed side by side and compared, one with the other. It is quite apparent that the scribes failed to do this while editing the Kebra Nagast, and thus this gem of information has slipped through the ecclesiastical net. While these deductions are interesting in themselves, the most convincing piece of evidence that this section of text from the Kebra Nagast provides is the name of this mysterious princess from Egypt, who is normally referred to only as 'pharaoh's daughter'.

While the Biblical scribes were busy cutting the name of this Egyptian princess out of every single Biblical reference to her, all of their work would be in vain; for a single and solitary reference to this princess has remained hidden – within this relatively obscure document known as the Kebra Nagast – for two or more millennia, waiting like a loaded pistol to discharge its evidence into the rapidly retreating theologians. While the Kebra Nagast may eventually name this Egyptian princess, it never names the Maakhah Tamars, and so the following deduction cannot be made in isolation – which infers, once more, that the editing of these texts was done separately. The primed cartridge in the Kebra Nagast is the passage that says this mysterious 'pharaoh's daughter' was actually called Maakshare:

> And (Solomon) loved very greatly the daughter of pharaoh, the king of Egypt, whose name was Maakshare. KN5

The Kebra Nagast is stating that the mysterious 'pharaoh's daughter' was called Maakshare, while the Bible says that King David's daughter (and daughter-wife) was called Maakhah (Egyptian Maakare). Not only is this text confirming that Maakhah Tamar II and the pharaoh's daughter (Maakshare) were the same person, it is also confirming the position of King David once more. It is axiomatic that if King David's daughter was known as the 'pharaoh's daughter', then King David must have been a pharaoh. In which case, it is all rather understandable that King Solomon should have loved this Egyptian princess, because in reality she was his mother.

The text that follows this revelation is also confirming that this 'Queen of the South' was of Theban Ammonite ancestry, and she had brought with her many idols of the gods. According to the Kebra Nagast, it was primarily this 'pharaoh's daughter' (Maakare) who tried to turn King Solomon away from his Hyksos-Israelite beliefs, and to induce him into worshipping various idols. This story is very similar to the tale of the later Maakhah Tamar III, who tried to influence King Rehoboam, the son of King Solomon, with her worship of an erect phallus. Since the Kebra Nagast has passed through so many translations it is impossible to determine exactly what these idols were, but I have no doubt that they were exactly the same phallic effigies. In the Kebra Nagast, Princess Maakshare (Maakhah Tamar II) is said to have introduced King Solomon to the worship of these Egyptian idols and to have succeeded to such a degree that the Judaic god was said to have deleted twenty years from Solomon's life-span for his sins.

This is not all, for the Kebra Nagast, having already confirmed that the Queen of Sheba was known as Maakhah Tamar II, now provides us with yet another title for her that simply reinforces this fact. The title in question is that of Makeda. While the earliest translations of the Kebra Nagast that exist today are in Arabic, these same translations mention that the Arabic copies of this book were based upon Coptic originals, and it is equally certain that the Kebra Nagast has a longer history even than this. Undoubtedly, the original texts that the compiler was working from would have been derived from Hebrew originals, and the compilation of the original Kebra Nagast (minus the New Testament material that has been shoved into the text in rather odd places) could have taken place at any time prior to the tenth or eleventh centuries AD.

If the original text had been Hebrew, then the name 'Makeda' for the Queen of Sheba would have been spelt מעכדה. But, as we have seen on many occasions before, the Hebrew letter 'd' (ד) can easily be confused with an 'r' (ר), and if this mistake had been made in the distant past then the original name for the Queen of Sheba would have been Makera מעכרה rather than Makeda מעכדה. Once more, the unmistakable evidence is that the original Hebrew name for the Queen of Sheba was Maakera Tamar (Maakhah Tamar or Maakare Mu-Tamhat) and that she was a queen of Egypt, not Ethiopia.

Nevertheless, these Arabic legends of the Queen of Sheba do allow us to link the titles of this legendary queen into the later New Testament legends once more. One of the traditional Arabic tales of the Queen of Sheba was that she was born of a union with a *jinn* or, in the English translation, a 'genie' – thus, the queen had been conceived through a union with the world of the spirits. But the Arabic *jinn* is not simply a spirit that appears from the spout of a lamp, it is also a reference to one of the many dust-devils that traverse the arid deserts of Arabia. The Queen of Sheba was therefore thought to be a manifestation of a *jinn* or dust-devil, and this attribution quite possibly came about because the Egyptian word Sheba also means a violent wind 𓈖𓃭𓅓𓏏 .

The Egyptian scribes have always had a fascination with puns and wordplay, which was invariably used as a method of obscuring the subject being discussed – thus, in Biblical folklore the term Sheba was equated with wine and drunkards, while in Koranical folklore it became a *jinn* or genie.

> To Solomon We subdued the wind ... We gave him a spring flowing with molten brass, and a *jinn* who served him by leave of the lord. [K6]

In this quotation from the Koran, both the wind that was being subdued and the *jinn* that was given (as a wife) to King Solomon were references to the Queen of Sheba. But in what way does this quote dovetail with the New Testament accounts?

While the Egyptian title for the Queen of Sheba, that of Maakare Mu-Tamhat, has already been equated with the Biblical Mary, the mother of Jesus, this Arabic legend manages to confirm this assertion. It has also been previously shown that Mary Magdalene was said to have had seven devils come out of her, and that these 'devils' could actually be read as being *jinn*, or dust-devils. The clear inference is that Mary Magdalene, who was most probably the daughter of Mary, was following in the footsteps of the Queen of Sheba in having the same title and also in being identified with the *jinn*. Instead of being given to King Solomon, this New Testament *jinn* was instead being given to Prince Jesus, and so Mary Magdalene became his chief wife.

King Solomon's Mines

While the identity of the Queen of Sheba has been adequately settled, perhaps another of the many deductions that this identification can supply us with is an explanation for the design of the sarcophagus of Sheshonq I [King Solomon]. Before making this explanation, however, there is the little matter of the true ownership of this tomb to cover.

The temple complex at Tanis, in the Nile Delta, was first excavated by Auguste Mariette back in 1860, but he failed to locate the tombs. Their discovery was left to the later investigations of Pierre Montet in 1939; indeed, he had to clear a huge amount of material that had been dumped by Mariette to even get at the tombs. The results of these investigations were, however, to prove extremely fruitful.

Although grave-robbers had found the Tanis tomb complex in antiquity, for some reason they had failed to uncover all of the burials and one of the mausoleums was completely untouched. Inside this pristine tomb were four separate chambers, which contained several burials including the sarcophagi of a Psusennes and a Sheshonq. But, despite the cartouches on these coffins all being intact and perfectly legible, there is still the usual confusion over the ownership of these burials – although, at first glance, the cartouches do point towards these burials being prepared for the pharaohs Psusennes I and Sheshonq II.

The burials themselves were richly adorned with gold and silver artifacts, with Psusennes having a solid silver coffin and a solid gold death-mask, while Sheshonq had a magnificent solid silver falcon-headed sarcophagus. Such extravagance is almost the equal of the ornate funerary artifacts that were discovered in the tomb of the pharaoh Tutankhamen, a fact that points towards the Tanis regime being almost as rich and as powerful as the New Kingdom pharaohs. In fact, an inscription of the pharaoh Uasorkon I from Bubastis, who ruled after Sheshonq I, lists the inventories of the temples and appears to record some 400 tonnes of gold and silver. [7] Such a fantastic amount of precious metals has to be doubted, and the suspicion has to be that either there has been some deliberate exaggeration, or perhaps the incorrect unit of weight has been used in the translation.

Nevertheless, leaving the precise amounts of treasure aside for the minute, the myths of this era are in general agreement with the Tanis pharaohs having an inordinate amount of precious metals, and these myths are conveniently ascribed to King Solomon himself. According to legend, the Tanis pharaohs were not the only monarchs of this era to revel in material wealth; Sheshonq's alter ego, King Solomon, was reputed to have been equally well endowed with precious metals. But the source of this wealth is rather interesting because the myths of King Solomon ascribe it to a specific and mysterious location – the legendary King Solomon's Mines.

The myths of King Solomon's Mines are an enduring, if elusive, feature of the United Monarchy era; and the historical basis of this myth involves a need to explain the origins of the great wealth of King Solomon. The United Monarchy was based upon the foundations of the Judaean era of the Judges, a period of Jewish history that was far from successful and prosperous. Suddenly, when King Solomon came onto the scene, the kingdom was transformed both economically and politically, and the new Judaean monarchy was not only indulging in a host of impressive building projects, but these temples and palaces were also being lavishly appointed with fittings and embellishments made from copious amounts of gold, electrum and silver. The question has to be asked – in respect of both the United Monarchy and the twenty-second dynasty at Tanis – as to where all this wealth originated.

Historians, if they contemplate these myths at all, try to off-load the story onto the extensive copper mines at Timnah that have been attributed to the era of the United Monarchy. As we saw in an earlier chapter, although these mines near modern Elat have been attributed to King Solomon, they bear every indication of having been an Egyptian industry. While the association in this book between King Solomon and Sheshonq I would explain this Egyptian heritage, the site at Timnah would not explain the myths of King Solomon's Mines. While the copper at Timnah may well have been used to fabricate the bronze pillars of Jachin and Boaz, the myths would suggest that the wealth derived from King Solomon's Mines was primarily of gold.

While these enduring myths indicate that this king's ransom in gold and other precious metals came from the legendary King Solomon's Mines, unfortunately, like most things in this era, the precise location of these mines has somehow been lost to us. This has not, of course, stopped adventurers from searching and novelists from dreaming, and it was on this basis that H Rider Haggard's novel of the same name was written in 1885. The reason for this story being written at this time probably has something to do with the travels of the great Scottish adventurer, James Bruce. It was Bruce who brought back the first copies of the Kebra Nagast to Europe in the late eighteenth century, but the first of the English translations was not made available until Professor Wright published his version in 1887. The publication of the Kebra Nagast brought with it a renewed interest in the life and times of the Queen of Sheba and the era of King Solomon, and so the coincidence between these two dates would suggest that Haggard based his best-selling book, at least in part, on the characters and events contained in the Kebra Nagast.

Further evidence, which shows how close Haggard must have been to this whole subject, is contained within the story he narrates. The story revolves around a character called Allan Quatermain and his search for the mythical mines that made King Solomon so incredibly wealthy and, being set in the Victorian era, this adventure takes Allan into the wild Veldt of South Africa. The location Haggard chose for his mines was rather incongruous in terms of a likely trading partner with King Solomon of Israel, but Africa was in the process of being opened up to European eyes at this juncture in history, and so this location probably added a degree of topical spice to the story.

That Haggard's mythical mines were something to do with the historical accounts of King Solomon [Sheshonq I] and the underground legends that surround the Queen of Sheba is fairly certain, and the evidence for this lies in the location that Haggard chose for these mines in his novel. As Richard Knowles pointed out to me, the path to the mines, as was noted on the map that these adventurers had obtained, ran straight through a valley between two mountains that were known as Sheba's Breasts. The likelihood of Haggard producing such terminology in a context that involved a close relationship with King Solomon – but without knowing the significance of the title 'God's Wife' and her association with the pyramids at Giza – is relatively small. But if Haggard knew of this association between Sheba and the breast symbology of the pyramids, then why did his map locate King Solomon's Mines in South Africa and not in Egypt?

It is entirely possible that Haggard did not want to give the game away because, even if the location of these mines were known, it may not have been wise to divulge the location. This reticence would not have been to prevent the masses from descending on this location in search of booty, as these mines are now empty; rather, it was because the identification of King Solomon's Mines may actually be a little embarrassing in some circles. So where, in Egypt, would there once have been a lost hoard of precious metals and gemstones? And why should such a location produce any feelings of 'embarrassment'?

The truth of the matter is perhaps rather startling, for the ancient myths of Sheba and Solomon were absolutely correct: King Solomon's Mines were a historical reality, and if one travels down the valley that runs alongside Sheba's Breasts (the Nile valley alonside the pyramids of Giza), these legendary mines will eventually be found. Even the historical records of Egypt obliquely tell us of the discovery of these legendary mines:

> ... there was a drastic upheaval in the necropolis of Western Thebes (the Valley of the Kings) ... Pinudjem II died and was succeeded by Psusennes [II or III] ... Now at last it was decided to guard the ancestral dead in the same way as had been used by the priests themselves to secure the burials of their own company: by interment in one or two large groups in secret hiding-places. So the bodies of the revered Amenophis I, and of Ramesses I, Sethos I and Ramesses II were lodged in the secret tomb of Pinudjem II and his wife. Psusennes [II or III] then proceeded to inter almost forty mummies of empire pharaohs and their relatives... [8]

This passage is describing the looting of the New Kingdom tombs in the Valley of the Kings, which occurred during the twenty-first and twenty-second dynasties. Kenneth Kitchen tries to make this sound like a pious act of salvage: the saving of the vulnerable corpses of the New Kingdom pharaohs from the predation of wicked thieves. While this may sound like a reasonable argument upon first reading, this whole concept seems to leave so many questions unanswered.

What of the incredibly valuable burial artifacts and sarcophagi – what did the high priest Psusennes do with these? If this was a pious re-burial of a New Kingdom pharaoh, then why were all the mummies stripped bare, even of all the jewellery that was deep within their wrappings, before they were re-interred? Conversely, if all this pillage and destruction was the work of thieves, then how on Earth did they lay their hands on so many mummies, seemingly with impunity? Was security really so lax in the Valley of the Kings that vagabonds could tour the valley, deciding which tomb to plunder next? Could they really drag out massive pieces of funerary equipment, including granite sarcophagi, and sail them up the Nile without anybody noticing this activity?

The traditional concept of this event being common tomb-robbing by disaffected workers in the Valley is simply not credible. In reality, the tomb-robbing began at the very same time that the Tanis pharaohs of the twenty-first dynasty came to power, and the suggestion has to be that this clandestine activity was actually state sponsored. The evidence for this comes from the records of the trials that were held for those accused of breaking into the tombs during the last years of the Ramesside dynasty's reign.

The first of these trials involved two important officials, Peser and Pewero, the mayors of Thebes and the Valley of the Kings respectively. Peser had received information that ten tombs were being robbed, and he sent this information to the vizier, Khamwese, the most important official in the land. In view of the grave accusations being made, the accused men were questioned and an official investigation of the tombs was begun. The results of this thorough investigation showed that of all these tombs, only one showed signs of entry; but in the final analysis even this evidence was overlooked:

> We inspected the tombs, where the mayor of the city (Peser) said that the coppersmiths ... had been. We found them uninjured; and all that he said was found to be untrue ... It was found that the (coppersmiths) did not know any place in the (tombs) of pharaoh, of which the mayor had spoken the words. He was found wrong therein. [11]

Not only did the judgement ignore the evidence of the tomb that had been entered, but investigations some years later would eventually show that Peser had been correct, and that the tombs *had* been entered. Breasted says of these events, and the resulting judgement, that: "it arouses the suspicion that there was some reason for such action that was not apparent on the surface". [12]

The suspicion this does raise is that this trial was a complete whitewash. The officials in the Valley knew that there was wholesale robbery going on, and the last thing they wanted was for some diligent official from the east bank (Thebes) interfering with their lucrative little trade. The only question that this does raise, however, is whether this plunder was a private affair arranged by the Valley mayor, or something that was sanctioned at a higher level. The fact that Pewero, the Valley mayor, was able to successfully bamboozle the vizier to the pharaoh, and the fact that he was able to dispose of (fence) these valuable and easily recognisable items, suggests that there was high-level collusion.

As every professional villain knows, there is absolutely no point in stealing something unless there is a market for the goods. While it is true that the precious metals could be melted down and reworked, much of the funerary furniture and relics in these tombs were marked with the owner's name and could easily have been traced back to the tombs from which they were stolen. There would have been no point in taking any of these items unless there was a reasonably secure market for this produce that would not arouse too much suspicion – a market that may also have had strategically placed officials in the Egyptian hierarchy, who could frustrate any subsequent investigations.

The rising power of the local rulers in Tanis was just such a market, and they had a valuable commodity to trade – food. For much of the twentieth dynasty, it would seem that the food supplies to the Valley workers were intermittent at best.

> There are no clothes, no oil, no fish, no vegetables', they said. 'Send to pharaoh ... concerning them, and send also to the vizier our master that a means of sustenance be provided for us.' [13]

The cause of these shortages was most probably the continuing raids from the north by the Sea People (Hyksos mercenaries). No doubt this war, which had simmered on for about eighty years or more, caused havoc with the Theban economy. A disproportionate proportion of workers would have been required for the army and weapons production, leaving the agricultural and domestic trades short of workers, while the embargo on trade with the north would have deprived Thebes of the plentiful agricultural supplies that originated in the Nile Delta. The resulting food shortages caused general discontentment and many strikes in the Valley of the Kings, and doubtless these disaffected workers, having been so well looked after previously, would have been easy targets for coercion and bribery.

In return for a steady supply of smuggled food and supplies from the north, the Valley mayor could have supplied a steady stream of valuables to the Tanis regime, secure in the knowledge than none of this material would come back onto the Theban market and arouse too much suspicion. Since the trade was both illegal and born of desperate circumstances, no doubt the Tanis regime got a good price for their produce too. As this enterprise became routine and successful, so the tombs being plundered rose in both status and numbers. The scam started with the tombs of lesser officials and queens, but as the twenty-first dynasty rose in influence and wealth in their northern power base at Tanis, the emboldened thieves in the Valley started to rob the tombs of the pharaohs.

Ramesses II and Seti I's tombs were entered during the reign of Ramesses X, while the bulk of the tombs of the eighteenth dynasty pharaohs were stripped bare during the middle part of the twenty-first dynasty. By the reign of the Tanis pharaoh Amenemopet (Obed), the tombs of Amenhotep I, Tuthmoses II, Ramesses II, Ramesses III and Seti I had all been plundered; and we know that some of this contraband was finding its way to Tanis, because all of the burials in the Tanis necropolis contained grave-goods that had been plundered from Thebes. Despite all this activity in the Valley over a period of several decades, this still left a considerable number of valuable tombs for King David [Psusennes II] and King Solomon [Sheshonq I] to plunder.

Some of the later royal mummies from the Theban necropolis were even transferred to the Deir el Bahri cache by a high priest who was called Psusennes, a name that suggests he could have been related to the Tanis regime. This could have been King Psusennes II [King David], or even Menelek, the son of King Solomon, who was also called David [David II or Psusennes III]. Either or both of these individuals could have entered the priesthood at Thebes prior to ascending to the throne, as was common practice for royal princes. Thus, the person who had been transferring many of these mummies of the New Kingdom pharaohs to the great mummy-cache at Deir el Bahri may have been a prince of the Tanis regime, and it was the Tanis regime that was the main beneficiary of this trade.

The bitter truth is that the legendary King Solomon's Mines were nothing more or less than the royal tombs of the New Kingdom pharaohs, which lay in the Valley of the Kings. Note that the mythology of this location always refers to King Solomon's Mines in the plural; in other words, this was not a normal mine-shaft that branched off into separate tunnels, but a whole host of separate passageways all extending out of the same valley – just as is to be found in the King's Valley. It would appear that the rich 'veins' of precious metal and gemstones that King David [Psusennes] and King Solomon [Sheshonq] had discovered were not natural, mineral-rich seams of ore located in some distant mountain-range in the heart of Ethiopia or South Africa; instead, they were the tombs in the royal cemetery at Thebes, which contained a rich source of ready-made jewellery, gems, silver and gold. This incalculable wealth was then used to finance these pharaohs' administrations and armies, and also to finance the lavish appointment of the Temple and Palace at Jerusalem. While King

Solomon may have revelled in his new-found wealth and delighted in the destruction of his enemy's tombs at Thebes, the loss to history of this great treasure of the pharaohs is incalculable.

The scale of this looting was, according to the Tanis records, simply prodigious. As was mentioned previously, the pharaoh Uasorkon I, the son of Sheshonq I [King Solomon], compiled an inventory of the treasures that had been presented to the various temples in Egypt. The listed items comprise 20,500 *deben* (two tonnes) of gold and 72,800 *deben* (seven tonnes) of silver, while the larger donations (or grand totals?) suggest another 200 tonnes of silver and 230 tonnes of gold and silver were in the temple inventories. [14] (The reference to gold and silver may be a reference to electrum, the alloy of gold and silver mixed.) James Breasted, who quotes these figures, makes little of them, but clearly these amounts have to be in error. The inflation of these weights, and the proportion of the likely exaggeration, seems to be mirrored in the later accounts contained in the Copper Scroll, which was the most interesting exhibit of the famous Dead Sea Scrolls.

It has been calculated [15] that the total amount of gold in circulation throughout the world in this era was about seventy tonnes. While the donations of the pharaoh Uasorkon I would have represented a large proportion of this total, the larger figures appear to eclipse it by a considerable margin. While this anomaly could be explained in terms of exaggeration, these accounts were supposed to have been a temple record – an inventory of the temple treasure. While it is possible that such things are still prone to inflation and exaggeration, as most of the Soviet production records of the 1980s were, it is more likely that these figures represented a true reflection of the temple deposits. If so, then the only alternative possibility is that the units of weight being used were somehow in error, as they also appear to be on the Copper Scroll.

These measures were supposed to have been recorded in *deben*, which weighed some 100g. But this implies that a golden sphinx, given to the temple of Ra-Harakhte, weighed some 1.5 tonnes, and a statue that was given to the temple of Amun-Ra contained 1.9 tonnes of silver. Both of these figures are highly unlikely. A master-craftsman can beat gold, especially, into thin sheets that nevertheless retain enough structural strength to form a statue or sarcophagus. The result of the artisan's work is a large and striking artifact that, considering the density or 'weight' of gold, is surprisingly light. A good example of this, which may give us a much better idea of what a golden statue should weigh, is the life-size solid gold sarcophagus of Tutankhamen. Although this artifact is large enough to surround a wrapped mummy and is strong enough to be lifted (complete with mummy inside) into the outer sarcophagus, it weighs just 110 kg.

The implication is that the units being used in the Uasorkon inventory are all ten times too large, and had the intended unit of weight been the *kite* instead of the *deben*, then exactly this proportion of error would have occurred. The *kite* weighs only 10g and if this were the unit of weight intended, then all of the figures given in the inventory would need dividing by ten. The resulting inventory figures would then be:

Uasorkon's donations of gold	200kg
Uasorkon's donations of silver	700kg
Total silver available	20 tonnes
Total electrum available	23 tonnes

While these figures are still impressive, they are now in a manageable proportion that has some relation to reality. What this does mean, however, is that King Solomon's Mines had produced a staggering amount of precious metals over the preceding two hundred years; a continuous stream of precious metals and artifacts that underpinned the wealth and authority of the Tanis regime and saw them rise to power as the dominant force in Egypt and the Near East. This predation of the Theban necropolis not only furnished the tombs at Tanis with gold and silver, but also with granite sarcophagi for the kings of the United Monarchy. The provenance of all these sarcophagi has not been established, but it is known for certain that those of Psusennes [II] and Amenemopet were usurped from Theban tombs and that much of the funerary equipment in the latter's chamber was taken from the tomb of Seti I.

The possibility that this looting of the tombs in the Valley of the Kings was officially sanctioned at the highest levels within the Tanis administration, rather than the work of local Theban criminals, may also explain the seemingly fortuitous survival of the tomb of Tutankhamen. Like the Tanis line of pharaohs, the Amarna regime, which included the young pharaoh Tutankhamen, had distinctly Hyksos leanings – both these royal Houses maintained an essentially monotheistic religion and both, I maintain, were linked to the history of the Biblical Israelites. Very little evidence of the Amarna regime now survives as their faith was despised by the Theban priesthood and nobility, and the Amarna tombs and temples were systematically looted and destroyed by the later Ramesside pharaohs.

The Tanis pharaohs, being of the same Hyksos-Israelite stock as the Amarna pharaohs, were intent on paying the same respect to the Theban tombs as the Thebans had shown to the tombs at Amarna, and so each and every New Kingdom tomb was systematically opened and robbed of any valuables. However, when the Tanite government officials, who were in charge of this official looting, came across the tomb of Tutankhamen, they left it alone. Actually, it is known that the tomb of Tutankhamen had been entered twice previously in the ancient past, but whoever had broken into the tomb had not done much in the way of damage and the entrance had been officially sealed with the seal of the royal necropolis. Some of the funerary items in the tomb appeared to have been rearranged by these intruders, some boxes and caskets may have been opened, but it would appear that very little was stolen and the vast majority of the valuables were left completely untouched. So was this evidence of bandits that had been caught in the act, as has been suspected, or was it something else?

Under the circumstances, I believe that all of the destruction in the Valley of the Kings was the work of officially sanctioned tomb-robbers, who were ordered by the Tanite pharaohs to fill the northern pharaohs' coffers with gold. The only exception to this, was to be the tomb of Tutankhamen. This was the only tomb of the Amarna regime that managed to survive the pogroms of the Ramesside period against the Amarna family, no doubt because the boy-king had been persuaded that he should renounce the Atonism faith of the Amarna regime and convert instead to Ammonism. This same tomb had then survived the much later predations of the Tanis pharaohs because it was known to be the tomb of a member of the Amarna regime – Tutankhamen most probably being the younger brother of Akhenaton.

This claim may be disputed, however, because it is traditionally thought that the workers' cottages that were built upon the entrance to the tomb of Tutankhamen date from the reign of Ramesses VI. If this were true, then it is unlikely that this tomb could have been entered by the Tanis regime's officials and deliberately left intact, as the entrance lay underneath these huts.

The evidence that points towards the official view being incorrect is twofold. Firstly, why should workers' huts have been left directly outside the tomb of Ramesses VI? No doubt a number of highly placed officials, royalty and priests would come to see the interment of the previous king, and the presence of some scruffy workmen's huts just outside the tomb is unlikely to have been tolerated. Secondly, there is the discovery of a scarab of Tuthmoses III, which was found amongst the debris that concealed the entrance to this tomb. The presence, under these workmen's huts, of a scarab from a pharaoh who had died more than a century before Tutankhamen, and perhaps three centuries before the tomb was supposed to have been last entered, is a little incongruous. However, as was mentioned previously, these scarabs of 'Tuthmoses III' that seem to litter the archaeology of the United Monarchy may well have been scarabs of the high priest Menkheperre. This high priest not only had the same name as Tuthmoses III's throne name, he also used the royal cartouche for this name, hence the confusion.

Had this scarab actually been that of the high priest Menkheperre, it is relatively certain that the tomb of Tutankhamen was entered during the twenty-first dynasty, and that this particular high priest must therefore have been a Tanite sympathiser who was actively participating in the plundering of the New Kingdom tombs at Thebes. That this particular high priest may have had Tanis sympathies would also explain the predominance of these same scarabs in the Hyksos-held lands of Judaea and Israel; he was not simply a long-serving pontiff, but also a trusted ally. In which case, these workmen's huts must have been built by Menkheperre, and presumably they were put there to deliberately disguise and conceal the precious tomb of Tutankhamen that lay below.

Fig 36.   The pharaoh Tutankhamen.

VIII *Sheshonq*

While the Tanis regime maintained its power and prestige on the back of the Theban gold reserves, such regimes are never stable in the long term. Like the Middle Eastern oil states of the modern era, the Tanite dynasties underpinned their power and influence with imported products, immigrant labour and foreign mercenary defences; and while this type of economy may be convenient and comfortable for a ruling dynasty, it produces an over-reliance on foreign states and workers who have no commitment to the nation. Without indigenous technology and industries, and indigenous citizens to run them, today's empire can be rapidly transformed into tomorrow's vassal state – as Britain has also belatedly discovered to its cost.

Meanwhile, an over-reliance on mercenary armed forces is equally flawed as it leaves a nation open to similar political and social complexities. Mercenary armies are particularly fickle organisations as they have absolutely no commitment to the land or the indigenous people. If the money runs out, if another nation makes them a better offer, or if the military odds look too daunting, the impressive army of today's parade-ground is likely to become the future battle ground's ghost squadron. Worse still, the tame tiger that once obeyed every command of its master may decide that it is easier to bite the hand that used to feed it. Such may have been the fate of the Tanis regime, which eventually succumbed to the Persian army's advances some four centuries after Sheshonq I's [Solomon's] rule.

The result of these constant cash demands on the once immense Tanis treasury is that only a minuscule proportion of this treasure, which was originally taken from King Solomon's Mines, has turned up in the modern era: the majority of it has been frittered away thousands of years ago, and dispersed across the continents. Much of this treasure would have been spent on the maintenance of the Greek mercenary army, the Phoenician navy and the various tributes that were required to keep the inquisitive easterners at bay. Any remaining wealth would have been taken from the Hyksos-Israelite capitals of Jerusalem and Tanis when the Babylonians and Persians invaded Judaeo-Israel and Egypt respectively.

In turn, much of this same wealth would have subsequently been taken from Persia to Athens when Alexander the Great sacked the Persian capital city of Persopolis, and no doubt the Romans helped themselves to any remainders when the power of Athens started to fade. The constant recycling of this treasure – with much being lost, buried, melted down and destroyed in the process – has probably left just one or two items still in current circulation. King Solomon's Mines once represented one of the largest treasure-troves in the history of mankind, but the politics and theology of this region has seen it squandered and scattered to the four winds.

Some of these precious metals, however, may have been recycled and reworked at Tanis, and a few of the artifacts that were manufactured in this city were buried in the tomb of Psusennes I or II (and Sheshonq I or II) and eventually survived the millennia. It was most probably for this reason that both of the tombs discovered at Tanis were found to be resplendent with solid silver sarcophagi of extraordinary originality and beauty. Although the granite sarcophagi in this tomb had been usurped from previous burials, the metalwork and engraving on the coffins appears to have been the work of Tanite (Hiram Atif's) craftsmen; a fact that attests not only to the obvious skills of these new artisans who were employed by Psusennes and Sheshonq, but also to the ready availability of precious metals. Here, in the tomb of Psusennes and Sheshonq, there remains some of the last vestiges of the great treasures of King Solomon's Mines.

Sepulchre

The problem of the true ownership of these two royal burials at Tanis has still not been settled, and since the characters who may have been interred there are so internationally important, this is not a topic that can be brushed aside. The historical chronology of this era ascribes one of the coffins to a Psusennes I, a pharaoh that the new Biblical chronology in this book has already disposed of; while the second burial is then said to be that of Sheshonq II, an ephemeral pharaoh who apparently ruled for less than a year. So can the historical record be relied upon in these identifications? Is it sensible to believe that a pharaoh can be identified by a single coffin, as in the case of Sheshonq II, and no other inscriptions whatsoever?

The argument eventually has to come down to the perennial discussion as to whether the spelling of pharaonic cartouches ever changes. The simple answer to this is that it does, as the funerary equipment for this Psusennes at Tanis demonstrates. The name of this pharaoh is generally spelt as Pasebakhae_n_-nuit, but the 'incision plaque' on this mummy spelt this same name as Pasebakhae_s_-nuit. This was only a change of a single glyph, but it was a change nonetheless. Likewise, the name being used for Sheshonq III on the 'Lesser Vaults Stele' from the Serapeum changes from Usermaatre-Setepen_amun_-Sheshonq, to Usermaatre-Setepen_ra_-Sheshonq: the god-names of Amun and Ra being interchangeable. Although these are only small changes in spelling, it is clear that the names of pharaohs were not fixed in stone and some variations are likely to be found in the record.

This is actually a very important point, as the differentiation between these pharaohs, especially those of the twenty-second dynasty, often comes down to a slightly different arrangement of glyphs in the pharaoh's cartouche.

Since the new Biblical chronology, which is being championed in this book, has done away with the need for a pharaoh called Psusennes I, the next obvious question to ask is: could all the references to Psusennes I have actually been intended for Psusennes II? Could the cartouches of Psusennes I, for instance, ever be written in the same manner as those intended for Psusennes II? Well, the two names are pronounced as:

Psusennes I

Pasebakhaen-nuit, Meryamun.
My Star that Appears in his City, Loved by Amun.

Aakheperra, Setepenamun.
Great Image of Ra, Amun's Carpenter.

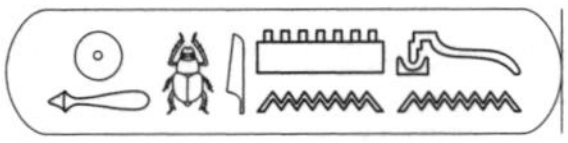

Psusennes II

Pasebakhaen-nuit, Meryamun.
My Star that Appears in his City, Loved by Amun.

Titkheperre, Setepenre.
Image Image of Ra, Ra's Carpenter.

The differences between the two cartouches of these two pharaohs are relatively minor; they all occur in the right-hand of the two cartouches – the throne name – and they are listed below:

a. The god-name has been changed from Amen 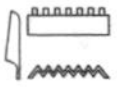 to Ra . As has already been pointed out, this change is entirely acceptable, and several of the reference books write the name of Setepen<u>amun</u> as Setepen<u>ra</u> anyway, despite the spelling change.

b. The three strokes of a plural sign have been added.

c. The *aa* 'pillar' glyph  has been changed into a *tit* 'lock of hair' glyph . The *aa* glyph simply means 'great', while the *tit* glyph means 'image' and is the direct counterpart of the *tut* in Tutankhamen.

In actual fact, this alteration in spelling makes no difference whatsoever to the resulting name for Psusennes. If a subject requires emphasis in the Egyptian language, it can either acquire an adjective like 'great', or it can be duplicated for greater emphasis. In the second version of this name, instead of writing 'Great Image', the scribes have used 'Image Image' instead, but the end result is much the same.

d. As an aside, note that the final attribute of Psusennes was the title Setepenre, or 'God's Carpenter'. It hardly needs pointing out that this was a title that was eventually to be inherited by the New Testament Jesus.

It can be seen that the meaning of the titles for these two pharaohs are actually complementary, and so the final decision as to which pharaoh to ascribe this burial at Tanis to comes down to a choice of king-lists. If one prefers the king-list of Manetho, which refers to a long reign for a pharaoh called Psusennes I, then the obvious choice would be that the sarcophagus belongs to this pharaoh. If the Biblical chronology is the favourite, however, then the decision has already been made. According to the Bible, the tomb *must* be that of Psusennes II, because there was no Psusennes I in this record – in which case, the two different spellings that can be observed in these cartouches simply represent two variations of the same name.

So, can this situation be resolved at all? Personally, I think that it can, and the evidence that could decide this matter is contained within the names of the immediate family members who were buried alongside this particular pharaoh. While the first piece of this evidence is not terribly clear cut, the later sections clearly show that this tomb complex belonged to Psusennes II and the immediate family of the Biblical United Monarchy.

The tomb of this Psusennes (I or II) at Tanis was designed to take four burials, and these included the king himself, his wife, an elder son and a (related?) army commander. The chief wife of this pharaoh was known as Mutnodjmet, and while the chamber adjacent to Psusennes was prepared for this queen, she was never interred there. Although the titles of Mutnodjmet show that she was Psusennes II's chief wife and that she was allowed to use the royal cartouche – which should equate her with the influential Maakare Mu-Tamhats – unfortunately this name does not equate to any of the known wives of King David. But the absence of this queen's mummy from the Tanis tomb may give a clue as to who she may have been.

The Maakhah Tamars (I & II), the chief wives of King David [Psusennes II], were both Theban princesses, and as such one would expect to find the tombs of these individuals somewhere in the Valley of the Queens near Thebes, rather than at Tanis. Accordingly, when the first cache of royal mummies was discovered at Deir el Bahri on the west bank near Thebes, by Maspero in 1881, the beautiful sarcophagus of a certain Maakare Mu-Tamhat was discovered. This mummy is traditionally ascribed to Maakare I, the daughter of the high priest Pinedjem I and a contemporary to Psusennes I. But under the revised chronology, this same Maakare I would have been the daughter of Pinedjem II instead, and she married Psusennes II. Since the names of the daughters of these two high priests (and all the other characters that surround them) were substantially the same, this provides for a rich source of confusion between the two generations.

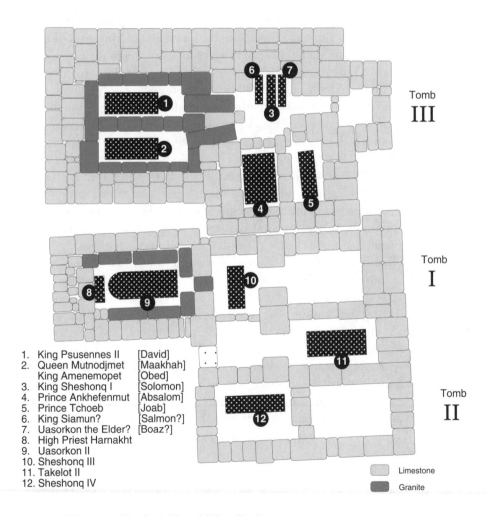

Tomb
III

Tomb
I

1. King Psusennes II   [David]
2. Queen Mutnodjmet   [Maakhah]
    King Amenemopet   [Obed]
3. King Sheshonq I   [Solomon]
4. Prince Ankhefenmut   [Absalom]
5. Prince Tchoeb   [Joab]
6. King Siamun?   [Salmon?]
7. Uasorkon the Elder?   [Boaz?]
8. High Priest Harnakht
9. Uasorkon II
10. Sheshonq III
11. Takelot II
12. Sheshonq IV

Tomb
II

Limestone

Granite

Fig 37. Tombs I, II and III at Tanis.

The titles attributed to this sarcophagus indicate that this Maakare was the 'King's Daughter' and the 'Daughter of the Chief Wife'; and although High

Priest Pinedjem I (the presumed father of Maakare Mu-Tamhat I) was supposed to have claimed the kingship at some point in his career, he is hardly to be regarded as a true pharaoh of Egypt. Likewise, from the Biblical perspective, the father of Maakhah Tamar I was Jesse, and again it is unlikely that this character was actually a king.

As this Maakare Mu-Tamhat from Thebes proudly claimed to be the 'King's Daughter', the much more likely identification of this mummy is that she was Maakare Mu-Tamhat II [Maakhah Tamar II], the daughter of King Psusennes II [King David], who must, by definition, have held the dual titles of 'King's Daughter' and 'Daughter of the Chief Wife'.

The reason for the traditional preference of Maakare I, rather than Maakare II, is that this mummy also held the title of 'God's Wife', and yet Maakare II had been promised children by the gods. Since the traditional view is that the office of God's Wife demanded a virgin, this would exclude an association with Maakare II. But, like the Biblical 'virgin' Mary, the God's Wife was supposed to eventually have children, and so this title does not exclude this mummy being attributed to Maakare II. In addition, this mummy was the very same Maakare Mu-Tamhat who had been interred along with the mummy of a small baboon. As has already been explained, this was probably an allusion to the virginal God's Wife who was 'raped' by Ammon (Amnon), and this would positively identify this mummy as being Maakhah Tamar II (Bathsheba), the daughter-wife of King David-Psusennes and the mother of King Solomon-Shoshenq. Therefore, the evidence that has been presented by the discovery of this sarcophagus at Deir el Bahri suggests that it actually belonged to the second chief wife of King David-Psusennes, who was eventually buried at Thebes; which is possibly why the chamber at Tanis was found to be empty.

A possible reason for the disparity in names between the tomb at Tanis and the sarcophagus at Thebes, therefore, is that the names 'Maakhare' and 'Mu-Tamhat' were Theban titles, and not the titles that were preferred by the Tanis regime. Tentative evidence that supports this claim can be seen in the similarity between these two titles. The Theban title of Mu-Tamhat (Mutemhat) has already been shown to mean 'Mother of the Breast'. In comparison, the Tanis title of Mu-Tenodjmet (Mutnodjmet) is said to mean 'Sweet (smelling) Mother', which it can do. But since Egyptian ritual was more concerned with fertility than perfume, I would tend to prefer the alternative translation of this title, which is 'Mother of Copulation'. As can be seen, these two names, and therefore these two chief wives, do seem to have some distinct ritual similarities with each other.

VIII *Sheshonq*

Ankhefenmut

The historical evidence seems to be supporting the deletion of the pharaoh Psusennes I from the king-list of the twenty-first dynasty, and so this tomb at Tanis should really belong to Psusennes II [King David] rather than to a fictitious Psusennes I. In fact, even the chronology of the tombs at Tanis tends to support this idea. Five tombs have been excavated on this site and they were associated with the following pharaohs:

(The following list is arranged in chronological order, rather than tomb-number order. Two of the tombs have a primary burial, plus one or more secondary burials.)

Tomb Nº	Classical occupant	New occupant
Tomb IV	Amenemopet	Amenemopet
Tomb III	Psusennes I	Psusennes II
	Sheshonq II	Sheshonq I
	Amenemopet*	Amenemopet*
Tomb I	Uasorkon II	Uasorkon II
	Takelot I	Takelot II
	Sheshonq ?	Sheshonq ?
Tomb V	Sheshonq III	Sheshonq III
Tomb II	Pimay	Pimay
Tomb II & VI	Unused	Unused

* Amenemopet was transferred from Tomb IV to Tomb III.

The classical list of occupants for these tombs starts with Psusennes I, but then misses out the pharaohs Uasorkon the Elder, Psusennes II and Sheshonq I; it is not explained why these pharaohs should be missing from the necropolis in this fashion. Having deleted Psusennes I from the record, however, the new chronology of the necropolis now contains an almost unbroken line of kings from Amenemopet all the way through to Pimay.**

The reason that the pharaohs Uasorkon the Elder and Siamun may be missing from this necropolis is that the city of Tanis was known as the 'City of David' or the 'City of Psusennes II', rather than the 'City of the twenty-first Dynasty'. Under this new Biblical chronology (leaving aside the complexities of Jesse-Harsiese), the pharaoh Amenemopet becomes the father of Psusennes II, and after Psusennes had built this new capital city it

---

** There are actually another three pharaohs missing from both of these lists: Uasorkon I, Takelot I and Sheshonq II. Various pieces of evidence, including Manetho's king-list, suggest that these three pharaohs are a simple duplication of the three pharaohs who were interred in Tomb I; in which case, they should be deleted from the chronology completely.

is not so surprising that he would have had his father interred there when he died. But Uasorkon the Elder and Siamun would have been buried long before the founding of Tanis as a capital city, and so their original tombs were most probably located in another town. Later investigation of some of the grave-goods at Tanis has shown the possibility that these two pharaohs may have been brought to Tanis at a later date and hurriedly re-interred in very simple coffins in Tomb III.

In Tomb III there was also interred the son of Psusennes II (burial number four), who was known as Ramesses-Ankhefenmut, a name which again has no similarities whatsoever to the Biblical sons of King David. As usual, however, this son of the pharaoh did have other titles and one of these was *Ur* 🔱, meaning 'great man' or 'prince'. This name has immediate associations with King David's son Absalom, who was also known as <u>Ur</u>iah אוריה or <u>Ur</u>iel. While such a loose identification cannot be considered to be certain, these two individuals also appear to have had similar duties and professions. Both of these individuals were elder sons of the king; both appear to have been the king's favourite son; both were generals in the army; and both appear to have predeceased the king.

The comparison between Prince Ankhefenmut and Prince Absalom seems to be moderately compelling, but if this was so, then why should Absalom have been buried in a prime location next to his father? Absalom, remember, was the rebel son who had challenged the rule and throne of King David and was killed for his impertinence, so why should this 'traitor' to the realm have been honoured in such a fashion? The simple and succinct answer to this is that he wasn't! Although this chamber was prepared for Ankhefenmut [Absalom], it was never used and most of the names of the intended occupant were rubbed out. The question that has been asked by many Egyptologists is: why should this have been so? Now the seemingly reliable Biblical history can possibly supply us with the answer – the crown prince was hung and killed as a traitor to the realm and his body was thrown into a crevasse, and so not only was this tomb unoccupied, but the scribes had also deleted the traitor's names.

In a similar fashion, the Bible makes it clear that Prince Absalom [Ankhefenmut] had already made preparations for his burial or epitaph, although the precise location of this monument is not given:

> Now Absalom in his lifetime had taken and reared up for himself a pillar, which is in the Valley of the Kings ... and he called the pillar after his own name: and it is called unto this day, Absalom's place. [B16]

The term 'pillar' is actually written as *matstsebeth* מצבה, and the modern equivalent of this word is mastaba, meaning a tomb or step-pyramid. The text is indicating that Absalom had made a tomb for himself in a place called the Valley of the Kings, and while Absalom had fled to the land of his mother's family (Thebes) for a number of years, it is still unlikely that this monument was located in what we term today as the Valley of the Kings. Although the Valley at Thebes contains many tombs, it is not known for its mastaba-type monuments; and despite his mother's protection, I am not so sure that the Thebans would have appreciated the tomb of a Tanis prince being built in the Valley at this time.

There are a couple of possibilities that this quote could be referring to. Firstly, it could have been a reference to one of the pyramid tombs in Jerusalem. Secondly, it could have been a reference to the family tomb at Tanis, in which Absalom's chamber lay unused. Since this tomb at Tanis was the royal family's necropolis and a rival to the traditional necropolis at Thebes, it could easily have been called the 'Valley of the Kings'.

Joab

So far, there is evidence to show that two out of the three additional chambers in Tomb III at Tanis may have been related in some way to King David, but what of that third chamber? Sarcophagus number five in this tomb was set aside for an army general who was known as Un-Tchoeb-en-Djed 〰🜲, but since this was a bit of a mouthful he was known as Tchoeb 🜲 for short. This individual's titles included:

> Superintendent of the Sole Friend
> Hereditary Prince and Count
> Seal-bearer of the King of Lower Egypt
> God's Father
> General and Army Leader of the Pharaoh
> High Steward and Prophet of Khons
> Prophet of Osiris, Lord of Djedet
> Superintendent of the Prophets of the Gods

Having such illustrious titles, it is not surprising that this man was eventually interred in the king's mausoleum. But in this era, could a person have attained such a high office, and be buried alongside the king, without actually being directly related to the king? It would seem to be obvious that there should have been some form of direct kinship, even if this fact is not directly claimed among this person's many titles. The proof of this assertion is that we seem to have the same problem with the equivalent character in the Biblical history.

It should not be quite so surprising by now to learn that this Lower Egyptian army commander was also mentioned in the Bible, and this gives us another, highly detailed, perspective on this man's life and achievements. The rather startling and convincing piece of evidence is that the general of Psusennes II's army was called Tchoeb 𓉐 , while the general of King David's army was called Joab יוֹאָב. Like the Egyptian army general, Tchoeb, the Biblical Joab was not just an army commander, but perhaps the most trusted man in the royal court of King David – if there were any important deeds that the king required doing, Joab was there to assist, however ruthless the task. Quite plainly, these two characters from the historical and Biblical records must have been one and the same, an observation that proves, once more, that King David was Psusennes II.

Fig 38.   Name of Un-Tchoeb-en-Djed, or Joab.

While the exact paternity of Tchoeb is not certain, it is likely that he was the king's son. Likewise, the paternity of the Biblical Joab is equally uncertain and again, it is entirely possible that he was the king's son. I initially included Joab as a son of King David because his mother's name was Zeruiah, which, as a reminder, means 'full-breasted'; and so this name can be directly linked to the Maakhah Tamar queens. In addition, there is also the fact that King David married Zeruiah's sister, Abigail, which would suggest that Zeruiah was of sufficient status to have been the king's wife. Equally interesting is the deafening silence in regard to the name of Zeruiah's true husband. When the Bible manages to mention that Joab's mother was called Zeruiah on no less than thirty-nine occasions, but does not mention the identity of his father once, there is bound to have been a cover-up. But what, in this case, was there to hide?

I had initially thought that the cover-up was Biblical. However, the fact that the historical record is similarly evasive about Tchoeb's (Joab's) paternity implies that there was more to it than this – perhaps Joab was simply born out of wedlock or some other such scenario. At the very least, the Biblical history confirms that Joab was the nephew if not the son of

King David [Psusennes II], and hence we have the presence of a related military commander at the family mausoleum in Tanis.

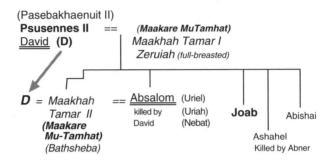

Fig 39.   Family tree of Joab / Tchoeb.

This coincidence in both names, titles and family relationships is compelling enough, but if further evidence were required to show that Tchoeb and Joab were the same individual, it is to be found in the Bible once more. The Biblical scribes like to entertain us with witty puns, as has already been demonstrated, but on this occasion the name 'Joab' was less of a pun and more a title that simply described his position within the armed forces:

> And David consulted with the captains of thousands and hundreds, and with every leader. [B17]

> And David numbered the people... and set captains of thousands and captains of hundreds over them. And David sent forth a third part of the people under the hand of Joab (the son of Zeruiah), and a third part under the hand of Abishai the son of Zeruiah, Joab's brother, and a third part under the hand of Ittai. [B18]

Joab was a captain of the army, but here he was being described in the text as a captain of 'hundreds and thousands'. This designation was exactly the same as the Romans chose for their armed forces, where commanders were known as centurions, or 'Captains of Hundreds' – no doubt the Roman army inherited the concept from this Egypto-Judaic methodology and terminology. However, the Biblical Joab (Tchoeb) was not a mere centurion; instead, he was a 'Captain of Thousands', and he commanded a third of the Egypto-Judaean army.

The Egyptian title that was conferred upon this same commander,

Tchoeb 𓏤, confirms both his position in the army and also his direct equivalence to the Biblical Joab, because the Egyptian word *tchoab* 𓍿𓃀𓏤𓏢 means 'hundreds and thousands' in general or the number 'ten thousand' in particular. The meaning of this army commander's title, in both the Biblical and Egyptian records, is therefore precisely the same – Joab was a 'Captain of Thousands', while Tchoeb was a 'Captain of Ten Thousand'. Thus, it is as plain as it can possibly be that the Biblical army commander known as Joab was the Egyptian army commander called Tchoeb.

Thus far, this royal tomb at Tanis has been shown to have been constructed to contain the sarcophagi and remains of King Psusennes II [King David], Mutnodjmet [Maakhah Tamar II?], Ankhefenmut [Uriah-Absalom?] and Tchoeb [Joab]. All of these individuals have been shown to have been directly related to the United Monarchy and to the reign of King David. Therefore, in the equivalent historical record, the occupants of this tomb must have been similarly related to the reign of Psusennes II, and *not* to the illusionary Psusennes I. This is yet another indication that the Biblical chronology of this era is correct, and that all of the details and family relationships that have been traditionally associated with Psusennes I should be assigned instead to Psusennes II.

As a short addendum to this section, the new Biblical account of this family indicates that their mausoleum contains one other poignant link between its occupants. The two adjacent side-chambers contained the mummies of Absalom [Ankhefenmut] and Joab [Tchoeb], who may have been brothers or cousins. But the Bible indicates that it was Joab who killed Absalom with a spear during the latter's failed rebellion, then threw the body into a chasm and filled it with stones. The empty and unused tomb of Ankhefenmut [Uriah-Absalom], which resides next door to Joab's, stands in mute testimony to that execution.

Falcon of Sheba

The same chronological problems that have been explored with the Psusennes II burial are also to be seen with the last of the mummies to be interred in this same tomb. This sarcophagus was hastily interred in the tomb's vestibule, indicating that it was probably an unplanned burial in this tomb, at a later date than the burials of Psusennes II and his immediate family. The cartouches on this sarcophagus indicate that this burial belongs to a pharaoh who has been identified as Sheshonq II in the classical chronology. But the chronology of this twenty-second dynasty is even more problematic than that of the twenty-first.

VIII *Sheshonq*

Two versions of Manetho's history mention only three pharaohs in this dynasty, while the other version mentions nine, with six of them only being identified by the duplicated term 'three other kings'. Although the classical king-list follows that of Manetho very closely, there are a number of interpretations that could be placed upon this dynasty. As with the pharaoh Psusennes, a number of cartouches belonging to a Sheshonq have been discovered, each with slightly different spellings, and so it has been presumed that these were the 'other pharaohs' mentioned in one of Manetho's accounts. But only one version of Manetho mentions this possibility, and even this does not directly say that these 'extra' pharaohs were definitely Sheshonqs. As Kenneth Kitchen admits:

> Of this series (of Sheshonqs), numbers 1,2 and 5 are distinct entities ... But the individuality or otherwise of numbers 3a, 3b, 4, 6 and 7 has remained a matter for discussion. [19]

What Kitchen is trying to say here is that the cartouches of seven or more Sheshonqs have been found, and yet no Egyptologist would dare entertain that so many pharaohs of this name actually existed. By tacit admission, therefore, it is certain that the spelling of cartouches can vary, and that some of these Sheshonq titles must have been references to the same individual. In fact, Kitchen is proposing an amalgamation of no less than five of these pharaohs, leaving us with three or perhaps four Sheshonqs. The more immediate problem for this enquiry, however, is the likelihood of Sheshonqs I & II being the same individual.

The first thing to note here, is the scanty evidence in favour of this ephemeral Sheshonq II. Apart from the sarcophagus itself, there seems to be no other information whatsoever, and genealogies like those on the Louvre Serapeum stele (below) – which details the high priests of Memphis and the kings that they served under – simply miss out this monarch completely:

High priest	Pharaoh
Shedsunefertem	Sheshonq I
Sheshonq C	Uasorkon I
Uasorkon A	Takeloth I
Takeloth A	Uasorkon II

According the records of Memphis, it is entirely possible that Sheshonq II did not exist – so could Sheshonqs I & II have been confused with one another in any way? In actual fact, it can be seen once more that these two cartouches only differ by one glyph. The titulars of these two Sheshonqs are:

Sheshonq I

Sheshonq, Meryamun.

Wise Leader,* Loved by Amun.

Hedj-kheperre, Setepenre.

Theban Monarchy is the Image of Ra, Ra's Carpenter.

Sheshonq II

Sheshonq, Meryamun.

Wise Leader,* Loved by Amun.

Heq-kheperre, Setepenre.

Hyksos Monarchy is the Image of Ra, Ra's Carpenter.

*   There are many interpretations that could be placed upon this name, which range from 'Wise Leader' and 'Nomadic Leader', to 'Wise Hill' and 'Nomadic Hill'. In essence, all of these terms simply refer to the rituals that were conducted upon the Giza plateau.

The only difference between these two titles is that one uses the *Hyk* (*Heq*) glyph of the Hyksos pharaohs ⌐ , while the other uses the white *Hedj* crown of the Theban pharaohs ⌐ . One can easily imagine that this difference between these titulars was simply due to political expediency, rather than there being two distinct monarchs. The two or three dynasties who ruled from Tanis were primarily Lower Egyptian monarchs, which is self-evident not only from their perceived Mashuash ancestry, but also from the fact that the crown of Psusennes II is adorned only with the *Uraeus* (serpent) of Lower Egypt, instead of the *Nekhbet* and *Uraeus* (vulture and serpent) symbols that represented the 'Two Lands' of a united Egypt.

If any of these northern monarchs 'ruled' Thebes and Upper Egypt, as Sheshonq I claimed to have done, this was most probably achieved though diplomacy and delicate marriage alliances rather than through popular adoration of the pharaoh and automatic respect for his authority.

The point being made here is that when Sheshonq I went down to Thebes and started the new construction work at the Karnak Temple, and made his inscriptions on the walls of the Bubastite Gate, it may have been politically advisable for the scribes to change the Hyksos *Heq* glyph in his cartouche into a Theban *Hedj* glyph. The Hyksos were still a despised people in Upper Egypt, as the theological disputes with these northern tribes had already precipitated two civil wars and two exoduses, so the overt use of Hyksos symbology would have been viewed as being highly provocative to the Theban priests.

Whilst this explanation for a change in the spelling of Sheshonq's name is largely hypothetical, this is nevertheless exactly what we seem to find – all of the inscriptions at Karnak refer to the name of Sheshonq using the *Hedj* glyph of Upper Egypt. What is lacking in the historical record, in order to confirm this argument, is a list of artifacts and cartouches that show how the name of Sheshonq I was spelt within this pharaoh's own home territory of Lower Egypt. What Sheshonq I's sarcophagus at Tanis may represent is exactly this. When given the security of Lower Egypt and the capital city of Tanis, Sheshonq I could afford to discard the *Hedj* glyph $\mathcal{Q}$ of southern Egypt, which the Tanites despised, and to use instead the contentious *Hyk* glyph $\left\lceil\right.$, which had been bequeathed upon Tanis by the previous Hyksos dynasties. In which case, the burial at Tanis does not belong to an ephemeral and otherwise unknown Sheshonq II; instead, this burial belongs to the mighty and illustrious Sheshonq I, which probably means that Sheshonq II is nothing but a figment of the classical chronology's imagination.

This reasoning would actually make more sense of the burials that are to be found in the Tanis mausoleum. The sarcophagus of Sheshonq 'II' contained a pair of bracelets that were adorned with the cartouche of Sheshonq I. To explain away this slight anomaly, it has been argued that Sheshonq 'II' had been interred with some family heirlooms that had belonged to his late grandfather, Sheshonq I. While this may sound like a reasonable explanation, had Sheshonq I & II been the same person there would be no need for any storytelling at all – Sheshonq I was buried with his own personal artifacts, much as one would expect.

Furthermore, the classical interpretation would have Amenemopet, Psusennes I and Sheshonq II all together in the same tomb, with some 100 years and several generations separating their burials. If these mummies were instead of the pharaohs Amenemopet, Psusennes II and Sheshonq I (plus Maakhare, Absalom and Joab) – with the reign of Amenemopet being allocated its place according to the Biblical chronology – then the family unit would consist of a grandfather, father, his wife and three of his sons. The latter is a much more satisfactory arrangement and it demonstrates that this mausoleum was more of a private family tomb than a state sepulchre.

In addition to these burials, the vestibule of this tomb also contained two unadorned wooden coffins of uncertain provenance, which had been hastily re-interred in this position along with the silver sarcophagus of Sheshonq I. The ushabti figurines that were found adjacent to these coffins indicate that one of these may well have belonged to the pharaoh Siamun, while it is reasonable to assume that the other belonged to Uasorkon the Elder. The hurried re-burial of Siamun and Uasorkon was probably due to the transfer of these mummies from a tomb in another city;

they were only able to join this family group after the city of Tanis had been founded by King David [Psusennes II].

These extra hasty burials in Tomb III still manage to leave the chronology of this cemetery in order. Tomb III now contains the remains of the kings and sons from Siamun through to Sheshonq I, while the adjacent Tombs I & II contain the mummies of the subsequent pharaohs from Sheshonq I through to Pimay.

Perhaps at this point a mention should be made of David Rohl's argument that Tomb I was built before Tomb III, and therefore the occupants of this tomb must predate those in Tomb III. It has to be acknowledged that this possibility would upset the entire Biblical and classical chronology, and so the problem has to be addressed. The argument lies in the fact that an annex to Tomb III protrudes into a cutout in Tomb I, which is a strange architectural feature. Rohl maintains that a portion of Tomb I was cut away to allow the annex to Tomb III to be built, and so Tomb III must have been built after Tomb I. The construction sequence being proposed by Rohl can be seen in the following diagram.

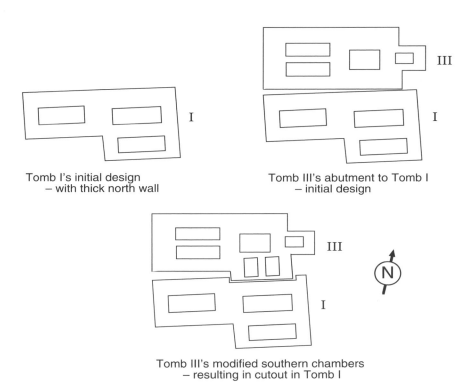

Tomb I's initial design
– with thick north wall

Tomb III's abutment to Tomb I
– initial design

Tomb III's modified southern chambers
– resulting in cutout in Tomb I

Fig 40.   Rohl's argument – Tomb III cuts into an existing Tomb I.

But this argument does not seem to be substantiated by the facts. Tomb I was primarily fabricated by a single course of megalithic blocks, and to have had an extra-thick wall on the northern side would have been out of character with the rest of Tomb I's design. If Tomb I's design was all designed and constructed using a single course of blocks, there would have been no extra-thick wall on the northern side for Tomb III to cut into.

In addition to this, the remaining single-block thickness wall on the northern side of Tomb I appears to be formed from blocks of equal thickness; but this is not how a double-thickness wall is built. As the rest of Tomb III demonstrates, double-thickness walls are made from blocks of varying thickness in order that the blocks key into each other to form a cohesive structure, just as a bricklayer would lay alternate lengthwise and widthwise bricks when building a double-width wall.

Outer face of double-thickness wall

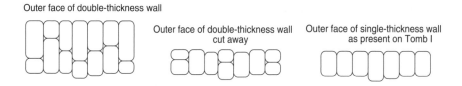

Outer face of double-thickness wall
cut away

Outer face of single-thickness wall
as present on Tomb I

Fig 41.   Wall construction techniques employed at Tanis.

Both of these arguments point towards the northern wall in Tomb I being an original, planned construction, rather than a cutaway afterthought by another dynasty. But if this was so, then why do we see this peculiar interlocking design for these two tombs at Tanis? The answer may well lie in a last-minute redesign of the main chamber of Tomb I.

If the original design of Tomb I specified a single layer of limestone for all the chambers, then the entire tomb would have been neatly abutted to the edge of Tomb III, as in the third diagram below. However, either someone found some more granite blocks to line the main western chamber of Tomb I with, or the sarcophagus that they finally used was much larger than had been expected (and it has to be said that this particular sarcophagus is inordinately large). Whatever the problem was, this additional feature suddenly made this chamber much wider than was originally planned. The result was that the northern wall of Tomb I had to overlap parts of Tomb III, in the fashion that we see below, in order to accommodate this extra width. This explanation demonstrates that Tomb III could easily have been built before Tomb I, as was originally thought, and that the twenty-first and twenty-second dynasties do not need to be transposed as Rohl has suggested.

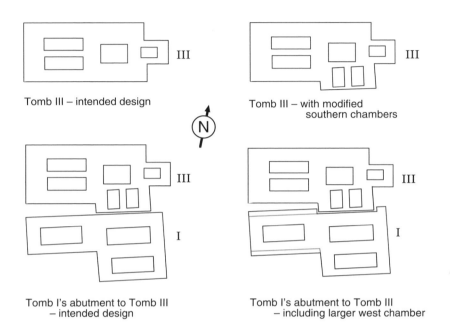

Tomb III – intended design

Tomb III – with modified
southern chambers

Tomb I's abutment to Tomb III
– intended design

Tomb I's abutment to Tomb III
– including larger west chamber

Fig 42.   *True construction sequence:*
a larger than expected chamber in Tomb I envelops Tomb III.

Perhaps the most significant result of the identification of these pharaohs as being the kings of the United Monarchy of Judaea and Israel is that it transforms this otherwise relatively insignificant tomb at Tanis into one of the most important religious and historical sites in the world. Here, in a remote and desolate location in the Nile Delta, lies the tomb of King David and King Solomon – two of the most celebrated figures in Biblical history. What is more, the mummified remains of both these individuals have survived the predations of the millennia, and they are now on display in the Cairo Museum.

Sokar

This disputed sarcophagus from Tomb III, which has now been attributed to Sheshonq I, was beautifully formed and engraved in solid silver, and its design is unique in Egyptian history. The sarcophagus has been fashioned into a very striking image of a hawk or falcon, and this image has often been linked to the funerary god Sokar. But is this the real reason for Sheshonq I deciding upon a silver, hawk-headed sarcophagus?

There were three main deities that took the form of a hawk or falcon – Sokar, Horus and Qebehsenuef, and any of these three deities could have been the role model for this sarcophagus. The god Sokar would have been appropriate because he was often considered to be the god of metalworkers, and the sarcophagus itself represents the apex of their abilities in this era. Perhaps the main reason for choosing this design, however, is that the popular symbolism of the era was of the infant Horus being suckled by his mother, Isis.

Fig 43. Sokar - Osiris.

But, during the twenty-first dynasty, the role of Isis was being represented by the high priestesses who were called Maakhah Tamar. If Sheshonq I [King Solomon] was a son of this influential line of Maakhah Tamar queens and priestesses, as the Bible indicates, then he would naturally have been represented as the Horus figure who was being nursed by his Isis-like mother.

One possible reason for the falcon-headed design of Sheshonq's [Solomon's] sarcophagus was, therefore, the famous and potent symbolism of Horus sitting upon the knee of Isis. The symbolism being generated here was, of course, repeated endlessly within the imagery of the Biblical New Testament and even Michelangelo's famous Pietà sculpture follows the same kind of symbolism. This same mother and child symbolism was represented in the different eras of Egyptian history by the following characters:

Fig 44.   Isis and Horus,
Madonna and Child.

VIII *Sheshonq*

Symbolism	Mother	Child
New Kingdom	Isis	Horus
United Monarchy	Maakhah Tamar	Solomon (as Horus)
New Testament	Mary	Jesus

Hiram Atif

If this falcon-headed burial at Tanis really was that of Sheshonq I, and if this pharaoh really was the Biblical King Solomon, then it would not be surprising to discover that King Solomon had inherited some bird-like attributes. The only link of this nature that I could find comes from the Koran, which says:

> Solomon said ... 'Know my people, we have been taught the tongue of birds and endowed with all good things. [K20]

It would seem that King Solomon could speak the language of the birds. But, to be honest, this is not a good enough explanation for the design of this falcon-headed sarcophagus; it would have been much more convincing if the owner of this coffin were directly associated with a falcon-god, like Sokar or Horus. In fact, that may be exactly what originally occurred, but in order for this to be so, then this cannot have been Sheshonq I's [King Solomon's] original sarcophagus. Since the mummy of Sheshonq I was obviously not in its intended tomb and had been re-interred in the tomb of Psusennes II at a later date, this possibility may not be too surprising.

The reason why Sheshonq I [King Solomon] may have used another family member's coffin is an interesting tale in itself, and it may shed some light on the true identity of the Masonic hero known as Hiram-Abif (Hiram Atif) 𓄿𓄿𓊪𓈖 .

As was demonstrated in the last chapter, the Biblical and Masonic architect known as Hiram Atif was actually the historical chief architect of Sheshonq I (or Psusennes II) who was called Haram Saf (Haram Atif). Since the historical version of his name has been inscribed in a number of locations around Thebes, Hiram Atif is known to have been a real historical character. Although there is no known tomb or mummy ascribed to Hiram Atif, the mummy that has been traditionally ascribed to the pharaoh Seqenenre Tao II seems to have met exactly the same death as the Masonic traditions mention in regard to Hiram Atif. It is entirely possible that this mummy from the Deir el Bahri cache has been mislabelled, and that these were really the remains of the chief architect rather than a pharaoh.

However, if Hiram Atif was laid to rest alongside all the great pharaohs and priests of the eighteenth dynasty, he must have been a rather important character, so who exactly was this chief architect of the Tanite kings? Why was his mummy discovered in Thebes? And why was he so famous that *his* name, rather than that of a famous pharaoh, has been revered in the Masonic world for nearly three thousand years? A tentative answer can be given to this question, and while this explanation may be based more on circumstantial evidence than fact, it is a scenario that would explain a great deal about the history of this era. The bare bones of the Masonic history of Hiram Atif are as follows:

Hiram was not simply a secular architect, he was also a high-ranking Masonic Architect; reputedly, he was one of the three people in the world who hold the true secrets of Masonry at any one time. However, while Hiram was working on the construction of the Temple of Solomon, three 'ruffians' tried to get him to divulge these secrets. For some reason that is not explained in the Masonic texts, all of these men were called Jubel. During the ensuing struggle with these people, Hiram Atif was killed by three blows to the head, thrown into a pit and covered with earth. Some of Hiram Atif's fellow Masons later found his body, and immediately ran back to tell King Solomon. The king was distraught at this murder, and ordered that Hiram's body be dug up and disposed of in a manner befitting his rank. [21]

This story is centered around the reign of King Solomon, and yet it appears to have a number of striking parallels with the murder of Prince Absalom, which has been covered in a previous chapter. Just to recap the details of Absalom's life and death, the story went as follows:

Prince Absalom was the son of King David. Having lost his sister-wife to his father, Absalom was exiled to Thebes where he formed a rebellion against the rule of his father in the north. After a pitched battle on the Great Plain, Absalom was killed by Joab, who thrust three spears (or clubs) into Absalom's heart. Absalom's body was then tossed into a pit and covered with rocks. Two messengers were immediately sent to King David, who was apparently distraught with grief at the news of his son's death. A large mausoleum was, or had been, made for Absalom.

While there are a number of minor points of difference between these two stories, there are also a great number of similarities, and so it is worth exploring some of these differences to see if they can be explained. The discussion points are as follows:

a. The Masonic story refers to King Solomon, whereas the Biblical version refers to King David. In actual fact, this may be more of an explanation than a problem. While King Solomon is credited with building the Temple of Jerusalem, the materials were assembled and the construction was actually started by King David. In addition, both the Biblical texts and the historical texts from Egypt indicate that there were two generations of Hiram Atifs, who were probably related to each other. Since there were two Hiram Atifs – perhaps a father and his son – who worked for two different kings, a slight confusion between the two is not so unexpected. Although the Biblical texts indicate that Hiram Atif was the younger of the two Hirams, the link with Prince Absalom means that it is likely that the Masonic hero was actually Hiram the elder, the 'King of Tyre'.

b. Hiram Atif was not, of course, from Tyre (Tchar) in Lebanon. As has been explained previously, this name actually refers to either the stone quarries in which this architect worked, or to the city of Tanis, which was known as Thar. In deciding the identity of Hiram Atif, we may therefore be looking for a prince or king of Tanis who was known as both a secular architect and a ritual Architect (Mason), and who was brutally killed. To decipher this riddle, we need look no further than Prince Absalom, who manages to fulfil all of these requirements.

Absalom was not only a Prince of Tanis, he was also the King of Tanis for a short while during his rebellion against his father, King David [Psusennes II]. In addition, the Kebra Nagast rather deliberately explains that King Solomon was an architect, and since Solomon was demonstrably a replacement prince for the murdered Prince Absalom, it is highly likely that Absalom was also an architect. Of course, the profession being alluded to here was as much Architect as architect, and so both Solomon and Absalom would have been Masons.

c. The three murderers of Hiram Atif were called the 'three Jubels', while in a similar fashion the eventual executioner of Prince Absalom was called Joab. In fact, this Biblical story has a greater affinity with the Masonic version than it might at first appear. The name 'Joab' was actually a military title meaning 'Commander of Ten Thousand'. Since King David had three military commanders on the field of battle when Prince Absalom was killed, it could be said that Absalom was actually killed by the 'three Joabs' – King David's three military commanders.

d. Both Hiram Atif and Prince Absalom were killed by three blows, which were delivered by the three Jubels (three Joabs). Both Masonic lore and the evidence from the mummy at Deir el Bahri indicate that these three blows were delivered to the head of Hiram Atif, while in contrast, the Biblical texts say that the three blows were to Absalom's heart.

While this may be a genuine difference between these texts, it is more likely that this was just a simple confusion of meanings. In Egyptian terms, the organ of thought and consciousness was the heart instead of the brain, and so a later translator may have confused these two terms. The Hebrew word being used here, *lebab* לבב, reflects this exact same confusion as, in addition to 'heart' it also means 'mind', 'knowledge', 'memory' and 'thought'. Remember that this same point of confusion also occurs in the Egyptian text known as the *Instructions of Amenemopet*, as mentioned in chapter VII, where the seat of knowledge was said to have been the heart.

e. Hiram Atif was prominently known in Masonic literature as the 'Son of the Widow', but Prince Absalom still had a father – King David – a fact that appears to nullify this comparison between Absalom and Hiram Atif. Actually, this may not be so. Absalom's mother was Maakhah Tamar I, whose role as chief wife was usurped by her own daughter, Maakhah Tamar II. It is likely that upon losing her status as chief wife, Maakhah Tamar I became known as the 'widow', because she was no longer able to obtain sexual access to the king.

The Biblical texts seem to confirm that this was the terminology that was being used in this era, when it mentions King David's concubines. Ten of David's concubines were made into guardians of the house (harem), and since this new position no longer gave them sexual access to the king, they were then known as widows. [B22]

This explanation is further supported by the story that was told to King David, of the fight between two brothers and the subsequent death of one and the exile of the other. The story was actually an allegorical tale concerning Absalom's fight with his 'brother' Amnon and his exile to Egypt [Thebes]. The interesting thing about this particular tale, however, was that the mother of these two brothers was pointedly said to have been a widow. The widow in question would have been an allusion to Maakhah Tamar I, who had been 'widowed' because her daughter, Maakhah Tamar II, had become the new chief wife of King David. This story confirms the fact that Absalom himself was known as the 'Son of a Widow'. [B23]

f. The Masonic texts indicate that Hiram Atif was a hero, while the Biblical texts indicate that Prince Absalom was a traitor to the realm. Again, this is less of a point of contention and more of a question of perspective – one man's terrorist is inevitably another man's freedom-fighter. Quite simply, the Bible was a book that was written by the scribes of King Solomon's court who were the victors in this particular battle, while the Masonic texts must have been penned by the supporters of Absalom.

g. The historian, Josephus, says that Hiram Atif's father was called Ur, a name that has already been linked to Absalom, who was called Uriah. [24]

h. The evidence seems to indicate that the Masonic Hiram was actually Hiram the elder, the 'King of Tyre', and so it may have been a 'son' of Absalom who finished off the construction of the Temple of Jerusalem during the reign of King Solomon. Since it was Solomon who inherited Absalom's position of prince regent, and since the Kebra Nagast pointedly states that King Solomon was the architect who supervised the construction of the Temple, it is not beyond the realms of possibility that Hiram the younger was actually King Solomon himself.

Likewise, both Josephus and the book of Chronicles state that it was King Solomon who made the brass artifacts for the Temple, including the 'brazen-sea'. Like most researchers, I initially took this to mean that Solomon had *commissioned* these items and that Hiram had fabricated them, but the texts actually say on several occasions that King Solomon *made* them. Being the Masonic Chief Architect (Grand Master), it is possible that King Solomon took all the credit for the Temple's construction, and he was also considered to be its secular architect.

For whatever reason, when it came to the construction of the Temple, it would appear that both of these Architects (architects), Absalom and Solomon, were called Hiram.

All in all, a good case can be made to show that the Masonic Hiram Atif was actually Hiram the elder – a prince or king of Tanis and chief architect to the United Monarchy – and that he was also known in the Biblical texts as Prince Absalom, the favourite son of King David who was killed while organising a military coup against his father. While the name Hiram Atif does not equate in any way to the names that were held by Absalom or Ankhefenmut (Absalom's possible Egyptian title), it is known that the princes of Egypt picked up strings of titles during their lives. It is not beyond the realms of possibility that Absalom was given the new title of Hiram Atif either while he was exiled in Thebes or perhaps when he was initiated into the craft. If this was so, then Masonic history can be suitably amended to reflect the new realities that this story provides.

Hiram Atif was a famous individual from his very birth, as he was the elder prince and heir apparent of King David [Psusennes II], who was the king of Lower Egypt and Judaea. After a domestic tiff with his father over the 'rape' of Absalom's sister-wife and the resulting death of Absalom's 'brother' Amnon, Hiram Atif was exiled to his mother's province of Thebes. Being a prince, he would have held many of the high offices of the priesthood, and this quite possibly included the title of Chief Architect. The secrets of astronomy, alchemy, geometry and mathematics were not simply the domain of artisans and officials, they were a part of the mystique and power of the monarchy in this era. Knowledge is power and, as the verse from the Kebra Nagast in the last chapter has shown, King Solomon in particular boasted of his great Masonic knowledge. No doubt Solomon was simply following in his elder brother's (Absalom's) footsteps.

Although Absalom was the prince regent who would have taken the throne upon the death of King David [Psusennes II], Absalom decided to organise a rebellion against his father; and one might suspect that he was being urged on and backed militarily by the Theban priesthood, who would have done anything to diminish the power of Tanis and Jerusalem. The opposing armies met on the Great Plain, and during the ensuing battle Absalom was slain by three blows to the head, which were delivered by King David's three military commanders, who all held the title of 'Joab'. Absalom's body was thrown into a pit and not discovered for some days, which is why his mummy, discovered at Deir el Bahri, is semi-decomposed. Although King David was 'distressed' by his son's death, he was not about to have a traitor to the realm buried in his mausoleum at Tanis, so Absalom's name was cut out of the chamber that had been set aside for him and his body was sent back to Thebes for burial, which is where it was eventually discovered.

Since Absalom was the heir apparent to the throne of Egypt, an ornate silver sarcophagus had already been commissioned for him; but after his precipitous fall from grace and eventual execution, his mummy had been sent back to Thebes in a plain wooden coffin. This left the artisans at Tanis with two magnificent unused sarcophagi (an inner and an outer one), which were eventually used by King Solomon, who was the younger brother of Absalom. But the title that Absalom had been given while he lived in Thebes was Hiram Atif, which means 'Horus is my father', and so these two magnificent sarcophagi belonging to Absalom had been fabricated in the image of Horus, the falcon-headed god of Egypt. In truth, it was Absalom who had been the 'Falcon of Sheba', but it was to be King Solomon who eventually inherited that title.

Fig 45.   Historical name of the Masonic Hiram Abif (Hiram Atif).

Queen of the South

As we saw in an earlier chapter, the original homeland of the Queen of Sheba was most probably Thebes and Upper Egypt. It was to be the much later New Testament gospel writers who reinforced this argument with the assertion that the Queen of Sheba was known as the 'Queen of the South':

> The queen of the south (Sheba) shall rise up in the judgment with the men of this generation, and condemn them: for she came from the utmost parts of the earth to hear the wisdom of Solomon. [B25]

Although these princesses were married to both King David and King Solomon, who were Lower Egyptian monarchs, the line of Maakhah Tamar queens are likely to have been of Theban extract. As such, the Theban aristocracy would have looked towards these queens in times of adversity, just as Spain tried to influence Catherine of Aragon, the Spanish first wife of King Henry VIII. The Koran tends to support this hypothesis, when it says of the Queen of Sheba:

> The Queen of Sheba said '... I have received a message ... from Solomon. (it reads) '... Do not exalt yourselves above me, but come to me in all submission'. [K26]

> (Solomon said to the envoy from Sheba) 'Go back to your people: we will march against them with forces they cannot oppose, and drive them from their land humbled and condemned.' [K27]

While the Koranical texts may indulge themselves in a piece of bravado, the quotes do succeed in throwing a very different light on the visit by the Queen of Sheba to the court of King Solomon. The Koran indicates that King Solomon [Sheshonq I] was in a position to threaten the land of Sheba, and these same texts also infer that the treasures that were brought to Solomon were actually a tribute; which was intended to prevent Solomon's attack on the lands that were governed by the Queen of Sheba.

It would seem that the famous journey by the Queen of Sheba to Jerusalem was not simply a trade mission, nor was it a pilgrimage to pay homage to the great 'king of Judaea'; it was primarily a peace mission that secured an uneasy truce between these two kingdoms. The fact that the Queen of Sheba was sending such a vast tribute to King Solomon indicates that the Judaean king was firmly in control of this province and could manipulate the territories that were governed by the Queen of Sheba at will. It also indicates that these two countries must have been neighbours of each other, which would exclude any notion of the Queen of Sheba being from Ethiopia or Yemen as it is unlikely that Judaean sovereignty or influence could have extended that far. Once again, the finger must point towards Thebes as being the land from which the Queen of Sheba originated, and therefore this diplomatic posturing was actually occurring between the Tanis-Jerusalem empire and Thebes.

A similar story to this, which once again shows that relations between the Queen of Sheba's kingdom and the United Monarchy were not always amicable, is to be found in the Biblical texts. This story goes back to the reign of King David and it gives an addendum to the story of Absalom, the son of David [Psusennes II]. Prince Absalom had challenged the rule of King David and been killed for this presumption, but the historian Josephus then goes on to say that David's rule was further threatened by someone known as 'Sheba'.

To be honest, I think that this may well be a simple repetition of the story of the rebellion by Absalom, who may have been called 'Sheba' in this version in honour of his father. Just as Maakhah Tamar II was called the Queen of Sheba, because she was the wife of King David (King Sheba), Absalom was similarly known as the Prince of Sheba. A possible confirmation of this is that the father of this rebel called Sheba was known as Bicheri (Bakkari) בכרי or Bakar בכר, and exactly the same word means hawk or falcon in Egyptian 𓂝𓏤𓃀𓅃 . As has already been shown, the Masonic name of Absalom was Hiram Atif, which means 'Horus is my Father'.

Absalom, as we have already seen, took refuge in the lands of his mother, Maakhah Tamar I, who was of Theban descent. The fact that this story of the rebel called 'Sheba' could have been speaking about the rebellion of Absalom once more, seems to be confirmed as this story develops:

> Now as (David) pursued Sheba through all the country ... one told him he was in a strong city called Abel-Beth-Maakhah. Now there was a woman of small account, and yet both wise and intelligent, who seeing her native city (besieged), ascended the wall ... and called for Joab (the military commander)... [28]

The Biblical texts do contain some interesting stories, and here they have preserved a wonderful piece of evidence pertaining to the name 'Sheba'. The story is of a prince called Sheba who tries to overthrow King David [Psusennes II] and who is chased by David's army to a town called Abel-Beth-Maakhah אבל-בית-מעכה, according to Josephus, meaning 'Princess of Maakhah' – or Abel *and* Beth-Maakhah in the Biblical account – which has been translated as the 'House of Maakhah'.

Here, we not only find a direct correlation between the names 'Sheba' and 'Maakhah' (Tamar), but it can also be seen that this woman was a princess or perhaps the monarch of this city. The latter is possibly confirmed by the fact that the negotiator of the ensuing siege of this city was a woman. Although the text tries to belittle this woman rather than saying that she was its monarch, it is unlikely that a female would have been mentioned as being the chief negotiator if she had not been a very influential character within this city's hierarchy.

What the Biblical-type texts have preserved here is an account of a queen whose House, or family name, was called Maakhah. This same queen then gave shelter to a prince who challenged the rule of King David [Psusennes II] and who was called Sheba. If these two individuals were related, as seems likely, then this queen would have been both Queen Maakhah and also the Queen of Sheba. Once more, it would seem likely that the real Queen of Sheba was one of the wives of King David – Maakhah Tamar II.

Bearing in mind the turbulent relations that seem to have existed between the land ruled by the Queen of Sheba and the kings of the United Monarchy, and the fact that Solomon was receiving tribute from this queen, it is quite obvious that these two nations were in fairly close proximity to each other. Not only were the kingdoms of Ethiopia and Saba too far from Judaea to have posed a threat to Judaean sovereignty, it is extremely unlikely that either Ethiopia or Saba were a political force of any kind during this era. Even if they had some kind of political cohesiveness, which historians very much doubt, their politics were entirely remote from that of

Egypt or the Levant. For the threat of war to exist between two nations, there has to be a cause for the friction between the two combatants – reasons that normally revolve around the thorny issues of theology, geography or economics – and yet there seems to be no evidence of any such frictions between Judaea and these African or Arabian principalities. The two nations that did have a history of political unrest and feuding, however, were Upper and Lower Egypt – but since the monarch of Lower Egypt now controlled all of Palestine, this province was now included in these perennial disputes.

The dispute between Judaea and the kingdom of the Queen of Sheba was essentially a continuation of the constant bickering between Lower and Upper Egypt, and so these brief extracts from the Koran and Josephus confirm once more that the Israelite kings were also Tanite pharaohs. But these new verses also contain a slight twist in the developing story, for if Tanis was posturing militarily against Thebes, then the equivalent implication is that King Solomon was threatening his mother in Thebes. While this might initially seem to be improbable, this possibility is easily explained in terms of the complexities of dynastic alliances, where close relatives of the royal families have often found themselves on opposite sides in a political dispute. An example might be the fate of George V of Britain, who found his country at war against his immediate relatives in Germany from 1914 to 1918, and had to change his name from Saxe-Coburg-Gotha to Windsor, in order to appear a little more British.

One of the prime reasons for royal dynastic alliances was to stabilise the relationships between nations; but despite this good intention, history is still littered with royal brothers, cousins, sons and fathers who have been warring against one another. The fact that the Queen of Sheba was Solomon's mother would not necessarily have prevented diplomatic posturing and military threats between the aristocracies in Tanis and Thebes.

Mother

There is one other aspect of this relationship that has not been covered in quite enough detail up until now. If the Queen of Sheba were Maakhah Tamar II, the mother of King Solomon, this relationship would have had one other titillating implication – Maakhah Tamar II would have had one of the strangest married lives on record. According to this new history of the United Monarchy, she was:

a. The daughter of King David, who was raped by her 'half-brother' Amnon.

b. The husband of Prince Absalom, her full-brother.

c. The widow of Absalom, who married her father, King David.

d. The widow of King David, who 'married' her son, King Solomon.

At first I doubted that this was physically possible, as it would have made her too old to bear a child for Solomon, but a quick estimate of the generations proved that this scenario was entirely feasible. The first thing to note is that Maakhah Tamar II was still a teenager when she married King David. Maakhah Tamar II was a daughter of King David and so she was separated from him by a whole generation. This is also clear from the deathbed scene, where King David was dying of old age but Maakhah Tamar II was still a youthful wife. It would seem that King Solomon was the elder son of a very late union between Maakhah Tamar II and King David, and so Solomon would have been yet another generation removed from his father. A possible chronology of Maakhah Tamar II's life might, therefore, look something like this:

(In each case, the 'age' refers to the age of Queen Maakhah Tamar II.)

a. Maakhah Tamar II had been elected as both God's Wife and the Royal Virgin. Age 9-14.

b. She married her brother Absalom as a teenage bride. Age 14.

c. She had at least one child by Absalom. Age 16.

d. Absalom was killed by his father, King David. Age 17.

e. She married King David and had their eldest child, Solomon. Age 18.

f. She had at least another three children by King David. Age 24.

g. After the death of King David, Solomon was crowned king at the age of fourteen. Queen Maakhah Tamar II then returned to her mother's homeland in Upper Egypt. Age 32.

h. Solomon was married and had his first son by his chief wife, Naamah, at the age of fifteen. Age 33.

i. In the seventh year of the reign of King Solomon, Maakhah Tamar II (the Queen of Sheba) travelled back to Jerusalem see her eldest son. King Solomon's first son, Rehoboam, was six years old. Age 39.

j.   Maakhah Tamar II had conjugal relations with her son and bears another child, Menelek. Tamar then returns to Egypt. Age 40.

k.   At the age of twenty-two, Maakhah Tamar II's son, Menelek, travelled to Jerusalem to be anointed by King Solomon, his father. Solomon would have been forty-three years old at this time and have reigned for twenty-nine years, so Menelek's visit was planned to coincide with Solomon's jubilee. Age 61.

The Kebra Nagast indicates that when the Queen of Sheba visited King Solomon, the king's first son, Rehoboam, was six years old and it was the seventh year of Solomon's reign – the inference of these dates being that the marriage and coronation of the youthful King Solomon were coincident; a dual ceremony that was common practice in this era. Since it was Bathsheba (Maakhah Tamar II) who had manipulated Solomon onto the throne of Israel (and Lower Egypt), she must have been present at the coronation of King Solomon, but she most probably left Jerusalem for Egypt just after the coronation as she disappears from the Biblical account at this point.

By the time that Maakhah Tamar II, the Queen of Sheba, travelled back to Jerusalem to see her son, he could have been a strapping 21, while she may have still been in her prime, aged 39. The purpose of the visit was most probably just as the Koran records it. It was not simply a trip to see the achievements of her famously wise son; instead, this queen was bringing a fortune in spices and gold for the coffers of King Solomon's treasury – with most of the gold probably originating from King Solomon's Mines (the Valley of the Kings). The Koran indicates that this visit was the result of a diplomatic dispute between these two nations, in which case the purpose of the Queen of Sheba's visit was to bring a fortune in tribute to placate the Tanis regime, and perhaps to sign a peace treaty between the two nations.

The royal diplomacy obviously went well, and perhaps it was suggested that this new union between Upper and Lower Egypt should be cemented in rather more tangible terms. Had such an oedipal union taken place in the liberal social climate of the Egypto-Judaean royal court, Maakhah Tamar II could easily have been capable of bearing a child for her son, King Solomon. Moreover, in having such an illustrious mother, such a child may have taken royal precedence over the other children of Solomon. Would such a union have been allowed in these times? Much as we like to think of our era as being enlightened and decadently liberal, our attitudes are surprisingly Victorian in comparison with those acceptable in the Egypto-Judaean royal court of the tenth century BC:

> Ritual prostitution of both sexes was rampant, and the variety of evil
> practices is attested by the multiplicity of names employed to designate
> these professions. The cinaedus (homosexual) formed a recognised guild
> in Canaanite temples ... Asherah was represented as a beautiful naked
> prostitute, called 'Holiness' in both Canaan and Egypt ... (while) Anath
> and Astarte are called 'the great goddesses that conceive but do not
> bear'. [29]

The author of this great tome on Israelite history, Louis Finkelstein, was a
respected Jewish historian; and while he was happy to write about Canaan
and Egypt in this manner, I think he may have thought twice had he
realised that the Egyptian and Judaean royal courts were one and the same.
But even within the Biblical texts it can be seen that such practices were not
exclusively Egypto-Canaanite, and the court of King Solomon seems to
have had very similar tendencies. Think of the furore that would be
generated today if a member of the modern royal family had a public
mistress or two. According to the Bible, such things were a mere trifle a few
millennia ago and it is recorded that King Solomon had rather more than a
mistress or two:

> But King Solomon loved many strange women, together with the daughter
> of Pharaoh, women of the Moabites, Ammonites, Edomites, Zidonians, and
> Hittites ... And he had seven hundred wives, princesses, and three hundred
> concubines: and his wives turned away his heart. [B31]

Even allowing for the normal Biblical exaggeration, it is clear that King
Solomon kept a substantial harem. Since his brother's (Absalom's) entry
into their father's harem was considered to be a treasonable offence, as has
already been explained, it is also clear that this harem was for the king's
personal consumption alone. Bearing in mind the variety of intermarriages
that have already been demonstrated (and consummated) within the royal
court of King Solomon, this union between Solomon and Sheba – between
mother and son – would have barely raised an eyebrow among the court
officials. Besides, as has already been hinted, the court officials may have
even urged such a union in order to seal the new diplomatic ties between
Upper and Lower Egypt with a common son.

But, in the eyes of the Biblical scribes who were compiling these
accounts in later generations, such shenanigans would have appeared
desperately immoral. The problem they faced was; what should they do
about it? Both King David and King Solomon (Psusennes II and
Sheshonq I) were considered to be the two most important 'Judaic'

individuals in the whole of this millennia, so there was no way they could have been left out of the story. On the other hand, there was also no way that the entire truth could be shown to the Judaic population, especially in the more restrictive moral environment that pervaded the post-exilic age in which these texts were being revised and edited.

Luckily, the problem was easily solvable by the simple tactic of using different portions of a person's title in different sections of the Bible. If the scribe did not wish to divulge that King David not only killed his son but also took his wife for his own, the technique was to call the son Absalom, and the character who had his wife taken, Uriah. As long as it is not mentioned anywhere in the Bible that this person was actually called Absalom-Uriah, then nobody need know that David married his own daughter. In much the same fashion, not saying that another famous character was actually called Maakhah-Tamar-Sheba, the pharaoh's daughter, prevented anyone from finding out that King Solomon had conjugal relations with his mother.

Separate the names and events, and the whole thing can be smoothed over beautifully. But just in case, the clergy then insist that this was all the word of god and anyone who said otherwise would be burned at the stake; which was a fairly effective way of stifling any debate and dissent that may uncover the truth.

The final point to make about the life of the Queen of Sheba is that she appears to have ended her life back in Thebes, along with her son Menelek [David II]. If this was so, then it is also likely that she would have been buried in Thebes and honoured as a great Queen of the South. As mentioned in the last chapter, the titles that were inscribed upon the sarcophagus of Maakare Mu-Tamhat, which was discovered at Deir el-Bahri, included that of 'King's Daughter' and 'First Wife'. This would indicate that this coffin belonged to Maakhah Tamar II, rather than Maakhah Tamar I, as the former was both the daughter and daughter-wife of King David [Psusennes II]. If this was so, then this sarcophagus must also be that of the legendary Queen of Sheba, and so this unique piece of Biblical history resides today in the Cairo museum.

Shishak

There was one more thing that the scribes needed to cover up. Those who are well versed in the events of this era may have been wondering how the campaigns of the Egyptian pharaoh Sheshonq I fit into the arguments being championed in this book. Despite my equating King Solomon with

Sheshonq I, it is an undoubted fact that the pharaoh Sheshonq I is already an established figure within the Biblical texts where he is called Shishak שׁישׁק – the two names are exactly the same in the Hebrew spelling. So, if this pharaoh called Shishak (Sheshonq) was in the Biblical story all along, and if Shishak was said to have robbed the Temple of Solomon, then how can King Solomon be Sheshonq I?

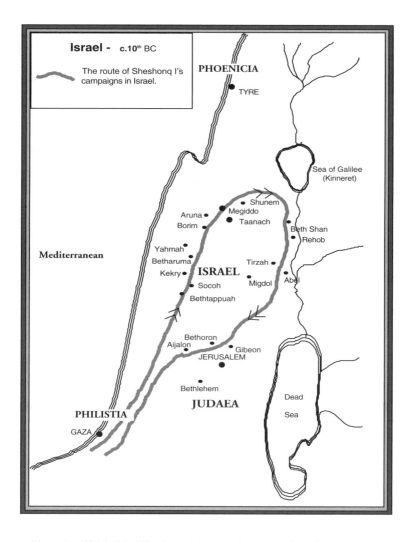

Fig 46. Shishak's (Sheshonq's) campaigns into Israel.

VIII *Sheshonq*

The campaigns of the pharaoh Shishak (Sheshonq I) are reasonably well attested to, in both the historical and the Biblical record. Sheshonq led a major campaign up and across much of Israel, conquering many of the towns in this province. In addition, the Bible also reports that Sheshonq conquered Jerusalem and took away the treasure of the Temple. But this was, of course, the Temple of Solomon; so how can one reconcile the story of King Solomon (Sheshonq) robbing his own temple? This may initially appear to be a major flaw in this whole thesis, one that proves it all to be a complete fabrication. But in actual fact, instead of the Sheshonq-Solomon correlation being a problem, it actually explains a perennial problem with the classical history of the region.

The standard theory is that the pharaoh Sheshonq I was the Biblical Shishak, which is all very reasonable at this stage. However, as David Rohl pointed out in *A Test of Time*, the campaign records of Sheshonq I show that this military invasion was primarily conducted in northern Israel rather than Judaea, and that Jerusalem was not touched. But, according to the Biblical account, the northern province of Israel was supposed to have been an ally of the pharaoh Shishak-Sheshonq, under the leadership of the rebel, King Jeroboam. According to the Bible, it was King Rehoboam, the king of Judaea, who was being threatened in his capital city of Jerusalem by this pharaoh, not King Jeroboam.

There seems to be no rational explanation for the historical evidence showing that King Sheshonq I skirted the lands of Judaea and attacked his ally in the north. The two accounts seem to be completely at odds with each other, a fact that seems to undermine the whole Shishak-Sheshonq correlation. To overcome this anomaly, which was one among several perceived anomalies, Rohl attempted to show that Ramesses II (Shessy) was the true invader of Israel and the true equivalent of the Biblical pharaoh called Shishak. But Rohl's explanation is unwieldy and unwarranted; the chronology of this era is not that far adrift, in my opinion, that three centuries need deleting from the Third Intermediate Period, as this alternative scenario requires.

The simple answer to this anomaly is, in fact, to say that Sheshonq I *was* Shishak, who *was* in turn King Solomon, as we shall see. But how, then, can a recently deceased pharaoh called Sheshonq-Shishak-Solomon be seen to be attacking his own city of Jerusalem? As is usual, the explanation for this seeming impossibility is not difficult, just lateral.

Towards the end of his reign, King Solomon was at the height of his powers, with tributes and princesses being donated from all the surrounding provinces, and his magnificent Temple and Palace being fitted out with all their bronze and gold ornamentation. Then, according to the

Bible, Solomon suddenly 'dies' and his son Rehoboam reigns in his stead. But the Biblical text is lacking detail at this point.

Conversely, the account of the death of King David is extremely detailed, and every intimate feature of his death is explained; including the attempt to get a fresh young virgin called Abishag אבישג to revive the ailing king with a bit of old-fashioned rumpy-pumpy. The name Abishag was derived from *ab*, meaning 'father' and *shag* meaning 'ravish'; and so the name Abishag means 'to shag my father', which is no doubt the origin of this slang word.

The Bible seems to be quite emphatic about the great age and infirmity of the dying King David, and if the theory that David was Psusennes II is to retain any credibility, the body of Psusennes II would have to be that of an old man.* Luckily for the theory, that is exactly what was found when the mummy of Psusennes II was finally unwrapped back in the 1940s. Not only has the advanced age of this monarch been remarked upon by several historians, but Kenneth Kitchen himself argues for an age of 87 years; and this is just the sort of age that the touching Biblical deathbed scene infers. [32]

In complete contrast to the vivid deathbed scene of King David, and despite King Solomon being the most famous of all the Judaean monarchs, absolutely no details of Solomon's death are given whatsoever. Instead, the text just refers us to the books of 'Solomon, Ahijah and Nathan', which the Bible no longer contains, even within the Apocrypha.

I think that this unremarked 'death' of King Solomon is rather unusual and too convenient to be true, and that the truth of the matter is that the king actually 'retired' from Judaea. Having done so, he either allowed his son, Rehoboam, to rule in a co-regency or allowed him to be the regional governor for Judaea. As we shall see later, it may well have been at this same time that his other son, Menelek, was anointed as king of Upper Egypt. Despite this anointing of his sons, Rehoboam and Menelek, King Solomon [Sheshonq] was alive and well and ruling his heartlands of Lower Egypt from Tanis.

The policy of a co-regency was well established within the Egyptian royalty; indeed, it was probably an absolute necessity. The pharaohs often had many wives, yet not all of these wives had the same status, and so a much younger son born of a very high-status wife might have a much stronger claim to the throne than an older son from a lesser wife. While such a policy was devised to ensure that the pure bloodline

---

* The mummy is traditionally explained as being that of Psusennes I, but the Biblical chronology confirms that these were instead the remains of Psusennes II.

flowed into the next royal generation, it also gave rise to bitter rivalries between the many princes.

This is exactly the same scenario that is so graphically illustrated in the Biblical story of the Old Testament Joseph. Of the twelve sons of Jacob, it was a younger son, Joseph, who was to inherit Jacob's position and this caused sufficient jealousy amongst the other brothers that they wished to kill him. It matters not that this story is part of an old Egyptian tale and that much of it may be apocryphal; the point is that this scenario was believed to be entirely possible. The solution to these rivalries, which if unchecked could well result in a civil war erupting, was to give the favourite son a 'trial run' at the monarchy in a co-regency with the king. This not only gave the prince valuable experience, under the guidance of the king, it also graphically displayed to the public exactly who was going to be the next king. There was to be little disputing the legitimacy of the next king because he was already king – appointed into a co-regency by the reigning monarch, no less.

Such a scenario would easily explain the confusion that seems to exist in the Bible over this 'invasion' of Israel by the pharaoh called Shishak [Sheshonq I]. Although the Bible states that this 'invasion' by Shishak occurred during the fifth year of the reign of King Rehoboam, the son of Solomon, this is by no means acceptable to all commentators. Even without the co-regency explanation just given, several classical authors question the Bible's accuracy in this matter:

> According to (the book of) Kings, (Sheshonq's invasion) happened in Rehoboam's fifth year, but the chronology at this point is unclear, and it has been suggested that the event may have taken place late in Solomon's reign. [33]

While they may seem at odds with each other, it is entirely possible that both the Bible and the Jewish historians are correct in their assumptions. If there had been a co-regency between King Solomon and King Rehoboam, then the 'invasion' of King Solomon-Sheshonq into Israel could well have taken place both during Solomon-Sheshonq's last years and also during the fifth year of King Rehoboam's co-regency. This, I believe, is what the Bible was trying to explain happened to King Rehoboam.

King Solomon had appointed his son, Rehoboam, as co-regent in Jerusalem and then he himself retired back to Lower Egypt, perhaps to observe how much wisdom his son had acquired from his illustrious father. The reason for King Solomon (Shishak-Sheshonq) then 'invading' his own lands of Judaea and Israel, as the Bible maintains, is as follows:

VIII *Sheshonq*

As soon as Solomon had retired to Tanis, the exiled Prince Jeroboam, who was mentioned in chapter VI, left Egypt at this point in time and travelled back to Jerusalem. Jeroboam probably saw that the possibility of usurping the position of King Rehoboam was a much more promising prospect, now that King Solomon had left Judaea. As expected, Jeroboam immediately challenged King Rehoboam over his intended policies in Israel and in return, Rehoboam indicated that he was going to be even tougher than his father had been:

> You shall say unto them, My little finger shall be thicker than my father's penis ... whereas my father laid upon you a heavy yoke, I will add to your yoke. My father chastised you with whips, but I will chastise you with scorpions. [B34]

In other words, Rehoboam was going to be twice the man that his father Solomon was. His elder counsellors advised caution, but the novice King Rehoboam and his cadre of young-bloods rejected their entreaties with much verbal abuse. It may have been brave fighting-talk, but the people were appalled by the prospect of even tougher taxes and workloads. The final straw for the people of Israel – those in the north of the province who supported Prince Jeroboam – was probably that:

> When Rehoboam had established the kingdom, and had strengthened himself, he forsook the law of the Lord, and all Israel with him. [B35]

It is not entirely clear if this means that Rehoboam had forsaken the word of god, or instead forsaken the word of the 'Lord' his father. On balance, this verse probably refers to god, as there was nothing worse in Israelite eyes than a monarch who disregarded the law of Moses. Accordingly, the northern tribes of Israel backed the Israelite traditionalist, Prince Jeroboam, while only the provinces of Judaea and Benjamin supported the overtly Egyptian traditions that King Solomon and possibly King Rehoboam had lapsed into (with the assistance of their Theban wives). Here we see the point at which the northern Israelite traditions became increasingly more Jewish, while the Egyptian Hyksos traditions that had been observed in the south of Palestine became less and less influential.

Eventually, King Rehoboam sent an emissary to talk to the northerners in Israel, but they stoned him to death and Rehoboam had to flee Jerusalem by chariot. Unfortunately for King Solomon, who was trying to enjoy his retirement in Tanis, it would appear that neither of his sons (if that is what Jeroboam was) had absorbed much of his wisdom, and eventually the whole province subsided into factional fighting once more. In response to this worsening situation, King Rehoboam mustered a huge army to crush the rebels in the north, but he was cautioned against this action by 'god':

> But the word of the Lord came to Shemaiah the man of god, saying. Speak unto Rehoboam ... You shall not go up, nor fight against your brethren: return every man to his house. [B36]

Again the question has to be asked: Was this really 'god' who had just cautioned King Rehoboam against military action, or was this in reality the Lord Solomon (Sheshonq I)? As a pharaoh of Egypt, King Solomon would have been regarded as a son of god or perhaps even a god in his own right, and so this time it seems much more likely that this verse was speaking about King Solomon. In reality, it was the mighty pharaoh in Tanis who was telling his newly appointed co-regent son not to start a civil war in Palestine. Seemingly as confirmation of this, the intermediary with this 'Lord' was called Shemaiah שמעיהו, who was a brother of King Solomon.

Following this warning from 'god', King Rehoboam of Judaea immediately started to fortify all his towns and to stockpile provisions. But why? He was already confident enough to threaten Jeroboam in Israel so why, after hearing 'gods' advice, did he become so afraid? Again, the only logical answer was that this warning actually came from his father, King Solomon, and perhaps the warning came along with a veiled threat to dissolve the co-regency and liquidate yet another wayward royal son if he did not behave. Accordingly, right on cue, the very next thing to happen in these Biblical texts was the invasion of Judaea by the Egyptian pharaoh Shishak:

> And it came to pass that in the fifth year of king Rehoboam, Shishak king of Egypt came up against Jerusalem, because they had transgressed against the Lord. [B37]

Under the circumstances, the 'Lord' who had just been transgressed against was probably not 'god'; instead, it just has to be King Solomon-Sheshonq, and therefore this invasion of Judaea was also organised by King Solomon-Sheshonq, the father of King Rehoboam. Once more, the father was faced with a wayward son; once more, the provinces of Israel and Judaea faced the threat of civil war; once more, Egypt faced the prospect of having an unruly neighbour on its doorstep; once more, an Egypto-Judaean king had to punish his own son.

VIII   *Sheshonq*

Perhaps, more importantly, King Solomon-Sheshonq also risked losing all that he had worked for over the many years of his reign. He had striven to raise Israel out of its perennial position as a downtrodden backwater and it seems that he may have given it a fine temple in its capital city, Jerusalem. It might not have been quite the equal of the mighty stone temples in Heliopolis and Thebes, but it was nevertheless an expensively ornamented cathedral, with a lofty interior of cedar pillars, and its accompanying palace was similarly known as the 'Forest of Lebanon'. The last thing that King Solomon wanted was for all that time and expense to be wasted on a couple of squabbling children. To prevent this happening, he simply marched his army into Judaea and demanded obeisance:

> And when the Lord saw that they humbled themselves, the word of the Lord came to Shemaiah, saying, They have humbled themselves; therefore I will not destroy them, but I will grant them some deliverance; and my wrath shall not be poured out upon Jerusalem by the hand of Shishak. Nevertheless they shall be his servants; that they may know my service, and the service of the kingdoms of the countries.
>
> So Shishak king of Egypt came up against Jerusalem, and took away the treasures of the house of the lord, and the treasures of the king's house; he took all: he carried away also the shields of gold which Solomon had made. [B38]

The Bible blames this attack on Jerusalem by Shishak on the transgressions by the Israelites against their 'Lord' (god), and then goes on to say that the people had to humble themselves before this 'Lord' (god) in order to prevent the attack by this Egyptian pharaoh. In its own peculiar and convoluted style, the Bible is simply saying that the people of Judaea had to humble themselves before the pharaoh to prevent the attack – in other words, the 'Lord' being mentioned was actually the pharaoh, Sheshonq I. Note also that it was Shemaiah, the brother of King Solomon, who was again the intermediary for the 'Lord' (Solomon-Sheshonq).

So could this reference to the pharaoh Shishak entering Jerusalem also be a reference to the King Solomon of Israel? I think that if you look at these problems from the perspective of King Solomon, the Egyptian pharaoh who was living in semi-retirement in Lower Egypt, the verses make every sense. Try reading these extracts again, replacing 'Shishak' with 'Solomon'.

Note that Jerusalem was apparently neither besieged nor sacked. Note also that the Temple was not burned to the ground or even desecrated by these 'foreigners' from Egypt. Unlike the assaults on Jerusalem by the Romans and the Persians – which resulted in long sieges, bloody conflicts and the destruction of the Temple – the pharaoh Shishak simply walked in, said "Can I have all your (my) treasures, please?", and left again.

Historians will say that Shishak was simply bought off with this heavy tribute in gold, which was a commonplace event in ancient times to prevent the destruction of a town. But this process of giving tribute was normally arranged while the enemy stayed firmly outside the city walls; to ask a potential enemy in through the city gate, to personally hand over tribute, would have been folly in the extreme. But, according to the historian Josephus, this is exactly what happened in Jerusalem:

> (Shishak) took the strongest cities of Rehoboam's kingdom without fighting ... he came last of all to Jerusalem ... So when Shishak had taken the city without fighting, because Rehoboam was afraid and <u>received him into it</u> ... he emptied the treasures of god ... and left nothing behind him. [139]

Fig 47. The campaigns of Shishak, from the Bubastite Gate, Karnak.

It would seem that Shishak was not simply bought off with tribute, as is often assumed; instead, he conquered and entered the city of Jerusalem without firing so much as an arrow, and simply confiscated all the temple treasure. While it is difficult to explain how an enemy Egyptian pharaoh could have achieved this, it is much easier to explain how King Solomon – who was still the reigning monarch of Israel and Judaea (and Egypt) – could have had the authority to command that the gates of the city be opened to him.

It is likely that Solomon [Sheshonq-Shishak] was not about to leave all the fabulously expensive artifacts, which he had commissioned himself for the Temple of Jerusalem, to be destroyed or sold off by his wayward princes. This was neither a siege nor a campaign; Solomon-Sheshonq simply used his authority, as the incumbent king of the Egypto-Judaean empire, to retrieve his own treasures and take them back to Egypt for safekeeping. The Temple was left untouched, of course, because it was still Solomon's pride and joy, despite all these power struggles and bickering.

Not only does this explanation show how the Biblical Shishak can still be King Solomon, without any implied contradictions, it also explains why the Biblical and historical accounts of this campaign differ so much. The explanations for this are as follows:

a. The historical campaigns of Sheshonq I, as listed upon the Bubastite Gate at Karnak, are actually the records of the early campaigns by King David-Psusennes, which resulted in Israel being conquered in the first place. The reason for these campaigns being in Israel, rather than Judaea, is that Judaea was already an ally of Tanis. King David-Psusennes' right to rule in Judaea was not in dispute, and the campaign in Palestine was all about trying to usurp the northern Israelite kingdom of King Saul.

The account of this campaign, as recorded at Karnak, mentions Sheshonq I rather than Psusennes II because the latter monarch did not have sufficient control over Thebes to record his expedition into Palestine. This prerogative was left to the later Sheshonq I, and as well as recording these events he also took the liberty of usurping his father's triumphs.

b. The Biblical account of a campaign by Shishak [Solomon] against Judaea and Jerusalem does not appear in the records at Karnak, as this was not a part of the original campaign in Israel. The Jerusalem event occurred during the reign of Shishak [Solomon] and it was just a domestic incident involving a father reprimanding his wayward son. The people of Jerusalem may have seen this incident as a major international crisis, whereas the officials in Lower Egypt probably regarded it with the same avid interest as one reserves for swatting an annoying fly!

c. The assertion that Prince Jeroboam was an ally of Shishak is a red herring. The Biblical account actually infers that Jeroboam fled to Thebes, not Tanis, and so this prince was never an ally of Shishak [Solomon].

Rather than the Biblical account of Shishak [Solomon] attacking his own city of Jerusalem being a problem for this new, revised history of this era, it actually explains a great deal about the politics that underpinned the United Monarchy. In addition, this same reasoning may also explain the peculiar funerary arrangements that were made in Tanis for King Sheshonq I.

One of the reasons for the orthodox view – that the falcon sarcophagus at Tanis belonged to the ephemeral Sheshonq II – was the hurried and simplistic nature of its interment. The sarcophagus was laid in the vestibule of King David-Psusennes' tomb with very little in the way of burial goods, which would tend to suggest that these were the mortal remains of an inferior and ineffectual pharaoh who could not afford to construct his own sepulchre. While this logic may be entirely reasonable under normal circumstances, it does not explain why this same ineffectual pharaoh could have afforded the rich craftsmanship of this solid silver, falcon-headed coffin. It also does not take into account the unique reign of Sheshonq I.

This particular pharaoh was not simply the monarch of Upper and Lower Egypt; it can now be seen that he was also King Solomon of Judaea, and according to the Biblical perspective he appears to have spent a lot of his reign organising and governing this otherwise troublesome province. Having spent so much time, trouble and expense in preparing a palace and temple at Jerusalem, it is possible that Sheshonq also intended to be buried in this capital city. Remember that Tanis was essentially a new town that had been hastily thrown together during the twenty-first dynasty, with King David-Psusennes being responsible for the bulk of the work. Because of this, Tanis was largely a mud-brick citadel, with any quality masonry being looted from the previous capital at Avaris. It is entirely possible that the city of Jerusalem may have been a more prestigious and luxurious capital than Tanis during this era – especially if the temple and the new royal palace had just been constructed there.

Bearing this in mind, it is entirely possible that a large and elaborate tomb was prepared at Jerusalem for Sheshonq's burial – perhaps this was even one of the pyramidal tombs that are now known as the tomb of the Pharaoh's Daughter and the tomb of Zechariah. But the impending civil strife in Judaea would have halted any such plans and left the king without a final resting place, and possibly without a sarcophagus either. In the end, the ever-patient administrators did the only logical thing possible under the circumstances: the two elaborate, hawk-headed sarcophagi belonging to Hiram Atif [Absalom?] were suitably amended to include the cartouches of the pharaoh Sheshonq I [King Solomon], and the king was eventually given a very simple burial in the anti-chamber of King David's tomb at Tanis.

While the touching Biblical deathbed scene of King David allowed us to confidently say that this king was quite elderly, unfortunately there are no equivalent details given for the death of King Solomon. Despite this omission, and a general lack of information about this monarch's age, it is nevertheless obvious that this legendary king had had a long reign and must have been a mature individual. Luckily for the theory once more, the mummy of Sheshonq I * was found to be that of a man of about fifty years of age. [41]

Entrance

The earlier chapters of this book have discussed the Maakhah Tamar queens and their illustrious décolletages in some detail. The purpose of the following paragraphs is to explore the connection between the Maakhah Tamars' breasts and the outline of the pyramids in more detail, to see if this assertion can be supported in any way. It may sometimes appear that every reference to high ground or a rounded piece of flesh is interpreted by the author as being a pyramid, a tendency that some readers may blame on an over-active or fevered imagination. But I do not think that these claims are in any way fanciful, and the evidence for this resides on the floor of every Masonic lodge.

This investigation begins with the duties that were expected of the Master of the Palace or Vizier, which was the title of a high official who managed and controlled the royal courts of Egypt and Judaea. The duties of the vizier are explicitly given in the Biblical book of Isaiah, where it is said of the Master of the Palace, who was known by the name of Elyaquim:

> And the key of the house of David will I lay upon his shoulder; so he shall open, and none shall shut; and he shall shut, and none shall open. [B42]

---

* This mummy is traditionally explained as being that of Sheshonq II, but the historical chronology infers that these were instead the remains of Sheshonq I.

In other words, this official held the keys to the royal palace, and as such this must have been a position of great trust and status. This rank and position stemmed, of course, from Egyptian royal court. As far back as the sixteenth century BC, the Biblical patriarch Joseph – who was the Vizier to an unnamed pharaoh – can be seen to be inheriting the 'keys' (or seals) to the palace:

> (Pharaoh said to Joseph), thou shalt be <u>over my house</u>, and according unto thy word shall all my people be ruled: only in the throne will I be greater than thou. [B43]

Joseph was given the position of Master of the Palace and so held the 'keys' of the royal palace. While this duty was most probably a secular position, it is also likely that there was a similar position for the official who held the keys (or seals) to the innermost sanctums of the great temples of Egypt. Since the Biblical Joseph was also a high priest of Heliopolis, it is likely that he held the temple's keys (or seals) too. While being responsible for the keys to the temples was more of a sacred duty, the high priest had another, even more esoteric role to perform, and the evidence for this can be seen in the unique and sacred role that was given to St Peter in the New Testament:

> Thou art Peter, and upon this rock (Peter) I will build my church ... And I will give unto thee the keys of the kingdom of heaven. [B44]

This extract from the gospel of Matthew demonstrates that the keys held by the Vizier were not necessarily just the keys to a secular palace or sacred temple, they also included the keys to the celestial heavens. But what was being inferred by this position? In what way could the heavens, be they either spiritual or physical, be unlocked?

   The answer to this may lie in the equivalent title that was given to the master of the Egyptian royal palace. In Egypt, this same rank of steward (or major-domo) was given the Egyptian title of Mer-Per 𓄟𓉐 . Once more, the two components of this title can be broken down and analysed. On the surface, it would appear that *mer* means 'high official' and *per* means 'palace', and so the Mer-Per was the Master of the House, the Vizier. But this is not the only possible translation and a simple pun can transform the word *mer* into the word *mer* 𓄟𓏏𓉴 meaning 'pyramid'. This simple alteration would now infer that the vizier was also connected in some manner to the pyramids. So what kind of palace was being locked (or sealed) up: a royal palace or a mighty stone monument?

Peculiar as it may sound, the answer to this question may well lie in the names that were chosen by the pharaohs of the twenty-first dynasty. The birth name of the pharaoh Psusennes II [King David] included the star glyph, which could be read as either *djuat* or *seba*. While both of these words may mean 'star', the term *seba* can also mean 'door', which can be used either as a reference to 'palace gates', or even the 'door of heaven'. In each case, the determinative that is used for 'door' is the 🚪 glyph, which is pronounced *seba*. Here we have this same kind of confusion between the gates of a secular palace and the entrance to the sacred netherworld – apparently, the same door can access both of them. In some respects, this confusion is to be expected, as the temples themselves were only envisaged as being Earthly representations of the heavens above; but the fact that the word *seba* can mean both 'door' and 'star' does indicate that the celestial heavens were the dominant symbolic factor here.

One of Psusennes II's ancestors, and several of his descendants, had the birth name of Uasorkon. While it has been claimed that this name is of foreign origin, it has already been shown that it actually contained a reference to the god Osiris. The glyph that was used to spell this god-name, Osiris, was the *sa* glyph 🔲, which has a very similar style to the *seba* glyph 🚪. The Griffith Institute book, *Egyptian Grammar*, indicates that the *sa* glyph is supposed to represent a razor, no doubt for shaving the heads of the priests. However, this glyph does not seem to have razor among its many usages and in fact, one of its prime meanings is 'back'. How a razor can be taken to mean 'back' is not explained.

Personally, I think that the designation given to the *sa* glyph 🔲 is wrong, and that it was, in reality, a representation of a door with a knob or handle attached. Indeed, the glyph on its own can mean 'gateway', 'wisdom', or even 'a sanctuary in which a god was housed', all of which tends to indicate a doorway function rather than an article of toiletry. But precisely which type of door was being inferred by the *sa* glyph , and how was this connected to the concept of 'wisdom'? Is there any way of knowing such precise little details from such an ancient lexicon?

The clue that may provide an answer to this question may lie in the associated glyph that is also pronounced as *sa* ▱. It is not said what this strange-looking glyph was supposed to represent in real life, but I will give the reader one guess. Like the *sa* glyph, this peculiar glyph ▱ also means 'wisdom' or 'knowledge', and so both of these symbols therefore have the same characteristics that have been associated with the pharaoh Sheshonq I [King Solomon the Wise]. Somehow, the concept of 'doors' was being linked to 'wisdom', and no doubt this arcane knowledge had something to do with knowing what lay behind those doors.

The question still remains, however, as to which door concealed this great wisdom, which was linked in some manner to the stars and heavens. Was *sa* the entrance to the Holy of Holies deep inside the temple, where only the high priest and the pharaoh were allowed to enter, or did it refer to something even more esoteric? Actually, to remain true to form, I think that all of these glyphs are really alluding to the Great Pyramid once more, and there is a very startling piece of evidence that will be shown to support this assertion. The first thing to note is that the *sa* glyph was most probably a door with a handle attached, and since its partner glyph *sa* ⬛ looks suspiciously like a pyramid (from above), it is only reasonable to suspect that the 'razor' was actually a symbolic representation of the original entrance door to this pyramid, as we shall see.

According to the early Biblical liturgy, the great god of the Israelites was supposed to have inhabited a rough-hewn chamber at the very base of Mt Sinai. But Mt Sinai has already been identified in the book *Tempest* as being the Great Pyramid at Giza, and if this were so then the Israelite god actually inhabited the Great Pyramid's lower chamber. Therefore, the entrance door to this pyramid would naturally have been regarded as being very special indeed. I believe that this was not only true, it was for this reason that these two glyphs – which were designed to represent a door and a pyramid respectively – were also said to represent the deeper concepts of 'a sanctuary in which a god was housed' and 'wisdom'. The wisdom being referred to here was the sacred knowledge of what happened in the chamber that lay deep inside the Great Pyramid, where the great god himself was supposed to reside, and which may have been known as the *Uasekh* ⳼, or the Hall of Osiris.

Lewis

The final piece of evidence that positively confirms all of these suspicions is a curious device known in Masonic circles as a Lewis. The Lewis is a small mechanical model that is placed upon the floor of every Masonic lodge; it consists of a tripod with a pulley system that holds up a block of stone by means of a large metal ring inserted into the top of the stone. It so happens, of course, that the stone block of the Masonic Lewis looks exactly like the *sa* ⬜ glyph that has just been discussed in some detail. This may initially sound like a huge assumption on my part, for the two items appear to have nothing whatsoever in common, and an association could be made between the *sa* glyph and any old block of stone with a ring in it – a stone block from a harbour wall, for instance, would look very much like a *sa* glyph. But there is more to this story than a simple block of stone.

The prime constituents of the Masonic Lewis are the stone with a metal ring in the top, and a rope that is looped around the pulley system and is used to lift the stone up. Looking once more at the name of the pharaoh Uasorkon a striking parallel can be seen, as the initial two glyphs of this name comprise a loop of rope with a knot on the end and the familiar stone block with a ring on the top. Amazingly enough, the two main components of the name Uasorkon and the two main components of the Masonic Lewis are absolutely identical.

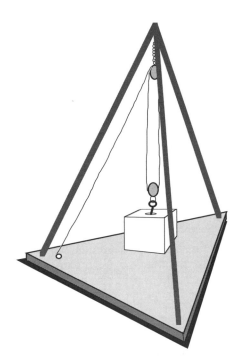

Fig 49. Masonic Lewis - or L'Uas.

Somehow, through the long years of oppression and exile of the Hyksos people, this same imagery, which was originally used in the cartouche of a long-forgotten pharaoh, has been preserved as a central piece of Masonic ritual furniture. More than that, however, the original name of this piece of sacred machinery has been perfectly preserved too. To the ancient Egyptians, the original name of this device must have been the Uas, which is the pronunciation of the first two glyphs of the name 'Uasorkon'. But since the modern name for the Lewis has come down to us from the Knights Templar and their immediate ancestors, who were primarily French, they no doubt added a definite article, 'the', to the word. It was through this process that the original Egyptian name for this device, the Uas, was changed into Le Uas or, indeed, L'Uas. The resulting compound name was deemed important enough to have been used as a title for royalty, and the first of the various European monarchs who inherited this name was Louis I, who was a son of Charlemagne. The most famous of these kings, however, was Louis XIV, who was known as the Sun King; the latter title is supposed to be a reference to the 'splendour' of his reign, but in reality this was just a poor allusion to Ra and the pharaonic ancestry of the European monarchs.

In which case, this peculiar little artifact known as a Lewis not only preserves within its design the outline of the hieroglyphs that spell the name of a long-lost pharaoh, it also preserves the original pronunciation of that name. But it is entirely possible that the name of this Egyptian pharaoh was in itself only representational – it was probably the pharaoh who was basing his title upon the name of the machine and not the other way around. If this were so, however, it would mean that for some strange reason, the pharaohs of Egypt were using a similar pulley system, called a *uas*, way back in the tenth century BC. While this might seem to be a bold assertion, the evidence to demonstrate that this may be true can be derived from the Lewis' modern usage.

If the Lewis was a sacred piece of the original Egyptian rituals, which has been adopted by modern Masonry, the question remains as to what it was supposed to represent. The Masonic Lewis is supposed to be a representation of a stone plug that once sealed a vault under the Temple of Jerusalem, which was hauled up by means of this rope and pulley system. The fact that this device was reputed to have been used under the Temple of Solomon places it in exactly the right context to be associated with the twenty-first dynasty, but not necessarily in the right era.

Unfortunately for the theory that has just been presented, it was not supposed to have been King Solomon who was pulling on the end of this rope but the Knights Templar, who were not in Jerusalem until the twelfth century AD. But, as with most things Masonic, these explanations about the Knights Templar and the Temple of Solomon are only for the lower degrees of initiation. Like the artifact itself, the true roots of Masonry do not stem from Jerusalem; instead, they go right back into ancient Egypt. In which case, it would not be too surprising to find that this block of stone originally had nothing whatsoever to do with the Temple of

Jerusalem, but it must instead have represented some aspect of the Hyksos' pyramid theology.

While the Egyptian origins for the name of this pulley system demonstrate that it considerably predates the Templar search in the ruins of the Temple of Solomon, perhaps the original functions of this device have nevertheless been preserved within these Masonic explanations. The lower-degree Masonic explanations indicate that the Lewis pulled up a stone plug from the top of a secret chamber, and while this is probably true in some respects, this was not the much later entrance to a tomb under the Temple of Solomon but a much earlier chamber known as the Hall of Osiris. The name Lewis (L'Uas), as previously mentioned, has just these kinds of connotations; it can refer to a large chamber, the god Osiris, and also to the Chamber of Osiris – the latter being pronounced as *uasekh* 𓌾𓉐𓏏 . It also has secondary inferences alluding to the two geese of Osiris (Usar)𓌾𓎡𓅬𓅬 , which have already been shown to be an allusion to the two great pyramids at Giza.

If this piece of ancient imagery, in the form of two glyphs from the name of the pharaoh Uasorkon 𓌾𓉐 , were quite so important that it has been passed from generation to generation for several thousand years, then where was this sacred Chamber of Osiris?

Stone plug-type entrances to chambers are not that common in Egypt, but it is known that the pyramid of Zoser (Djoser) had this exact same layout (minus the iron ring in the plug). The presence, in the Masonic version, of the tripod may tend to indicate an outdoor usage, in which case some of the entrances around the Giza plateau may have been stoppered in this manner. The entrance to the 'Tomb of Osiris' at the back of the Sphinx may be one such passageway, but the reference here to Osiris' tomb is thought to be a very recent invention and so no correlation with the name of Uasorkon can be gained from this.

It is always possible that the correct location for this plug is no longer known, and the number of recent surveys of the Giza plateau looking for 'Secret Chambers' and 'Halls of Records' may be a testimony to this possibility. But it is equally possible that somewhere, either at Giza or Dahshur, there may be a large stone plug just waiting to be raised by a Lewis-type apparatus, with a secret chamber lying below. Personally, however, I think that the Great Pyramid is the key to this conundrum.

It has already been demonstrated in chapter III that the opening of the Great Pyramid's door was the primary ritual of the Hyksos priesthood. It was so important that the term used to denote their holy day, the Sabbath, was directly derived from the name that was used to describe the Great Door of Heaven, *saba* 𓊽𓂋𓈖𓇳𓉐 – indeed this was probably the name given to the door of the Great Pyramid itself. Similarly, the Egyptian word *sefekh* ⌐⌐⌐ , which was the term used to describe the unbolting of this same door, also became synonymous in the Biblical texts with the Great Pyramid, as the verse from Ezekiel mentioned earlier has already demonstrated. In short, whichever way one looks, the concept of opening a sacred door in Egypt is consistently linked to the door that once plugged the entrance to the Great Pyramid.

The term *Uas* appears to have been similarly endowed with Great Pyramid symbolism. This word not only meant 'chamber', it also had connotations of an unfinished chamber, just as is to be found at the base of the Great Pyramid. (Remember that the upper chambers to this pyramid had not been discovered in this era.) The book *K2* gives a full description of how the original entrance door to the Great Pyramid was supposed to have been fabricated, and the explanations there showed that it could have been finely balanced on a pivot and relatively easy to operate.

Nevertheless, the possibility also exists that the door was not quite so finely balanced after all, and that a pulley system and ropes very similar in appearance to the *Uas* were required to heave the entrance block into the open position. Ancient pulley blocks that may have been used for this very purpose have been discovered at Giza, and while these are not as sophisticated as the items shown in the following diagrams, they could easily have been adapted to fulfil this exact same role.

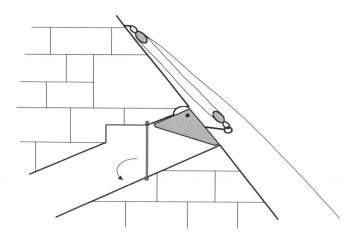

Fig 50.   The Great Pyramid access stone, closed.

As the glyphs that form the name Uasorkon comprise just the rope and stone block, and omit the tripod, it is entirely possible that the tripod was a recent addition that allowed the device to be freestanding on the floor of a Masonic lodge. In its original usage, however, the *Uas* may have used the side of the pyramid itself to gain its leverage. The resulting arrangement may have looked something like these two diagrams (figs. 50 and 51):

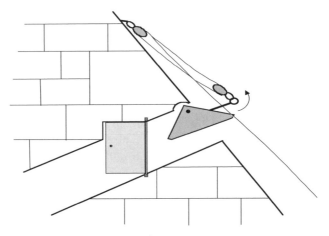

Fig 51. Opening the Great Pyramid access stone.

The assertion that the *sa* glyph was a razor never did explain any of the attributes of this glyph. On the other hand, the possibility that it may instead refer to the stone access-door to the Great Pyramid explains all of them. It certainly explains why the *sa* glyph 🗝 was used to denote a 'door', and why this door could sometimes be considered to be a 'doorway to heaven'. It would also explain why the *sa* glyph was a truncated door glyph. The original glyph for a door was always quite tall 🗝, as are most doors, but the Great Pyramid's access door is unusually squat and so the design of the glyph reflects this shape 🗝. It also easily explains why this glyph would be equated with the concept of 'wisdom', for there were and are many mysteries to be found in and around the Great Pyramid: the priesthood who controlled access to this pyramid not only knew many of the deepest secrets of Egyptian theology, they also held the 'keys' (the seals) to the chamber of god. If anyone was to be considered wise in this era, it would have been the Heliopolian and Giza priesthood who were the Guardians of the Giza plateau.

This same explanation also explains the prime, and seemly

obscure, meaning for the ⌂ glyph – that of 'back' or 'hind parts'. A razor cannot begin to fathom such intricacies, whereas the Great Pyramid's entrance-door concept explains everything – because the entrance door to the Great Pyramid was situated part of the way up the northern face of this pyramid. Around the Great Pyramid there are a great number of significant constructions: the east face had the mortuary temple and the causeway; the south face had pits for the two solar boats; while the western face contained much of the necropolis. The northern face not only had no significant artifacts or constructions to its credit, it also faced away from the god Ra. If any part of this pyramid was going to be declared the 'backside', it was going to be the northern face. It was for this reason, I believe, that the ⌂ glyph also gained the meaning 'back' or 'hind parts'.

The function of this glyph, not simply as a doorway but also as a plug-door on a pyramid, would also explain the shape of the 'handle'. Had this simply been a plug of stone in the ground, the shape of the metal ring on the top would have been like that in the modern Lewis – a simple ring at the top. Such a design on a pyramid door, however, would be quite useless. The pyramid door's 'handle' would require three attributes:

a. To stand out from the stone to prevent the block and tackle from fouling on the entrance stone itself.

b. To be inserted into the middle, thicker section of the plug, to prevent the stone plug from breaking under the lifting force.

c. To be angled downwards, to regain the leverage lost by item b. above. This angle would also help to regain the leverage lost by the slope of the side of the pyramid.

The curious angle displayed by the 'handle' on the *sa* ⌂ glyph would be difficult to explain under any circumstance, yet the function of a handle on the entrance plug to the Great Pyramid would explain each and every aspect of it. If nothing else, this scenario is most comprehensive in its list of successful explanations.

Finally, the doorway explanation would most certainly explain why the L'Uas or Lewis contraption was considered to be sacred for so long after it had ceased being used to open the Great Pyramid's door. Only a few centuries after the rule of Uasorkon, the pyramids themselves were no longer accessible to the Hyksos-Israelites due to the invasion of the Persians, and so the Guardians of the plateau were relegated to being just the Guardians of its secrets. Having been deprived of their sacred 'mountain', it was to be the form and function of the L'Uas that was handed down from generation to generation as being the ultimate in sacred artifacts, because it was the device that once gave the priesthood access to god – it was the 'key' to the Kingdom of Heaven.

Like everything in Egypt, the language of this pious nation was not inspired by bathroom implements, it was instead primarily influenced by, and dependent upon, theology and the ritual artifacts that were employed by this trade. In addition, while historians have shunned the idea for centuries, this trilogy of books has also positively shown that the center of Egyptian theology did not simply revolve around the great temples of Upper and Lower Egypt, but that the megalithic pyramids of Giza and Dahshur were equally central components. One of the basic accoutrements required by the Giza priesthood was the pulley system needed to open the 'doorway to god', and if anything was going to be remembered as being sacred, it was the L'Uas or Lewis.

Like the glyphs that were explained in some detail in the book *Tempest*, here are another two glyphs whose origins were firmly based upon the pyramid theology of the Hyksos. Once more, however, the acceptance of this concept will give some people, and Egyptologists in particular, a bit of a headache. Like the three-hills glyph ᴍ , the pyramid-door glyph is to be found at the beginning of dynastic Egypt and thus, according to the established chronology, this glyph predates the construction of the pyramid upon which its design was based. Once more, the linguistic evidence from Egypt points towards the Great Pyramid being much older than the established chronology will currently allow.

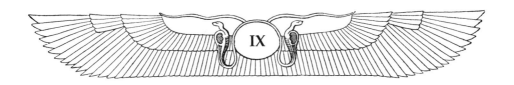

Menelek & Saba

The preceding chapters have shown concrete evidence that demonstrates that the Egyptian monarchy invaded Judaea and Israel during the tenth century BC and became regarded, by the later Judaean scribes especially, as being purely local Judaic monarchs. But the history of the United Monarchy and their descendants does not end there, of course; the court intrigues and political machinations of this royal family continued right through to the Persian invasion and the Babylonian exile, and they eventually found their way into the first century world of Jesus the Nazarene. So, who were these later Judaic monarchs, like Rehoboam and Abijam? Were they, in reality, yet more pharaohs of Egypt?

Much of the evidence, which shows exactly what happened subsequent to the reign of King Solomon, is actually to be found in the Kebra Nagast once more. After her visit to King Solomon, the Queen of Sheba is said to have returned to her native country, and that country has now been positively identified as being Upper Egypt. When her son (Menelek) was twenty-two years of age, however, he demanded to see his father, King Solomon-Sheshonq. The reason for this visit to the reigning monarch was as follows:

> Harken O King (Solomon) unto the message which thy hand-maiden (the Queen of Sheba) ... has sent by me: Take this young man (Menelek), anoint him, consecrate him, and bless him, and make him king over our country, and give him the command that a woman shall never again reign (in this country), and send him back in peace. KN1

The obvious question here is why King Solomon of Israel should have the authority to anoint a prince and invest him as king over a foreign land. Even if Prince Menelek was Solomon's son, this family relationship would not normally give a monarch jurisdiction over another nation. Why, then, was King Solomon of Judaea and Israel being asked to crown a foreign king? In addition to sending his son back as king, it is also said that King Solomon sent a complete ruling elite – comprising the elder sons of all the government officials in Jerusalem – to this foreign land ('Ethiopia') to control and rule this kingdom and its people. Again, the question has to be asked, why should a foreign nation willingly subject itself to this invasion of aristocrats and government officials from lowly Judaea?

The answer can only be found in this radically new account of the history of this region during this era. King Solomon, the pharaoh Sheshonq I, had already reigned for twenty-nine years when his son made the visit to see him in Jerusalem. Since the Egyptian Sed festivals of rejuvenation – which are now known in Britain as royal jubilees – were originally held every thirty years, the visit of Solomon-Sheshonq's son was probably arranged to coincide with the king's first jubilee celebrations. Achieving this rather satisfactory result, from the dates given in the Kebra Nagast, gives some confidence in assuming that the data being presented in this work is correct. A jubilee celebration would indeed be the very occasion for princes to make the long and hazardous journeys involved in visiting a reigning pharaoh, especially as this one may have resided in a distant part of his empire.

The reason, therefore, that a Judaean king was able to anoint and consecrate a foreign prince and to make him king of a 'foreign land', is that in the guise of Sheshonq I, King Solomon was also the king of Upper and Lower Egypt. While Solomon-Sheshonq appears to have spent much of his time away from Upper Egypt and even away from Lower Egypt, his mother, the Queen of Sheba, is reported to have travelled straight back to her homeland. There, she ruled as *de facto* queen, but the population were obviously not greatly impressed with this arrangement as rule by a female pharaoh had always been a touchy subject in Egypt.

Since this queen had a true bloodline son who had now come of age, it would appear that the pharaoh, Solomon-Sheshonq, was being asked to crown his son as either king of Upper Egypt, or perhaps as co-regent with his primary jurisdiction being Upper Egypt. This arrangement neatly solved a festering problem for the Theban elite. While they did not fully trust Sheshonq I to be their monarch, especially since he was a confirmed Tanite (Hyksos) ruler, his son by a confirmed Theban queen would have been eminently suitable as a local leader.

While Solomon the Israelite would have had no jurisdiction

whatsoever over foreign lands like Ethiopia, it is most certain that Solomon-Sheshonq had some form of jurisdiction over Upper Egypt; in which case, the circumstances of this coronation of Prince Menelek can be fully explained. The Kebra Nagast seems to encapsulate the political uncertainty that was generated by this delicate situation beautifully:

> ... the first-born sons of the nobles of Israel were given to rule over the country of Ethiopia, with the son of Solomon the king (Menelek). Then they assembled together and wept together with their fathers and their mothers and their relations ... And they cursed the king (Solomon) secretly and reviled him because he had seized their sons against their will. [KN2]

The trepidation of the elder sons in the royal court of Jerusalem was not just due to the impending and imposed separation from their parents; it was primarily due to the knowledge that their task was far from straightforward. They had been told to go and govern a foreign land and to stop the inhabitants there from worshipping idols. One can readily imagine the concerns these sons must have felt, not knowing what kind of reception that these foreigners would give them.

The whole scenario is very reminiscent of Abraham's journeys into Upper Egypt and his crusade against idolatry there, which was also fraught with political uncertainties. The royal sons would also have recalled the era of Akhenaton, where exact same scenario was played out during the reign of this 'heretic pharaoh'. Unlike Abraham's cautious approach, Akhenaton played a no-holds-barred high-risk game of bluff with the Theban hierarchy – and lost. It was for this reason that these same sons from the court of Solomon hatched a plot to steal the Ark of the Covenant from Jerusalem and take it with them on the journey, so that its protective powers would assist them in their dangerous task. The suggestion has to be that the sons of the Egypto-Judaean empire were setting off to govern the troublesome province of Thebes, not Ethiopia, and were charged with preventing the influential priesthood there from worshipping idols.

Further evidence to support this notion can be found in the journey that Menelek and his companions took in order to get back to 'Ethiopia'. The journey took them from Jerusalem to Gaza and thence to the Nile. From there, they went to Mt Sinai, for some strange reason. According to the classical geography of this region, this detour not only represented their route doubling back on itself, it also required an unnecessary crossing of the Red Sea. The unlikely nature of this route alone would suggest that Mt Sinai was not in its classical location, and the assumption that I have made previously in the book *Tempest* is far more sensible: namely, that Mt Sinai was actually the Great Pyramid at Giza. A route that went from Gaza to the Nile and on to the pyramids near Memphis would make a great deal more sense.

This revised location for Mt Sinai is rather dramatically supported by the next location in Menelek's itinerary, a story that was apparently related to the Kebra Nagast's editors by an Egyptian government official:

> ... Having set out from Alexandria I came to Kehera (Cairo) ... and on my arrival these men of Ethiopia of whom you speak arrived there also. They reached there after a passage of three days on the Takkazi, the river of Egypt (the Nile). [KN3]

So, from Mt Sinai, the party of princes and aristocrats eventually ended up in Cairo, and once more the itinerary of the journey only makes sense if Mt Sinai lay in close proximity to Cairo. This confirms once more that Mt Sinai was a man-made mountain located next to a major Egyptian city, rather than a jagged peak in a remote part of the Sinai peninsular. The town of Kehera (Arab. Qahira) is reliably being translated as Cairo, and this name is taken from the original Egyptian name of Kheraha 𓈖𓉐𓂝𓏤, the city that was known as the 'Babylon of Egypt', which stood across the Nile from the Giza plateau.

The Kebra Nagast is indicating that the route to Ethiopia was made via the Nile, which in itself is a peculiar suggestion. While it is true that the river Nile does flow out of Ethiopia, backtracking this great river to its source is not exactly the easiest way of reaching Ethiopia. Not only does the Nile meander and loop back on itself, but this river is also completely unnavigable in many places, and so such a journey would have been a major expedition to be attempted by only the hardiest of explorers. By far the most preferable route from Israel to Ethiopia would be down the Red Sea by boat to modern-day Asmera or Djibouti, and then a short overland journey into the highlands of Ethiopia. What, in this case, was Menelek doing in Cairo?

The Kebra Nagast then continues its improbable explanations by indicating that the rest of the journey to 'Ethiopia' took just one day. While this might be just dismissed as the stuff of fairytales and not to be taken seriously, the text may be correct in some respects: it was simply trying to indicate that the remainder of the journey was the shortest part. It is reported that the journey from Jerusalem to the Nile took Menelek three days and the remainder of the journey was only a third of that amount. It is some 500 km from Jerusalem to the Nile, and even if the journey were made by boat down the Mediterranean coast, it is unlikely that such a schedule could be maintained. But the texts seem to indicate that this was actually an overland journey, and if this was so, then the journey would take more like three weeks than three days.

This, of course, may be the answer to this problem: the term for 'week' or 'month' may have been confused at some time with the word for 'day'. It is known that the Hyksos-Israelites were using a seven-day week, as the number seven was the basis of the word used for the Sabbath. In this case, the entire journey from Jerusalem to Thebes may have taken just twenty-eight days, and although this is still a reasonable pace, it is entirely feasible.

While the distance from Jerusalem to Cairo is much the same as from Cairo to Thebes, the river journey down the Nile (travelling with the wind) could easily have been only a third as long as the overland journey from Jerusalem. If the party travelled for ten hours a day, which is normal for trekking expeditions, they would only need to have maintained some 2.5 km/hr on the overland section and 7.5 km/hr on the river journey; all of which is within the capabilities of the transport infrastructure of the day. If the journey from Cairo to 'Ethiopia' took just one week, the most probable explanation is that Prince Menelek and his party of aristocrats simply cruised up the Nile to Thebes, as that was their intended destination.

That Ethiopia was in fact a pseudonym for Egypt is further confirmed by the description of the boundaries of the land of Ethiopia that Menelek was supposed to have ruled. Menelek's kingdom apparently stretched along the 'lands of the Garden, where food is in plenty'. The translator has taken this to be a reference to the heavenly paradise, but the text may not be referring to something quite so intangible; the reference to the 'Garden' may simply have been a reference to the irrigated lands of the Nile. The conclusive evidence that shows this to be so is contained within another description of the eastern borders of Menelek's kingdom of 'Ethiopia'. This border is described as follows:

> And the eastern boundary of the kingdom of the King of Ethiopia is the beginning of Gaza in the land of Judah, that is, Jerusalem; and its boundary is the lake of Jericho... KN5

The text is indicating that the eastern borders of 'Ethiopia' terminated in Judaea, and therefore all of Egypt came within 'Ethiopia's' sphere of influence. While the Kebra Nagast has obviously been doctored by many later editors and redactors, none of these could be quite so confused as to think that Ethiopia governed all of Egypt, right up to the borders of Judaea. The reverse of this situation, however, it entirely possible; namely, that Egypt governed all of Nubia (not Ethiopia as we know it). Quite plainly, the Kebra Nagast's 'Ethiopia' was simply a pseudonym for Egypt.

That the land of Egypt has been mistranslated as Ethiopia is probably no accident. By the time the Kebra Nagast came to be assembled from the various scattered texts, the Hyksos-Israelites were most probably enduring their exile at the hands of the Babylonians, and by this time the land of Egypt was not simply a fading memory but also a pariah state. In the eyes of the Judaic priesthood, Egypt was the origin of all Israel's woes – a nation to be derided and scorned. Not only was it unacceptable to have the kings of Israel associated with Egypt, it was also politically undesirable for the Queen of Sheba to have any such affiliations.

The simple answer for the scribes was probably to use another of the many titles that graced the priests and kings of Egypt. The High Priest Herihor, for instance, was known as the Viceroy of Nubia, while the pharaoh Solomon-Sheshonq is reported to have led a military campaign into Nubia. Clearly, Nubia was under Egyptian control throughout the twenty-first and twenty-second dynasties and, undoubtedly, the scribes were trying to deflect attention away from Egypt and towards Nubia. Although the term 'Nubia' is traditionally thought to refer to modern Sudan rather than Ethiopia, the Bible often refers to Nubia as being the land of Ethiopia, as we shall see shortly.

Taking this into account, the text of the Kebra Nagast therefore makes sense. It is likely that the Queen of Sheba was from Thebes rather than Ethiopia, as has already been demonstrated, and that the Theban aristocracy had long been independently minded. The people of Upper Egypt were probably complaining that they had been prevented from having a Theban monarch for far too long and, instead of having King Solomon's mother as a *de facto* ruler in the region, they were demanding that the king anoint his son, Menelek, as co-regent or king of Upper Egypt. This Solomon-Sheshonq did, and the name that he gave his son during the coronation ceremony was said to be David (David II). As it is already known that the name David is synonymous with the Egyptian name Psusennes, the task is to find another pharaoh called Psusennes who would equate with the arrival of this northern prince or king. Menelek [David II - Psusennes III] was said to be the son of Solomon-Sheshonq but, unfortunately, the historical record does not show a son of Sheshonq I with this name. The historical data that is available to us does, however, tentatively indicate that a high priest called Psusennes III of Thebes existed at about this time, but his parentage is not thought to have involved Sheshonq I.

While this is disappointing, it should not be so surprising. Solomon-Sheshonq was reputed to have had a vast harem and, doubtless, hundreds of children, yet very few of these show up in the records. It is true that the Kebra Nagast says that King Solomon only had three children, but unless Solomon had a problem fathering children, this was probably just a reference to the three children who were born to his chief wife, Karamaa (Naamah). The Biblical sources indicate that Solomon's sons were called Rehoboam, Menelek (David II), and possibly Aadrami; while the equivalent historical sources say that Sheshonq's sons were known as Iuput and Nimlot. With the data being so meagre, it is not surprising that another possible son, known as David-Psusennes, has been omitted from the few records that are still available.

While the historical record does not seem to provide us with a similar name or title for this son of Sheshonq I who was sent to rule Thebes, it nevertheless agrees with much of the rest of this hypothesis:

> Sheshonq I quickly took over all four leading posts in Amun's hierarchy at Thebes. He appointed his second son Iuput as High Priest of Amun – a mark of honour ... but this son was naturally also a royal representative in personal charge at Thebes ... later monuments add the title Governor of Upper Egypt. [6]

So, the historical evidence supports the Biblical story once more, and it shows that Sheshonq I's son, Iuput, was placed in charge of Thebes as a regional governor. While the name of this son of Sheshonq is not the same as the Kebra Nagast gives for the son of Solomon, the general thrust of this account, and the political intentions of the northern pharaoh, are precisely the same. Solomon-Sheshonq wanted control over the troublesome southern states of Egypt that were traditionally governed by Thebes, and this was achieved by installing his son, plus some sundry government officials, into leading positions within the hierarchy of Upper Egypt. It would seem that the Kebra Nagast, like the Bible, contains a complete history of the pharaohs of Egypt during the twenty-first and twenty-second dynasties.

The final point to make in this respect is that the Queen of Sheba appears to have ended her life back in Thebes, along with her son Menelek (David II). If this was so, then it is also likely that she would have been buried in Thebes and honoured as a great Queen of the South. As mentioned in the last chapter, the titles that were inscribed upon the sarcophagus of Maakare Mu-Tamhat, including that of King's Daughter, indicate that she was Maakhah Tamar II, the daughter and daughter-wife of Psusennes II [King David] and the mother of King Solomon. If this was so, then this sarcophagus is actually that of the legendary Queen of Sheba, and it now resides in the Cairo museum alongside the mortal remains of King David and King Solomon.

Rome

The Bible only mentions one son of Solomon, known as Rehoboam; it is the Kebra Nagast that records the additional two sons who were called Menelek and Aadrami. This same text then relates that the latter son also became a king of yet another foreign land. This time, the son Aadrami was sent to Baltasar, who was said to be the king of 'Rom' or 'Rome'. Baltasar was said to have had no male offspring of his own and so he asked for a son from King Solomon, in order to continue the 'Romany' royal line. This son of Solomon was, however, related to king Baltasar as he was the son of a princess who had been sent to Solomon by a relative of Baltasar. Aadrami was not, therefore, a son of Solomon's chief wife Naamah [Karamaa].

There are three possible explanations for the Kebra Nagast's story of an additional son of Solomon, who was supposed to have become the king of Greece/Constantinople (Rom) in such similar circumstances to that of Menelek. Firstly, this could well be a simple repetition of the life of Menelek, with added variations. Secondly, it could have been a true account and therefore a fortuitous opportunity for Solomon-Sheshonq to place another of his sons as the ruler of yet another country. Thirdly, it was again based upon a true story but these events really happened in another, much later, era.

While I had initially considered it improbable that a king of Greece/Constantinople would have asked for a son of Solomon-Sheshonq to become the king of this region, this option could have been true in the light of a common Greek-Hyksos ancestry, through the pharaoh called Danaus who fled to Greece. If King Baltasar was a descendant of the pharaoh Danaus [Ay], and if Solomon was also a descendant of the Amarna regime, as is entirely possible, then there would have been every reason to have made a dynastic alliance.

But then I began to doubt the location that had been given for the kingdom of Rom, and began to think that the last of these explanations was the more probable – that this all occurred in a much later era. So why did the Kebra Nagast identify this location as being Constantinople? The answer to this question was fairly simple. The Roman Empire was eventually split into two halves by the emperor Diocletian in 293 AD, and the city of Constantinople became temporarily known as 'New Rome'. It would seem that Archbishop Domitius found the 'original' copy of the Kebra Nagast in the libraries of the Aya Sophia in Constantinople, and that he was known as the Archbishop of Rom; so, the traditional connection that has been made between the Kebra Nagast's nation called Rom and the city of New Rome (Constantinople) is understandable.

But there seemed to be a glaring problem with this association. My suspicions were being driven by the two words that have been traditionally used to denote the Gypsy or Rom (or Romany) nation. The term 'Gypsy' may have been derived from the pharaoh known as Danaus [Ay], the brother of Aegyptus, who had fled to Greece nearly 400 years before the reign of King Solomon. If this association were true, however, it would place the origins of this name at a rather early date. The same seems to be true of the term 'Rom', and it would appear that the texts of the Kebra Nagast were using the term 'Rom' some 1,200 years before the naming of New Rome (Constantinople) by Diocletian. So how did the Kebra Nagast know of Rom before it came into existence? Have later translators and redactors inserted 'Rom' where another name once stood?

While it may be logical to refer to a town by its contemporary name – as was demonstrated by the Biblical exodus originating in Pi-Ramesse rather than Avaris – referring to a monarch in this way does not make so much sense. While Nebuchadnezzar may have visited 'Baghdad' during his lifetime, he was most certainly not the King of Iraq! By the same argument, would a compiler of the Kebra Nagast have referred to a King of Rom who had reigned a thousand years before Rom (Constantinople) was founded? Personally, I think it much more likely that the Kebra Nagast was referring to another location called Rom entirely, and this has been wrongly assumed to be a reference to New Rome because that was where the manuscript was found.

If anything, the traditions of the Romanies tended to suggest that they had Persian rather than Anatolian origins; so, in order to progress further, the search for the country of Rom – if there was ever such a place – had to turn its attention to Persia during the era between Solomon and the fall of Jerusalem.

While this era may be far too early for the classical history of the Romanies, these classical explanations have to be questioned. The origins of the Gypsies have been assigned to the north-west of India in about 1000 AD, primarily on the basis of linguistic comparisons. But, as one researcher on this subject points out, this evidence does not preclude there having been a root language from which both Sanskrit and Romany were derived. It was also pointed out that the Persian poet, Firdusi, reported that

Gypsy musicians were being imported from India in 420 AD, a date that precedes the classical chronology of the Romany nation by a considerable margin. [7]

I was on the trail of a king who was known as Baltasar, a king 'Rom' who could have had close relations and sympathies with the Judaean regime in Jerusalem; close enough to have asked for a Judaean son to marry his daughter. After a long search I eventually found the king I was looking for, and the evidence can be seen in the Bible once more, in the book of Daniel. After the fall of Jerusalem, the Babylonian king, Nebuchadnezzar, ordered that some of the princes of Judaea should be brought to his royal court in Babylon. There were five princes who were taken to Babylon, and one of them was called Daniel (the Daniel who ended up in the lion's den). On their arrival these princes were all given local names, and the name that was given to Daniel was Baltashazzar.

Although the names Baltashazzar and Baltasar look remarkably similar, and although Daniel (Baltashazzar) was a prince of Judaea and so was likely to have wanted a Judaean son for his daughter, Daniel was just a prisoner in Babylon and not the king that the Kebra Nagast makes out. However, like Joseph in Egypt, Daniel was reputed to have become the fortune-teller to his captor, King Nebuchadnezzar of Babylon, and because of this talent he obtained a position in the royal court and was eventually promoted into high office.

The Biblical history then jumps over a decade of Babylonian history and says that Belshazzar, the son of Nebuchadnezzar, became king of Babylon. The fact that Daniel (Baltashazzar) had such a similar name to the new king is possibly explained by the tradition of high officials in the royal court taking on the royal title, as we have seen before. But the book of Baruch, in the Biblical Apocrypha, confuses this simplistic argument by saying that the new king of Babylon was actually called Baltasar. [B8] Since the names Baltashazzar and Baltasar are now so similar, it is possible that Daniel may have become king of Babylon.

Though historians may dismiss the Biblical Apocrypha as being unreliable, this Biblical account was actually written by <u>Baruch,</u> a name that sounds rather similar to the Babylonian priest and historian known as Berossus, whose name was originally pronounced as <u>Bel-reuchu</u>. Berossus has been used by modern historians as the standard-bearer of Babylonian history, so if these two ancient authors were actually the same person, this would not only reinforce the reliability of this Biblical account, it would also give us a complete family history of this otherwise shadowy Babylonian historian – a family history that indicates that Berossus (Bel-reuchu or Baruch) was actually of Judaean descent.

So how, if at all, could the Biblical Daniel have been related to the Babylonian King Nebuchadnezzar? A brief look at the Babylonian royal succession is perhaps required. The historical record indicates that the son and successor to Nebuchadnezzar was actually called Amel-Marduk, who was reputed to have been a demagogue and was deposed by his brother-in-law, Nerigglissar. The son and successor to Nerigglissar, Labashi-Marduk, was then deposed by Nabonidus, who may have been related to Nebuchadnezzar. It was Nabonidus' son who was called Prince Bel-sharusur and who was identified in the Bible as Baltashazzar or Baltasar.

Now all of this may seem to be a long and convoluted history, but in actual fact it only represented a brief, ten-year interlude in Babylonian history and it may well have been a traumatic episode that the scribes wanted to forget about. For simplicity and stability's sake, the scribes decreed that Nabonidus succeeded Nebuchadnezzar and Prince Baltashazzar (Baltasar) was the prince regent. So how, if at all, does the Biblical Daniel fit into this history? How could Daniel (Baltashazzar) have become king of Babylon?

The Bible could be right in this assertion, but only if one of the reigning monarchs of Babylon, either King Nebuchadnezzar or King Nabonidus, married a Judaean princess. Since the taking of foreign princesses into the royal harem was an established practice in this era, and since the Babylonians had just besieged and taken Jerusalem and most of its royalty, this is all rather likely. Since the Judaic royal succession ran though the female line, as did the Egyptian, then the Judaeans would have regarded the offspring of such a union as being Judaean rather than Babylonian royalty. The enslaved Egypto-Judaean princess would have been more cuckoo than captive, implanting her Egypto-Judaean offspring into the heart of the Babylonian royal court.

The only difficulty for the Judaean wife of the Babylonian king would have been promoting the son of this union into a position of power within the extended Babylonian royal family, and perhaps the close connections between the Judaean royalty and the Egyptian monarchy helped in this process. If this revision of Babylonian history is correct, then it may also solve the little mystery of what happened to Prince Baltasar after the Persian invasion of Babylon. Historians assume that he must have died, whereas the Bible indicates that he actually became one of the Persian administrators – a puppet king or a vizier. The Biblical assertion is that the Persian monarchs subdivided the kingdom into three provinces and Baltasar became the ruler or administrator of one of those regions.

The confusion that seems to exist between Daniel's Babylonian name of Belshazzar (Bel-shar-usur), and the alternative Biblical translations of Baltashazzar or Baltasar, may actually have been deliberate. The Bible has used both versions of this name and so the scribes must have known its real pronunciation; in which case, the alternative spelling that they used may have been yet another witty pun designed to show Baltasar's Egypto-Judaean heritage. The scribes may well have been making a play on words between the name 'Baltasar' and the very similar Egyptian word *Bata-Sar* 𓃒𓈖𓏛 𓂋𓈖𓇋 , which means the 'King of Lower Egypt'. While this name may have been inappropriate for a ruler of Persia, it would make a great deal of sense in terms of a prince who was of maternal Egypto-Judaean descent. The simple insertion of the letter 't' into the prince's name may have discreetly signified what was otherwise unmentionable – that the king (vizier) was not of pure Babylonian descent.

To add to this intrigue at the royal court, a mysterious event then happened – a magical finger appeared from nowhere and wrote a message on a wall:

> Immediately the fingers of a man's hand appeared and wrote on the plaster of the wall of the king's palace, opposite the lamp-stand; and the king saw the hand as it wrote. Then the king's colour changed, and his thoughts alarmed him; his limbs gave way, and his knees knocked together. [B9]

The Bible indicates that the king involved in this episode was Baltasar, but since Baltasar never gained the throne and remained a prince, it is more likely that this king was actually Nabonidus, the father of Baltasar, and so this event would have occurred before the Persian invasion of Babylon. Nobody could translate the magical finger's script, so in desperation the king eventually promised the third highest office in the land, a gold chain, and a purple robe to the man who could translate this script. Predictably enough, it was Daniel (Prince Baltasar) who translated the text for the king and, like the patriarch Joseph before him, he received the golden necklace and the exalted rank of vizier for his services. History suggest that Prince Baltasar did indeed become vizier or prince regent to King Nabonidus during the latter's absence.

Again, it is fairly predictable that the enigmatic writing on the wall foretold the Persian invasion and the downfall of the king [Nabonidus], the 'son' of Nebuchadnezzar. It was in this manner that King Darius I, the Mede or Persian, was reputed to have taken the throne of Babylon. Daniel's (Baltasar's) translation of this writing on the wall was:

MENE;   God hath numbered thy kingdom, and finished it.

TEKEL;   Thou art weighed in the balances, and art found wanting.

PERES;   Thy kingdom is divided, and given to the Medes and Persians. [B10]

Again, the Biblical account has skipped a generation or two here, as it was Cyrus II who incorporated Babylon into the Persian empire and then bequeathed it to his son, Cambyses II. Darius I did not reign for another seventeen years or so, when he took the throne from Cambyses II by force.

It is from these ancient myths that the modern term 'the writing is on the wall' has been derived. It never ceases to amaze me that a saying such as this can still be in current usage some 2,500 years after it was first coined. The same is true of the saying 'to eat your words', which was derived from the ancient tradition of washing off sacred verses and then drinking the resulting colloid of water and ink. This tradition comes from Numbers 5:23 in the Bible, but it may have had an even older heritage as the technique is also noted in Egyptian texts.

So, is the Kebra Nagast's account, of another son of Solomon being married off to the king of Rom, in any way based upon fact? The fact that the Bible is studiously silent about this event serves to undermine the Kebra Nagast's account, but if these events really did occur in a later era then perhaps this is not so surprising. What may have happened here is that the Kebra Nagast has picked up a tradition about Daniel that the Bible has missed. The destruction of Jerusalem and the resulting Babylonian exile resulted in many famous names ending up in strange places, and not all the stories of these people have been able to make their way back into the texts that became the Torah (Old Testament). The Bible did get to hear of some of Daniel's experiences, however, and if Daniel (Baltashazzar - Baltasar) had been raised as a Babylonian prince and worked his way up through the princely ranks to become second in command of the Babylonian nation, and if he had requested a son from Judaea for his daughter, then this action would most certainly have been worth recording somewhere.

Not quite knowing where to put this particular account, and knowing very little of the later Old Testament history, the Kebra Nagast's compilers must have presumed that this story came from the history of King Solomon. But the fact that this was really a later account about the Babylonian exile is confirmed by the fact that the Kebra Nagast links the nation of Rom and King Darius, saying that Darius built twelve great cities, including Rom. The text then goes on to say that between Darius and Solomon was eighteen generations, which, if the order is reversed, is about correct – the Bible gives twenty generations between Solomon and the Babylonian exile. Although it is now sitting in the wrong position, the fact that this snippet of history has survived may be of some value.

The point of this investigation is to highlight the many pieces of circumstantial evidence that indicate that the descendants of Daniel were something to do with the origins of the Gypsy nation. This particular piece of text from the Kebra Nagast helps considerably in this regards and so these points of interest are as follows:

a. Daniel was of the tribe of Dan, as was Danaus who fled to Argos. Danaus has already been identified as the pharaoh Ay, who had a brother called Aegyptus, from whence the name 'Gypsy' was derived. No meaning is given for the modern name 'Egypt', but a stab in the dark at an Egyptian derivation could result in 'Stairway to Heaven'
[hieroglyphs] .

b. Daniel was known as Baltasar (Baltashazzar), the king of Rom. The alternative name for Gypsies is the Romany people, and so it would seem that the titles 'Gypsy' and 'Romany' were both derived from associations with the tribe of Dan.

c. Daniel was of Hyksos-Israelite stock, and these people had become known as the 'travellers' ever since the exodus (or perhaps before, due to the 'circling rituals' at Giza and Dahshur). Like the Shasu and Mashuash tribes, the Gypsies and Romanies are also famed for being travellers.

d. Of all the trades that the Romanies have developed over the centuries, the most noteworthy is that of fortune-telling. Daniel was reputed to have been the chief fortune-teller of the Babylonian/Persian empires.

e. The Romanies were said to have originated in Persia, which is where Daniel lived and where he rose to power.

Having highlighted all these points, does this represent an argument in favour of the Gypsies being descended from the Persian nation, which was known as Rom? Personally, I don't think that we shall ever know one way or the other. The truth of the matter is that the Romany people have no written history; they have not conserved an oral tradition that explains their origins; nor do they follow any recognised religious practice from which deductions could be made. Indeed, the absence of these two basic human traits is remarkably striking. Everywhere that mankind has settled throughout the world, the resulting tribes and nations have invoked some kind of religious practice and have attempted to explain the origins of their society; the Romanies, in complete contrast, seem content to exist in the present.

That the Gypsies have shunned this basic human need for a tribal history and a rationale for their existence may have something to do with their decentralised, nomadic lifestyle. Religion is primarily a power base for social control: remove the society, and the requirement for an organised religion and its accompanying tribal history rapidly diminishes. Having said that, on a personal level I as an individual would still like to know something about my origins, and so the Romany indifference to these social norms could equally be construed as being a deliberate attempt to distance themselves from their former lives.

Like an individual blanking a traumatic event out of their minds, the Romany nation may have collectively deleted their troubled history and former religious strife from their social traditions. But if the latter scenario were so, then there must be a social scar that runs through this travelling nation and prevents these people from getting involved with such contentious institutions ever again. Most immigrants into new countries pick up the traditions of the local population within a few generations; yet although the Romanies have entered every European country and have assimilated the local languages (in addition to their own), they have deliberately distanced themselves from the local populations and from the local belief systems for tens, if not scores, of generations.

While this lack of history and religion may make the Romanies very different from every other nation on this planet, this very difference demonstrates their close association with some of the tribes of the Hyksos. As I have already observed, the history of the world shows that immigrants into a country tend to assimilate with the local population; a process that inevitably modifies their language, culture, customs and religion. There are only two nations who have consistently bucked this trend, and they are the Jews and the Gypsies – but despite this similarity, these two nations are still like chalk and cheese. Both of these nations have been dispersed from their original homelands in the Near East, and yet one has spread throughout the world as a settled people with a long history and an obsessive passion for god, while the other spread throughout the world as a nomadic people with no history and no gods whatsoever. The equivalence in the differences between these two nations is quite striking.

But if the Romanies have a peculiar affinity to the Jews, is there any evidence to show that they once incorporated the same traditions? While the Gypsies do not hold a tribal history as such, they do maintain some traditions about nature and the outdoor environment in which they live;

rules and adages that (in their once truly rural existence) assisted them in their everyday existence. Some of these traditions, being less political or contentious, may well contain kernels of much older traditions. The most noteworthy of these that I could find was in a peculiar book on Gypsy history by Samuel Roberts, which he penned in 1836. As a complete aside to his thesis, Roberts mentions that his Gypsy tutor said:

> On seeing a mouse, she said that they used often to have dormice, which they called the Seven Sleepers. [11]

While dormice are known for sleeping, as that is what their name means, the designation of Seven Sleepers is still unusual. Considering the possible similarities between the Jews and the Gypsies, the mention of the Seven Sleepers just has to recall the account of the Seven Sleepers in both the Koran and the Gloria Martyrum, as translated by Gregory of Tours. Both of these accounts originated somewhere in the Arabias and the common source, I believe, was the exiled Hyksos. As I narrate in the book *Tempest*, the tradition of the Seven Sleepers was probably derived from a Hyksos initiation ceremony at Giza, and the sleepers were actually the sarcophagi of seven of the Hyksos kings.

So, could the Gypsy and Koranical Seven Sleepers be one and the same? It is difficult to say on this evidence, but it has to be said that the era, location and traditions do favour a common source.

Division

If the rest of the Biblical story of the sons of Solomon-Sheshonq can be taken at face value, it would be entirely in keeping with the politics of the era for this pharaoh's two favourite sons to have inherited the two provinces of Egypt and Judaea. The Bible also gives the possibility that another close relation or son, Jeroboam, gained control over the northern provinces of Israel after a show of force. Both Upper Egypt and Palestine had historically been difficult provinces for the Tanite pharaohs to control, and the installation of sons in each of these provinces would have been a sensible political manoeuvre. While this action may have divided the empire, it also gave a sense of autonomy to increasingly fractious local populations and it may have prevented the tendency towards internal disputes and even the possibility of civil war.

The account of the Kebra Nagast has therefore answered many of the question as to what happened to Solomon-Sheshonq's empire after his death. The story-line suggests that the empire was split into three provinces, with capital cities at Jerusalem, Tanis and Thebes. It would be unlikely that the Judaean arm of this disintegrating empire would have held the primary claim to the throne of Egypt, and so the Lower Egyptian twenty-second dynasty pharaohs, who followed Sheshonq I, are unlikely to have been recorded in the continuing lists of Biblical Judaean kings. Accordingly, when looking through the list of the kings of Judaea, there are no sensible matches of names to the corresponding list of pharaohs from Tanis.

It would seem that, subsequent to the reign of Solomon-Sheshonq, the Bible only recorded the kings of Judaea and Israel, while the Kebra Nagast recorded the achievements of the regional king (Menelek) at Thebes. What is not given by either of these texts is the history of the succeeding pharaohs at Tanis. In the historical record, the pharaoh who succeeded Sheshonq I is said to be Uasorkon I and he is thought to have been a son of Sheshonq. The Egyptian monarchs had retreated back to Tanis, while the Bible was now only concerned with the successors to the two pharaonic princes (now kings) who ruled Judaea and Israel.

This scenario would, however, have meant that the monarchs in both Judaea and Egypt were closely related. If this were so, then it is likely that these Judaean monarchs could have called upon their relatives for assistance during times of great need. There is a convincing piece of evidence in the Bible that appears to confirm that these monarchs were prepared to assist each other, as it would appear that more than one of the kings of Judaea had an alliance with a pharaoh of Egypt. The first of these stories concerns the campaigns of the Assyrian king, Shalmaneser, who took his armies down into Israel in the eighth century BC.

> And it came to pass in the fourth year of king Hezekiah ... that Shalmaneser king of Assyria came up against Samaria, and besieged it. And at the end of three years they took it ... And the king of Assyria did carry away Israel unto Assyria. [B12]

Of course, Shalmaneser was not satisfied with Israel – the northern lands of Palestine – he had his eyes on the province of Judaea and the wealthy city of Jerusalem as well. But it wasn't for another eight years that the next king of Assyria, Sennacherib, came into Judaea and started plundering its cities. Eventually, Jerusalem itself was besieged and a campaign of disinformation began on both sides. The Assyrians indicated that King Hezekiah's stripping of the gold from the Temple, to pay a tribute to the Assyrians, had defiled the Temple and that their god would desert the

Israelites. Hezekiah was deeply troubled and sought the advice of his chief prophet, Isaiah, who had an ingenious solution to this problem:

> And when (the Assyrian king) heard (rumour) of Tirhakah king of Ethiopia (saying) "Behold, he is come out to fight against thee". (The Assyrian king) sent messengers again unto Hezekiah, saying ... "Let not thy God in whom thou trusts deceive thee, saying, Jerusalem shall not be delivered into the hand of the king of Assyria". [B13]

In other words, Isaiah's ploy was to spread a rumour that the king of 'Ethiopia' would come to save the city of Jerusalem. But the problem with this story is that there is no reason to believe that any Ethiopian king would have come to the aid of the Judaeans, and equally there is no reason to suspect that the Assyrians would be unduly worried by the Ethiopian army even if they did come. So can this tale be given any credence whatsoever?

I think that the answer to this is yes, because the king involved was known as Tirhakah and, far from being an Ethiopian king, he was in fact the pharaoh Taharqa (Taharkhah) of the twenty-fifth dynasty. The Egyptologist, Donald Redford, dismisses the Bible as being wholly unreliable on this point of detail:

> And if we remind ourselves that the pharaoh ... Taharqa is wrongly identified in the Biblical narrative, we cannot help but conclude that the Biblical writers ... lacked precise knowledge of Egypt. [14]

While Redford likes to dismiss each and every statement in the Bible as being unreliable, this great history book of the Hyksos nation is not quite so mistaken as one might expect in its 'confusion' between an Ethiopian king and an Egyptian pharaoh. In a similar fashion to the text of the Kebra Nagast, it would seem that the Bible was simply confusing the term 'Ethiopia' with the province of Upper Egypt, and there are two possible explanations for this muddle. Either the scribes were deliberately altering the references from 'Upper Egypt' to 'Ethiopia', in order to distance all things Egyptian from the history of the Israelites, or perhaps they were instead genuinely confused by the terms 'Ethiopia' and 'Nubia'.

This confusion between Ethiopia and Nubia has been primarily precipitated by a confusion in the later translation process, as the Torah was being made available in English. The term that the Hebrew Bible was using to denote Ethiopia was Cush כוש, which actually refers to Nubia and which was derived from the Egyptian word Kush ⳩, which also means Nubia. While the Torah was absolutely correct in its identification, the King James Bible consistently translates this same word as 'Ethiopia' for some reason; whereas later Bibles translate it as either 'Ethiopia' or 'Nubia', a process that is seemingly dependent upon a translator's whim.

The theological assertion that Kush or Nubia should include the lands of Ethiopia is completely unjustified and I am not sure how this strange translation has come about – certainly it is quite an established tradition, as my 1657 King James Bible uses this exact same translation. From the historical point of view, however, the lands of Kush (Nubia) are assumed to denote the far south of Egypt and the Sudan, and so the lands of Kush have nothing whatsoever to do with Ethiopia.

The confusion between Nubia and Upper Egypt is a different matter, however, and this error may have been exacerbated by the history of the Egyptian monarchy. While the twenty-first and twenty-second dynasties had Nubian associations and possessions, the twenty-fifth dynasty was actually known in the historical record as a line of 'Nubian' pharaohs of Egypt. Although the Bible's confusion between Egypt and Nubia is therefore understandable, the confusion between Nubia and Ethiopia is much less so.

The Biblical writers then go on to relate how the rumour of military intervention by King Tirhakah of 'Ethiopia' was not simply a rumour. According to the Bible, the 'Ethiopians' (the Upper Egyptians) attacked the Assyrian camp and won a great victory. Sennacherib was then said to have retired back to Assyria and, at some unspecified point in time Adrammelech and Sharezer, the Assyrian king's sons, murdered their father. This assassination is acknowledged as being a historical reality and the date for this murder is given in the historical record as being in 681 BC.

Far from 'lacking knowledge', it would seem that the Biblical scribes knew a lot about this era and its events. The only confusion in their Biblical history was in regard to the origins of this attacking force from the south, but that, as we have just seen, was probably deliberate.

Not only do the names and circumstances of these two histories match, but the dates are reasonably accurate too. The classical chronology of Egypt gives a reign for the Egyptian pharaoh, Taharqa, of 690-644 BC. On the other hand, the reign of the Judaean king, Hezekiah, is reckoned to be from 728-698 BC, a reign length of thirty years. The siege of Jerusalem occurred at some date after the fourteenth year of the reign of King Hezekiah, but obviously before his thirtieth year when he died. The Bible gives this siege of Jerusalem as being the last event in the life of Hezekiah, but this could either mean the siege was in the last years of his reign, or that nothing else of significance occurred before his death. If the period between the twentieth and thirtieth years of his reign is assumed to be the most likely for the siege, it should have occurred – according to the Biblical timescale – between the years 708 and 698 BC.

On the other hand, from the historical perspective, the siege could not have been lifted before the year 690 BC, when the pharaoh Taharqa came to the throne, and it must have been lifted before 681 BC, the date that marked the assassination of Sennacherib by his sons. In this case, we have just an eight-year discrepancy between the Biblical and Egyptian histories and the associated royal chronologies of this era.

All in all, a discrepancy of such a small magnitude is quite remarkable. However, it has to be remembered that this is a relative and not an absolute date. Because the known dates of Israel and Egypt are matched against each other and then against the Babylonian and Persian campaigns, there is bound to be a broad agreement between the two histories – but that does not necessarily infer that the absolute date is correct. If the date of the Babylonian conquest of Israel were slightly wrong, for instance, this would have a consequential knock-on effect for the dates in Judaea and Egypt. The two chronologies would stay synchronised, but the absolute date could shift significantly.

But the accuracy of the chronology of this era, however interesting a subject, was not the point of this particular investigation. The question posed was, were the subsequent kings of southern Palestine, Judaean or Egyptian monarchs? The answer to this has to be the former. King Hezekiah of Judaea was besieged in his capital city of Jerusalem, and it was the Egyptian pharaoh Taharqa who came to his rescue. The main point of this particular event is that there were two distinct royal lines at this period, one Judaean and the other Egyptian; although it is still likely that there were close blood-ties between the two families.

Saba

If the empire of King Solomon-Sheshonq was divided after his reign, the evidence that has been presented so far indicates that Menelek, the hero of the Kebra Nagast, eventually became an (Upper) Egyptian monarch rather than an Ethiopian king. Although this appears to rule out any links to Ethiopia, it is an undoubted fact that Ethiopia has inherited many traditions that are somehow linked to the Israelites and to the story of the Queen of Sheba. One question that still remains, therefore, is how these traditions found their way into Ethiopia.

One possible route would have been via the kingdom of Saba. As was mentioned in chapter III, despite a complete lack of archaeological evidence, it has long been assumed by many historians that the Queen of Sheba was a monarch of the Sabean nation, who once occupied modern Yemen; the reason for this 'close' association between Saba and Sheba being based upon a dodgy chronology, a few Arabic myths and a similar-sounding name. Having previously dismissed the notion that the Sabeans were anything to do with the Queen of Sheba, I will now completely turn that position around and say that they were very much a part of the Sheba story – but not quite in the fashion that historians imagine.

I think that the established chronology of the Sabean people is approximately correct. Although a reasonable amount of serious archaeology has been completed in Yemen, and although a significant number of translatable texts have been discovered, the weight of evidence shows that the Sabeans did not rise to a position of relative power until somewhere between the sixth and seventh centuries BC. This chronology presents historians with a problem, because it is far too late to have had anything to do with the kingdom of the Queen of Sheba. Yet, despite acknowledging this fact, the respected authorities in the field, like Alessandro de Maigret, continue to link the Sabeans with the Queen of Sheba.

Although it may appear to be a major stumbling block, this chronology is not so much a problem as an answer. The evidence I will now present indicates that the land of Saba did not *spawn* the traditions of the Queen of Sheba – instead, the complete opposite of this is true and the Sabeans actually *inherited* these traditions from this legendary queen. The clear inference of this evidence, if it is judged to be true, is that the Sabeans were actually the descendants of the court of Solomon-Sheshonq, who migrated into Southern Arabia in a later era. It was through this process that a new city state, which had close links to the Queen of Sheba, was eventually founded in a remote spot on the Arabian peninsular.

So, who were the Sabeans? This wealthy nation grew from the occupation of a town called Marib, whose ruins now lie in the highlands to the north of Aden in modern Yemen. It is widely thought that these people were invaders who arrived in Southern Arabia from an unknown location to the north. They appear to have brought into this region a whole range of new technologies, from architecture and literature to agriculture and irrigation. Of all the walled cities and irrigation projects that were initiated by the Sabeans, their most obvious legacy – which shows their mastery of a whole range of technologies – was the walled city of Marib, its associated temple of Awwam, and the great Marib dam.

The Marib dam was a tremendous achievement for the era; it consisted of a wide, earthwork dam with two massive stone sluicegates, one at either end. The dam contained the seasonal waters of the Dhana Wadi, and these two exquisitely constructed sluicegates regulated the irrigation of the lower plains, producing some 40 sq km of fertile arable land.

From these small beginnings the people of Marib, under the rule of their first leader Karib'il I, set out on an aggressive campaign of expansion; and it would appear that these Sabean wars involved a comprehensive defeat and subjugation of the local population. In the fifth and sixth campaigns alone, which are documented in the inscriptions of Karib'il, the Sabeans conquered the cities of Ashr, Bayhan, Nashan, Nashq, Qawm, Jaw'al, Dawr, Fadhm, Shibam, Ayk, Zalam and Hurmat: the result of this rapid expansion being that Saba was propelled from a small city state to a cosmopolitan empire encompassing most of the Yemen in the space of one generation. The speed of this advance demonstrates how much more advanced than the indigenous population this new, invading force really was.

With their new irrigation and agricultural techniques, the Sabeans were then able to dominate the spice trade and it would appear that much of their later wealth and regional influence was based upon the export of cash crops, assisted by their extensive trade links with the rest of the known world. The Sabeans apparently still held this privileged position at the beginning of the Roman period and, in order to secure continued supplies of aromatic spices, the Roman emperor Gallus dispatched a large army to subdue Saba. No doubt the Sabeans were charging too much for their produce and the Romans found it cheaper to send in the army rather than be subjected to extortion.

The historical texts cheerfully say that this all-important European trade, which eventually required a military assault on Saba, was all down to the Romans' love of 'aromatic spices' and incense for their religious rituals. While historians may be happy with this explanation, I personally do not think it is the full story. In reality, much of the 'aromatics' that the Sabeans were trading were probably based upon hemp, a plant that is native to central Asia and grows well in these hot but well-irrigated environments. While hemp is a useful raw material for rope-making, its main value lies in its resin, which is the basis for hashish or cannabis. Hashish was not only smoked throughout the Middle East, as it is today, it was also well known and widely used in much of first century Europe. This would have been an ideal product for Sabean exports as, considering the transport restrictions of the era, cash crops for export had to be relatively small and of high value. Both traditional spices and cannabis fitted that category precisely. It is equally certain that the nation that controlled the production and distribution of this narcotic would be inordinately wealthy, just as the Sabeans were.

This rapid expansion for the Sabean nation; their undoubted technical expertise; and their (later) trading links that reached out across much of Europe, once more demonstrates that the Sabeans were most probably an invading force who were able to control, manipulate and dominate the local population of the Yemen almost at will.

The era in which the local Sabean leader, Karib'il, came to power is variously given as anywhere between 500 and 700 BC; and although the location that Karib'il came from and the cultural origins of his people are not expressly given, if we were to take an average of the various guestimates given for the date of the Sabean invasion of Yemen and call it 600 BC, there might be a logical contender for this role.

In 597 BC, after a battle with the Egyptians, the Babylonian king Nebuchadnezzar invaded Israel and Judaea. After a siege of unknown duration, the city of Jerusalem surrendered and a great number of its citizens were taken into exile in Babylon. While the people licked their wounds and rebuilt their houses, calamity was about to strike the land once more. Zedekiah, the new puppet king of Judaea and Israel rebelled against his Babylonian overlords and so, less than ten years later, the Babylonians were back with a larger force. After decimating the countryside and all of the outlying towns, Jerusalem finally fell for a second time. This time the Babylonians finished the job more thoroughly – not only was the Temple and much of Jerusalem destroyed, but so too was the line of kings from Judah, the Judaic arm of the Hyksos monarchy that was descended from King Solomon-Sheshonq.

Is it entirely possible that, with the grim reaper gathering in his grizzly harvest throughout the lands of Judah and Israel, one or two Judaic leaders and a body of its citizens decided to evacuate these troubled lands. They would probably have set out from Elat on the Red Sea, and made their way down the Arabian peninsular towards modern Yemen. Did these same people find a warm welcome in the town of Marib, whose leaders happily accepted their own subjugation in return for a promise of technical assistance and great wealth? I think that this is exactly what happened, and the first piece of evidence for this comes from the Biblical texts:

> Then a breach was made in the city wall and the king with all the men of war fled by night by the way of the gate between the two walls ... and they went in the direction of the Arabah. [B15]

It would appear that a substantial portion of the Judaean army fled into the Arabias. Although their exact destination is not given in this account, a good case can be made to show that they actually went to Saba (perhaps via Egypt) and the evidence for this lies in the philology of the Sabean people.

The initial leaders of the Sabeans were known locally as Mukarribs, a term that infers a leader but not exactly the role of a king. The Mukarribs of Saba did not become kings for another two or three hundred years, when they exchanged titles and became known as Melek Saba, or kings of Saba. What the historians fail to point out, however, is that the term *melek*, meaning king, is actually Hebrew. The equivalent Hebrew word, *melek* מֶלֶךְ, has exactly the same pronunciation and meaning, and the son of the Queen of Sheba was called Menelek for this very reason – because he became a king.

But if the Sabean word for king was Judaic, then what of that initial term for leader? Was this word supposed to be Mukarr-ib or, by using a slightly different emphasis in the pronunciation, was it instead Maakare-ib? The original Egyptian pronunciation of the title for the Maakhah Tamars was either Maakare or Maatkare, and so it was interesting to see that the Italian transliteration of this same Sabean title was Maadkar-ib – the words could not be more similar if they tried. But this is not simply a case of similar phonetics, because the myths of the region strongly associate the lands of Saba with the Queen of Sheba, who has already been identified as being one of the Maakhah Tamar (Maatkare Mu-Tamhat) queens.

Under the circumstances, having a leader who was called a Maadkar-ib would have been quite appropriate. In addition, the suffix of *ib* has already been explained as being the Egyptian term for 'wisdom', a word that may still have echoes in the Hebrew word *leb* לֵב, which also means 'wisdom'. The resulting compound title for these early Sabean leaders would therefore have been the 'Wisdom of Maakare', or the 'Wisdom of the Queen of Sheba'.

These small snippets of information seem to be pointing towards a Judaic origin for the nation of Saba, and perhaps more specifically, a Judaic sect who were influenced by and worshipped Maakhah Tamar II [the Queen of Sheba], who had undoubtedly undergone some kind of deification in the centuries since King Solomon's death.

That this process of deification may have taken place at an early date is perhaps confirmed by a recent discovery at Bubastis, a city that lies to the south of Tanis and that rivalled it in status during later dynasties. To one side of the main temple complex at Bubastis, a large statue dedicated to one of the Uasorkon pharaohs has been unearthed. Bearing in mind the fact that Uasorkon I married one of the Maakare Mu-Tamhat princesses, and the fact that this statue's design closely mimics that of Maakare Mu-

308

Tamhat's sarcophagus, it is hard not to associate this statue with the deified Queen of Sheba. (See the colour section for a comparison, and note the possibility that this statue may be bare-breasted.)

If the titles of these Sabean kings may seem to have had Judaic origins, then what of the kings of Saba themselves? What can they tell us about the origins of these people? The first of the Sabean leaders was called Karib'il, and I have no doubt that this name was based upon the formal title of Mu-<u>Karrib</u>, but with the initial *Mu* being dropped. This dropping of the initial *Mu* is rather similar to the dropping of the *Mu* at the beginning of the name Mu-Tamhat (Tamar) and one could speculate that *Mu* had become a silent syllable in the Semitic languages, like the redundant 'p' in the spelling of psychology. The suffix of *il* (*el*) that was being used in the name Karib'il was, according to Alessandro de Maigret, simply the Semitic god-name El. Yet again, there seems to be a direct Semitic influence over the Sabean people.

The reason why this similarity between the Sabean titles Karib and Maadkarib (Maakare) is so important, is to be found within the remaining names of the kings of Saba. The early monarchs of Saba only had five different names, which were repeated endlessly throughout this dynasty. Surprisingly enough, all of these Sabean leaders seem to have had names with Judaic origins. The names were:

Sabean king	Judaic name
Karib'il	Maakhah (ib)
Thamar	Tamar
Sumhuali	Samuel
Yakrub-Malik	Jacob-King
Yada	Yada
Yatha-Amar	Yatha

Note how the name Tamar is conspicuous in the Biblical and Egyptian texts by its repeated association with the name Maakhah [Maatkare]. It would seem that in Saba there is the same kind of association, thus two of the kings of Saba were none other than Kare-ib (Maakare) and Thamar (Tamar). The direct transformation of Sumhuali and Yakrub into Samuel and Jacob is also quite a striking transliteration of two famous Judaic names.

If the other names in the list, Yada and Yatha, do not seem to be quite so obviously Judaic, that is probably because the English equivalents of these names have been badly translated. Within the court of David and Solomon, however, there were important officials and royal princes with the following names:

Hebrew name	English translation
Ab-Yathar	Abiathar
El-Yathar	Eliathah
El-Yada	Eliada
Yow-Yada	Joiada
Baal-Yada	Beeliada
Yehow-Yada	Jehoiada

Note that, in a similar fashion to the list of Sabean names, the Judaic equivalents have various god-names attached to them; presumably this was done as a method of differentiating between the otherwise identical names. But if the names of the early Sabean kings may look distinctly Semitic, then so too do the names of the gods that they worshipped.

The Semitic god-name of *El* has already been mentioned, but another Sabean word that was often used to prefix the names of their gods was *djuat*. According to the translations of these texts, this word is supposed to mean 'she of', but this word also looks rather similar to the Egypto-Semitic word *djuat*, which was a reference to the entrance door of heaven. The prime god of the Sabeans was called Athar, who was a direct counterpart of the Phoenician/Semitic god Astarte. Another of their prominent gods was called Wadd-Ab, and while the word *wadd* may be elusive, the term *ab* אב is simply the Hebrew word for 'father', and it is translated as such directly from the Sabean. The last of these Semitic deities is the Sabean Sun-goddess, Shames, which just has to have been based upon the Hebrew name for the Sun, which was *Shemesh* שמש, and which was in turn based upon the Egyptian *shemu* and *shemm* , meaning 'summer' and 'hot' respectively.

Thus far, the gods of the Sabeans have taken on a distinctly Semitic flavour, which surely links this culture with the Semitic tribes of Judaea and Israel. Although all of these suggestions are being driven by the desire to link the Queen of Sheba with the Sabeans, as the myths of the region infer, this proposed Semitic history is nevertheless roughly in line with current historical thinking, which places the influences of the Sabeans and the adjacent Maaneans back into Phoenicia and Greece:

> We have here evidence of four principal (Arabic) alphabets ... All of these have written similarities to Phoenician, but also enough differences to exclude a direct derivation. The most likely answer is that the Arabian alphabets are very ancient and were derived, along with Phoenician, from a common root.

...coins started to bear an owl motif typical of Athenian currency ... We also find a strong Greek influence in the arts, especially in the later period.[16]

In the search for a nation that could be considered the 'common root' to both Phoenicia and Greece, we need look no further than the Hyksos-Israelites. It is known that the Hyksos had close contacts with and similarities to the Minoan empire, which is but one step away from Greece. It is also an established fact that the Greeks formed a part of the Sea People alliance, and also came to the aid of the Saite (Lower Egyptian) pharaoh, Psamthik II (Psammetichus II); and the Hyksos (Semitic) sympathies of this particular pharaoh were subsequently confirmed by his foray into Palestine in support of the Judaean king, Zedekiah. Likewise, I have already outlined the possible Hyksos (Semitic) origins of the Phoenicians in the book *Jesus*.

In fact, much of the Sabean artwork appears to be quite reminiscent of Minoan art and architecture. Perhaps the most striking example of this is the figurative decoration carved on the doorway of the Temple of Aathtar. These friezes contain a number of female figures, which seem to bear a striking resemblance to the famous faïence figurine from the Temple of Repositories in Knossos. Indeed, in baring her breasts quite so prominently, this Minoan figurine was quite possibly emulating the role of the Maakhah Tamars, the 'Lady of the Breast'.

But if the Sabeans were descended from yet more Hyksos refugees (later refugees, from Judaea), then we should also be able to find Egypto-Semitic influences within their culture. This is indeed the case, and so it can be seen that the symbol for the Sabean god El was a 'crescent Moon with a circle inside'; a design which has immediate Egyptian connotations as this was the symbol for the Egyptian Moon-god Yah 𓇹𓏏𓀭 . In the book *Tempest*, I have already equated this Moon-god with the Biblical Yahweh, and yet the Biblical texts use this same name interchangeably with the god El. Since the Israelites were only supposed to worship one god, Yahweh must be the same god as El, but the hieroglyph for Yah [Yahweh] was the god Thoth, wearing his usual crescent-moon and circle headdress. When expanded for more clarity, the headdress looks like ☺ , and this glyph is, of course, a superimposition of the Egyptian Sun-god Ra and the Moon-god Yah.

In addition to the Egyptian El, we also find that the storm god of the Sabeans was called Dju(at)-Qabd. The *Djuat* is the equivalent of the Egyptian *Djuat* 𓇼𓃀𓈖𓏏 , while the *Qabd* is the Egyptian *Qabhu* 𓈎𓃀𓊖𓈖𓈖 , which refers to 'cool water' and the 'waters of heaven'. In other words, the Sabean storm god called Dju(at)-Qabd can be translated in the Egyptian as 'Storms from Heaven'. Another name for the Sabean god *Qabd* was *Sharqan*, and it is a little remiss of the archaeologists not to point out that the Egyptian title *Sharqan(sa)* 𓏏𓅓𓈖𓏤𓉐 was the Nubian name for the Egyptian god, Amen (Amun).

While the following translation is not quite so certain, the last name for this Sabean deity was pronounced as 'Theban', which could well have been derived from the Egyptian word *teban* (*djeban*) ⌒𓏤𓂻𓏥, meaning 'to revolve', or 'to wander around in circles'. The connection between the gods and the wandering in circles may stem from the circling ritual, a ceremony that I have argued originally took place around the pyramids but eventually became the origins of the circling of the Qa'ba (Ka'ba) in Mecca. If this association were true, however, it may go some way towards explaining the oval design of the temple of Awwam at Marib. If an Islamic-type circling ceremony was a central part of these Sabean rituals, then an oval enclosure like Awwam's would have been an obvious design for any temple.

If these associations with Mecca can be taken one step further, then perhaps this oval enclosure once contained a rectangular shrine at its very center; in which case, this Sabean temple would have been the original model for the later Al-Haram mosque at Mecca. Indeed, the whole of modern Islamic culture and religion may well have been descended from these Sabean people, who seem to have migrated northwards towards the Euphrates after their precious dam at Marib failed for the fourth and final time. This would infer that Islam is simply a corrupted, fifth-hand rendition of the original rituals that once took place at Giza, and since the Koran is primarily a garbled synopsis of the Judaic Torah, this scenario is entirely plausible.

A possible confirmation of these Islamic origins can be seen in the name of a Sabean governor, a <u>Kabir</u> (Arabic - Kafir; English - Gaffer), which has links to the Egyptian language once more. The determinative glyph being used in the Egyptian word *teban* was the 'intestines' glyph ⌒, which, for obvious reasons, can also have connotations of 'coils' or 'circling', and these intestinal coils were also associated with the image of a coiled snake. Thus, the Egyptian word for the intestine, which is *qab* (*kab*, <u>kabir</u>) 𓂝𓃭⌒ , could be taken to mean 'coiled snake', 'intestine' and 'to circle'. In which case, the Sabean governor known as a Kabir could be regarded as the leader of these circling rituals.

The link between the Egyptian word for intestines and the city of Mecca is that this same word (*qab*) is also used to denote the 'middle', especially the 'middle of the body', just as one might expect (as does the Hebrew word *qerab* קרב). In a similar fashion, the Ka'ba in Mecca is known as the Navel of the Universe and the Islamic faithful circle around this sacred shrine during the Hajj. Quite surprisingly, the Islamic Ka'ba can be seen to be the same as the Egyptian intestine glyph in no less than three ways: they are both known as Ka'b(a); they both refer to the navel; and they both refer to a crowd perambulating in a circle.

In the book *Tempest*, I pointed out that the word 'Ka'ba' could have been based upon the Egyptian *Ka* and *Ba*, the 'body' and 'soul'; but in some respects these two explanations are complementary. The Egyptian scribes loved the odd pun or two, and so to be able to make the 'body and soul' sound the same as the intestines (the viscera) was probably quite satisfying to them. The fact that these same intestines could be considered to be 'circles' and were used for the purpose of sacrifice and divination at these ceremonies was doubly satisfying. This ritual usage infers that the intestines were not simply treated as coils of offal; they were considered to be special elements of the body, perhaps the seat of the body's soul or life-force.

Although I have suggested that the circling ceremony of the Hyksos-Israelites originally took place at the Giza or Dahshur pyramids, there were other locations and constructions of equal importance for these people. Perhaps the most important temple in all of Egypt once lay at Heliopolis, and a quote from the texts of the historian Josephus indicates that this temple once housed a tall tower that was surmounted by the sacred Benben stone. In the book *Jesus*, I follow the history of these towers and find that they have been reproduced in many of the countries that the exiled Hyksos-Israelites have fled to. From the foothills of the Himalayas, to many of the islands in the Mediterranean and onto the barren moors of Ireland, large enigmatic stone round-towers have been constructed, and their many and varied locations seem to be coincident with countries that I have proposed for the exiled Hyksos.

It has been argued by historians that these towers, which are called *nuraghi* on the island of Sardinia, were defensive positions, but my subsequent investigations have shown that they must have instead had a religious purpose. My original proposal was that these round-towers were actually phallic totems, which were based upon the original Benben tower at Heliopolis, which was in turn a representation of the phallus of Atum. Since Maakhah Tamar was known as the 'Handmaiden of God', and since it is also reported that she was caught in the act of worshipping an erect penis, it is extremely likely that both she and her adherents would also have been familiar with and associated with the cult of the phallic round-tower.

If the Sabeans were indeed these same exiled Hyksos people, who had fled from either Egypt or Judaea at a later date, one might expect that the highlands of Yemen should not only be associated with the deified Maakhah Tamar, but also be populated with the ubiquitous (often truncated) round-tower. Not surprisingly, this is exactly what has been found in this region:

> Turret tombs are distinguishable from the others by their shape – they look like small Sardinian *nuraghi*... [17]

While historians love to label these truncated Mediterranean round-towers as being defensive positions, the purpose of the Sabean *nuraghi* conforms much closer to my alternative interpretation of their role. Not only are the Sabean versions far too small to have been defensive positions, they were overtly used as ritual (burial) monuments. But perhaps the most convincing piece of evidence for the ritual and phallic nature of these round-towers is yet another linguistic comparison.

Since these monuments were based on Egyptian ritual and practice, they would originally have been called *maktal* 𓏏𓎡𓈖𓇋𓊖 or *magdjal* 𓍑𓏤𓈎𓇋𓊖 ⊗ , meaning 'tower'. As has been demonstrated earlier, it was from these ancient roots that the Hebrew word *migdal* (*magdil*) מגדל, meaning 'tower', was derived. But as this word spread out across the Near East, it underwent modification: the Greeks transliterated it into *magdala* μαγδαλα or *magadan* μαγαδαν, while the Indians managed to reverse it completely and form the Sanskrit word *lingam* (the 'd' being changed to an 'n' to make the word pronounceable). The point about this latter transposition is that the resulting Sanskrit word has managed to preserve the meaning of the original ritual purpose of these towers, because this word means 'penis'. In fact, this same word has crept into the English language too, and the English word lingam also means 'penis'. [18]

Here, at last, the complete reason for Mary Magdalene receiving her second title can be clearly seen. The name Magdalene means 'tower' and it was directly derived from the Egyptian original, *maktal*. As a descendant of the long line of Maakhah Tamars, Mary Magdalene would also have been a 'Virgin' and a 'Handmaiden of God' (God's Wife), who caressed the erect phallus of Atum. But since the round-tower was a representation of this same phallus (or the *magdal* was a *lingam*), no doubt this ancient ritual involved much caressing and anointing of these round-towers by the Maakhah Tamars and the later Marys. To reflect this sacred and exalted role, Mary was given the subsidiary title of Magdalene, which not only meant 'Mary of the Tower', but also more graphically referred to 'Mary of the Penis'.

When relating this evidence to the Sabean round-towers, it is entirely possible that this phallic ritual became unacceptable to the priesthood in Judaea during the seventh century BC, and evidence for this will be presented shortly. In order to continue their devotions, the followers of Maakhah Tamar would have had no alternative but to find another location in which they could practice their beliefs and rituals; and it is for this reason that these phallic towers can be seen as a prominent feature of the Yemen landscape. It is estimated that, like the *nuraghi* of Sardinia, there are several thousand of these ritual (burial) towers scattered throughout southern Arabia, and their presence in the region can only serve to support the links with the United Monarchy and the exiled Hyksos-Judaeans hypothesis.

But if the presence of round-towers in southern Arabia supports the notion of a cultural link with the United Monarchy of Judaea, then the converse of this argument should also be true. If the round-towers were intimately connected with the Hyksos-Judaeans, and if a substantial proportion of this population worshipped the deified Maakhah (Tamar), then shouldn't some of the other countries that sport these round-towers be linked with Maakhah (Tamar) too? What about Ireland? While the cult of the later New Testament Mary (Maakhah) is notably strong in Ireland, is this due to recent Christian influences or to a much earlier priestess called Maakhah (Mary), whose cult arrived on the shores of the Sacred Isle along with the design of the round-towers themselves?

Many books have been written on the links between Egypt and Ireland, and most of these have highlighted the similarities between the Tuath-de-Danaans, the mythological ancestors of the Irish, and the pharaoh Danaus, who was evicted from Egypt. As has already been explained, Danaus has been linked with the Daanu Sea People from Argos (Greece) and his brother Aegyptus with the Gypsies, but did Danaus also travel to Ireland, as these speculative Irish authors claim?

In actual fact, this is a subject worthy of a complete book in its own right, but perhaps a couple of small snippets from the great body of evidence that is available in favour of this argument are due. The term 'Tuath-de-Danaan' is reputed to refer to the 'People of Danu', who arrived in Ireland at some time in the dim and distant past and defeated the Fir Bholg, the original rulers of Ireland. While the word *tuath* is said to mean 'people', it has to be noted that this term is remarkably similar to the Egyptian term *djuat*, which is so closely linked with the Hyksos rulers who eventually formed the United Monarchy of Judaeo-Egypt. In which case, the term 'Tuath-de-Danaan' may well have originally referred to the 'Star of Danus'.

The second strand of evidence is contained within Keating's *History of Ireland*. It would appear that the three female deities of the Tuath-de-Danaans were known as Badhha, Moriagen and Macha. Alternatively,

Robert Graves indicates that these deities were actually called Badb, Ana and Macha, and these three were together called the Morrigan. The reference to a goddess called Macha, when mentioned alongside a reference to the *djuat*, just has to be an allusion to the Egypto-Judaean princess, Maakhah Tamar.

Thus, in three separate locations – Lower Egypt, Saba and Ireland – the deified Maakhah (Tamar) and the cult of the round-tower are to be found co-located and revered. The possibility that the modern Irish cult of burning candles to the Virgin Mary was originally based upon the pre-Christian ritual of burning incense to Maakhah (Tamar), would serve to explain Mary's near-universal attraction in that land. But which of the two Marys was being venerated here: was it the Virgin or was it the Magdalene? Since the name 'Magdalene' has been derived from the Hebrew word *migdal* and the Sanskrit word *lingam* – meaning 'tower' and 'penis' respectively – and since Ireland is littered with these phallic round-towers, it is entirely possible that the primary focus of early Christian worship in Ireland would have been the Magdalene (although it is likely that both of the Marys would have held this same title). Whichever of the two Marys was the more important, this Irish cult of Mary (Maakhah Tamar) would appear to have transcended the worship of god himself, and yet this is the very same impropriety that the Biblical prophet Jeremiah accused the Sabeans of – as we shall see shortly.

Having fully explored the history of the Sabean round-towers, yet another example of Hyksos-Israelite building technology in Saba is to be found in the construction methods that were employed on the magnificent Marib dam's sluicegates. The walls of these two constructions employed a distinctive decoration, which involved leaving raised sections of some stones uncut. This is merely a modification of the walling technique that was used in early Israeli architecture, and examples of this can be seen in the excavations that were undertaken at the city of Samaria, where walling attributed to the reign of Ahab in the ninth century BC displays a very similar style. [19]

Another example of the close association between Judaea and Saba are the people themselves, for it is known that the region around Saba was once the home to one of the oldest known Jewish diaspora communities. The Teman Jews (Yemen Jews) claim to have been the direct descendants of Jews who had fled the destruction of the Temple by the Babylonians in about 586 BC. While this claim has often been doubted, the history and chronology that is being unearthed in this chapter would strongly support the claims being made by these Teman Jews. [21] The Torah also narrates a similar story about a group of 80,000 priests who fled the destruction of the

Temple and went to the lands of the Ishmaelites, or the Arabs; a tale that sounds very similar to the Biblical verse previously mentioned, and the history of the Teman Jews.

The final piece in this extensive jigsaw puzzle, which may finally determine the origins of the Sabeans, may well be contained in the name of one of their greatest monuments. Just across the river from the city of Marib lies the Temple of Awwam, which is known locally as Mahram Bilqis. Since the name Bilqis is just the Arabic name for the Queen of Sheba, then this temple is known locally as the Temple (or sanctuary) of the Queen of Sheba. But the archaeologist, Eduard Glaser, discovered an inscription on the outside of this temple that stated that the temple was dedicated instead to the god Al Maqah, as was the Temple of Al Maqah at Sirwah. While Al-Maqah is known to have been the patron god of Saba, the meaning of the Sabean term 'Maqah' is not known; but since this name occurs in the same context as the Egypto-Judaic terminology that has already been covered in great detail, the Sabean Temple of Maqah just has to have been dedicated to the worship of Maakhah [Maakare].

Surprising as it may seem, the Temple of Awwam in the distant lands of Saba, which is also known as the Temple of the Queen of Sheba, was originally known as the Temple of Maqah, or the Temple of Maakhah Tamar II. Once more, we see this inescapable union between the terms Maakhah and Sheba. This rapidly growing body of evidence seems to conclusively show that Maakhah Tamar II was indeed the Queen of Sheba; that she had become deified by the exiled Judaeans who had fled to Saba; and that temples dedicated to her worship had been constructed all over this region.

This would again indicate that the Sabean people were actually Hyksos-Judaean exiles, most probably from a period long after the era of the United Monarchy, and that the Queen of Sheba [Maakhah Tamar II] had made such a strong impression on the people of Judaea that she had gained cult status. Some members of this cult must have evaded the predations and invasions of the Babylonians and sought a new life in Yemen, and it was for this reason that the Sabeans considered themselves to be the 'progeny of Al-Maqah', or the 'descendants of Maakhah Tamar II'. [22]

Mashuash

This brings us to the people of Maa-in, who inhabited a region just to the north of the Sabeans. The Maa-in are thought to have arrived in Yemen at about the same time as the Sabeans, and if the term Saba has similarities to the Biblical Sheba, then the Maa-in has striking similarities to the Lower Egyptian people of Ma, the Mashuash. In fact, Maa-naean history further confirms the assumption that all of these people were exiled Hyksos-Israelites, and this can be seen upon a Maanean text that is simply known as RES 3022, which says:

> '... gratitude to the gods ... who delivered them from danger in Egypt during the (war) between Medys and Egypt'. [23]

Here we see a direct association between the Maaneans and the Egyptians. The text is implying that the gods delivered the Maaneans from Egypt, and that they had fled from Egypt during a war between the Egyptians and Medys. It has been assumed by some historians that this war refers to the revolt of Prince Inaros of Heliopolis, which was quelled by the Persian king, Artaxerxes I's invasion into Egypt in the fourth century BC. But was this so? Since the Maaneans were supposed to have been resident in Yemen for almost as long as the Sabeans, should they not have been escaping the disruption of a much earlier war in Egypt?

Both historians and the Bible identify the Medys as being the Persians, but the Bible goes one stage further and specifically identifies the Medes (sic) as being associated with Darius I, the Persian prince who took control of Persia after the assassination of Nebuchadnezzar's 'son', (Nabonidus?) and the promotion of Belshazzar [Daniel] to the position of vizier. The Biblical chronology has managed to jump some 20 years here, and has missed out the reigns of Cyrus II and Cambyses II completely. As Cambyses II had already conquered Egypt, the empire of the Persians included all of Egypt during this era, and so Darius I became pharaoh of Upper and Lower Egypt in about 520 BC. I have already proposed that the Sabeans may have fled Judaea during the campaigns of Nebuchadnezzar in about 600 BC, and the Maanean text just quoted would seem to confirm this – the Maaneans fled Egypt during the invasion of the Medes (Cambyses II and Darius I) into Egypt, an event that is classically dated to around 525 BC.

Just prior to this Persian invasion, the Egyptians, who had probably sent an army in support of their neighbours and allies in Judaea, suffered a great defeat at Carchemish on the Euphrates and had to retreat all the way back to the traditional Egyptian borders, where a number of skirmishes with the Persians were fought. Although it is not thought that Egypt itself was attacked at this time, the threat to her sovereignty must have been grave and it was at this time that the Lower Egyptian pharaoh, Psamthik II, sought the assistance of the bronze-clad Greeks:

... not long afterwards certain Carians and Ionians (Greeks) ... disembarked, all
equipped in their brazen armour ... Psammetichus made friendly advances to
the strangers and engaged them to enter into his service. He then, with their aid
... attacked the eleven (other princes) and vanquished them. [H24]

Herodotus is perhaps not the most trustworthy of all the ancient historians,
but this report is not that unreasonable. It has often been wondered why
Greece was so willing to give military support to the Lower Egyptian
princes; but if one of their ancestors had been the Amarna pharaoh Ay
[Danaus], and if the Egyptians were still able to pay handsomely with
gold plundered from King Solomon's Mines, then the reasons are plain
enough.

However, these Greek mercenaries were not just being used by
Psamthik II to conquer domestic enemies in Egypt; they were also being
used to repel the Persian incursions. The Persians came again to Egypt in
about 525 BC, under the rule of Cambyses II. Whether the Egyptians were
assisted on this occasion by the Greeks or not, this time the defeat for Egypt
was absolute, and Cambyses II was eventually crowned as pharaoh of all
Egypt.

Herodotus goes on to say that Cambyses was half Egyptian
through his mother, Nitetis, who was an Egyptian princess. It is difficult to
say how much truth there is in this account, but plainly it is another version
of the Biblical story of Baltasar-Daniel. Daniel was himself of Judaean
origins and the Bible indicates that he became a vizier of Babylon, while the
Kebra Nagast further suggests that Daniel's daughter married another prince
from Judaea. All of these events took place just before Cambyses II came to
the throne, and so the assertion by Herodotus that Cambyses II was half
Egyptian suggests that Cambyses was somehow descended from Baltasar-
Daniel.

While the invasion of Egypt by Cambyses II was reputed to have
been relatively swift and painless, undoubtedly there would still have been
turmoil and civil unrest throughout Egypt. It is not unusual for there to be
population migrations at such times, and the Lower Egyptian lands of the
Mashuash at Tanis and Avaris would have been the first in line for Persian
immigration and oppression. Although the evidence is only tentative, it
would certainly be in keeping with the history of this region for an
emigration of the Mashuash out of Egypt to have taken place at this time.
While it was not perhaps the most obvious of choices, a tribe of the
Mashuash may have thought the relatively remote and unpopulated lands
of Yemen were an ideal location in which to practice their religion
unhindered and unoppressed.

The evidence that shows this suggestion to be a distinct possibility was discovered in an excavation in the Yemen by R. Hamilton. During a season in the Wadi Jirdan, which lies to the south-east of Saba, he discovered a bronze warrior that was:

> ... to all intents and purposes, a Peloponnesian work of the sixth century BC. [25]

In other words, a piece of Greek armour was found near Saba that exactly matches the bronze armour that Herodotus said the Greeks who fought alongside the pharaoh Psamthik II (Psammetichus II) were wearing. It was Psamthik II who had gone to the aid of the Judaean king Zedekiah, and it was Psamthik II who had fled back to Egypt with the Persians in hot pursuit. Again, it was Psamthik III, only some sixty years later, who surrendered Egypt to the Persians and ushered in a whole dynasty of Persian pharaohs. If elements of Psamthik's court and soldiery had evacuated Egypt – either before or after this eventual defeat – in search of a safe refuge, they would have had access to exactly this kind of Greek armour. Indeed, it may have been one of Psamthik's Greek mercenary warriors who took this style of armour to Saba.

Jeremiah

Was this what happened all those years ago? Did a group of exiles really escape from Egypt and start a new, successful civilisation in Yemen? What we are looking for is a historical report of a group of Hyksos-Israelite people who venerated the Queen of Sheba, and who were evicted from Egypt at about the time that Jerusalem or Egypt fell to the ravages of the Babylonian and Persian empires. Could such an ancient text still exist?

Believe it or not, the complete account of the setting up of the kingdom of Saba is reported to us in great detail in the Bible. This account is contained in the book of Jeremiah, the Judaean priest of Jerusalem who officiated during the turbulent years of the last kings if Judaea. His tenure covered the period from the thirteenth year of King Josiah's reign, through to the Babylonian exile of King Zedekiah (about 625 – 587 BC); which in Egyptian terms covers the reigns of the pharaohs Necho, Psamthik II and Wahibre. (Jerusalem is supposed to have fallen to the Babylonians some sixty or so years before Egypt succumbed to the Persians.)

The account of Jeremiah begins after the second of the Babylonian incursions into Judaea. The first invasion had secured large tribute from

Jerusalem, whereas the second incursion destroyed the city and the Temple and saw the majority of the city's prominent citizens taken into exile in Babylon. Following this utter defeat for the Judaeans, Nebuchadnezzar had left a small force in Jerusalem to administer the region, under the command of Ahikam. Although Jerusalem had been destroyed, there were still many remnants of the Judaean army that had been scattered across the lands and, on hearing that there was only a token force of Persians left in the region, they started to drift back. Their discontent led to talk of yet another uprising, and two Judaean army commanders came to the fore in these discussions: Ishmael the son of Nethaniah and Johanan the son of Kareah. Ishmael was the more radical rebel of the two and so:

> Then arose Ishmael the son of Nethaniah, and the ten men that were with him, and smote Gedaliah the son of Ahikam ... with the sword, and slew him, whom the king of Babylon had made governor over the land. [B26]

Ishmael, the Judaean rebel commander, then took the daughters of the exiled Judaean king and fled to the relative safety of Ammon, a location which has already been identified as Egypt. It is said that Johanan disapproved of these actions, attacked the fleeing Ishmael and rescued the daughters, but this may just be a small deceit to distance Johanan from the murder of the Babylonian governor. Knowing the consequences of this murder, Johanan sought the advice of Jeremiah, the prophet. Jeremiah said they should stay in Jerusalem and god would protect them. The rebels wanted to go to Egypt, but Jeremiah prophesied that if they went to Egypt they would be annihilated by the sword and famine. The subplot in this discussion was probably that the high priest Jeremiah did not want the Judaean army, having just murdered the Babylonian governor, to leave the remaining population of Jerusalem unprotected. But despite the prophesy and the pleading by Jeremiah, Johanan, his army, and the princesses of Judaea all left for Egypt:

> So Johanan the son of Kareah, and all the captains of the forces, and all the people, disobeyed the voice of the Lord, to dwell in the land of Judah, (instead they) took all the remnant of Judah, that were returned from all nations ... Even men, and women, and children, and the king's daughters, and Jeremiah the prophet, and Baruch the son of Neriah. So they came into the land of Egypt ... even to Tahpanhes. [B27]

Here we have a tale of a band of exiles who had been forced out of

Jerusalem by the Babylonian invasion, and their choice of sanctuary was, not surprisingly, Egypt. In fact, they did not just go to the borders of Egypt, they went directly to the Egyptian royal court, for the word Tahpanhes (Tahpenes) was derived from the Egyptian phrase *Tah-Pa-Nesu* [hieroglyphs], meaning the 'King of the Two Lands' or, in other words, the 'King of Egypt'.

Since the phrase 'Tahpenes' refers to a person or to the royal court of Egypt, rather than to a location or a city, where did these people travel to, exactly? Is it possible to find out such trivial details after such a vast amount of time has elapsed since these events? The truth of the matter is rather surprising, for we may know exactly where these people went and exactly what they did there. It would seem that the pharaoh of Egypt, who was probably Wahibre (Apries), granted these refugees an old Hyksos fort at Yehudiyeh, which lies to the north east of Heliopolis and is more usually known as Leontopolis. Note how the name of this fort has retained its Judaic associations even to this day, with the name Yehudiyeh meaning the 'City of the Jews'.

The reason that I can confidently assert this as being the location in which Johanan and Jeremiah settled is the action that they may have taken upon reaching this fort. According to Flinders Petrie, a Judaic people made an extension to this fort at some point in time, which included a temple area. This extension to the fort was designed so that:

> It comprised a town and an isolated building higher than the rest ... the precious part of the whole place. This building had just the proportions of Solomon's Temple, and had an inner and outer court before it. The bricks were partly supplied by Jews (and the names in the cemetery were Jewish). Together, they seem to leave no possibility of the question that we have here the New Jerusalem and Temple...[28]

Petrie goes on to show that the arrangement of this temple and its proximity to the fort at Yehudiyeh were all designed to exactly mimic the layout of the Jerusalem Temple in the Old City of Jerusalem. It would appear that somebody had deliberately set out to recreate the city of Jerusalem and Temple of Solomon in the middle of the Nile Delta. The question is, however, which of the many Jewish exiles would have gone to all this trouble? Petrie explains that this must have been the work of Simon Onias, the high priest of Jerusalem who petitioned Ptolemy to build a temple at Yehudiyeh in about 160 BC. The reply from the Egyptian monarch was as follows:

> King Ptolemy and Queen Cleopatra* to Onias, send greeting. We have read thy petition, wherein you desire permission to be given to you to purge that temple which is fallen down at Leontopolis (Yehudiyeh), in the Nome of Heliopolis ... So Onias took the place, and built a temple, and an altar to god, like indeed to that in Jerusalem, but smaller and poorer.[J29]

Since Josephus says that the temple at Yehudiyeh was supposed to look like the Temple of Jerusalem, Petrie not unreasonably takes this as being evidence that Simon Onias built this temple at Yehudiyeh (Leontopolis). However, in the book *Jesus*, I noted that this same letter from Ptolemy definitely indicates that this was an existing temple that had 'fallen down'. The fact that Simon Onias was *rebuilding* a temple suggested to me that Petrie was wrong about the location and that Simon Onias may have made repairs to the temple at Heliopolis instead. But perhaps the accounts of Josephus and Petrie were not so wrong in identifying this location after all. It is highly likely that this temple at Yehudiyeh was indeed already in existence, and that Simon Onias was making repairs to a temple that had been constructed some 400 years earlier by the exiles from Jerusalem, who were under the command of Johanan and Jeremiah. The evidence for this again comes from the Bible:

> Then came the word of the Lord unto Jeremiah in Tahpanhes, saying. Take [many] stones in thine hand, and hide them in the clay [pots?] in the brick pavement, which is at the entry of Pharaoh's house in Tahpanhes, in the sight of the men of Judah. [B31]

The translation normally says 'great stones', but in terms of the archaeology of the site at Yehudiyeh, the equally valid translation is 'many stones'. What Petrie found at Yehudiyeh is that the lower brick walls of the entrance gate had had burnt sacrificial clay pots inserted into niches, which had then been walled up with burnt bricks. The pots contained ashes of wood and lamb bones, which probably came from a sacrificial feast, plus lots of small marl stones. Petrie thought that these stones had fallen into the pots at a later date, but the Biblical account might suggest that they were intended to be there, as Jeremiah had been advised (by god) to place these stones into the clay (pots) to 'hide them'. [32]

If this is indeed what happened at Yehudiyeh, then the history of

---

* This was not the famous Cleopatra. Josephus, in his *Jewish War*, maintains that this event occurred at the time of Antiochus IV of Syria, which would place the date as being around 160 BC.

this site is a little different to that suspected by Petrie. The original fort was a Hyksos construction, which may or may not have been inhabited during the dynasties of King David-Psusennes and King Solomon-Sheshonq. By the time of Jeremiah, some 360 years later, the fort was most probably abandoned and the pharaoh (possibly Wahibre) gave the site to Jeremiah as a safe refuge from the ravages of Nebuchadnezzar. It was Jeremiah, Johanan and their followers who built the copy of the Temple of Jerusalem on this site, and who placed the clay pots in the walls of this new temple. In which case, the account of Josephus was correct when it said that the high priest, Simon Onias, was only rebuilding an existing structure that had fallen down – Simon Onias was asking for this concession from Ptolemy some 400 years after the era of Jeremiah, so there had been plenty of time in which this site could have fallen into ruin.

The Biblical account also gives us a compelling reason for the design of this new temple and for the burial of these clay pots in its walls, which were later discovered by Flinders Petrie. The politics of this group of Biblical refugees from Jerusalem was complex. It would appear that the army commander, Johanan, had been influenced by the rather relaxed theology of King Solomon's United Monarchy, and had been worshipping certain idols. High Priest Jeremiah, on the other hand, was most definitely a committed monotheistic iconoclast who had a distinctly puritanical Israelite, rather than Egyptian, outlook.

Jeremiah had opposed this expedition from the very start, and he blamed the entire destruction of Jerusalem on these people who had been worshipping idols and strange gods. In the warped and perverted sense of morality that only a devout theist can reach, Jeremiah now wanted the expedition to fail and its people to be destroyed, which would prove that his benign and forgiving god was looking after those who followed the true creed. Accordingly, Jeremiah ensured that the Temple at Yehudiyeh was made to look like the Temple of Jerusalem and that clay pots were buried in the walls, so that Nebuchadnezzar would be compelled to attack it – as he had attacked the real Temple of Jerusalem – and so destroy the fort, the rebel Judaeans, and all of Egypt too:

> Thus saith the Lord Israel; Behold, I will send and take Nebuchadnezzar the king of Babylon, my servant, and will set his throne upon these stones that I have hid; and he shall spread his royal pavilion over them. And when he cometh, he shall smite the land of Egypt, and deliver ... death to death; and ... captivity to captivity; and ... sword to the sword. [B33]

It would seem that the stones in the pots were placed into the wall of the fort so that the Judaic god could entice the Judaean enemy, Nebuchadnezzar, into attacking and destroying the Jews and Egyptians who had strayed from some idiosyncratic assumed path of righteousness. With opinions of this nature within the Hyksos-Israelite hierarchy and priesthood, it is no wonder that the provinces of Judaea and Israel have lurched from crisis to crisis throughout their entire history.

Thus far, we have seen evidence for a group of rebels who fled Jerusalem and created their own New Jerusalem in the Nile Delta. So what, if anything, connects these people with the nation that took over Saba in the Yemen at about this time?

There are two possible threads of evidence that link these refugees to the history of Saba. The first is that same short story from the Talmud, which indicates that some 80,000 children of the Judaean priesthood fled to the Ishmaelites after the destruction of the Temple of Jerusalem. Since the Ishmaelites are known to have been the ancestors of the modern Arab nations, this is a clear indication that some of these refugees fled to Arabia.

The second and strongest of these threads lies in the religion of these refugees. While Jeremiah may have been a devout monotheistic high priest who wanted to bring the might of Babylon/Persia down upon these people to punish them for their sins, the bulk of these people were far from being orthodox followers of Judaism. The differences and arguments between these two groups were diligently recorded in the Bible, and in these remarkably lucid exchanges, the hellfire, brimstone and damnation god of Jeremiah rants:

> I am determined to bring disaster upon you and destroy all Judah. I will take the remnant of Judah who have set their faces to come to the land of Egypt to live, and they shall all be consumed; in the land of Egypt they shall fall; by the sword and by famine .. and they shall become an execration, a horror, a curse, and a taunt. I will punish those who dwell in the land of Egypt, as I have punished Jerusalem, with the sword, with famine, and with pestilence, so that none of the remnant of Judah who have come to live in the land of Egypt shall escape or survive or return to the land of Judah. [B34]

This prophesy, similar examples of which were often amended or written with the benefit of hindsight, was that these people in Yehudiyeh would be destroyed and could not return to Jerusalem. The reason for god's displeasure with these people, was that they had offered incense to an idol. But despite god's ranting and raving against them for this indiscretion, which was delivered through Jeremiah, these people were not about to give up the worship of their alternative deity. Their leaders replied to god:

> We will not listen to you. But we will do everything that we have vowed, burn incense to the Queen of Heaven and pour out libations to her, as we did, both we and our fathers, our kings and our princes, in the cities of Judah and in the streets of Jerusalem; for then we had plenty of food, and prospered, and saw no evil. But since we left off burning incense to the Queen of Heaven and pouring out libations to her, we have lacked everything and have been consumed by the sword and by famine. [B35]

Here we come to the nub of this matter. These people who had fled to Yehudiyeh worshipped an idol known as the Queen of Heaven, rather than the ethereal and unknowable deity of the orthodox Jew. Jeremiah may have screamed abuse as much as he liked, and he did, but these people blamed their perilous predicament upon their not being allowed to worship their idol. When they worshipped their goddess, life was good; when they were forcibly stopped, Jerusalem fell and so the reason for this calamity was obvious.

So who was this Queen of Heaven that these people worshipped? The Hebrew version of this name was Meleketh Shameh מלכת שמה, and rather than meaning the Queen of Heaven, it actually refers to the 'Queen of the Stars'. Considering the arguments that have already been aired in this book, this name is both very interesting and very familiar. The most common Egyptian word for 'star' is *seba (Sheba)* 𓊪𓄿𓇼, which is, of course, the same word that was used in the title Queen of Sheba.

In the Egyptian, the name of this legendary queen of the south can be just as easily translated as the 'Queen of the Stars'; in which case, the goddess that these rebels at Yehudiyeh were worshipping was none other than the deified Queen of Sheba, or Maakhah Tamar II. Here, at last, we can see the reason for the deep veneration of the Queen of Sheba in the land of Saba, and the rationale for identifying their gods and temples with the name Maqah (Maakhah).

This same term, the Queen of the Stars, also invokes the same imagery that was used at a later date for Mary the mother of Jesus, who was also known as the 'Marie Stella' or 'Marie Celeste'. This observation shows that the veneration of Maakhah Tamar II was very widespread indeed, for these beliefs not only influenced the theology of Saba, they also determined the liturgy of the later Christian sect. The Catholic Church likes to pride itself on being a monotheistic religion, but many of their followers – especially the Irish, as already explained – prefer to venerate the Virgin Mary [the Virgin Maakhah Tamar LVI??] as much as they worship their strange ethereal and unimaginable being.

Here were the Sabeans, the people who worshipped the Queen of

Sheba, living in Yehudiyeh to the north of Heliopolis – so what happened to them? The final part of this Biblical account states that High Priest Jeremiah departed this fortified camp and left its occupants with a stinging rebuke ringing in their ears. He rants that god would destroy Egypt and deliver the pharaoh Hophra into the hands of the Persians, just as he had done with King Zedekiah of Jerusalem. Although this final rebuke probably fell onto deaf ears, it is rather useful to us as it once more confirms the precise era of these events.

The Bible is clearly stating here that the Egyptian pharaoh who Jeremiah and Johanan had fled to was called Hophra. When turning to the equivalent Egyptian chronology, the pharaoh who was in power at about this time was called Wahibre Haaibre  . It is not too difficult to see that the names Haaibre and Hophra had precisely the same origins. This small snippet of Biblical text confirms that the historical chronology of this particular era is correct, and that Jerusalem did indeed fall to the Babylonians in the early years of the reign of Wahibre Haibre.

Fig 55.   Cartouche of Wahibre Haaibre.

Unfortunately, the account of Jeremiah breaks off at this point as the high priest probably returned to Jerusalem, and so we are not informed of the fate of the Sabeans. What *is* known, however, is that we have a large party of exiled Judaean soldiers who had a number of court officials and princesses within their party; in effect, they were a complete Hyksos-Judaean nation in miniature, complete with their own royalty. While they may have been safe in the Nile Delta for a few decades, less than sixty years later a Persian monarch, Cambyses II, was going to roll through this region creating yet more havoc and destruction, just as Jeremiah (retrospectively?) predicted.

It is highly likely that at this point in time, the Sabeans decided to vacate the disputed territories of Judaea and Lower Egypt and to find a new homeland in which to practise their religion. Significantly, their worship of the Queen of Sheba (Maakhah Tamar) involved the burning of incense, and so it is likely that these people had trading links with the incense-producing region of Yemen. No doubt one of their envoys to the area saw a new and sparsely populated land that was ripe for the picking, a land in which the superior armour, military tactics and irrigation skills of these Judaean-Sabeans could reap great rewards.

Like the Pilgrim Fathers of a later era, these people would have crossed the (Red) sea to a new life in a new land, where their technical superiority propelled them into being the dominant people in the region. A new nation was born of a few renegade Judaean soldiers and its reputation eventually spread all over the Near East and Europe. The success of the descendants of these refugees continued for some six hundred years or so, until the Romans placed a garrison in the area to control the lucrative trade in Sabean incense and narcotics.

This, then, was the true history of this nation, which built a small empire on the tip of the Arabian peninsular; and this is also the reason why later Arabic historians so strongly linked the Sabeans with the Queen of Sheba. This nation had venerated the memory and history of this legendary queen ever since her visit to Jerusalem, and they had maintained these rituals throughout their exile in both Egypt and then the Yemen. In this latter homeland, in their new capital cities of Sirwah and Marib, they built two of their greatest cathedrals. Naturally, both of these temples were dedicated to the Queen of Sheba, and so they were known by the Sabeans as the Temples of Maqah – the Temples of Maakhah Tamar II.

Grail legends

Although it may seem incomprehensible and almost impossible that a nation could have covered up its history quite so comprehensively and successfully, this new interpretation of Biblical history is actually the true history of the United Monarchy of Israel. As I suggested in the books *Jesus* and *Tempest*, in reality the history and religion of the Judaic people were all pure Egyptian, and a brief overview of this history is as follows:

There had long been a simmering dispute between the theology of Upper and Lower Egypt, with the northerners accusing the southerners of idolatry and polytheism. Into this climate of mutual animosity came the eruption of the volcano at Thera (Santorini), an event that proved the gods were upset with all this bickering. Rather than this perception solving the dispute, however, each blamed the other for this calamity, and so the situation deteriorated into civil war. The result was that the Hyksos nation were evicted from Lower Egypt in what became known as the great exodus. But the Hyksos-Israelites were a powerful enough nation to be able to evacuate Lower Egypt on their own terms, and to demand a vast tribute from the Theban pharaoh, Ahmose I, which made the journey to Palestine infinitely more palatable.

But this overt and disproportionate accumulation of wealth probably made the Hyksos-Israelites a target for the aggressive campaigns into Palestine by the New Kingdom pharaoh Tuthmoses III, who comprehensively conquered the region and no doubt confiscated much of this Judaean wealth. In return, the Hyksos-Israelites succeeded in placing one of their princes, Joseph, back into the heart of the Egyptian monarchy, whose descendants eventually came to power under the unstable patronage of the pharaoh Akhenaton. But this pharaoh's revolutionary reforms of the Egyptian religion proceeded too rapidly and too comprehensively, and eventually he and his Amarna regime were evicted from Egypt in the second, smaller, exodus of 'lepers' and 'maimed priests'.

But the Hyksos-Israelites had still managed to hold onto small pockets of land in the north-eastern Delta region of Egypt, which slowly grew in power and influence. Eventually, the local leaders of Judaea, Israel and the northern Delta lands, who were known as the Judges, enrolled the services of foreign mercenary fighters, the Sea People, to overthrow the Theban monarchs. While these raids were not completely successful, the Hyksos-Israelites were still able to make great inroads into Theban-held territory and to extract significant amounts of tribute from the southern administration, which was used to pay off the Sea People mercenaries. The result of these battles was that the pharaohs of Tanis had established themselves as a revitalised force within Lower Egypt, and their power steadily grew with each generation.

This stalemate between Tanis and Thebes also appears to have brought with it the possibility of dynastic alliances, which held the exciting possibility of gaining control over Thebes through marriage rather than warfare. The first of these diplomatic unions appears to have been made during the reign of David-Psusennes, and this may have stabilised relations with Thebes sufficiently for David-Psusennes to concentrate more on his north-eastern borders. An alliance with King Saul, the local monarch of Israel, was sought in order to deal with the problem of some unwanted Sea People mercenaries who had overstayed their welcome – the Philistines. Having conquered most of the Philistine cities, David-Psusennes then made a bold and successful attempt to depose King Saul and assume control over all of Judaea and Israel. David-Psusennes was now in command of an empire that stretched from Memphis in Egypt to the borders of the Euphrates – but the independence of Thebes and Upper Egypt was still a sore point.

IX *Menelek & Saba*

David-Psusennes' marriage alliance with the Theban princess, Maakhah Tamar I, swung the balance of power backwards and forwards, as each of these sovereigns tried to influence the other in terms of theology and allegiances. David-Psusennes appears to have gained the upper hand in this regard, and was able to control Thebes to the extent that his officers could plunder the tombs of the New Kingdom pharaohs, which became known to history as King Solomon's Mines. Buoyed up by these unlimited financial resources, David-Psusennes was able to fortify and extend the Hyksos lands in Judaea and Israel. His son, King Solomon-Sheshonq, continued the predation of the 'gold mines' at Thebes, and used this power and wealth to build his father's dream – a sumptuous palace and temple, which may have been constructed in the Judaean capital city of Jerusalem. It was due to Solomon's continued demands for more and more gold from Thebes that his mother – Maakhah Tamar II, the Queen of Sheba – travelled up to Jerusalem to see her son during his jubilee Sed festival, and deliver to him a vast tribute of gold and spices. This event, and the subsequent mother-son partnership, was so infamous that the cult of Maakare Tamar II endured for centuries, if not millennia.

Yet the downfall of Solomon-Sheshonq was to be the influence of his Theban mother, Maakhah Tamar II. This highly independent queen not only undermined the monotheism of the Hyksos-Israelites and led the king astray theologically, she also persuaded Solomon-Sheshonq to crown their son, Menelek, as king of (Upper) Egypt. As the Judaean priesthood became resentful of these Theban influences, the empire of Solomon-Sheshonq began to come apart at the seams, and it was eventually split between two or three of his sons. While the division of the empire appeased the separatists, the truce between the various sons was always going to be uncertain. It is at this point in time that the Biblical texts part company with Egyptian history, and the subsequent history in the books of Kings and Chronicles merely records the factional fighting between Israel and Judaea.

This new Biblical history, which has been teased out of these ancient texts by this trilogy of revolutionary books, has shown irrefutable evidence that the bulk of the Biblical texts were nothing more or less than a complete chronicle of the history of the Hyksos leaders and their people. Theologians have taken these same texts and presented us with a colourful tale of a pious people at the mercy of a capricious and vengeful god, a deity that can also take part in each and every domestic event in the lives of these people. Historians like Donald Redford, on the other hand, regard these fanciful-sounding stories as being the equivalent of Grimm's fairytales or the Grail legends.

The truth of the matter is neither of these points of view. If we strip away the spiritual fairytales and try to comprehend the scribe's code words, the prosaic truth is that the Biblical texts are a simple chronicle of the political machinations within the Lower Egyptian royal court; a tale of monarchs and momentous events in the history of a highly influential nation. As historical works go, it is probably the most comprehensive and authoritative document to have survived from the very beginnings of man's recorded history, the greatest of all the ancient literary works to have survived the millennia.

White House

While the Bible may represent, in my opinion, the greatest body of real historical information about the history of Egypt that has ever been assembled, this same historical text can also be remarkably obtuse at times. Throughout the whole of this book, one of the primary unsolved riddles has been the precise location of the Temple of Jerusalem. Did Solomon-Sheshonq decide to build this magnificent new temple at the furthest reaches of his empire, in Judaea, or did he decide to build it at the very heart of his dominions, in Tanis?

The first piece of evidence that demonstrates that the Temple of Solomon was actually built in Egypt is the name of the great palace that Solomon constructed next to it. This palace is said to have been given the rather grand title of the 'House of the Forest of Lebanon', and in the Hebrew this is pronounced as *Bayith Yarah Lebanon* בית יערה לבנון. The question is, of course, what does this title really mean?

The traditional interpretation, which I have reproduced earlier in the book, is that this palace was fabricated from massive cedar timbers and pillars, and since these great balks came from Lebanon, courtesy of King Hiram of Tyre, the palace itself became known as the House of the Forest of Lebanon. But there are some problems with this name that have already been highlighted by this book, and perhaps the most troublesome of these is that King Hiram did not come from Lebanon. King Hiram of Tyre was actually Prince Absalom, the (stone) (M)ason from Thar (Tanis), and while Solomon-Sheshonq's palace would still have required timber from somewhere, this new identification immediately diminishes any close associations with Lebanon.

Since we are no longer looking for a link with Lebanon, the search can be broadened to include many other interpretations for this palace, and it is the literal Hebrew translation of Lebanon that gives away its true meaning. In the Hebrew language, *lebanon* לבנון means white, and if that clue is not clear enough, try placing the word 'white' into the name of this palace. The combined title is now 'House of the Forest of White', or when turned around a little this becomes 'White House of the Forest'.

Perhaps the word 'forest' is a bit of a distraction; what the Biblical scribes were trying to describe and explain here was that in Egypt, the second most important building after the temple was the treasury. As was shown in an earlier chapter, the treasury of Egypt was traditionally known as the White House, and in the Egyptian language this title was often pronounced as the *Per-Hetch* (⬚ or ⬚), which is literally translated as 'House White'. Unfortunately, this title included the much despised word *hetch*, which could also be taken to mean the White Crown of Upper Egypt; and since this term would have been unacceptable for a Lower Egyptian king, the word for 'white' was changed.

Actually, the term 'white' may be a slight misnomer here, for *hetch* is not just 'white', it actually refers to the brilliance of the rising Sun, or Ra. The solution for the scribes was therefore obvious: the light of the dawn was caused by Ra peeping over the horizon and taking a look at his favourite land of Egypt, and so the scribes could just as easily use the word *yira* or *yara* ⬚ , meaning 'Ra sees', instead of *hetch*. In addition to this, the scribes also changed the word *per* ⬚ into the word *baat* ⬚ , with both of these words meaning 'house'. The result of all this feverish scribbling was that the usual term for the treasury of Egypt, the *Per-Hetch* ⬚ , had now become the *Baat-Yira* ⬚ ⬚ ; but the meaning of this title for the royal treasury was unaltered, as both of these phrases still translate as 'House White' (White House).

It would seem that the confusing term *yarah*, meaning 'forest', was simply a poor translation of the term for 'white' or 'brilliance'; and the fact that the scribes did not understand what this word really meant is demonstrated by their next action. Knowing that this royal palace or treasury had always been called 'white', and not finding this term anywhere in the title, they then tacked on the Hebrew word for white, which is *lebanon*. What this resulted in is the slightly distorted compound title of *Bayith Yarah Lebanon*, which can now be translated as 'House White White', or 'White White House'. Clearly, the Hebrew title of *Bayith Yarah Lebanon* was based upon the Egyptian original of *Baat-Yira*, which refers to the ancient tradition of the treasury being called the White House. History likes to repeat itself wherever possible, however, and so the most important secular building in modern America is still known as the White House.

Zion

The next path to follow in this investigation is rather simple in concept. The Temple of Jerusalem was built in the mysterious location that is known in the Bible as Zion, and so if Zion can be found, so too can the Temple. Due to the fervour of the modern Zionists who have successfully pushed for a Jewish homeland, the mention of Zion has taken on almost mystical proportions. As the prime symbol of this campaign for a Jewish homeland, it has been assumed that the location known as Zion was synonymous with Jerusalem, which in many respects it is.

But the true answer to this riddle is not quite so simple as this. The Kebra Nagast, for instance, clearly states that Zion was the Ark of the Covenant, whereas the Bible indicates that Zion was synonymous with something completely different:

> And many people shall go and say, Come ye, and let us go up to the mountain of the Lord ... for out of Zion shall go forth the law, and the word of the Lord from Jerusalem. [B36]

> And the Lord will create upon every dwelling place of mount Zion, and upon her assemblies, a cloud and smoke by day, and the shining of a flaming fire by night. [B37]

> Behold, I and the children whom the Lord hath given me are for signs and for wonders in Israel from the Lord of hosts, which dwells in mount Zion. [B38]

There are many Biblical verses that give an alternative flavour to the term 'Zion', but from the three just given a number of pertinent points can be derived. In addition to being the city of Jerusalem or the Ark of the Covenant:

a. Zion was a mountain.
b. Out of Mt Zion came the law (of Moses).
c. Mt Zion was covered by smoke and fire.
d. God lived inside Mt Zion.

In the book *Tempest,* it was demonstrated that each and every one of the points that have been attributed to Zion can also be applied to Mt Sinai. The seemingly different claims of the Kebra Nagast and the Bible are therefore reconcilable because the Ark of the Covenant was conceived as a substitute for the sacred Mt Sinai. The evidence indicates that Mt Sinai

(Siynay סִינַי) and Mt Zion (Tsion צִיּוֹן) may have originally been one and the same location.

But in that same book I also demonstrated that Mt Sinai was simply the Hebrew name for the Great Pyramid of Giza, and so this new identification infers that Mt Zion must also have referred to this same pyramid. Since the term Zion (Tsion) is said to mean 'desert monument' in the Hebrew, and since it was also known as the Mount of Esau – a character I have previously associated with the Giza plateau – this association between Zion and Giza seems quite likely.

In summary, then, the Kebra Nagast clearly states that Zion was the Ark of the Covenant, while the Bible hints at Mt Sinai, while simultaneously insisting that Zion was actually the city of Jerusalem. The common link between these differing explanations is that Zion referred solely to the location that the Israelite god inhabited. The Israelite god originally inhabited Mt Sinai [the Great Pyramid] but, during the exodus, he was bundled into the transportable Ark of the Covenant for the journey to Palestine. It is therefore obvious that the city in which the Ark was finally placed would also become synonymous with the term Zion, but was that city Jerusalem, or was it somewhere else?

One point in favour of the Jerusalem location is that it is said that this city was built upon three mountains, comprising Mt Zion, Mt Moriah and Mt Gihon. But if one views the city of Jerusalem today, while the location might look a little craggy, it hardly conjures up an image of three mountains. So what did the Biblical chroniclers mean by the 'mountains' of Jerusalem? In reality, Jerusalem was not built upon three real mountains; instead, the nation that built this city was primarily influenced by three pyramids at Giza, which were now regarded as the three symbolic foundations of the Judaic people and their religion. When, according to the famous song, the Israelites sat down in Babylon and remembered Zion, they were not just reminiscing about their lost City of David, they were also remembering the long-lost days when they could physically visit their primary temple in Egypt – the Great Pyramid at Giza.

Since there were many facets to the imagery of Zion, the descriptions of this sacred chamber of god were made to vary accordingly. When the scribes reminisced about Giza, Zion was a mountain or a desert monument; however, when they had in mind the City of David, Zion became a castle instead:

> And the inhabitants of Jebus said to David, Thou shalt not come hither. Nevertheless David took the castle of Zion, which is the City of David. And David dwelt in the castle; therefore they called it the City of David. [B39]

Following the death of King Saul, King David-Psusennes had employed decisive military action to take control of the fortified city of Jebus, and this was the city that eventually became known as the City of David and the Castle of Zion. Because this account calls the fort at Jebus the City of David, it has always been assumed by the scribes and later theologians that the name Jebus was the original name for Jerusalem – but was it? Have they made an error here?

Personally, I think that the scribes have got it wrong. In reality, the City of David was not solely synonymous with Jerusalem – there could have been any number of 'Cities of David', just as there were multiple 'Cities of Alexander the Great' – and so the fort at Jebus could have been sited at another location entirely. I believe that the true location of Jebus יבוס, one of the cities that became known as the City of David, was probably a fortified city that was known in the Egyptian as Tchebet (Jebet 𓈖𓂋𓎡𓏏). Note that the reed-float glyph *Jeb* 𓈖 was also used for the name of King David's army commander Joab, and so this usage confirms its pronunciation in Hebrew as a 'j'. The name for the Egyptian town called Tchebet was probably derived from the word *tcheb* 𓈖𓃀𓏏 , meaning to 'replace' or 'discharge a debt'. Since the accounts of Manetho indicate that a city in this location was given to the Hyksos-Israelites in return for their leaving Egypt during the second exodus, this could well have been that city.

While the only association, at present, between Jebus and Tchebet (Jebet) is a similar-sounding name, there are other similarities that serve to confirm the close affinity between these two towns. Jebus, for instance, was known as the City of David; whereas Tchebet (Jebet) was known as the City of Psusennes II. Since the pharaoh Psusennes II has been positively identified as being King David, then both of these towns were associated with and named after the same king. In other words, Tchebet (Jebet) was also known as the City of David.

In addition to this, both of these locations were given alternative names, and these can also be compared with each other. The second of the names for the Biblical City of David was Zion, which is more accurately pronounced as Tsion ציון. In a similar manner, the second of the alternative names for the City of Psusennes was Tchian 𓏏𓈖𓏏𓊖 . Again, these two cities appear to have remarkably similar names – Tsion and Tchian, as well as Jebus and Jebet (Tchebet).

It is likely that there were two ways of spelling the name Zion ציון, and the second of these versions was Zoan צען. The Bible tries to maintain that Zoan and Zion were two separate locations, but these names not only sound very similar to each other, the name Zoan was actually used as the

Biblical name for the city of Tchian – Zoan was called the 'Field of Zoan' (Sadeh Zoan שׂדה צען), while Tchian was called the 'Field of Tchian' (Sekhet Tchian 𓈖𓈖𓈖 𓇋𓈖). While the Bible is happy to admit that Zoan was Tchian, the similarities just given make it seem likely that the Egyptian city of Tchian was also the same city as the Biblical Zion (Tsion) – but this association would mean that the two Biblical cities of Zion and Zoan were also the same.

In fact, the direct Biblical link that is made between the cities of Zoan and Tchian is doubly important here, as it also confirms that the Egyptian cobra glyph *tch* can be rendered in the Hebrew as a 'z'. This means that Tchian can be pronounced in the Hebrew as Zian, and so the proposed association between the Egyptian Zian (Tchian) and the Biblical Zion is even more likely.

The final similarity between these two towns involves their physical appearance. The previous Biblical quotation indicates that Zion was known as a castle. In a similar fashion, the Egyptian city of Zian (Tchian) is known to have been a fortress, as the site still has a substantial defensive wall around it. In addition, Zian (Tchian) was known by yet another name, that of Thar 𓈖𓂝𓇋𓈖 , a name that can be translated as 'fortress' or 'castle'.

Therefore, there are a number of linguistic and physical affinities and similarities between the two capital cities of the Judaean Zion and the Egyptian Zian (Tchian), which indicate that these two towns were actually one and the same. These points are probably worth listing for clarity:

The Judaean Zion was:	The Egyptian Zian was:
called Jebus	called Jebet (Tchebet)
called Zion	called Zian (Tchian)
known as a castle	known as a fortress (Thar)
closely identified with a rock	known as the 'Rock' (Tyre)
known as the 'Threshing Floor'	known as the 'Threshing Floor' (*tchian*)
similar in pronunciation to Zoan	called Zoan
called the City of King David	called the City of King Psusennes II [David]

It would seem that there was a city in Egypt that mimicked many of the features that have traditionally been attributed to the fortress of Jebus, and so it is entirely possible that Jebus was not necessarily the same city as Jerusalem. Instead, it is highly likely that there were two Cities of David, one at Jerusalem and one in Egypt. So, where was this Egyptian version of Tsion (Zion), the Egyptian City of David, and was this city the real historical location for the Temple of Solomon-Sheshonq?

Back in chapter V, it was shown that the birth name of the pharaoh Psusennes II contained hieroglyphic elements that could be translated as the 'City of Psusennes II'. It was further stated that the historical record was so fragmentary in this era that it was not possible to decipher which city King Psusennes II [King David] was claiming as his own – but that statement was not entirely correct.

The less evasive truth of the matter is that there is a city in the Nile Delta in which every mud-brick of this citadel's surrounding defensive walls had been stamped with the cartouche of Psusennes II.*⁴¹ If any city in Egypt could be said to have been closely associated with this king, this would be it. Needless to say, this 'City of David-Psusennes' was in actual fact the fortress at Zian (Tchian), the Biblical Zoan, and today it is known as Tanis.

Cornucopia

The evidence presented thus far in this chapter suggests that the Temple of Solomon was built somewhere in Egypt, and also that the Lower Egyptian capital city of Tanis was called the City of David. However compelling this evidence may seem, this does not in itself prove that Tanis was the location chosen for the Temple of Solomon. Somehow, a direct link has to be forged between the Temple of Solomon and the city of Tanis, and it is the historian Josephus who once more provides this crucial piece of information.

As was noted in a previous chapter, the city of Tanis was called Thar (and also Zian, Jebet or Zoan) and this particular name had close similarities and connections to the Biblical city of Tyre (Tsar) צר. The city of Tyre has traditionally thought to have been located in the Levant, but since the word *tyre* simply means 'rock', this name could instead have been a reference to the city of Tanis (Thar) being a fortress, or it could even have been an oblique reference to the fact that the kings of Tanis were all Architects (Masons). Whatever the reasoning, the possibility that Tyre (Tsar) was a reference to the city of Thar (Tanis) would explain a great deal about the history of the Masonic Hiram Atif, who was supposed to have originated from the former of these cities.

This brings us to a curious statement in Josephus' *Antiquities* that has until now defied all explanation. To locate the Temple of Solomon in the wider historical context of his religion, Josephus attempted to date the Temple's construction by reference to all the great events in the history of

---

* Egyptologists will argue that this city belonged to Psusennes I, but the Biblical record suggests that this pharaoh did not exist, and so this must be instead the 'City of Psusennes II'.

the Israelites. Thus we read that the Temple was founded 592 years after the exodus; 1,020 years after Abraham; 1,440 years after the flood; and 3,102 years after Adam. Referencing the construction of the Temple against these great epochs in Judaic history may seem entirely logical, but Josephus then says:

> Now the year on which the Temple was built was (also) the eleventh year of the reign of Hiram, (and) from the building of Tyre to the building of the Temple there had passed 240 years. [J42]

Now this conclusion to the historical context for the Temple of Solomon is truly puzzling. Why on Earth should the Temple of Solomon be placed within the chronology of the Judaic world by reference to a king of Lebanon? Likewise, why should the Temple's construction be dated by reference to the founding of a city called Tyre in the Lebanon? The classical history of Judaism has absolutely no answer to these questions, and they are merely dismissed with a shrug of the shoulders and a dismissive comment about the wondrous and mysterious ways of god.

In truth, the solution to this short verse from Josephus' *Antiquities* is rather more profound that most historians could have imagined. The answer to the first problem is that King Hiram of Tyre (Tsar) was actually a coded reference to Prince Absalom, a very famous and influential Judaean prince who came from Tanis (Thar). The Temple was dated from the reign of Absalom because he was the king of Lower Egypt and all Israel for a brief period before his premature death at the hands of his father, King David-Psusennes.

The second comment in this verse is perhaps even more mystifying, for it is utterly nonsensical that the Temple of Solomon should be placed within a Judaic historical context by reference to a Phoenician city. The only logical conclusion is that the scribes must have been doing what any historian would have done in this same situation – they were referencing the construction date of the Temple of Solomon against the founding of the city in which it stood. But this simple observation has a rather profound repercussion: for this verse to make any sense, the Temple of Solomon must have been constructed within the city of Tyre. While this suggestion would have been laughable while the city of Tyre was said to be in Lebanon, it would make every sense in terms of the city of Thar (Tanis) in the Nile Delta, which was the capital city of David-Psusennes. Once more, the available evidence points towards the Biblical city of Tyre (Tsar) being a reference to the Egyptian city of Tanis (Thar), which was in turn the Biblical City of David.

Indeed, the period of 240 years between the founding of Thar and the construction of the Temple of Solomon would be eminently sensible. If the Temple had been constructed midway during the reign of King Solomon-Sheshonq, then the city of Tanis must have been founded during the reign of Ramesses III. It so happens that this is exactly when some of the first attacks by the Sea People on Egypt commenced, and this is exactly the period when this coalition of Hyksos-led forces would have required a new fortress in the north-eastern Nile Delta. Since the expansion of Tanis by King David-Psusennes was made to an existing (Hyksos) city, its original founding during the reign of Ramesses III dovetails nicely with the known archaeology of this region and era.

Another snippet of evidence that shows the Temple of Solomon was built at Thar (Tanis) is that this great temple was also known as the Temple of Eternity. This title was probably another play on words between the name Thar and the word for 'eternity', which was *(n)tchar*. This pun was also being used to show that this Temple of Solomon-Sheshonq must have been very wealthy indeed, as the glyph used to describe 'something without limits' (eternity) was the horn with grain growing from it. This glyph was the original *cornucopia*, or 'Horn of Plenty', and so the city of Thar (Tanis) must have been well blessed.

Great Temple

At last, the truth can be told. The reason for the lack of archaeological evidence for the Temple of Solomon on the Temple Mount in Jerusalem is that it was never built there in the first place. In reality, King David-Psusennes specified that his great temple should be constructed in the most logical place possible – his Lower Egyptian capital city at Thar, and that is exactly where his son, Solomon-Sheshonq, built it. The rather provocative truth of the matter is that Zian, Jebet and Thar were all original names for the city of Tanis, the fortified capital city of David-Psusennes where both he and Solomon-Sheshonq were eventually buried. Surprising as it may seem, the Temple of Solomon was actually constructed at Tanis in the Nile Delta, where it may be known today as the Great Temple.

Jebus-Jebet (Tchebet)   –   *Zion-Zian (Tchian)*

Unfortunately for both historians and theologians alike, the city of Tanis and the site of the Great Temple itself have been thoroughly trashed over the many centuries that have passed since the era of King Solomon-Sheshonq, and absolutely nothing remains of the Great Temple bar an outline of the site and a few of the beautifully carved, pink granite palm-tree columns.

Indeed, as mentioned previously, the prevalence of these majestic, granite palm columns throughout the site at Tanis is very reminiscent of the account in the book of Judges that describes the Ammonites (Upper Egyptians) gaining hold of the 'City of Palm Trees'.

> And he gathered unto him the children of Ammon and Amalek, and went and smote Israel, and possessed the city of palm trees. So the children of Israel served Eglon the king of <u>Moab</u> eighteen years. [B43]

According to the new history of the region, the account of Judges describes the struggles between the Sea-People alliance and the pharaoh Ramesses III. Since this particular verse occurs right at the beginning of Judges and since the land of Mera 𓋴𓇌𓏤𓊖 or Merab (Moab) 𓄿𓂝𓏤𓉐 refers to Egypt, this Biblical verse may well record the reign and campaigns of Ramesses II – during which the Hyksos-Israelites would definitely have served under an Upper Egyptian ruler.

If these two verses do indeed represent an account of the campaigns of Ramesses II, then this shows that, for all his bravado, Ramesses the Great only controlled the Judaeo-Egyptians in the Nile Delta for eighteen years. This verse may also explain the prevalence of this pharaoh's cartouche at Tanis, which has been chiselled all over the site and obviously represents the usurping of existing structures. If these palm columns have been brought to Tanis by the twenty-first dynasty pharaohs, as has been suggested, then the original 'City of Palms' may have been at Avaris. On conquering this city, Ramesses II simply left his mark there, just as he did all over Egypt.

The meagre remains of this once great temple at Tanis do, however, allow us to confirm that the Hyksos-Israelites were indeed basing their concept of Zion upon the layout of the Giza plateau. The Hyksos people had been excluded from their primary sacred site at Giza ever since the great exodus in 1625 BC, and so the Tabernacle and Ark of the Covenant were constructed as mobile substitutes for Giza, in which the same ancient rituals could be performed.

Although the Hyksos-Israelites of the United Monarchy may have regained some of their lands and much of their previous influence in Lower and Middle Egypt, the Giza plateau probably remained a politically sensitive area and it may well have been inadvisable for the Tanis pharaohs and priests to perform their ancient rituals on the Giza site. The obvious solution available to the northerners was to replace the ageing Tabernacle and Ark of the Covenant, and to reproduce another copy of Zion at Tanis, with the Ark retaining its position as the temple's center-piece.

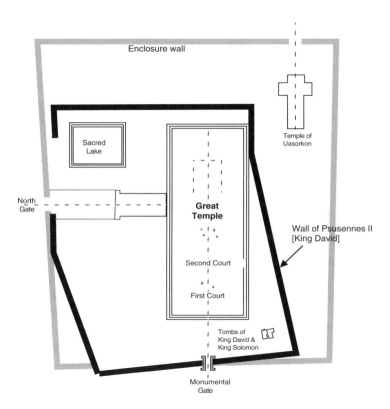

Fig 56.   The Great Temple at Tanis.

This new imitation of Zion was achieved by replicating the all-important measurements of the Giza site. The reason for the dimensions of the Giza pyramids being so important is fully covered in the books *Thoth* and *K2*, but even the most cursory glance at the Bible will confirm that metrology was deemed to be very important in this era. It was for this reason that the Tanis architect designed a temple that measured 230 meters or 440 royal cubits in length, which is, of course, exactly the same as the base-length of the Great Pyramid. In rod lengths, this same temple measures 80 x 28 rods, numbers that mimic the numerology of Giza very closely indeed. Clearly,

Zion was originally the Great Pyramid of Giza, and the Great Temple at Tanis merely attempted to recreate that sacred site in the safer environs of the Nile Delta.

The final piece of evidence that the Temple of Solomon actually resided at Tanis, rather than Jerusalem, are the names of the twin-pillars that graced the Temple's entrance. The names Jachin יכין – which is more properly pronounced Jakheen – and Boaz בעז have long remained enigmatic and indecipherable elements of Biblical lore, despite the many attempts at their translation (including my own). However, the two temples at Tanis provide us with a compelling answer to this ancient riddle.

I had already speculated that the name 'Boaz' may have had something to do with the patriarch (or king) Boaz, who has now been identified as B-Uasorkon, the father of David-Psusennes. But now, with this new interpretation of history, we can not only see that this king commissioned a small temple at Tanis, but also that the name 'Boaz' (B-Uas) has actually been inscribed on each and every one of these magnificent, pink granite palm-columns. But that is, of course, only half the story; to show that this identification and reasoning is correct, the name Jakheen (Jachin) has to be identifiable with a similar set of columns.

As it happens, the other temple at Tanis, the Great Temple, has similarly designed, pink granite palm-columns that are even larger. The columns of this temple have been usurped by Ramesses II, possibly while in their original location at Avaris, and so all of these columns have been inscribed with what appear to be this pharaoh's cartouches. While the names Ramesses Usermaatre Meryamun may not sound anything like the pillar-name, Jakheen (Jachin), it is entirely possible that this pharaoh had a nickname that was more familiar.

The twentieth dynasty saw a long line of Ramesside pharaohs on the throne of Egypt and one of these, Ramesses VIII, was called Ramesses Meryamun Usermaatre Akhenamun. The name Akhenamun 𓀀𓅷𓈖 , which is actually a variation on the name Akhenaton, is spelt using the ibis glyph 𓅷 . While this glyph can indeed be translated as sounding like *ah*, it could also be taken to be *yah*. If the latter were the original pronunciation, the resulting name would be Yakhen-amun, rather than Akhen-amun. In reality, it was not the two entrance columns to the Temple which were known as Jakheen and Boaz, it was the two temples at Tanis, and they could be identified by the names that had been inscribed on their respective columns. One of the temples was known as the Temple of Yakhen or Jakheen, a nickname of a Ramesside king, while the other was the Temple of B-Uas or Boaz, a nickname of an Uasorkon pharaoh.

This new interpretation may alter our perception of the Great Temple at Tanis, as it infers that this particular site was not identified exclusively with Solomon-Sheshonq, even during the United Monarchy era. It is entirely possible that although Solomon-Sheshonq was completing this massive project – which had been started by his father, David-Psusennes – the names that had already been inscribed on these usurped columns from Avaris became influential in their own right. Thus the Temples of Solomon also became famous for the two sets of columns that formed their cloisters, which called Jakheen and Boaz.

Coda

Having trawled our way through the complexities of the Torah – the Old Testament accounts from the Bible – and having turned up revelation after revelation upon the way, it is perhaps time to take stock of this rather novel situation.

The inescapable conclusion that has to be drawn from this new book of revelations is that the whole of Judaic, Christian and Islamic belief systems and iconography were based upon Egyptian antecedents. More importantly, perhaps, is the fact that the historical characters upon whose histories these three religions were founded, and the three books in which this entire history was eventually written, were also Egyptian. The time has come to take a deep breath, to reassess all that we know of these religious texts, and to completely rewrite the Torah, Bible and Koran so that they at last tell the truth. This book has started that inevitable process...

Appendix A

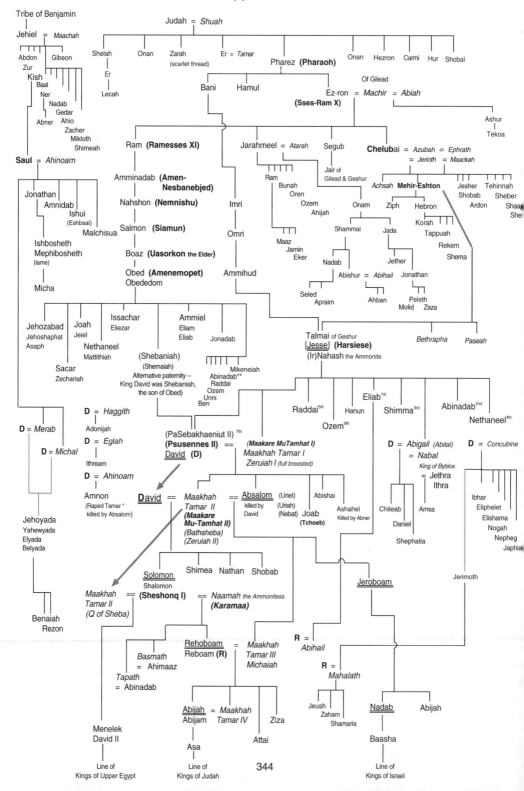

Tribe of Benjamin

Jehiel = Maachah

Abdon Gibeon
Zur
Kish
Baal
Ner
Nadab
Gedar
Abner Ahio
Zacher
Mikloth
Shimeah

Saul = Ahinoam

Jonathan
Amnidab
Ishui
(Eshbaal)
Malchisua

Ishbosheth
Mephibosheth
(lame)

Micha

Shelah

Er

Lecah

Onan

Judah = Shuah

Zarah
(scarlet thread)

Bani Hamul

Er = Tamar

Pharez (Pharaoh)

Onan Hezron Carmi Hur Shobal

Ez-ron = Machir = Abiah
(Sses-Ram X)

Of Gilead

Ashur
Tekoa

Ram (Ramesses XI)

Amminadab (Amen-
Nesbanebjed)

Nahshon (Nemnishu)

Salmon (Siamun)

Boaz (Uasorkon the Elder)

Obed (Amenemopet)
Obededom

Jehozabad
Jehoshaphat
Asaph

Joah
Jeiel

Sacar
Zechariah

Issachar
Eliezer

Nethaneel
Mattithiah

Ammiel
Eliam
Eliab

Jarahmeel = Atarah

Ram
Bunah
Oren
Ozem
Ahijah

Imri

Omri

Maaz
Jamin
Eker

Ammihud

Jonadab

(Shebaniah)
(Shemaiah)
Alternative paternity –
King David was Shebaniah,
the son of Obed)

Mikeneiah
Abinadab**
Raddai
Ozem
Unni
Ben

Segub

Jair of
Gilead & Geshur

Onam

Shammai

Nadab

Chelubai = Azubah = Ephrath
= Jerioth = Maackah

Achsah Mehir-Eshton

Ziph Hebron

Jada

Jether

Abishur = Abihail

Seled
Apraim

Ahban

Jesher Tehinnah
Shobab Sheber
Ardon Shaa
She

Korah
Tappuah

Rekem
Shema

Jonathan

Peleth
Molid Zaza

Talmai of Geshur
[Jesse] (Harsiese)
(Ir)Nahash the Ammonite

Bethrapha

Paseah

Eliab¹ˢᵗ

Raddai⁵ᵗʰ Hanun Shimma³ʳᵈ Abinadab²ⁿᵈ

Ozem⁶ᵗʰ Nethaneel⁴ᵗʰ

D = Merab

D = Michal

Jehoyada
Yahewyada
Elyada
Belyada

Benaiah
Rezon

D = Haggith

Adonijah

D = Eglah

Ithream

D = Ahinoam

Amnon
(Raped Tamar *
killed by Absalom)

(PaSebakhaeniut II) ⁷ᵗʰ
(Psusennes II) ==
David (D)

David == Maakhah
Tamar II
(Maakare
Mu-Tamhat II)
(Bathsheba)
(Zeruiah II)

== Absalom
killed by
David

(Uriel)
(Uriah)
(Nebat)

Abishai

Joab
(Tchoeb)

Ashahel
Killed by Abner

(Maakare MuTamhat I)
Maakhah Tamar I
Zeruiah I (full breasted)

D = Abigail (Abital)
= Nabal
King of Byblos
= Jethra
Ithra

Chileab Amsa

Daniel

Shephatia

D = Concubine

Ibhar
Eliphelet
Elishama
Nogah
Nepheg
Japhia

Solomon
Shalomon

Shimea Nathan Shobab

Jeroboam

Jerimoth

Maakhah
Tamar II
(Q of Sheba)

== (Sheshonq I) == Naamah the Ammonitess
(Karamaa)

Rehoboam
Reboam (R)

= Maakhah
Tamar III
Michaiah

R =
Abihail

R =
Mahalath

Basmath
= Ahimaaz

Tapath
= Abinadab

Abijah = Maakhah
Abijam Tamar IV

Asa

Ziza

Attai

Jeush
Zaham
Shamaria

Nadab Abijah

Baasha

Menelek
David II

Line of
Kings of Upper Egypt

Line of
Kings of Judah

344

Line of
Kings of Israel

Appendix B

Kings of Israel

Chronology

The classical chronology appears to have complicated the family tree of the twenty-first dynasty pharaohs by adhering to Manetho's argument that there was a pharaoh called Psusennes I, in addition to the more famous pharaoh known as Psusennes II [King David]. The following is a rough draft of the classical chronology of pharaohs and the high priests who served under them:

Pharaoh	High Priest
Smendes [Amminadab]	Pinedjem I
(Nesbanebdjed)	Masaharta / Pinedjem I
	Menkheperre / Pinedjem I
Amenemnisu [Nahshon]	Menkheperre / Pinedjem I
Psusennes I	Menkheperre / Pinedjem I
	HP Smendes
Amenemopet [Obed]	HP Smendes
	Pinedjem II
B-Uasorkon [Boaz]	Pinedjem II
Siamun [Salmon]	Pinedjem II
	HP Psusennes III
Psusennes II [David]	HP Psusennes III

If, however, the biblical chronology was maintained, a slightly simpler list would result; the main amendment being the complete removal of the pharaoh Psusennes I. Remember that the pharaoh's name does not occur on the vast majority of these historical references, just the year number of the reign; and so the ownership of each reference is therefore derived by comparison with the high priest that is mentioned. The game becomes one of matching up the various year lengths, using a coherent and sequential list of high priests' names. The early pharaohs in the list are an obvious case in point. Since the last high priest to officiate under the pharaoh Smendes was called Menkheperre, and since a pharaoh known as Amenemnisu also reigned over the high priest Menkheperre, one can fairly confidently say that Amenemnisu followed Smendes.

The Biblical chronology changes many aspects of the classical chronology, and the question is therefore: does the new, revised chronology fit together without any inconsistencies in the historical references? Since the main change in the Biblical chronology is the complete deletion of the pharaoh Psusennes I, this leaves a lot of references with no pharaoh attached to them. But since the pharaoh Siamun occurs much earlier in the biblical king-list, this pharaoh could inherit many of the references that are currently ascribed to Psusennes I. This would actually make a lot of sense: currently, there is a glaring gap in the records for Psusennes I, between years 9 and 18. On the other hand, Siamun now brings with him a separate group of references, under a new high priest, that range between years 12 and 17. Marry these two sets of records together, and the glaring gap just disappears. The resulting chronology then becomes:

Pharaoh	High Priest
Smendes [Amminadab]	Pinedjem I
(Nesba<u>nebdjed</u>)	Masaharta / Pinedjem I
	Menkheperre / Pinedjem I
Amenem<u>nisu</u> [Nahshon]	Menkheperre / Pinedjem I
Siamun [Salmon]	Menkheperre / Pinedjem I
	Psusennes III
B-<u>Uas</u>orkon [Boaz]	Menkheperre
Amenem<u>opet</u> [Obed]	Pinedjem II
	HP Smendes
Psusennes II [David]	HP Smendes

The main points to note about this new chronology are:

a. The pharaoh Smendes takes some of the later references that are normally ascribed to the pharaoh Psusennes I. Since the king's name is not mentioned in any of these references, this borrowing of references is quite permissible.

b. The majority of the early references to Siamun & HP Pinedjem II are therefore off-loaded onto the pharaoh Amenemopet. The classical lists indicate that this is likely anyway; the reversal of the reigns of Siamun and Amenemopet just make this assumption a certainty.

c. Since the pharaoh Siamun has been shunted nearly to the top of the list, the references for the early years of Siamun are taken instead from the missing pharaoh Psusennes I.

d. Again, Siamun is earlier in the list than before, and so the hotly debated and seemingly phantom HP Psusennes III moves up the list with him. The presence of a HP Psusennes III may have been a part of the general confusion that led to the belief that a pharaoh called Psusennes I existed.

e. The final high regnal year references that do mention a Psusennes (I) actually belong to Psusennes II. The reason for the mention of Amenemopet in relation to one of these is because Psusennes II now follows Amenemopet.

f. Uasorkon's references gain an entry to year 6. He loses a reference to year 2, as this should come earlier than a similar reference in the list of Siamun.

g. Notice how two of Amenemopet's high priests have reversed places. The original order had to try to agree with the HP Smendes, who seemed to belong to Psusennes I. Since this reference to Psusennes I has now been deleted, the reference to the HP Smendes can come at the end of the reign of Amenemopet instead of the beginning; thus, it matches with Psusennes II and not Psusennes I. This is permissible because there is no date attached to this reference; it could have been either at the beginning or the end of Amenemopet's reign.

h. Psusennes II now gains two new references that were originally ascribed to Psusennes I. However, he gives the reference that included the HP Psusennes III to the pharaoh Siamun, thus eliminating the need for another HP Psusennes.

The references to these pharaohs and high priests, as listed in Kenneth

Kitchen's textbook on this era, have a numerical order. For ease of cross-reference with this list, I have retained this order as the right-hand side of the two numbering systems. [1]

The majority of these references specify a year, but this refers to the pharaoh's reign, not the high priest's. So 'Year 1 of HP Pinudjem I' means 'Year 1 of the pharaoh ......, under the High Priest Pinudjem I'.[2] The years without any named king or priest are assumed to be in these particular positions either because a known scribe penned that reference or because it occurred in a known setting. Thus the position of the reference, relative to better documented references, can be guessed even if no names are given. The designation of a reference to either HP Pinudjem I or II is also a guess, because these two characters had exactly the same names. In which case, many of the references display a degree of fluidity between the pharaohs and the high priests that they can be matched against.

The new chronology has demanded a number of alterations to the assumed order of these references, as can be seen in the list below:

Reference N^{os}		Text message	K = King/Pharaoh
My	**Kitchen**		HP = High Priest

K Smendes & HP Pinedjem I

6	6	Year 1 of Pinudjem I
7	7	Year 4
8	8	Year 6
9	9	Year 6, HP Pinudjem I
10	10	Year 6, HP Pinudjem I
11	11	Year 6
12	12	Year 9, linen made by HP Pinudjem I
13	13	Year 10, linen made by HP Pinudjem I
14	14	Year 10, linen made by HP Pinudjem I
15	15	Year 10, coming to see the mountains ... HP Pinudjem I
16	16	Year 10,
17	17	Year 11, coming to see the mountains ... HP Pinudjem I
18	18	Year 11, coming to see the mountains ...
19	19	Year 11, coming to see the mountains ...

Note the references to visiting the 'mountains' at the necropolis. Since these pharaohs were based in Tanis and Heliopolis, they were probably more interested in the Giza necropolis than the Valley of the Kings.

20	20	Year 11
21	21	Year 12
22	22	Year 12, re-burial of Amenophis II by HP Pinudjem I
23	23	Year 12, coming to see the mountains by necropolis scribe ...

24 24 Year 13, coming to see the mountains ...

25 25 year 13, osirify Ramesses III, HP Pinudjem I

26 26 Year 15, day of bringing, HP Pinudjem I
Induction of HP Masaharta & 'K' Pinudjem I

27 27 Year 16, HP Masaharta son of Pinudjem I
Note that HP Pinudjem I was still alive. He had left the priesthood and claimed the throne of Thebes as king, although nobody at the time seems to have paid any attention to this.

28 28 Year 16, HP Masaharta

29 29 Year 18, linen by HP Masaharta

30 30 Year 19

31 31 Year 20

32 32 Year 20

33 33 Year 21
Induction of HP Menkheperre & 'K' Pinudjem I

34 34 Year 25, arrival of Menkheperre

35 35 Year 25, induction of Menkheperre

36 ?? Year 25, (Louvre 'Banishment Stele') Recall of exiles
The Maunier 'Banishment Stele' marks a significant event that can only be explained in terms of a change of policy. Such policy changes are often only brought about by a change in administration, hence I have placed the record at this point in time on the induction of a new high priest. The 'Banishment Stele' is also followed by a short reign, which it now is – that of Amenemnisu.

37 43 Year 30, linen by Menkheperre?

38 44 Year 40, inspection of temples under HP Menkheperre

39 45 Year 48, works by HP Menkheperre

40 46 Year 48, Menkheperre linen

K Amenemnisu & HP Menkheperre & 'K' Pinudjem I

41 36 Year 1, HP Menkheperre seeks oracle

K Siamun & HP Menkheperre & 'K' Pinudjem I

42 56 Year 2, (Karnak Annals 3b 1-3), induction of Nespaneferhor under Pinudjem I

43 38 Year 7

44 39 Year 7

45 73 Year 8, of K Siamun, linen by HP&K Pinudjem I

46 74 Year 8, of K Siamun, linen, mummy 124 or 134?
There is an oddity here, in that the mummy No 124 has linen from both King Amenemopet and King Siamun. Kitchen has played around with the mummy numbers, but the problem still exists in both the classical and the revised chronology. It is unlikely that linen was kept for quite so long before being used.

47   40   Year 8, K&HP Pinudjem I to re-osirify Ahmose I

48   ??   Year 8, linen by HP&K Pinudjem I, and his son Menkheperre, year 8 of K Siamun

49   41   Year 8, command to osirify prince Siamun

> Note that the command to bury a <u>prince</u> Siamun makes much more sense now. Here, the father was burying a son with the same name, whereas the classical chronology has a pharaoh called Psusennes I inserted at this point and burying *prince* Siamun.

50   77   Year 10, dockets under K Siamun

51   78   Year 10, same

52   79   Year 10, burial of HP&K Pinudjem I (priest for 64 years)

> While this is a surprisingly long period, there are two factors to bear in mind. Firstly, Pinudjem I effectively resigned after 16 years in office, in favour of his sons. Secondly, it is thought that Pinudjem I was rather old at his death.

53   80   Year 12, linen by HP Psusennes III

54   85   Year 15, linen by HP Psusennes III (actual year uncertain)

55   82   Year 16, K Siamun

56   83   Year 17, K Siamun (Karnak Annals 3b 3-5) induction of Hori, son of Nespaneferhor

57   84   Year 17, K Siamun

K Uasorkon & HP Menkheperre

58   37   Year 6, linen by HP Menkheperre

K Amenemopet & HP Pinudjem II & HP Smendes

59   51   Year 1, mummy linen, also year 48 of HP Menkheperre, plus braces of HP Pinudjem II enclosed

> The changes made to the chronology mean that the 48-year tenure for the HP Menkheperre is now substantially correct. The HP Menkheperre would have held his office for 22 years under Smendes, 4 years under Amenemnisu, 16 years under Siamun and 6 years under Uasorkon (remember that if a pharaoh dies in his 17th year, he has only completed 16 full years). The total is thus 48 years. Since HP Menkheperre had been in office for 48 years at the start of the reign of Amenemopet, both the royal reign lengths and the priestly office periods tally rather well.

60   57   Year 1, (linen from mummy of Pinudjem II)

> This linen was obviously made in advance of Pinudjem II's death, as were several other bandages on his mummy – they must have been stored for up to 13 years. This bandage fragment infers that Pinudjem II was inducted as HP in year one of Amenemopet.
>
> As references that include HP Pinudjem II cannot possibly now refer to the pharaoh Siamun, the references following No 57 (Nos 57-72) must now belong to Amenemopet – as was thought all along by historians.

61   ??   Year (2), also year 49 of (HP Menkheperre)

62	50	Amenemopet & HP Pinudjem II (no year)
63	58	Year 2, judgement of officials under Pinudjem II
64	59	Year 2, judgement of officials under Pinudjem II
65	60	Year 3, judgement of officials under Pinudjem II
66	52	Year 3, linen by Pinudjem II, mummy 143
67	63	Year 3, linen by Pinudjem II, mummy 143
68	61	Year 3, linen by Pinudjem II
69	62	Year 3, linen from mummy of Pinudjem II
70	66	Year 5, linen by Neskhons
71	67	Year 5, decree for Neskhons
72	68	Year 5, burial text for Neskhons
73	54	Year 5, dateline for Amenemopet
74	64	Year 5, decree for Henttawy
75	65	Year 5, judgement of Amun
76	69	Year 6, decree for Henttawy
77	70	Year 7, linen (renewal of) mummy of Ramesses IX
78	71	Year 7, linen by HP Pinudjem II, his mummy
79	72	Year 7, linen by Pinudjem II, mummy 124
80	75	Year 8, decree for Henttawy
81	76	Year 9, linen by Pinudjem II, his mummy
82	55	Year 10, linen by Pinudjem II, mummy 124
83	53	Year 13, K Amenemopet, linen by HP Pinudjem II, mummy 124
84	86	Year 13, Karnak annals (yr 13 after Siamun)
85	87	Year 13, linen by a Chief of Harim
86	81	Year 14, Karnak priestly annals (entry year 14 after mention of Pinudjem II)
87	49	Amenemopet & HP Smendes (no year)

K Psusennes II & HP Smendes

88	42	Year 19, Psusennes II, Dakhla stele
89	47	Year 49, linen fragment with K Psusennes II and K Amenemopet
90	48	Burial of K Psusennes II, bracelets of HP Smendes, son of Menkheperre

The bracelets of HP Smendes do not infer that this high priest was still alive at the death of King Psusennes II. While the sequence of HP Smendes following HP Menkheperre is correct, the HP Smendes would have been rather (but not impossibly) old at the death of Psusennes II. Had Menkheperre begun his office at the age of 20, and fathered Smendes at the age of 60, then the HP Smendes would have been 77 at the death of Psusennes II.

The question of the Daressy bandage fragment that reads 'King Amenemopet, year 49' is still a minor problem, as Amenemopet did not have a year 49, neither under this nor under the classical chronology. This fragment is best explained in much the same fashion as was argued by Kitchen, although this argument now applies to another king/priest relationship. The bandage probably once had two names upon it, and the high regnal year must have applied to the second king, not the first. In other words, the fragment originally read: 'Year ?? King Amenemopet – Year 49 King ????'.

I am not sure that Kenneth Kitchen is entirely correct on this point. Instead of a bandage mentioning two pharaohs, the normal format was for the name of a pharaoh and a priest to be given. Since the High Priest Menkheperre has already been shown to have been quite proud of his long tenure, which was very close to 49 years in length, the high regnal year most probably applied to him. The task now is one of filling in the blanks on the fragment. In this case, the fragment must have originally read, 'Year 2, King Amenemopet – Year 49, HP Menkheperre'.

Despite starting with a radical new chronology, which looked as though it would be impossible to match with the established historical records, the resulting new chronology fits rather precisely, with all the known factors that pertain to these references being fully covered. The newly derived reign lengths also follow the general thrust of the king-list of Manetho. The following table compares the reign lengths in Manetho's king-list with the revised chronology:

Pharaoh	Manetho	Revised
Smendes	26	48
Psusennes I	46	–
Amenemnisu	4	4
Siamun	9	16
Uasorkon	6	6
Amenemopet	9	13
Psusennes II	35	49

Funnily enough, although this was not the aim of the exercise, the total reign length for the whole dynasty is more or less the same in both cases. The only weak point in the entire argument for a new chronology is the extraordinarily long office of HP Pinudjem I, but this period is well within the realms of human possibilities, even in this era. Kings and high priests were, of course, well fed and housed, while the priestly dietary prohibitions and ritual ablutions may have assisted in maintaining their general health. It was not uncommon for these aristocratic individuals to have long lives, even in an era when the average life expectancy was probably not much more than 40.

There is also the case of the disappearing pharaoh, Psusennes I. While the biblical chronology has apparently deleted him from the records, this might not be the whole story. One of the problems for historians, both ancient and modern, is that the pharaohs Psusennes I and Uasorkon the Elder held exactly the same throne names. The throne name for both Psusennes and Uasorkon was Akheperre Setepenre, and so these pharaohs only differed in their birth names. The possibility exists that there may have been a slight case of mistaken identity; indeed, this did happen during the early periods of historical research, and all the cartouches for Uasorkon the Elder were originally ascribed to Psusennes I. It is entirely possible that Psusennes I and Uasorkon were one and the same individual, and that this is why the latter pharaoh has been so difficult to find in the historical record.

Addendum

Since the publication of the prototype edition of this book, some debate has erupted regarding the precise name of the daughter of Pharaoh Psusennes II – the inference being that I had invented this daughter in order that the historical record matched the Biblical record more closely. This is not so; Psusennes II's daughter *was* called Maakhare (B), as the following quote demonstrates:

> In turn, Psusennes II ends the (21ˢᵗ) dynasty because his daughter, Maatkare B (Maakhare II), marries Oasorkon I (Uasorkon I). K Kitchen para 5, see also para 49.

Thus the only real contention is whether or not this Maakhare (II) also held the matching title of Mutemhat (Mu-Tamhat). In answer to this question, I would observe the following points:

a.   The subsequent princesses of the 23ʳᵈ to 26ᵗʰ dynasties often added the Mu-Tamhat suffix (or prefix) to their names.

b.   The historical character Maakhare (I), who the Bible infers was King David-Psusennes's first wife, most certainly did carry the title 'Mu-Tamhat'.

c.   Historical references from this era rarely include all of a person's many titles, and so many of these alternate titles are often missing from the records.

d.   The Bible is equally unreliable in reporting all of these titles. The Biblical references regularly use either Maakhah or Tamar, but the composite name of Maakhah Tamar is never mentioned and had to be assembled from several different sources discussing the same individual.

Unfortunately, Psusennes II's daughter is only known in the historical record by three references, and these simply declare her to be called Maakhare (II). However, it not beyond any stretch of the imagination to assume that she also once held the title Mu-Tamhat, as did her [mother] Maakhare Mutamhat (I) and many of her descendants. This was a royal title that was passed down through the generations, and so we should expect that the senior princesses in each generation held this title.

Additionally, it is not entirely certain that the mummy that is traditionally ascribed to Maakhare Mu-Tamhat I really belonged to this person. This mummy has been identified as being Pinedjem's daughter, Maakhare I, because she was God's Wife, and the god's wives were supposed to be virgins. Since Maakhare II, the daughter of Psusennes II, was married, it is said that this cannot be the latter's coffin.

However, the Bible strongly indicates that although Maakhah Tamar II was a virgin, she nevertheless seems to have married Absalom, her brother, and had children. Likewise, the New Testament Mary was also a married virgin who had many sons. It would seem that this title of Virgin did not preclude marriage, and so it is entirely possible that the coffin of Maakhare Mu-Tamhat I might actually belong to Maakhare II. The subsidiary mummy of a baboon would support this interpretation, as I have suggested in chapter V.

An additional concern is that this mummy does not mention that she was a queen, and so again it is ascribed to Pinedjem's daughter (Maakhare I) as it is not known if this lady ever married. However, the titles we have for Maakhare II also do not specify the title 'queen', even though it is known that she married Uasorkon I. I would personally speculate that the title 'God's Wife' was more important that the term 'queen', as it inferred that she was the 'Chief Wife', rather than any of the king's many other wives, and this would negate the need for the term 'queen'. In addition, I interpret the term Mu-Tamhat as meaning 'First Mother', or 'First Lady', which would seem to confirm that the lady in this coffin *was* married, otherwise she could not have been a mother. Likewise, it would also infer that she was indeed the queen, just as the American term 'First Lady' directly refers to the president's wife.

Once more, the available evidence would suggest that this coffin belonged to Maakhare II, rather than Maakhare I, and she did indeed hold the title of Mu-Tamhat, as the coffin clearly shows.

List of diagrams

* Image courtesy of Dover Egyptian Designs.

Photo credits

Plate 1.   Silver outer coffin of King Solomon - Ralph Ellis, Cairo Museum.
Plate 2.   Wooden inner coffin of King Solomon - Ralph Ellis, Cairo Museum.
Plate 3.   Silver outer coffin of King David - Ralph Ellis, Cairo Museum.
Plate 4.   Gold death-masks of King David and Obed - Ralph Ellis, Cairo Museum.
Plate 5-8. Funerary artifacts - Ralph Ellis, Cairo Museum.
Plate 9.   Sarcophagus of Maakhah Tamar - Ralph Ellis, Cairo Museum.
Plate 10. Statue at Bubastis - Ralph Ellis, Zagazig Museum.
Plate 11. Image of the Queen of Sheba - Ralph Ellis, Cairo Museum.
Plate 12. Great Temple, Tanis - Ralph Ellis, Tanis Museum.
Plate 13. Eastern temple, Tanis - Ralph Ellis, Tanis Museum.
Plate 14. Tomb complex at Tanis - Ralph Ellis, Tanis Museum.
Plate 15. Shrine to Queen of Sheba, Karnak - Ralph Ellis.
Plate 16. The mummy of Nesperennub - SGI/British Museum.
Plate 17. Bubastite Gate, Karnak - Ralph Ellis.
Plate 18. Campaigns of Sheshonq-Solomon, Karnak - Ralph Ellis.
Plate 19. Battles with Sea People , Medinet Habu - Ralph Ellis.
Plate 20. Sea People captives, Medinet Habu - Ralph Ellis.
Plate 21. Valley of King Solomon's Mines - Ralph Ellis.
Plate 22. Marib Dam, Saba - Ancient Art and Architecture Ltd, Middlesex.
Plate 23. Temple of Awwam, Saba - Ancient Art and Architecture Ltd, Middlesex.
Plate 24. Gypsy travellers - Barrie Law, York.
Plate 25. A palmiform pillar at Tanis - Ralph Ellis.
Plate 26. Pyramidal tomb of 'Zechariah', Jerusalem - Adrian Gilbert.
Plate 27. Instructions of Amenemopet - British Museum.
Plate 28. Menorah, Tanis - Ralph Ellis, Tanis Museum.

Notes & references

Bible: All references taken from the King James edition, although the text is often modernised for clarity.

Josephus: AA = Against Apion, Ant = Antiquities, JW = Jewish war, L = Life.
Page references are to the Loeb Classical Library system.
Quotes taken from William Whiston's translation, which was first published in 1736; some references are from the Penguin Classics edition by G. Williamson, first published 1959.

Manetho   All page numbers are taken from the LCL edition, editor G. Goold.

Within the referencing system in this book, some of the reference numbers are prefixed with letters. This is to give the reader an idea of the source of the reference, without having to look up that particular reference. This only applies to the more popular reference works, and the following have been prefixed:

B = Bible, M = Manetho, J = Josephus, H = Herodotus,
T = Talmud, KN = Kebra Nagast, K = Koran, S = Strabo.

All references to Egyptian words are taken from:

An Egyptian Hieroglyphic Dictionary, E A Wallis Budge, Dover Publications. The entries in the dictionary are substantially in alphabetical (glyph) order, and so the references are easy to find and have not been listed in the references by their page number.

Abbreviations:

ECIiAT   = Egypt, Canaan and Israel in Ancient Times, Donald Redford.
TTIPiE   = The Third Intermediate Period in Egypt, Kenneth Kitchen.
EotP   = Egypt of the Pharaohs, Alan Gardiner.
ARoE   = Ancient Records of Egypt, James Breasted.
Kebra Nagast   = Translation taken from 'Queen of Sheba', W Budge.

Notes & References

Chapter I

1. ECIiAT, Donald Redford p264.
2. Geography, Strabo bk 16. 2-34.
3. ECIiAT, D Redford p366.
4. The Assayer, Galileo.
5. The Israelites, Isserlin.
6. The Galileo Affair, M Finocciaro.
7. The Crime of Galileo, G de Santilana.
8. SIS review, P J Crowe 2001:2.
9. ECIiAT, D Redford p 365.
10. New Scientist magazine, 9 March 2002.
11. Manetho, Aegyptiaca Fr 1.
12. Manetho, Aegyptiaca Fr 2.
13. Josephus, Ant 6:99.
15. Bible, 1Sa 18:11.
16. Bible, 1Sa 18:12.
17. Bible, 1Sa 18:17.
18. Bible, 1Sa 31:4.
19. Bible, 2Sa 2:15-16.

Chapter II

1. Bible, Joshua 12:2.
2. Brown, Driver, Briggs, Gesenius – Hebrew Aramaic English Lexicon, H2999.
3. Bible, Judges 11:22.
4. Bible, Joshua 11:16-19.
5. Bible, 1Sa 15:7.
6. TTIPiE, K Kitchen.
7. Semitic Words in Egyptian Texts, J Hoch,
   Hieroglyphic Dictionary, W Budge.
8. Bible, Jud 12:6.
9. A Test of Time, David Rohl p72.

Chapter III

1. Arabia Felix, A de Maigret.
2. Bible, 2Ch 9:9.
3. Josephus, Ant 8:165.

4. Bible, 1Ki 3:1.
5. Bible, 1Ki 9:16.
6. Bible, Isaiah 43:3.
7. Koran, 34:15.
8. Koran, 27:21.
9. Bible, 1Ki 3:1.
11. David, Solomon and Egypt, Paul Ash.
12. Ancient Egyptian Literature, Miriam Lichtheim.
13. Ancient Israel, Roland de Vaux p475.
14. Letter on file.
15. Signs in the Sky, Adrian Gilbert.
16. Bible, Lev 27:34.
17. Bible, Eze 29:10.

Chapter IV

1. Oxford History of Ancient Egypt, Ian Shaw, p333.
2. Bible, 1Ki 10:16-17.
3. Bible, 1Ch 22:14.
4. Bible, Rev 13:17-18.
5. Bible, 1Ki 10:14.
6. Bible, 1Sa 17:41.
7. Bible, 1Sa 16:12.
8. Josephus, Ant 7:243.
9. Josephus, Ant 8:249.
11. Gods of the Egyptians, Wallis Budge.
12. TTIPiE, K Kitchen para 225.
13. Signs in the Sky, Adrian Gilbert.
14. The Queen of Sheba & Kebra Nagast, W Budge.
15. Kebra Nagast, 117.
16. Kebra Nagast.

Chapter V

1. David, Solomon and Egypt, Paul Ash.
2. Herodotus, Histories, Euterpe 111.
3. ECIiAT, D Redford p366.
4. ECIiAT, D Redford p302.
5. ECIiAT, D Redford p313
6. EotP, Sir Alan Gardiner p318.

7. TTIPiE, K Kitchen para 153.
8. TTIPiE, K Kitchen para 151.
9. Bible, 2Sa 3:3.
11. Bible, 2Sa 13:37.
12. Koran, 38:22.
13. Bible, 2Sa 15:10.
14. Bible, 2Sa 15:12.
15. Josephus, Ant 7:232 - 242.
16. Bible, 2Sa 18:5.
17. TTIPiE, K Kitchen para 25.
18. Bible, 2Ch 13:1-2.
19. Bible, 1Ki 15:1-2.
21. Josephus, Ant 8:249.
22. Bible, 2Sa 13:19.
23. TTIPiE, K Kitchen para 48.
24. Ancient Israel, Roland de Vaux p117.
25. Bible, Lu 1:35.
26. Bible, Lu 1:38.
27. Oxford History of Ancient Egypt, Ian Shaw.
28. Bible, Mt 2:9.
29. Kebra Nagast, 33.
31. Bible, Lu 8:2.
32. Bible, Eze 29:10.
33. The Bible and the Ancient Near East, F Moore-Cross, chap VI.
34. The Jews, Finkelstein p10.
35. Bible, 1Ki 15:13.
36. Biblical Commentary, Adam Clarke.
37. British Museum Dictionary of Ancient Egypt, Ian Shaw.
38. Bible, 2Sa 13:37.

Chapter VI

1. ECIiAT, D Redford p273.
2. ECIiAT, D Redford p251.
3. ECIiAT, D Redford p289.
4. Bible, Jud 7:16, 7:20.
5. Bible, Jud 11:5.
6. Bible, Jud 11:32-33.
7. ECIiAT, D Redford p287.
8. Bible, Josh 12:1-2.
9. EotP, Sir Alan Gardiner.
10. ECIiAT, D Redford p315.

11. Bible, Wisdom of Solomon 8:2.
Note that the Wisdom of Solomon is only available in Bibles that contain the Apocrypha. Please consult with a quality bookseller for further details.
12. Bible, Wisdom of Solomon 8:8 & 7:21.
13. Manetho, Fr 53.
14. Apollodorus, J Berard, Syria 29 1952.
15. Egyptian Dictionary W Budge p1038.
16. Hyksos and Israelite Cities, Flinders Petrie.
17. ECIiAT, D Redford p272.
18. ECIiAT, D Redford p272.
19. The Cairo Museum Masterpieces of Egyptian Art.

Chapter VII

1. Bible, 1Ki 10:23 & 2Ch 9:22.
2. Kebra Nagast 22.
3. Bible, 1Ki 9:26.
4. Josephus Ant 7:181.
5. Herodotus, The Histories, Melpomene 42.
6. Kebra Nagast 25.
7. Bible, 1Ki 10:24.
8. Bible, 1Ki 4:34.
9. Bible, 2Ch 9:3.
11. Bible, 2Ch 6:13.
12. Josephus AA 1:109.
13. Ancient Egyptian Literature, Miriam Lichtheim.
14. Ancient Egyptian Literature, Miriam Lichtheim.
15. Bible, 2Ch 2:3.
16. ECIiAT, D Redford p228.
17. Bible, 1Ki 5:11.
18. Bible, 1Ki 9:11.
19 Ancient Records of Egypt, H Breasted.
20. Josephus Ant 7:62.
21. Josephus Ant 7:318.
22. Josephus Ant 8:142.
23. Josephus AA 1:113.
24. Bible, 1Ki 10:28.
25. ARoE, James Breasted, IV para 357.

26. ARoE, James Breasted, IV para 357.
27. ARoE, James Breasted, IV para 704.
28. Bible, 1Ki 5:15-17.
29. ARoE, James Breasted, IV p 347.
31. Bible, 1Ki 7:13-15.
32. Commentary on the Bible,
    Adam Clarke.
33. Hiram Hey, Lomas and Knight, 121.
34. Bible, 2Ch 2:13-14.
35. Bible, 2Ch 2:13.
36. Herodotus, Histories, Euterpe 111.
37. The Oxford History of Ancient Egypt,
    Ian Shaw p367.
38. The Israelites, Isserlin.
39. Hiram Key, Lomas and Knight.
41. ECIiAT, D Redford p228.
42. Bible, Ge 22:2.
43. Bible, 2Ch 3:1.
44. Biblical Commentary, Adam Clarke.
45. ARoE, Banishment Stele,
    J Breasted V4.
46. Ancient Egyptian Literature,
    M Lichtheim.

17. Bible, 1Ch 13:1.
18. Bible, 2Sa 18:1-2.
19. TTIPiE, K Kitchen para 66.
20. Koran 27:14.
21. Masonic Prayer-book.
22. Bible, 2Sa 20:3.
23. Bible, 2Sa 14:5 .
24. Josephus Ant 8:76.
25. Bible, Lu 11:31.
26. Koran, 27:30.
27. Koran, 27:37.
28. Josephus Ant 7:288.
29. The Jews, Louis Finkelstein p10.
31. Bible, 1Ki 11:1-3.
32. TTIPiE K Kitchen para 32, 64.
33. The Israelites, Isserlin p82.
34. Bible, 2Ch 10:10-11.
35. Bible, 2Ch 12:1.
36. Bible, 2Ch 11:2-4.
37. Bible, 2Ch 12:2.
38. Bible, 2Ch 12:7-9.
39. Josephus Ant 8:258.
41. TTIPiE K Kitchen para 94.
42. Bible, Isaiah 22:22.
43. Bible, Gen 41:40.
44. Bible, Math 16:18.

Chapter VIII

1. Kebra Nagast 25.
2. Bible, 1Ki 3:1.
3. Bible, 1Ki 9:16.
4. Kebra Nagast 53.
5. Kebra Nagast 63.
6. Koran 34:12
7. Oxford History of Ancient Egypt,
   Ian Shaw
8. TTIPiE, K Kitchen para 233.
11. ARoE, Papyrus Abbot Pl 7:11,
    J Breasted V4.
12. ARoE, Ancient records
    J Breasted, V4:504.
13. Papyrus de Turin, F Rossi de Turin,
    Strike Papyrus Ro2, 3-5.
14. ARoE, J Breasted, p362.
15. Proceedings of the NATO Advanced
    Research Workshop on Prehistoric
    Gold in Europe 1993.
16. Bible, 2Sa 18:18.

Chapter IX

1. Kebra Nagast 36.
2. Kebra Nagast 43.
3. Kebra Nagast 59.
5. Kebra Nagast 92
6. TTIPiE, K Kitchen para 244.
7. Gypsies of Britain, Brian Vessel-
   FitzGerald, p5.
8. Bible, Baruch 1:8.
   Note that the book of Baruch is only
   available in Bibles that contain the
   Apocrypha. Please consult with a
   quality bookseller for further details.
9. Bible, Dan 5:5-6.
10. Bible, Dan 5:25-28.
11. The Gypsies, Samuel Roberts, p90.
12. Bible, 2Ki 18:9-11.
13. Bible, 2Ki 19:9-10.

14. ECliAT, D Redford p258.
15. Bible, 2Ki 25:4
16. Arabia Felix, A. de Maigret.
17. Arabia Felix, A. de Maigret.
18. The Round Towers of Atlantis (1834), Henry O'Brian.
    This venerable old book is long out of print, but has been republished by Adventures Unlimited, whose address is in the forepages.
19. Harvard Excavations at Samaria G A Reisner, vol II plate 27.
21. Oxford Companion to Jewish Religion, Louis Jacobs.
22. Arabia Felix, A. de Maigret
23. Arabia Felix, A. de Maigret
24. Herodotus Euterpe 152-154.
25. La datazione della sudarabia di Ma'adkarib, G Garbini.
26. Bible, Jer 41:1-2.
27. Bible, Jer 43:4-7.
28. Hyksos and Israelite Cities, Flinders Petrie.

29. Josephus, Ant 13:70.
31. Bible, Jer 43:8-9.
32. Hyksos and Israelite Cities, Flinders Petrie.
33. Bible, Jer 43:10-11.
34. Bible, Jer 44:11-14.
35. Bible, Jer 44:16-18.
36. Bible, Isa 2:3.
37. Bible, Isa 4:5.
38. Bible, Isa 8:18.
39. Bible, 1Ch 11:5-7.
41. TTIPiE K Kitchen   para 224.
42. Josephus Ant 8:62.
43. Bible Jud 3:13-14.

Appendix

1. TTIPiE, K Kitchen para 381-391.
2. ARoE, J Breasted V 4 para 606-607,

Index

Index

Index

Index

Index

Index

Index

Index

Index

Index

Index

Index

Index